Gendered Lives
Communication, Gender, and Culture

THIRTEENTH EDITION

Natalie Fixmer-Oraiz

Department of Communication Studies
Department of Gender, Women's, and Sexuality Studies
The University of Iowa

Julia T. Wood

Lineberger Distinguished Professor of Humanities Emerita
The University of North Carolina at Chapel Hill

 CENGAGE

Australia • Brazil • Mexico • Singapore • United Kingdom • United States

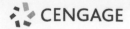

Gendered Lives: Communication, Gender, and Culture, Thirteenth Edition
Natalie Fixmer-Oraiz,
Julia T. Wood

Product Manager:
Kelli Strieby

Project Manager:
Julia Giannotti

Content Developer:
Katy Gabel

Product Assistant:
Camille Beckman

Marketing Manager:
Allison Moghaddasi

Content Project Manager:
Dan Saabye

Manufacturing Planner:
Doug Bertke

IP Analyst: Ann Hoffman

IP Project Manager: Kathryn Kucharek

Production Service:
Lumina Datamatics

Compositor:
Lumina Datamatics

Art Director: Marissa Falco

Text Designer: Diana Graham

Cover Designer: Marissa Falco

Cover Image: Ekely/Getty Images

For product information and technology assistance, contact us at Cengage Customer & Sales Support, 1-800-354-9706.
For permission to use material from this text or product, submit all requests online at **www.cengage.com/permissions**
Further permissions questions can be emailed to **permissionrequest@cengage.com**

Library of Congress Control Number: 2017944245

Student Edition:
ISBN: 978-1-337-55588-3

Loose-leaf Edition:
ISBN: 978-1-337-55597-5

Cengage
20 Channel Center Street
Boston, MA 02210
USA

Cengage is a leading provider of customized learning solutions with employees residing in nearly 40 different countries and sales in more than 125 countries around the world. Find your local representative at **www.cengage.com**.

Cengage products are represented in Canada by Nelson Education, Ltd.

To learn more about Cengage platforms and services, visit **www.cengage.com**.

Purchase any of our products at your local college store or at our preferred online store **www.cengagebrain.com**.

Printed in the United States of America
Print Number: 06   Print Year: 2019

DEDICATION

This book is dedicated to Susan B. Anthony, Ella Baker, Frederick Douglass, Charlotte Perkins Gilman, Emma Goldman, Sarah Grimke, Francis Ellen Watkins Harper, Alice Paul, Margaret Sanger, Elizabeth Cady Stanton, Maria Stewart, Sojourner Truth, Mary Wollstonecraft, and other women and men who began the conversation about gender in this country;

and to

Maya Angelou, Gloria Anzaldúa, Robert Bly, Judith Butler, Karlyn Campbell, Mary Daly, Angela Davis, Simone de Beauvoir, Marilyn French, Michael Kimmel, Betty Friedan, J. Jack Halberstam, bell hooks, Jackson Katz, Evelyn Fox Keller, Lady Gaga, Amy Schumer, Gloria Steinem, Beyoncé, and other women and men who have added to the cultural dialogue about gender;

and to

Emmons Fixmer-Oraiz, Jason Muehlhoff, Malia Obama, Sasha Obama, Niko Pezzullo Striphas, Daniel Wood Wilco, Harrison Wood Wilco, Michelle Wood Wilco, and other boys and girls whose voices will shape the next generation's understanding of women and men, masculinity and femininity, and the meaning of gender in our society.

Brief Contents

Contents

List of Exploring Gendered Lives Boxes

Preface

We wrote *Gendered Lives* for two reasons. First, we want to introduce students to a rich body of research that informs us about the intricate connections among communication, gender, and culture. Second, we think that learning about these connections empowers students to make more informed decisions about how they personally enact gender, address gender issues in their lives, and contribute to cultural attitudes, perspectives, laws, and policies related to gender.

Since the first edition of this book appeared in the early 1990s, our understandings of gender have changed as have issues related to gender. Society has acknowledged a greater range of options for individuals—in the military, in the home, in professional life, in social life, and in politics. During the past 25 years, society has become more accepting of gay, lesbian, and transgender, or trans, identities; new women's and men's movements have emerged; mass media have challenged some gender stereotypes while creating others; and social media have added to the content and forms by which gender is continually enacted and negotiated. Academic researchers have continued to map the ways that communication, gender, and culture influence one another. This new edition responds to social changes in the United States and around the world, as well as to feedback from students and faculty who generously offered ideas for ways to improve this book.

We discuss this book's origins and features in the Introduction ("Opening the Conversation," pages 1–13). Here, we want to describe changes that make this edition different from the last and identify supplementary resources available for students and instructors.

Changes in *Gendered Lives*, Thirteenth Edition

Five significant changes differentiate this edition from its predecessors.

Enhanced Coverage of Men's Issues

Since the first edition in the mid-1990s, *Gendered Lives* has included discussion of topics related to men and masculinity. In recent years, more research on men and masculinity has emerged and is reflected in this edition's increased attention to men's issues. For example, Chapters 3 and 4 include new coverage of the Black Lives Matter movement. Also, Chapter 9 highlights men's investment in fatherhood, and Chapter 10 covers the conflict between work and family that many men experience.

Attention to Gendered Dynamics in Public Life

This edition offers more focus on gender in the public sphere. For example, in Chapters 5 we attend to language used to describe male and female politicians and also the gendered ways in which voters view candidates of each sex. Similarly, Chapter 5 points out sexist language used in relation to athletes. We also discuss how public figures enact and challenge gender norms.

Integrated Emphasis on Social Media

With this edition, we continue to enrich our coverage of social media, which are not only sources of gender socialization, but also powerful platforms for rethinking gender and for gender activism. Accordingly, we have included discussion of social media throughout the book.

Expanded Emphasis on Application

Since the first edition, *Gendered Lives* has encouraged students to apply material in the book by reflecting on gendered issues in their lives and by taking a voice in their personal lives as well as the public sphere. This edition enlarges the commitment to application by providing more explicit invitations for students to do something active and personal related to what they learn in the book and the course it accompanies. The Exploring Gendered Lives boxes that appear in every chapter now conclude by asking students to take a stand on the topics discussed. At the end of each chapter, the Reflection, Discussion, and Action feature now includes a Gender in Action item that encourages students to apply or extend a concept or topic discussed in the chapter to their lives. The Gender in Action items are highlighted by this icon ⊚.

Up-to-Date Research

A final focus of this revision is updating research. Understandings of gender and issues connected to it change at lightning speed. To keep up with these changes, a textbook must be continuously updated to reflect the most current research and events. To ensure the currency of *Gendered Lives*, we've incorporated more than 275 new references into this edition.

Pedagogical Features to Engage Students

Five features are aimed to heighten students' engagement with the text and issues related to gender. First, each chapter opens with "Knowledge Challenge" questions, which focus on issues that are often misunderstood and which are covered in the chapter. Second, to encourage active engagement with material, Exploring Gendered Lives boxes conclude by asking students' opinion about issues raised in the feature. Third, each chapter concludes with questions for thought, discussion, and application. These may be assigned for students to think about or as journal entries. They may also be prompts for class discussion. Fourth, "Gender Online," which appears after each chapter summary, invites students to visit websites related to chapter content and to search online for videos and information about concepts and ideas in the chapter. Fifth, at the end of each chapter, we suggest two to four sources—films, articles, websites, and books. Our criteria for selecting these are that (1) we consider them either classic or especially insightful, and (2) they are accessible to undergraduate students.

In making these changes, we've avoided "page creep"—the tendency of books to grow longer with each new edition because old material is not deleted to make room for new material. We have eliminated dated references and coverage to make room for more current research and coverage of timely topics. We hope the changes make this edition of *Gendered Lives* a valuable resource for instructors and students who want to explore the complex and fascinating ways in which communication, gender, and culture interact and affect our lives.

MindTap

This edition is complemented by MindTap, a platform that propels students from memorization to mastery. It gives you complete control of your course, so you can provide engaging content, challenge every learner, and build student confidence. Customize interactive syllabi to emphasize priority topics, then add your own material or notes to the eBook as desired. This outcomes-driven application gives you the tools needed to empower students and boost both understanding and performance.

Access Everything You Need in One Place

Cut down on prep with the preloaded and organized MindTap course materials. Teach more efficiently with interactive multimedia, assignments, quizzes, and more. Give your students the power to read, listen, and study on their phones, so they can learn on their terms.

Empower Students to Reach Their Potential

Twelve distinct metrics give you actionable insights into student engagement. Identify topics troubling your entire class and instantly communicate with those struggling. Students can track their scores to stay motivated toward their goals. Together, you can be unstoppable.

Control Your Course—and Your Content

Get the flexibility to reorder textbook chapters, add your own notes, and embed a variety of content including Open Educational Resources (OER). Personalize course content to your students' needs. They can even read your notes, add their own, and highlight key text to aid their learning.

Get a Dedicated Team, Whenever You Need Them

MindTap isn't just a tool, it's backed by a personalized team eager to support you. We can help set up your course and tailor it to your specific objectives, so you'll be ready to make an impact from day one. Know we'll be standing by to help you and your students until the final day of the term.

Supplementary Resources for Students and Instructors

Gendered Lives, thirteenth edition, offers electronic supplements to assist in making the gender communication course as meaningful and enjoyable as possible for both students and instructors and to help students succeed. Cengage Learning has prepared the following descriptions for your consideration.

Instructor Companion Website. The password-protected instructor's website includes electronic access to the Instructor's Resource Manual, PowerPoints, CogneroTesting Program, Comprehensive Video Program, and links to Cengage Learning technology resources.

The Instructor's Resource Manual comprises two main parts, the first titled and addressing Special Issues in Teaching Communication, Gender, & Culture; and the second a Chapter-by-Chapter Guide for Teaching *Gendered Lives*, which provides chapter outlines and activities.

PowerPoint® presentations contain text and images and can be used as is or customized to suit your course needs.

Please consult your local Cengage Learning sales representative or cengage.com/login for more information, user names and passwords, examination copies, or a demonstration of these ancillary products. Available to qualified adopters.

Acknowledgments

One of the most gratifying aspects of writing a book is the opportunity to thank those who have offered support, insight, and advice. First and foremost, we thank our students. The individuals in our classes and those we meet when we visit other campuses are unfailing sources of insight for us. Their questions and ideas, their willingness to challenge some of our notions, and their generosity in sharing their perceptions and experiences have shaped the pages that follow in both obvious and subtle ways.

Among the undergraduate students who have pushed us to think in new ways about gender, communication, and culture are Jordana Adler, Cutler Andrews, Brandon Carter, Ethan Cicero, Alexis Dennis, Madeline Fitzgerald, Paige Pennigar, and Nisha Verma. Among the graduate students who have influenced our thinking are J. Beckham, Jen Cronin, Kate Harris, Naomi Johnson, Kristen Norwood, Tim Muehlhoff, Julia O'Grady, Phaedra Pezzullo, Stace Treat, and Grover Wehman-Brown.

Our thinking and writing also reflect conversations with colleagues. We are particularly grateful to Professor Bonnie Dow, Vanderbilt University, who has provided wise advice and challenges since the first edition of this book. We are also indebted to Lynn O'Brien Hallstein, Boston University, for her generative research and her passion for wrestling with questions about gender, communication, and culture.

We have benefited from the professional support of Nicole Morinon, Senior Product Manager for Communication Studies, and Katy Gabel, Content Developer, who made our job as authors far easier and far more satisfying than we had a right to expect. Along with Nicole and Katy, others at Cengage Learning have contributed in important ways to this edition of *Gendered Lives*. They are Colin Solan, Production Assistant; Karolina Kiwak, Associate Content Developer; Sarah Seymour, Marketing Manager; Daniel Saabye, Content Product Manager; and Ann Hoffman, Permissions Manager. Also, we thank Samantha Ross-Miller, who managed the production of this book.

Finally, we are indebted to the reviewers for this edition:

Sandra Alvarez, American International College
Sandy Berkowitz, Minneapolis Community and Technical College
Mary Carver, University of Central Oklahoma
Linda Dam, University of Connecticut
Abby Dubisar, Iowa State University
Charlotte Jones, Carroll College
Mary L. Kahl, Indiana State University
Myrna Kuehn, Clarion University of Pennsylvania
Amanda Martinez, Davidson College
Julie Mayberry, Meredith College/North Carolina State University
Kelly McKay-Semmler, University of South Dakota
Susan McManimon, Rider University and Kean University
Nina-Jo Moore, Appalachian State University
Kaneez Naseem, Monroe College
Jessica Papajcik, Stark State College
Kimberly Parker, Bellarmine University
Mairi Pileggi, Dominican University of California
Joquina Reed, Texas A&M International University
Henrietta Shirk, Montana Tech of the University of Montana
Erika Thomas, California State University, Fullerton
Joseph Velasco, Sul Ross State University
Justin Walton, Cameron University
Carrie West, Schreiner University
Debbie Wigington, Chemeketa Community College

And, always, we thank our partners. Natalie is ever grateful to Vanessa for sharing her mad smarts, generosity, compassion, and love. Julia thanks Robbie for his support, criticism, and, most of all, his steadfast presence in her life.

Natalie Fixmer-Oraiz
Iowa City, Iowa
Julia T. Wood
Chapel Hill, North Carolina
December 2017

About the Authors

Natalie Fixmer-Oraiz is an Assistant Professor of Communication Studies and Gender, Women's, and Sexuality Studies at the University of Iowa. She has published articles on rhetoric and reproductive justice, the commercial surrogacy industry, and third-wave feminism, as well as book chapters on the public debates surrounding birth control and communication activism pedagogy. She is currently at work on *Homeland Maternity*, a book that examines contemporary struggles over reproductive health and motherhood in the context of homeland security culture. In addition, Natalie has been honored by teaching awards from the University of North Carolina at Chapel Hill and the American Association of Colleges and Universities. She is committed to service-learning and experiential education as means of helping students make connections between theory and practice and the community and the classroom. She continues her involvement in reproductive health and justice initiatives in the United States and transnational contexts. She currently resides in Iowa City with her wife, son, and two cats.

Julia T. Wood is Lineberger Distinguished Professor of Humanities Emerita at the University of North Carolina at Chapel Hill. She joined the university at the age of 24. While on the faculty, she was named the Lineberger Distinguished Professor of Humanities and the Caroline H. and Thomas S. Royster Distinguished Professor of Graduate Education. She has authored 17 books and edited 10 others. In addition, she has published more than 100 articles and book chapters and has presented numerous papers at professional conferences. She has won 12 awards for undergraduate teaching and 15 awards for her scholarship.

Julia lives with her partner, Robert Cox, who is Professor Emeritus of Communication Studies at the University of North Carolina at Chapel Hill. Filling out their immediate family are two cats, Rigby and Always Rowdy, and a puppy, Sydney. When not teaching or writing, Julia works with, and consults on sex and gender issues, and serves on the Board of the Carolina Tiger Rescue.

Opening the Conversation

Knowledge Challenge:

- When was the term *feminism* first used?
- How many bras were burned in feminist protests in 1968?
- As a group, are heterosexual men happier in relationships with feminist or nonfeminist women?
- What is at stake in how we think about gender?

Textbooks typically begin with a preview of chapters and features, but we want to launch our conversation a bit differently. We think you're entitled to know something about the people behind the words you'll be reading, so we want to open the book by introducing ourselves and explaining why we wrote *Gendered Lives*.

Most people regard books as impersonal sources of information. Like anything that people create, however, books reflect the experiences, identities, and historical context of the authors who write them. Authors influence books when they decide which topics to include and which theories to present. This doesn't mean that books are not informative or reliable, but it does mean that authors' experiences and perspectives have an impact on books. By telling you a little about who we are and why we wrote this book, we are inviting you to think about how our backgrounds, experiences, beliefs, and values have shaped the book you're reading.

Let's start with some simple demographic information. Natalie is a white, femme, cisgender, middle-class woman in a committed 12-year relationship with her partner, Vanessa. Julia is a European-American, heterosexual, spiritually engaged, middle-class woman who has been in a committed relationship with Robbie (Robert) Cox for 42 years.

Yet, if you think about it, this information isn't simple at all. It implies a great deal about our identities and experiences. For instance, Julia became an adult when the second wave of the U.S. Women's Movement was ascending, and it influenced her personal life, political views, and perspective on gender and culture. Natalie grew up in a culture that presented far greater opportunities to girls and women than that of previous generations. But even as feminism seemed to be part of the air she breathed, she also began to notice how sexism and other forms of social and economic injustice remained stubbornly intact.

The "simple" demographic information also shows that Natalie and Julia are privileged by their race and economic class, as well as by their cisgender identities. Yet, because of persistent sexism in Western culture, Natalie and Julia have faced gendered forms of bias and discrimination, and homophobia has compounded those challenges for Natalie.

We did not earn the privileges conferred by our skin color, class, or gender identity, nor did we earn the inequities that come with being categorized as female and, for Natalie, being a lesbian. That is the nature of much privilege and inequity—they are unearned. They do not reflect the achievements, efforts, or failings of the individuals who enjoy or suffer them.

The Social Construction of Inequality

To speak of being privileged in some ways and disadvantaged in others does not mean that these aspects of life are fixed in stone. The fact that being classified female makes approximately half of the population vulnerable to job discrimination, violence, and other injustices is not unchangeable. Nor is it immutable that some people's sexual orientation or race or economic class or gender identity makes them vulnerable to inequity. In fact, one reason we wrote this book is because we believe society can change, and each of us can be part of bringing change about.

To participate in changing society, we cannot limit ourselves to our personal identities and experiences. We need to learn about the experiences, perspectives, and circumstances of people in other social positions: The anger and hurt experienced by trans people in a society that defines them as abnormal; the resentment felt by some heterosexual white men toward laws and policies that increase rights and opportunities available to women and other historically disenfranchised populations; what it means to be a person of color in a sea of whiteness; the sense of restriction many women feel knowing they cannot venture out at night without risking assault; the frustration felt by poor and working-class citizens whose needs and circumstances often are not represented in legislation that claims to help everyone.

We can never fully understand the lives of people who differ from us but we can realize that our feelings, identities, values, and perspectives are not everyone's. Recognizing the limits of our own perspectives and experiences encourages us to learn from people who have different perspectives and experiences. We do this by respecting the specific conditions that shape their lives and by recognizing that only *they* can define the meanings of their experiences, feelings, thoughts, hopes, beliefs, problems, and needs. We cannot speak for them and cannot appropriate their voices as our own (González, Houston, & Chen, 2012). But to listen is to learn, and to learn is to broaden our appreciation of the range of human experiences and possibilities.

Feminism—Feminisms

Finally, in introducing ourselves to you, we should tell you that we are feminists, as are 60% of women and 33% of men in the United States (Crary, 2014). Before you form an impression based on your understanding of feminism, let's define the term. The word *feminism*

■■■■■■■■■ EXPLORING GENDERED LIVES ■■■■■■■■■

Multicultural Perspectives on Gender

How do we define and express *gender*? It depends on which culture's perspective you take.

- The Agta in the Philippines and the Tini Aborigines in Australia see keen hunting ability as a feminine ideal (Estioko-Griffin & Griffin, 1997).
- In Melanesia, young Sambian boys perform fellatio on adult men. The Sambia believe that swallowing the semen of adult men helps boys grow into healthy adult males (Herdt, 1997).
- Berdaches are members of approximately 150 North American societies, many of which are Native Americans. Although berdaches often enact the behaviors of a gender other than that associated with their assigned sex, within their societies they are recognized as distinct third and fourth genders (Roscoe, 1993).

- In addition to male and female, several South Asian nations including India, Nepal, Pakistan, and Bangladesh, formally recognize *hijra* as a third gender. *Hijra* are biologically assigned male at birth but embrace a feminine identity (Human Rights Watch, 2016).In addition to males and females, Juchitán in Oaxaca, Mexico, recognizes *muxes*, who are biological males who, from an early age, identify as females and adopt the roles and practices assigned to females in their community. Many residents of Juchitán believe that *muxes* have special abilities (Lacey, 2008).
- In Samoa, there is a third gender called the *Fa'afafine*. *Fa'afafines* engage in sexual relations almost exclusively with heterosexual males (Bartlett & Vasey, 2006).

TAKE A STAND: Do you believe you would view masculinity, femininity, and sexual orientation differently if you were Samoan or belonged to one of the other cultures mentioned above?

---

was coined in France in the late 1800s. It combined the French word for "woman," *femme*, with the suffix *ism*, meaning "political position." Thus, *feminism* means "a political position about women." Ironically, although many people do not call themselves feminists, they do think that women's rights activism has improved the conditions and opportunities available to women. Also, many people of all sexes and genders believe that individuals should have equal rights, regardless of their sex, sexual orientation, or gender. This suggests that, for many people, there is greater reservation about the label *feminist* than about the actual goals, values, and achievements of feminism.

When we talk with students who say they aren't feminists, we often discover that we agree on most issues relevant to gender but disagree on the meaning of the word *feminism*. There's good reason for this. First, feminism is not one single belief or political position. Chapter 3 discusses a variety of feminist positions, and Chapter 4 explores the different stances—some feminist, some not—endorsed by men's movements. Second, most people's impressions of feminism have been shaped by bias in media portrayal of feminism and feminists. Beginning with the inaccurate report that feminists burned bras at a protest of the 1968 Miss America Pageant (no bras were burned at that protest), media have consistently misrepresented feminists as man-hating, shrill extremists. Many people, like a student named Andrea (see her commentary), say they aren't feminists because they associate feminism with media caricatures that emphasize bashing men and engaging in radical protests.

ANDREA

I would never call myself a feminist, because that word has so many negative connotations. I don't hate men or anything, and I'm not interested in protesting. I don't want to go around with hacked-off hair and no makeup and sit around bashing men. I do think women and men are equal and should have the same kinds of rights, including equal pay for equal work. But I wouldn't call myself a feminist.

Media stereotypes of feminists don't fit many women and men who identify as feminists. Most feminists are not extremists, and most, like the two of us, have strong and loving relationships with people of all sexes and genders. Those who identify as feminist claim a range of gendered identities, and including traditional femininity, from interest in fashions to activities such as cooking and caring for children. Research shows that heterosexual men in relationships with feminist women are happier and consider their relationships healthier than heterosexual men in relationships with nonfeminist women. The converse is also true: Women in heterosexual relationships with feminist men are happier and more satisfied with their relationships than women in heterosexual relationships with nonfeminist men (Rudman & Phelan, 2007). Being a feminist does not conflict with being feminine, but it does mean being reflective about how women define and express femininity. Likewise, being a feminist does not conflict with being masculine, but it requires conscious decision-making about how to define and express masculinity.

Because feminism means different things to different people, we want to tell you how we define the term. We understand feminism as an active commitment to equality and respect for all forms of life. For us, this includes respecting all people, as well as nonhuman forms of life and the Earth itself. Simply put, we see feminism as resisting oppression, be it the oppression of women, men, people with disabilities, people with any gender or sexual identity, people of any race, ethnicity or religion, elderly people, children, animals, or our planet. We don't think oppression and domination foster healthy lives for individuals or societies as a whole. We believe there are better, more humane, and enriching ways for us to live, and we are convinced each of us can be part of bringing these alternatives into existence. During the course of reading this book, you will encounter varied versions of feminism, which should shatter the myth that feminism is one position, and which should also invite you to consider where to locate yourself among diverse viewpoints.

Feminism does not just happen. It is a process and an achievement. Julia was not raised to be a feminist. In fact, quite the contrary. She was brought up to be a traditional Southern woman who deferred to men and devoted her life to home and family. In the 1970s when a friend first introduced Julia to some readings about discrimination against women, her initial response was denial. She tried to rationalize inequities or repress her knowledge of discrimination, perhaps because recognizing it was painful. When denial failed to work, Julia became angry about the ways in which women, including herself, were devalued and denied opportunities. She was also angry at herself for having been unaware of society's devaluation of women and for conforming to the roles assigned to women. Eventually, Julia transformed the anger into an abiding commitment to working for changes in society.

Natalie came to feminism somewhat differently. She was raised to believe that girls and women were equal to boys and men. Her parents, both of whom identified as feminists, encouraged her love of reading, music, dance, and math equally, and cheered her athletic and academic pursuits. She was fortunate to have a series of teachers throughout her schooling who believed in her and pushed her to excel. Upon entering graduate school, she was assigned to Julia's teaching team for the class, *Gender, Communication, and Culture*, using the very textbook you are reading right now (albeit an edition from a few years back!). The material resonated profoundly: Despite the fact that Natalie had grown up in a culture that proclaimed sexism to be over and feminism no longer needed, the new set of concepts she encountered in *Gendered Lives* named persistent patterns of inequity that she had noticed but had not had language to label and critique. Like Julia, sometimes Natalie's response to this new information was denial or anger, but it also ignited her curiosities and passions. She began exploring the histories of feminist social movements and contemporary gendered injustices and now devotes her research, teaching, and activism to these issues.

Becoming Aware

Whether you identify with feminism or not, you are gendered. Reading this book will expand your understanding of gender—how it is shaped and expressed in contexts ranging from the political arena to intimate relationships. The awareness you gain will enhance your insight into yourself and your society.

At the same time, you may feel unsettled as you read this book. If you identify as a woman, you may find it disturbing to learn the extent to which Western culture (and other cultures) devalues women's experiences and limits their opportunities. If you identify as a man, reading this book may increase your awareness of the ways in which cultural views of masculinity constrain your life choices. You may be uncomfortable learning about social expectations for men to succeed, to be self-sufficient, to repress feelings, and to put work ahead of family. You may also be surprised to learn that your sex and gender benefit you in ways that you may not have noticed, particularly if you are white. If you challenge gender norms or identify as LGBTQ, this book may give you language that helps you to define your identity and experience, while also specifying the unique challenges of living as LGBTQ in a cis- and hetero-normative world.

We also realize that a number of people reading this have been raped, sexually abused, sexually harassed, or battered. Some of you have eating disorders; some have suffered job discrimination; some of you have been taunted for not embodying current social expectations for women and men; and some of you have been bullied because of your sexual orientation or gender identity. Reading *Gendered Lives* is likely to stir up these issues. If you don't wish to deal with such difficult issues, then you may choose to forgo or delay study in this area. However, if you are ready to wrestle with serious personal and social matters, then this book should help you understand issues in your life as not only personal but also deeply rooted in social values and institutions.

Becoming aware of inequities in social life may lead you to speak out against practices and attitudes that sustain discrimination and disadvantage. Realize that some people will respond negatively if you make thoughtful criticisms of social attitudes and practices that foster inequity. Women who speak out against inequities and discrimination are sometimes accused of male-bashing. Men who speak out against discrimination against women are sometimes regarded as wimps or as disloyal to men. Such responses reflect an unwillingness to engage in the substance of the criticism. If you want to take an active role in shaping our shared world, you must anticipate struggles with those who are less willing to consider ideas that question familiar perspectives and behaviors.

PATRICK

I don't want to be lumped with all men. I am not sexist; I don't discriminate against women; I believe in gender equality and try to practice it in my relationships with women. It really makes me angry when people bash males as if we are all oppressors or something. I don't oppress women or anyone else, and I don't want to be blamed for unfair things that others do.

Patrick makes an important point. We need to distinguish between the actions and attitudes of individuals and the social practices and values of our culture. Most individual men do not aim to oppress women or gender-nonconforming people. The point is that Western culture as a whole has constructed gendered inequalities, and these inequalities continue in our era.

The problem, then, is not individuals, but rather a social system that accords unequal value and opportunity on the basis of sex assignment. This kind of prejudice diminishes us all. It limits our appreciation of human diversity by defining a very narrow zone of what is good, normal, and worthy of respect. Regardless of whether you are privileged or oppressed by social evaluations of what is normal and good, your study of gender, communication, and culture may be unsettling. If you are seriously disturbed by what you read, you might find it helpful to talk with your instructor or to visit the counseling center at your school.

Why We Wrote This Book

We wrote *Gendered Lives* because we believe that change is needed in how we view and embody gender. We also believe research presented in this book can empower you to make more informed choices about your personal identity and our shared world. Since the first edition was published, we've received many positive responses from colleagues who teach classes that use the book and from students in our classes as well as from students around the nation. We've also received helpful criticism and suggestions that have motivated us to rethink and improve the book.

In the chapters that follow, you'll learn about the extent to which gender inequities and discrimination persist and diminish individual and collective life. For instance:

■■■ EXPLORING GENDERED LIVES ■■■

About "Male-Bashing": Julia and Natalie—the Authors— Comment

Occasionally, a student tells one of us that *Gendered Lives* "bashes men." This comment puzzles us, because we don't see ourselves as male-bashers. Both of our lives include men we love. We have many male friends and colleagues, and we've done as much to mentor male students and colleagues as female ones. When we ask students to explain why they think the book bashes men, they tell us it gives more attention to discrimination against women than to discrimination against men and that it points out that some men harm women. They are correct in this observation, but the difference in attention to harms to women and men reflects findings from research rather than any personal views we hold.

Like all scholars, what we write depends largely on available information. Existing research shows that, although both men and women experience violence from intimate partners, 95% of people who are known to be physically abused by romantic partners are women (Haynes, 2009; Johnson, 2006). It would be inaccurate to give equal space to discussion of men who are physically abused by intimate partners. The same

is true of sexual harassment: Although members of both sexes and all genders are sexually harassed, most victims are girls and women and most perpetrators are men. The only way we could present a gender-balanced discussion of sexual harassment would be by misrepresenting facts.

You should also realize that this book includes more information about men and men's issues than any other textbook for a course in gender and communication. In the chapters that follow, you'll learn about men's movements, pressures men face to succeed and conform to stereotypes of masculinity, and consequences, such as depression, of social perspectives that limit men in the workplace and in personal relationships. You'll also learn that men, like women, can be victims of sexual violence. In addition, you'll discover that men find it stressful to balance work and family, yet men today are contributing more to raising children than previous generations of men. Research throughout this book shows how social expectations of women and men can restrict all of us. We hope that, as you read this book, you'll perceive the coverage as fair.

- Is there any way to justify the fact that, each day in the United States, at least four women are killed by their partners or ex-partners?
- Is there any way to justify the fact that the majority of the victims of hate violence murders are trans women and mostly trans women of color (National Coalition of Anti-Violence Programs, 2013)?
- Is it fair that men who want to spend time with their families are often evaluated negatively in professional contexts?
- Is it acceptable that a Pakistani court sentenced a woman to be gang-raped because of an offense allegedly committed by her brother?
- Is it just that most of the advances won by women's movements have benefited white, middle-class women more than poor women and women of color?

- Is there any reason why, for every dollar white men earn, white women earn 79 cents, Black women earn 60 cents, Native American women earn 59 cents, and Latinas earn 55 cents for doing the same job (Miller, 2016b; "Women Still Earn a Lot Less Than Men," 2015)?
- Is it fair that, in divorce proceedings, mothers have an advantage over fathers in gaining custody of children?
- Is it right that women bear the primary responsibility and nearly all of the risks in reproductive matters, including fertility, contraception, and parenting?
- Does it make sense that the United States is one of only four countries without a national policy requiring paid family leave (Oman, Tonga, and Papua New Guinea are the other three) (Rowe-Finkbeiner, 2014; Zarocostas, 2014)?

If you don't want inequities such as these to continue, read on. Becoming aware of how our culture establishes and normalizes inequities is necessary, but that alone will not lead to changes. In fact, concentrating exclusively on what is wrong tends to depress us, which can paralyze impulses toward reform. Awareness of inequities must be coupled with realizing that change is possible.

Through individual action and social movements, many blatant forms of sex discrimination have been eliminated. In the 1800s, women weren't allowed to vote. They also had no access to a university education, could not own property if they married, and were barred from participating in most professions. Until the mid-1970s, women in the United States could not get credit cards in their own names (Zeisler, 2016). In the past, sexual harassment, acquaintance rape, and marital rape were unnamed and generally unpunished. In recent decades they have been named and recognized as illegal. Women can now vote, attend

Contemporary views of masculinity differ from than those that prevailed in earlier eras.

g-stockstudio/Shutterstock.com

universities, own property, pursue professional careers, and have credit cards in their names, and they can bring legal action if they are harassed or raped.

Views of men, too, have changed. In earlier eras, our society defined *manliness* in terms of physical strength and bravery. After the Industrial Revolution, the ability to earn a good salary became the social standard of manliness. Today, many men are challenging social definitions of men as income providers and are seeking greater opportunities to participate in personal relationships. Forty years ago, it would have been almost unthinkable for a man to have been a stay-at-home dad. Today, a number of men are stay-at-home dads.

Gender is also increasingly recognized as fluid. Lesbian, gay, bisexual, trans and gender-nonconforming individuals enjoy greater visibility and acceptance than in previous decades. Long-standing forms of discrimination against LGBTQ people have been challenged and, in many cases, changed. For example, a few years ago, the Supreme Court ruled that same-sex marriages are legal. Despite these positive changes, many forms of discrimination against LGBQ people remain and strict gender norms create barriers to full acceptance.

Changes such as the ones we've discussed mislead many people into thinking that gender equality has been achieved. Some believe we live in a "postfeminist era" in which gender discrimination is history and that sexism has been overcome.

- Some say that women now have freedom of choice but fail to recognize that women have fewer reproductive rights in the United States than in a number of other countries.
- Some cite high-visibility politicians such as Hillary Clinton as evidence that the playing field in politics is now level but do not realize that women make up 18% of the U.S. House of Representatives and only 4.6% of CEOs of Fortune 500 companies (Remnick, 2015; Sandberg & Chávez, 2014 vanOgtrop, 2015).
- Some argue that the United States opposes discrimination against women but don't seem disturbed that the United States—along with a few other nations such as Somalia and Sudan—has refused to ratify the United Nations Convention on the Elimination of All Forms of Discrimination Against Women. Jimmy Carter signed the treaty in 1980, and the Senate has yet to act on it.
- Some believe that heterosexual women and men now have egalitarian relationships but don't seem concerned that, in two-worker families, women still spend twice as much time as men on housework and child care (Bruni, 2016).

As the listing shows, not all of the inequities based on sex and gender are history. Even in the United States, gender equity has not been fully achieved. In a ranking of measures that affect women's lives (health, education, economics, politics, and justice) the United States ranked eighth, behind Iceland, Sweden, Canada, Denmark, Finland, Switzerland, and Norway (Streib, 2011). Although we've made progress toward gender equity, there are more changes to be made before we have a truly level-playing field for everyone.

The consequences of how we define and embody gender are not abstract. There are very real stakes involved. Individuals' health and even their lives can be on the line. Consider a few examples of the concrete impacts of social views of gender:

- Women suffer far more adverse side effects, including potentially fatal heart arrhythmia, from sleeping pills than men because only men were used in trials when many of the drugs were in development (Rabin, 2013).

- Transgender people lack access to adequate health care because they often face outright refusal of services, discrimination, and/or lack of understanding and cultural competence from health care providers (National Center for Transgender Equality, 2016).

- Although female infertility accounts for only approximately one-third of heterosexual couples' trouble with conceiving, women bear the disproportionate burden and risks of fertility treatments. Regardless of the cause of infertility, virtually all treatments are interventions on women's bodies, and effects include bruising and soreness from shots, nausea, allergic responses, ovarian hyperstimulation syndrome, multiple miscarriages and stillbirths, gestational diabetes, maternal hemorrhage, and preterm labor and delivery (ASRM, 2017).

- Testosterone levels naturally decline as men age, yet men today are bombarded with advertising that urges them to treat "low T" or "low testosterone" (Jaret, 2014). Since 2001, prescriptions for testosterone have tripled. And prescription testosterone has some dangerous potential side effects, including adding massive numbers of red blood cells to the bloodstream, shrinking testes, and increasing the risk of heart attacks (LaPuma, 2014).

These facts make it crystal clear that the stakes are high when it comes to gender.

Communication as the Fulcrum of Change

The stakes we've noted provide a compelling reason to work for changes in how we understand and embody gender. Communication is the heart of social change. Through communication, we can identify and challenge current cultural views that constrain individuals and create inequities. We rely on communication to define alternatives to the status quo and to persuade others to share our visions. Public discourse often sparks and guides collective efforts at political reform. For example, in the mid-1800s Elizabeth Cady Stanton and other early feminists galvanized support for the women's rights movement through their eloquent speeches.

More recently, students are leading the way in persuading women's colleges to rethink policies that have excluded transgender students. One of the first challenges came in 2011 when students at Hollins, a women's university in Virginia, challenged the school's policy stating that any student who had hormone treatment, surgery, or changed her name as part of redefining her sex could no longer attend classes and could not graduate. As Hollins and other women's colleges were debating whether to allow transgender students to matriculate, The Department of Education, in 2014, ruled that Title IX protects transgender students from discrimination. A number of women's colleges, as well as coed colleges and universities, now admit and accommodate transgender students.

Other kinds of communication also instigate change. Perhaps you use social media to circulate articles about gender inequalities and as a result your friends see injustices they previously had not noticed. Maybe a teacher discusses sexual harassment with his class, and a student is empowered to bring charges against her supervisor who has been harassing her. You talk with your father about ways in which current leave policies disadvantage working mothers, and he persuades his company to revise its policies. Wherever there is change, we find communication. Through your interpersonal, social, and public communication, you can transform yourself and the society in which we jointly participate.

Information is the foundation of making effective choices about what you believe and what you want to change. Reading *Gendered Lives* will provide you with a great deal of information that you can use to develop knowledgeable stands on gender issues. Then, you can make informed choices about what you believe and about the identity you wish to fashion for yourself. You may decide to change how you define yourself, or you may be satisfied with your identity and the existing gender arrangements in our culture. Either stance is principled if it is *informed*—but no stance has integrity if it is not based on sound information and serious reflection.

The Challenge of Studying Communication, Gender, and Culture

Studying communication, gender, and culture involves us in perplexing and often painful questions about our society and our personal identities. You need courage to consider new ideas openly and to risk the turmoil of changing values and identities that are familiar. Further, with awareness comes responsibility. Once we are informed about gender and communication, we can no longer sit passively back as if they were not our concern. They *are* our concern, both because gender and communication affect each of us directly and because we are part of a collective world. Thus, how we act—or fail to act—influences our shared culture.

Although studying communication, gender, and culture is disturbing, it can be very worthwhile. By questioning constructed inequality, we empower ourselves to do more than unthinkingly reproduce the cultural patterns we grew up with. Instead, we can assume active roles in creating personal and collective lives that are fairer, more humane, and infinitely more enriching than what might otherwise be possible.

Features of *Gendered Lives*

Four features distinguish this book and support the views we've just discussed. First, we include **discussion of diverse classes, ethnicities, races, gender identities, and sexual orientations** whenever research is available. For instance, the Exploring Gendered Lives box titled "Multicultural Perspectives on Gender" identifies a range of ways in which cultures define *gender* and *sexual identities*.

A second feature of this book is **language that aims to include all readers**. We use terms such as *he, she,* and *they,* as well as *women, men,* and *people of all genders in* preference to *he, mankind,* and *men.* But inclusive language means more than including women and gender-nonconforming people; it also means using language that refuses to go along with cultural marginalization of any group. For instance, we generally refer to *committed relationships* rather than *marriages.* The terms *spouse, husband, wife,* and *marriage* exclude cohabiting partners who choose not to marry.

A third feature of *Gendered Lives* is inclusion of diverse perspectives. We present not only research that reflects different views but also **student voices that reflect widely ranging experiences, values, and identities**. In the pages that follow, you'll meet a lot of students—some like you, some quite different. In many courses on gender and communication, students keep journals or write reflection papers that link class concepts with their personal lives. Many of our own students gave us permission to include their reflections in this book. In addition, students at other campuses around the country have written in response to previous editions of *Gendered Lives*, and some of their comments appear in this edition. We've tried to return their generosity by including an array of individuals and viewpoints, including ones with which we personally disagree. In fact, including ideas with which we disagree, from both students and scholars, is necessary if this book is to reflect the variety of ideas about gender and communication that circulate in our culture. Hannah, a student from a northeastern college, makes a point in her commentary on this page.

> ### HANNAH
>
> *When I was reading Gendered Lives, I had to keep reminding myself that you were presenting information and that not all points were your personal values and beliefs. I didn't agree with all of your statements or the ideas of others, like the students in their commentaries, but I learned a lot about the ways others see gender. I also learned a lot about how I think about gender by seeing what ideas I agreed with and disagreed with.*

Hannah's comment reflects open-mindedness, which fosters learning. As you read this book, we hope you will think about research findings and students' voices and reflect on how they are similar to or different from your own beliefs and values. We have refrained from evaluating or interpreting the reflections that appear in this book. The students write clearly and eloquently, and we don't want to muffle their voices with our analysis.

Fourth, we encourage **your active engagement**. One way we do this is by asking you to think about issues both in the chapters and in questions that appear at the end of chapters. Second, we ask you to **Take a Stand** on issues presented in **Exploring Gendered Lives** boxes that appear in all chapters. Third, at the end of each chapter, we ask you to apply material in the chapter to your life. We hope you will embrace the challenge of engaging ideas in the chapters that follow.

GENDER ONLINE

1. The Organization for Research on Women and Communication (ORWAC) publishes the journal, *Women's Studies in Communication*. You can read back issues of the journal online at ORWAC's site: ***http://www.cios.org***

2. Terms for online searches: *sex-cultural views of, feminism, hijras*.

REFLECTION, DISCUSSION, AND ACTION

1. Using the authors' self-descriptions as guidelines, consider how your identity influenced your choice to take this course, as well as how it may affect your perceptions of topics in the book and the course. Have you been privileged or disadvantaged by your race, class, sex, gender, and sexual orientation? How have your privileges and disadvantages affected your opportunities, knowledge of issues, interests, abilities, goals, and so on?

2. How do you define *feminism*? Write your definition, and see if it changes during the course of reading this book and taking this class.

3. Interview two people who are from non-Western cultures. Ask them to explain what it means to be a man (or manly or masculine) and what it means to be a woman (or womanly or feminine) in their cultures. How do their cultures' definitions of gender cohere with and depart from those in the United States? Ask them what they find most interesting or surprising about U.S. views of gender.

RECOMMENDED SOURCES

1. Peggy McIntosh (2007). White Privilege: Unpacking the Invisible Knapsack. In P. Andersen and P. H. Collins (Eds.) (2016). *Race, Class, & Gender*, 9th ed. (pp. 98–102). Belmont, CA: Thomson-Cengage. This is a classic article that raises awareness of privileges many people enjoy without being conscious of them.

2. Allan Johnson (2017). *Privilege, Power, and Difference*, 3rd ed. New York: McGraw-Hill. This is an engaging and accessible introduction to thinking about inequalities and how they harm all of us, including those who seem to benefit from them.

We are looking for permission to be more than our society tells us we are.
—STARHAWK

The Study of Communication, Gender, and Culture

Knowledge Challenge:

- How many sexes are there?
- Do all males have the same sex chromosomes?
- What is the difference between gender identity and sexual orientation?

Google "male–female communication," and you'll find dozens of sites that offer advice on interacting with the "opposite sex." If you watch popular shows such as *Orange Is the New Black* or *Transparent*, you have seen transgender characters and actors. Listen to popular music, and you'll see artists engaging gender in their lyrics and videos, as in Beyonce's "Pretty Hurts" or Meghan Trainor's "No." The general public's fascination with gender and communication is mirrored by college students' interest. Around the United States and in other countries, many campuses cannot meet student demand for courses on gender and communication.

This chapter introduces you to communication, gender, and culture as an area of study and defines key concepts that form the framework of this book.

Communication, Gender, and Culture as an Area of Study

Had you attended college in the early to mid-1980s, you would not have found a textbook like this one, and it's highly unlikely you could have found a course such as the one this book accompanies. Today, most colleges and universities offer courses on gender because there is now an impressive base of research to inform teaching.

Research on Gender, Communication, and Culture

Research on gender comes from multiple fields, including anthropology, communication, history, neuroscience, philosophy, psychology, sociology, and women's studies. Scholars in these disciplines rely on a number of research methods.

Quantitative research methods[1] gather and analyze data that can be quantified. Three of the more common quantitative methods are descriptive statistics, surveys, and experiments. Descriptive statistics describe populations, proportions, and frequencies. They answer questions such as: How often do women and men interrupt in conversations? How much do men and women in the same professional positions earn?

Surveys, which may be written or oral, ask people to report their feelings, thoughts, and experiences. They ask women and men what they do with close friends or what kinds of online activities they prefer.

Experiments are controlled studies that manipulate one thing (called an independent variable) to determine how it affects another thing (called a dependent variable). They test the impact of reading fashion magazines on women's self-esteem and how a particular teaching method affects boys' and girls' learning.

Qualitative research methods, sometimes called interpretive methods, aim to understand meanings that cannot be quantified. Two popular qualitative methods are textual analysis and ethnography. As the name implies, textual analysis involves studying communication texts, which may be written, oral, or nonverbal. Textual analyses have illuminated the meaning of speeches such as the *Declaration of Sentiments*, which was given at the first Women's Rights Convention.

Ethnography relies on extensive observation to discover what things mean to people. Ethnographic study has provided detailed descriptions of how gender is enacted in diverse cultures.

Critical research methods identify and critique the means by which power relations are created or challenged. For example, critical research has given us insight into ways in which organizational structures and practices create work environments that women and minorities perceive as unwelcoming.

Mixed research methods are exactly what the name implies—a combination of two or more of the methods described above. For example, a scholar might document the frequency (descriptive statistic) of men's and women's smiling in social situations and then interview men and women (qualitative method) to learn why they smile.

■ **EXPLORING GENDERED LIVES** ■

Journals That Feature Research on Gender and Communication

Communication Education	*Journal of Men's Studies*
Communication Monographs	*Journal of Social & Personal Relationships*
Communication Studies	*Men and Masculinities*
Communication and Critical Cultural Studies	*Sex Roles*
Gender and Society	*Sexuality and Culture*
Journal of Applied Communication Research	*Signs*
Journal of Cross-Cultural Research	*Women and Language*
Journal of Gender, Culture & Health	*Women's Studies in Communication*

TAKE A STAND: Read one article focused on gender in one of the journals listed here. What did you learn as a result of reading the article?

---

[1]Boldface terms appear in the glossary at the end of this book.

Reasons to Learn about Communication, Gender, and Culture

Learning about communication, gender, and culture serves three important goals. First, you will gain increased appreciation of complex ways in which cultural values and practices shape understandings and expectations of masculinity and femininity and men and women. Second, as you become more aware of ways cultural expectations of gender are communicated to you, you will more deeply understand your personal gender, both as it is now and as it might be if you choose to remake it. You will be empowered to think critically about the extent to which you wish to identify with cultural prescriptions for gender.

Third, studying communication, gender, and culture will strengthen your effectiveness as a communicator. Learning about gendered differences in communication will enlarge your ability to appreciate and adapt to diverse communication styles. In addition, learning how your own communication does or does not conform to prevailing cultural prescriptions for gender allows you to make informed choices about how you want to communicate in the future.

Gender in a Transitional Era

You probably don't subscribe to your grandparents' ideals of manhood and womanhood. You may believe that people of all sexes and genders should be able to pursue careers and that both should be involved in homemaking and family life. You are probably not surprised when a woman knows how to change a tire or when a man cooks a good meal. Yet, if you're like most of your peers, there are also a number of gender issues about which you feel conflicted.

- You may think that both parents should participate in child rearing but assume that the mother, not the father, should be the primary caregiver during the early years of children's lives.
- You may support gender equality in the military but remain uncomfortable with women serving in combat roles.
- You may believe in equal opportunity but think that colleges and universities should be allowed to offer more scholarships to male athletes.
- You may believe that gender is fluid but are unsure how to respond when your roommate identifies as trans.

TRACY

The issue of women in combat really troubles me. I have a son who is 17 and a daughter who is 15. I don't want either of them in combat, but I've always known my son could be in combat. Would I argue that my son should be and my daughter shouldn't be? That's like saying I value her life more than his. I can't say that.

When we grapple with issues like these, we realize that our attitudes aren't always clear or wholly consistent. Many of us no longer accept all traditional views, yet we haven't become comfortable with alternative views and their implications for our identities and relationships. This makes our lives and our relationships interesting, unsettling, and, occasionally, frustrating.

> **MICHAEL**
>
> *The other day in class, we were talking about whether women should have combat duty. I'm really uncomfortable with where I stand on this, since I think one way, but I feel another. I do think women should have to serve just as much as men do. I've never thought it was right that they didn't have to fight. And I think women are just as competent as men at most things and could probably be good soldiers. But then when I think about my mom, my sister, or my girlfriend being in the trenches, having to kill other people, or maybe being a prisoner who is tortured and assaulted, I just feel that's wrong. It doesn't seem right for women to be involved in killing when they're the ones who give life. Then, too, I want to protect my girlfriend, sister, and mom from the ugliness and danger of war.*
>
> *But then, this other part of me says, "Hey, guy, you know that kind of protectiveness is a form of chauvinism." I just don't know where I stand on this except that I'm glad I don't have to decide whether to send women into combat!*

Differences between Women and Men

Are women and men really as different as pop psychologists proclaim? Certainly, there are some differences between the sexes, but there are also many similarities. In addition, there is substantial variation within each sex as a result of experience, heredity, sexual orientation, gender identity, race, economic class, and other factors.

> **KATHERINE**
>
> *I am really skeptical of books that describe women and men as "opposite" sexes. They focus on a few ways that most women and most men are different. They totally ignore all of the ways that women and men are alike. Even worse is that they act like all women are the same and all men are the same. People are just such individuals that you can't sum them up as "man" or "woman."*

Katherine's commentary is insightful. Terms such as *women* and *men* are troublesome because they imply that all women can be grouped into one category and all men into another. When we say, "Women's communication is more personal than men's," the statement is true of most, but not all, women and men. Yet some women don't engage in much personal talk, and some men do. Many factors, including race, economic class, and sexual identity, shape how individuals communicate.

Essentializing is reducing something or someone to certain characteristics that are assumed to be central to its nature and present in every member of its group. When we essentialize sex, we mistakenly assume that all members of a sex share defining qualities. Essentializing ignores characteristics that differentiate individuals from one another. In this book, we will discuss generalizations about sexed and gendered identities, but this does not imply there are essential qualities possessed by all members of a particular sex or gender.

In these opening pages, we've used the words *gender* and *sex* several times, but we haven't yet defined them. The remainder of this chapter provides definitions of key concepts that inform this book.

Relationships among Gender, Culture, and Communication

When asked to discuss a particular aspect of nature, John Muir, founder of the Sierra Club, said he could not discuss any single part of the natural world in isolation. He observed that each part is "hitched to the universe," meaning that every part of nature is connected to all other parts. Likewise, gender, culture, and communication are hitched together. We cannot really understand any one of these concepts without knowing about the others.

Although many people use the terms *gender* and *sex* interchangeably, they have distinct meanings. **Sex** (female or male) is a designation based on biology and assigned at birth. Gender is far more complex. **Gender** is socially constructed and expressed. It includes one's internal sense of self as a woman, man, or neither (**gender identity**), the external communication of one's gender identity through clothing, hairstyles, behavior, and voice (**gender expression**), as well as the cultural expectations assigned to one's sex (**gender role**). For many people, sex and gender are consistent; most children assigned male at birth eventually identify as men and most assigned female eventually identify as women. For some, however, sex and gender do not neatly align. We'll now elaborate the meanings and complexities of sex and gender and discuss how each is related to culture and communication.

Sex

Sex is a biological classification based on external genitalia (penis and testes in males, clitoris and vagina in females) and internal sex organs (ovaries and uterus in females, prostate gland in males). Genitalia are determined by chromosomes. In most cases, human development is guided by 23 sets of chromosomes, one of which determines sex. In most cases, people who are biologically male have XY sex chromosomes, whereas people who are biologically female have XX sex chromosomes.

■ EXPLORING GENDERED LIVES ■

Grown-Up Tomboys

University of Southern California professor Jack Halberstam says many girls are tomboys because "a lot of the really fun activities get allocated to men. That's where the action is" (Williams, 2012, p. B13). But, says Halberstam, "Tomboyism is tolerated as long as the child remains prepubescent; as soon as puberty begins, however, the full force of gender conformity descends on the girl" (1998, p. 6). Wanting to challenge the pressure for girls to become feminine, Halberstam (1998, 2011, 2012) argues that we have to separate masculinity from male bodies— and, by extension, femininity from female bodies. For Halberstam, the goal is to learn to think about female masculinity— and, by extension, male femininity. And don't assume masculine women or feminine men identify as LGBTQ. If you follow Halberstam's logic, those linkages are just as constructed and questionable as the ones between masculinity and male and femininity and female.

TAKE A STAND: How do you envision female masculinity and male femininity?

But sex is not as neatly binary as Western culture represents it to be. One challenge to binary sex categories is chromosomal variations. For every 500 individuals, 1 does not have XX or XY sex chromosomes (Harper, 2007). This means that of the approximately 300 million individuals in the United States today, roughly 600,000 do not have XX or XY sex chromosomes. They have XO, XXX, XXY, or XYY sex chromosomes. Occasionally, some of an individual's cells have XY chromosomes and some have XX chromosomes.

Another challenge to the traditional male/female dichotomy is **intersex people**, the approximately 1% of the population that is born with biological characteristics of both sexes (Sapolsky, 2013). For many years, infants who were born intersex were assigned one sex or the other, and they underwent "normalizing surgery" to make their genitals appear consistently male or female. This surgery, however, carries significant risk to sexual pleasure and reproductive function, and many intersex people resented the surgery that was imposed on them. They argued that intersex is simply another sex category that is neither pathological nor in need of "fixing."

Largely as a result of intersex activism, doctors and the broader culture have reconsidered the assumption that everyone must fit into either the male or the female biological category. In 2013, Germany and Australia joined Nepal and New Zealand in adopting guidelines that allow parents to choose among more than two sex categories on birth certificates (Bendavid, 2013). The United States has not yet recognized intersex as a distinct sex category, but U.S. surgeons are increasingly reluctant to recommend "normalizing" surgery for intersex infants (Bendavid, 2013). The Intersex Society of North America opposes surgery, hormone treatments, or a third sex category for intersex infants. They advocate instead for approximating sex within the current male-female binary at birth through various tests and then supporting children's natural gender exploration and development over time before considering surgery (Dreger, n.d.).

EXPLORING GENDERED LIVES

Social Views of Intersex

Not all species insist on strict sex dichotomies. One species of fish changes sex as necessary to maintain its population. If the only male fish in a group dies, a female becomes male and facilitates reproduction (Sapolsky, 2013).

Intersex is not new among humans, either. Deborah Rudacille (2006) found records from 1629 describing Thomas Hall, who lived in the Jamestown settlement and claimed to be both a man and a woman. A number of groups, including several Native American tribes, historically recognized and celebrated "two spirit" people, who were both male and female.

Albania recognizes burneshas, biological females who live as men, often to enjoy the freedoms traditionally allowed to men and not women: voting, driving, earning money, drinking, swearing, wearing pants. Becoming a burnesha also allows people born female to avoid the plight of being forced into an arranged marriage (Zhang, 2012).

The Intersex Society of North America (ISNA, **www.itpeople.org**) has three primary missions: (1) to affirm a positive identity for intersex people; (2) to change social attitudes toward intersexuality; and (3) to stop "normalizing surgery."

TAKE A STAND: Do you think intersex should be recognized as a distinct sex?

Sexual development is also influenced by hormones. When pregnancy proceeds routinely, fetuses with a Y chromosome are bathed in androgens that stimulate development of male sex organs, whereas fetuses without a Y chromosome receive fewer androgens, so female sex organs develop. In some cases, however, a genetically female fetus (XX) is exposed to excessive progesterone and may not develop the customary female genitalia. The opposite is also true: If a male fetus is deprived of progesterone, standard male genitalia may not develop. The influence of hormones does not end at birth. They continue to affect our development by determining whether we menstruate, how much body hair we have and where it grows, how much fat and muscle tissue we develop, and so forth.

Biological sex *influences* aspects of our development, but it does not govern the meaning that members of a culture assign to sex. This moves us into discussion of a second concept: gender.

Gender

Gender is the social meaning assigned to sex. Related to gender are the concepts of gender identity, which is an individual's perception, and subjective experience, of gender, and gender expression, which is how one communicates gender to the outside world. Gender, gender identity, and gender expression are not innate. They also tend to be less stable and more fluid than sex. Most of us are born male or female (sex), but we have to learn to see ourselves as gendered (gender identity) and to act in masculine and/or feminine ways (gender expression). Gender varies across cultures, over time within a given culture, over the course of individuals' life spans, and in relation to other genders. We'll elaborate these aspects of gender.

Consider current meanings of masculinity and femininity in the United States. To be masculine is to be strong, ambitious, successful, rational, and emotionally controlled. Although these requirements are less rigid than they were in earlier eras, they remain largely intact. Those we regard as "real men" still don't cry in public and are successful and powerful in their professional and public lives.

Femininity in our era is also relatively consistent with earlier views, although there is increasing latitude in what is considered appropriate for women. To be feminine is to be physically attractive, emotionally expressive, nurturing, and concerned with people and relationships.

Gender is learned. From infancy on, we are encouraged to embody the gender that society prescribes for us. Young girls are often cautioned, "Don't be selfish—share with others" and "Don't be bossy." They are praised for looking pretty, taking care of others (including dolls), and being nice. Young boys, in contrast, are more likely to be admonished, "Don't be a sissy" and "Don't cry." They are rewarded for strength, independence, and success, particularly in competitive arenas.

BISHETTA

I remember when I was very little, maybe 5 or so. My brother and I were playing outside in the garden, and Mom saw us. Both of us were coated with dirt—our clothes, our skin, everything. Mom came up to the edge of the garden and shouted, "Bishetta, you get out of that garden right now. Just look at you. Now, what do you think folks will think of a dirty little girl? You don't want people to think you're not a lady, do you?" She didn't say a word to my brother, who was just as dirty.

■ EXPLORING GENDERED LIVES ■

T Troubles

In 2014, 18-year-old Dutee Chand, one of the fastest runners in India, was preparing for her first international competition as an adult, when her competitors reported to the Indian government sports authority that she had a "suspiciously masculine" physique. Chand was subjected to invasive medical examinations and testing (Padawer, 2016). Chand was stunned when she was banned from competition because of her testosterone level.

Like Chand, a number of female athletes have had their sex challenged. The International Olympic Committee (IOC) and, for decades, the International Association of Athletics Federations (IAAF) have tightly regulated sex in women's sports. In the 1940s, female athletes were required to submit "medical 'femininity certificates' to verify their sex" and in the 1960s, officials mandated genital checks and chromosomal testing to verify female participants' gender (Padawer, 2016). In 2011, the IOC initiated a new guideline based on T (testosterone) levels. Female athletes whose T levels exceed what is considered "normal" are subject to sex testing, which may include blood tests, genital examinations, and psychosocial evaluations (Karkazis & Jordan-Young, 2014; Schultz, 2014). Under this policy, female athletes with higher T levels than customary for females were given two options: Either cease competing as women or have their gonads and part of their clitorises removed, which leads to sterilization (Karkazis & Jordan-Young, 2014).

But are T levels a surefire way to determine sex? In one study of 693 accomplished athletes, 14% of women had T levels that exceeded the range designated as typical for females, and 16.5% of men had T levels that fell in the range designated for females (Karkazis & Jordan-Young, 2014). Further, no study has proven that T levels in the "male range" provide female athletes a competitive advantage, whereas researchers have identified over 200 genetic and biological variations that offer athletes competitive advantages (such as exceptionally long limbs or flexible joints) that are not subject to scrutiny or regulations like those imposed on hormonal variation (Padawer, 2016).

In July 2015, the International Court of Arbitration for Sport ruled in Chand's favor, finding the policy "unjustifiably discriminatory" (Padawer, 2016). But the ruling is temporary. The IAAF was given two years from the date of the ruling to provide sufficient evidence that elevated T levels provide female athletes a competitive advantage comparable to that of men.

TAKE A STAND: How would you determine an athlete's eligibility to compete as a woman or man?

Although individuals learn gender, it is not strictly personal. Rather, cultures stipulate the social *meaning* and *expectations* of each sex. Because society's views of gender permeate public and private life, we tend to see them as normal, natural, and right. When society constantly represents women and men in particular ways, it is difficult to imagine that masculinity and femininity could be defined differently. But, as we will see, gender varies widely across cultures and history.

Conventional views of both sex and gender are challenged by people who define themselves as trans (transgender), genderqueer, or gender nonconforming. Although some trans people identify with the sex other than the one that they were assigned at birth, others reject the binary categories of male and female, and still others self-identify as a third gender or a unique blending of femininity and masculinity or describe themselves as agender—without gender. In Chapter 2, we'll look more closely at queer theory, which gives insight into a range of gender identities and ways of performing gender.

Meanings of gender also change as the result of role models, who embody visible alternatives to traditional gender identities. When a woman embodies professional ambition, she may challenge what others see as appropriate behavior for women. Similarly, when a man tells another man that time with his family is a top priority, his friend may reconsider his own views of men's roles. When one person lives openly as trans, that person may make it easier for others whose gender identity doesn't fit neatly into conventional categories.

ETHAN

What I always thought was unfair in my family was the way my folks responded to failures my sisters and I had. Like once my sister Maryellen tried out for cheerleader, and she wasn't picked. So she was crying and upset, and Mom was telling her that it was okay and that she was a good person, and everyone knew that and that winning wasn't everything. And when Dad came home he said the same things—telling her she was okay even if she wasn't picked. But when I didn't make the junior varsity football team, Dad went bonkers! He asked me what had gone wrong. I told him nothing, that other guys were just better than I had been. But he'd have none of that. He told me I couldn't give up and had to work harder, and he expected me to make the team next season. He even offered to hire a coach for me. It just wasn't okay for me not to succeed.

A good example of remaking the meaning of gender is the concept of androgyny. In the 1970s, researchers coined the word **androgyny** by combining the Greek word *aner* or *andros*, which means "man," and the Greek word *gyne*, which means "woman." Androgynous individuals embody qualities that our culture considers both feminine and masculine. For example, androgynous individuals might be both nurturing and assertive, both strong and sensitive. As Miguel points out in his commentary, there is value in the full range of human qualities—those currently labeled feminine and those labeled masculine.

MIGUEL

I like to be strong and to stand up for myself and what I think, but I would not want to be only that. I am also sensitive to other people and how they feel. There are times to be hard and times to be softer; there are times to be strong and times to let others be strong.

To realize the arbitrariness of the meanings of gender, we need only to consider different cultures' views of masculinity and femininity. Many years ago, anthropologist Margaret Mead (1935/1968) reported three distinct gender patterns in the New Guinea societies she studied. Among Arapesh people, both women and men were passive, peaceful, and deferential, and both nurtured others, especially young children. The Mundugumor tribe socialized both women and men to be aggressive, independent, and competitive. Mothers were not nurturing and spent very little time with newborn babies, weaning them early instead. Within the Chambri society, genders were the reverse of current ones in America: Women were domineering and sexually aggressive, whereas men wore decorative clothes and curled their hair so they would be attractive to women.

Body ideals for women provide another example of the constructed and arbitrary character of gender. Currently, Western culture regards thinness as desirable in women. Yet in the 1950s, fuller-figured women exemplified femininity and sexiness. Even today, some cultures regard heavier women as particularly beautiful and desirable. For example, in the Islamic Republic of Mauritania (sub-Saharan Africa), young girls are often overfed so that they become obese and thereby signify their family's wealth (LaFraniere, 2007).

Even within a single culture or social group, the meanings of genders vary over time. Consider changes in the United States. Prior to the Industrial Revolution, men and women worked together to raise crops or run businesses, and both sexes were involved in home-making and child rearing. The Industrial Revolution gave rise to factories and paid labor outside the home. With this came a division of life into separate spheres of work and home. As men took jobs outside the home, masculinity was redefined as earning income; as women increasingly assumed responsibility for family life, femininity was redefined as nurturing and making a good home (Cancian, 1989).

The meaning of gender also changes over the course of an individual's lifetime. Being masculine at age 10 may mean being good at soccer or baseball. At age 35, however, most men regard a job and salary as measures of their masculinity. Similarly, a 10-year-old girl may regard bows in her hair as feminine, whereas a 35-year-old woman may define femininity as succeeding in her career and being a good mother. Our sense of what is feminine or masculine changes not only because we age but also because we respond to broad social changes.

EXPLORING GENDERED LIVES

Pink Is for Boys?

Valerie Steele, director of the Museum at the Fashion Institute of Technology, offers some intriguing examples of how gender assignments have changed (Boboltz, 2014).

In 1918, the color pink was first assigned to males in the United States. A retail publication announced that pink, "being a more decided and stronger color, is more suitable for the boy," and the article stated, "while blue, which is more delicate and dainty, is prettier for the girl" (Boboltz, 2014). Only in the 1950s did pink began its transformation to feminine and blue to masculine (Paoletti, 2012).

Shoes with high heels were originally designed to keep cavalry men secure in stirrups when they were shooting from the saddle. By 1600, upper-class European men wore high heels, which increased their height and established dominance over others.

Originally, both cheerleaders and secretaries were usually males. Through the early 1900s, cheerleading was considered too physically challenging for women, and secretarial work was thought to require abilities beyond those women possessed.

And lace? You guessed it: Originally, it was deemed masculine. From the 1700s until the 1900s, lace was perceived as a marker of high status in Europe and was worn by men in the aristocracy.

TAKE A STAND: Identify two current gendered roles or styles that you think could be equally associated with another gender.

In my day, women were a lot different than they are today. We were quieter, and we put other people ahead of ourselves. We knew our place, and we didn't try to be equal with men. Today's women are very different. Some of the younger women in my classes put their careers ahead of marriage, some don't want children, and many think they should be as much the head of a family as the man. Sometimes, I feel they are all wrong in what they want and how they are, but I have to admit that a part of me envies them the options and opportunities I never had.

Finally, gender is a relational concept because most cultures define femininity and masculinity against each other. As meanings of one gender change, so do meanings of the other. Challenges to the idea that there are only two sexes and two genders complicate the cultural tendency to define one gender as opposite to another.

In summary, we have noted that gender is the meaning that a society constructs and attaches to sex. The meaning of gender varies across cultures, across individuals' life spans, and over time in particular cultures. This reminds us that, even though what our society defines as feminine and masculine may seem natural to us, there is nothing necessary or innate about any particular meaning for any gender. This suggests that we have more choice than we sometimes realize in how we enact gender in our lives.

Beyond Sex and Gender

Western culture assumes connections between sex, gender, and sexuality so that male, man, masculinity, and heterosexuality are presumed to be naturally linked and female, woman, femininity, and heterosexuality are presumed to be naturally linked. The term **cis** functions as a prefix—cisgender, cisman, ciswoman—to describe these links, designating a person who fits conventional social expectations of gender. In other words, a female who identifies as a woman would be labeled cisgender or ciswoman. *Cis* means "on the same side of." So people who stay on the side of the gender identity assigned at birth are cisgender. The use of this term disrupts the assumption that saying "woman" necessarily connotes someone who was assigned female at birth.

As we have seen, sex, gender identity, gender expression, and preference for romantic partners don't always go together. Think of these departures from what mainstream culture prescribes:

- A feminine cisgender man who is sexually attracted to women
- A masculine cisgender woman who is sexually attracted to women and men
- A masculine trans man who is sexually attracted to women
- A feminine cisgender woman who is sexually attracted to women
- A masculine cisgender man who is sexually attracted to women and men

Sexual orientation refers to a person's preference for romantic and sexual partners. People who have heterosexual orientations are romantically and sexually attracted to people of a sex different than their own. Gay men are sexually and romantically attracted to men, whereas lesbians are sexually and romantically attracted to women. Bisexuals are attracted to men and women. While some have questioned the possibility of being bisexual, recent research documents bisexuals' subjective and genital arousal to women and men (Denizet-Lewis, 2014; Rosenthal, Sylva, Safron, & Bailey, 2011). A recent survey found that 66% of 18–29-year-old Americans say they are completely heterosexual or completely gay or lesbian. The remaining third place themselves somewhere in the category of bisexual (Blow, 2015).

Changing views of gender and sex are evident in the increasing recognition of individuals who don't fit into orthodox sex and gender categories. **Transgender**, or trans, individuals find that their biologically assigned sex and its accompanying gendered expectations don't match their gender identity—they are women, despite having male chromosomes and genitalia, or men, despite having female chromosomes and genitalia. Some trans people have hormonal treatment and/or surgery so that their bodies more closely match the sex with which they identify. Very recent evidence suggests that trans people may be right about their "true" sex. Scientists have mapped a number of differences in regions of the brain in males and females. Tests reported in the past few years show that trans individuals have brain regions that are more like the sex with which they identify than their biological sex (Sapolsky, 2013).

SEAN

In high school my closest friend was Megean. In our junior year she tried to kill herself and nobody knew why because she was pretty, popular, and smart—the "girl who had everything." Later she told me that she had never felt she was female, that she'd always felt she was a guy and just didn't think she could keep going if she had to live as a girl. If I hadn't been so close to Megean, I would have found it totally weird, but we were close—still are, in fact, although now he's Mark—and what I mainly felt was sad that somebody I loved was so unhappy. He's a much happier person now that he's Mark.

Sex may be easier to change than gender. Deirdre (formerly Donald) McCloskey is a professor of economics. According to her, surgery and hormones changed her sex, but she had to learn gender. She studied all of the small actions—gestures, facial expressions, postures—that women use and practiced them until they were second nature to her. Reflecting on this, McCloskey (2000) wrote that gender is "an accretion of learned habits, learned so well that they feel like external conditions, merely the way things are. It is a shell made by the snail and then confining it" (pp. 83–84). Because of their experience with gender transition, trans people have keen insight into gendered dynamics in cultural life. For example, Ben Barres (Vedantam, 2006) wryly commented on his experience: "By far the main difference that I have noticed is that people who don't know I am transgender (female to male) treat me with much more respect. I can even complete a whole sentence without being interrupted by a man" (p. 135).

Sexual and romantic interests do not necessarily change just because a person transitions from one sex to another. Some trans people stay in previously heterosexual marriages or committed relationships after transitioning. In 2008, Thomas Beatie attracted a lot of attention when he gave birth to a girl. You read the sentence correctly: *He* gave birth. In fact, he did so through vaginal delivery. How can this be? Thomas is a trans person who is legally

---

EXPLORING GENDERED LIVES

Bathroom Battles

In January 2014, the first statewide legislation granting trans students self-determination in their use of school facilities and extracurricular programming went into effect. Under California's new law, AB 1266, students who identify as trans select which athletic teams, extracurricular groups, bathrooms, and locker rooms correspond with their gender identities (Lazo, 2014).

California's law follows a number of efforts to make schools more hospitable to transgender students. But not all states agree. In 2016, the state of North Carolina passed HB 2, a law that required individuals to use the restroom that corresponds with the sex designated on their birth certificate. The Obama administration denounced the law as a violation of federal civil rights protections and North Carolina compromised in 2017—repealing part of the law while placing a moratorium on local antidiscrimination policies designed to protect LGBTQ people (Associated Press, 2016; Binker, 2016; Marusak, 2017). Federal guidelines have wavered recently too. In 2016, the U.S. Department of Education affirmed that protections for trans students are covered by Title IX, but in 2017, the Trump administration withdrew the federal guidelines to protect trans students under Title IX (Kreighbaum, 2017).

Rigidly gendered public facilities pose challenges that are not exclusive to trans individuals. For example, people caring for opposite-sex children or persons with disabilities struggle to provide adequate care in public settings, which affects where those people are able to travel, and for how long. Like most laws, those regulating bathroom use tend to reflect most citizens. In so doing, they often constrain the rights and quality of life for others.

TAKE A STAND: How might we create public facilities that affirm access for everyone?

---

male and legally married to a woman named Nancy. Thomas's sex reassignment surgery was limited to chest reconstruction and testosterone therapy, but he kept his reproductive organs. Nancy had had a hysterectomy, so when she and Thomas wanted a child, they decided that Thomas would carry it (Beatie, 2008). Thomas later carried and gave birth to a second child. People like Thomas prove that the links between sex, gender, and sexual orientation are not always clear, stable, or absolute.

There is yet another aspect of sex and gender identity. We've seen that some people transition away from their biological sex; but what of people who reject the idea of being one or the other sex? Consider the case of Norrie May-Welby. Born biologically male in 1962, young Norrie preferred dolls to contact sports and imagined herself as a girl. In 1989, Norrie had gender reassignment surgery to make her appearance conform to the identity she embraced. However, Norrie didn't like being disconnected from all aspects of identity that are regarded as masculine. Asked if this meant that she was renouncing being a woman, Norrie replied, "It's not so much about not being female as not being exclusively female. I am both a man and a woman" (Baird, 2014). For Norrie and others, binary sex categories are insufficient.

Jennifer Finney Boylan was born James Richard Boylan but later transitioned to female.

SLOAN

It's great that some people finally realize there are more than two sexes and two genders. Ever since I came to college, I found lots of people like me who don't identify as exactly male or female and not as straight or gay. There is so much gray area in between the dualities society has imposed.

Trans and intersex people challenge the idea that male and female, woman and man, masculine and feminine are opposite, stable, and the only two possibilities. They also disrupt society's assumption that sex, gender, and sexual orientation correlate in consistent and natural ways. As a result, we may realize that links among sex, gender, gender identity, and sexual orientation are not nearly as clear-cut as we sometimes believe.

Culture

Our discussion of sex, gender, and sexual orientation has noted that culture influences how each of these is defined and embodied. Now we focus more closely on **culture**, which is structures (also called institutions) and practices (also called activities) that reflect and uphold a particular social order. They do this by defining certain identities, values, and patterns of behavior as natural, good, and important and defining other identities, values, and patterns of behavior as unnatural, bad, or unimportant. Because gender is central to cultural life, society's views of gender are reflected in and promoted by a range of social structures and practices.

One of the primary practices that structures society is communication. We are surrounded by communication that announces social views of gender and seeks to persuade us that these are natural, correct ways for men and women to be and to behave. We stream videos and see commercials showing women cleaning toilet bowls and kitchen floors and men going for the gusto after a pickup basketball game; we play a video game that awards points to players for attacking women characters who are prostitutes; a working woman receives maternity leave, but her husband does not take paternity leave. Each of these practices communicates society's views of gender.

Another cultural practice that upholds Western views of gender is the custom whereby a woman takes her husband's name if she marries. In taking a man's name, a woman's identity is linked to his, but his identity is not equivalently linked to hers and he is not defined by his relationship to the woman. Within families, too, numerous practices reinforce social views of gender. Parents routinely allow sons greater freedom than daughters, a practice that encourages males to be more independent. Daughters, much more than sons, are assigned housework and care for younger siblings, thus socializing women to be concerned with home and family.

Now think about social structures, or institutions, that uphold gender ideology. One institution is the judicial system. In divorce proceedings, it is often difficult for a father to gain child custody even when he might be the better parent or might be in a better situation to raise children. Only 3% of the designated National Historic Landmarks are associated with women, minorities, or LGBTQ communities (Bridges, 2017).

In many respects, Western culture, as well as many other cultures, is **patriarchal**. The word *patriarchy* literally means "rule by the fathers." Because the United States was originally governed by men, historically it reflected the perspectives and priorities of men more than those of women. For example, it would be consistent with men's interests to consider women property, which was the case in colonial times. Similarly, from men's point of view, laws against marital rape would not be desirable, and they did not exist until very recently. Today, some of the most overt patriarchal tendencies and practices of U.S. culture have been tempered, yet the patriarchal history of the country persists in more subtle ways. In other cultures, such as Dympna's home culture, patriarchal traditions are more pronounced.

DYMPNA

In 1974, I traveled to New York for my college education…. I'm a member of the Ibo tribe of Nigeria, and although I've lived in the United States most of my adult life, my consciousness remains fixed on the time and place of my upbringing…. When I left Nigeria at 18, I had no doubts about who and what I was. I was a woman. I was only a woman…. My role was to be a great asset to my husband…. I was, after all, raised within the context of child brides, polygamy, clitorectomies and arranged marriages…. I've struggled daily with how best to raise my daughter. Every decision involving Delia is a tug of war between Ibo and American traditions (Ugwu-Oju, 2000).

Because messages that reinforce cultural views of gender pervade our daily lives, most of us seldom pause to reflect on whether they are as natural as they have been made to seem. Like the air we breathe, they so continuously surround us that we tend not to notice them. But we can learn to notice and think critically about them. Reflecting on cultural prescriptions for gender empowers you to chart your own courses of action and identity.

Communication

The last key concept we will discuss is **communication**. Communication is a dynamic, systemic process in which two levels of meanings are created and reflected in human interaction with symbols. To understand this rather complicated definition, we will focus on one part of it at a time.

Communication Is a Dynamic Process   Communication is dynamic, which means that it continually changes. Not too long ago, the word *queer* was strictly derogatory but has been reclaimed by many who identify as LGBTQ. And before trans activists questioned the stability of sex and gender, "cisgender" was unnamed because it was simply assumed.

Because communication is a process, communicative interactions have no definite beginnings or endings. Suppose a friend drops by while you're reading this chapter and asks what you are doing. "Reading about gender, communication, and culture," you reply. Your friend then says, "Oh, you mean about how men and women talk differently." You respond, "Not exactly—you see, gender isn't really about males and females; it's about the meaning our culture attaches to each sex." Did this interaction begin with your friend's question, with your instructor's assignment of the reading, with our writing this chapter, or with something else?

Think also about when this communication ends. Does it stop when your friend leaves? What the two of you talk about may influence what your friend thinks and does later, so the impact of your conversation extends beyond the immediate encounter. Communication is a dynamic process without clear beginnings and endings.

Communication Is Systemic   Communication occurs in particular systems that influence how we interact and what meanings we attach to messages. For example, suppose you observe the following interaction. In an office building where you are waiting for an appointment, you see a middle-aged man walk to a woman's desk, put his arm around her shoulders, and say, "You drive me crazy when you wear that outfit." She doesn't look up from her work but responds, "You're crazy, period." How would you interpret this interaction? Is it an instance of sexual harassment? Are they coworkers who are comfortable joking about sexuality with each other? Is he not an employee but her friend or romantic partner? We can't interpret this interaction, because we don't understand the systems within which it takes place.

Recall John Muir's statement that each part of nature is "hitched to the universe." As a system, all aspects of communication are hitched together, so they interact with one another. Who is speaking affects what is said and what it means. In the foregoing example, the woman would probably attach different meanings to what the man says if he is a friend or a coworker with a reputation for hitting on women. Communication is also influenced by how we feel: When you feel tired or irritable, you may take offense at a comment that ordinarily wouldn't bother you. The time of day and place of interaction may also affect what is communicated and how our words and actions are interpreted.

The largest system affecting communication is our culture, the context within which all our interactions take place. As we saw in our discussion of culture, a society's view and treatment of men and women changes over time. Thirty years ago, it would have been rude for a man not to open a car door for his date and not to stand when a woman entered a room. Today, most people would not regard either as rude. Just a few decades ago, sexual harassment did not have a name and was not considered cause for grievance or legal action. Today, laws and policies prohibit sexual harassment, and employees may bring charges against harassers. The systems within which communication occurs interact; each part affects all others.

Communication Has Two Levels of Meaning

Perhaps you noticed that our definition of communication referred to meanings, rather than a single meaning. That's because communication has two levels of meaning. Years ago, researchers noted that all communication has both a content level and a relationship level of meaning (Watzlawick, Beavin, & Jackson, 1967).

The **content level of meaning** is its literal meaning. If Ellen says to her partner, Ed, "You can't buy that car," the content level of the statement is that he can't buy a car. The **relationship level of meaning** defines the relationship between communicators. In our example, Ellen believes she has a right to tell Ed what he can and cannot buy. Ed could respond by saying, "I certainly can buy it, and I will." Here, the content level is again clear. Ed is stating that he will buy the car. On the relationship level, however, he may be arguing about the power balance between himself and Ellen, and he may be refusing to accept her control. If she says, "Okay, then buy it," she accepts Ed's claim that she is not running the relationship.

The relationship level of meaning reflects and influences how people feel about each other. It tells us how to interpret the literal message. Perhaps, when Ed says he is going to buy the car, he uses a teasing tone and grins, in which case the relationship level of meaning is that Ellen should not take the content level seriously. If, however, he makes his statement in a belligerent voice and glares at her, the relationship level of meaning is that he does mean the content level and is angry with Ellen.

Relationship levels of meaning are particularly important when we try to understand gendered patterns of communication. A good example is interruption. Elyse is telling Ty how her day went. He interrupts and says, "Let's head out to the soccer game." The relationship level meaning declares that Ty has the right to interrupt Elyse, dismiss her topic, and initiate his own. If she he does not protest, they agree to let him control the conversation. If she does object, then the two may wind up in extended negotiations over their respective power in their relationship.

Meanings Are Created through Human Interaction with Symbols

This premise highlights two final, important understandings about communication. First, it calls our attention to the fact that humans are symbol-using creatures. Symbols are abstract, arbitrary, and often ambiguous ways of representing phenomena. For example, ♀ and ♂ are symbols for *female* and *male*, respectively. Words are also symbols, so *female* and *male* are symbols for particular humans.

Because human communication is symbolic, we have to think about it to figure out what it means. Symbols are ambiguous; that is, their meanings may not be clear. Recall our earlier example, in which a man tells woman assistant, "You drive me crazy when you wear that outfit." To interpret what he said, she has to think about their relationship, what she knows about him, and what has occurred in their prior interactions. After thinking about all these things, she'll decide whether his comment was a joke in poor taste, a compliment, sexual harassment, or a flirtatious show of interest from someone with whom she is romantically involved. Because symbols are abstract, ambiguous, and arbitrary, meaning is not inherent in symbols themselves. Each of us interprets communication by drawing on our past experiences, our knowledge of the people with whom we are interacting, and other factors in a communication system. Differences in interpretation are the source of much misunderstanding between people. However, you can become a more effective communicator if you keep in mind that people's perceptions and interpretations often differ.

SUMMARY

In this chapter, we introduced four central concepts: sex, gender, culture, and communication. Sex is a biological classification, whereas gender is a social, symbolic system through which a culture attaches significance to biological sex. The third key concept, culture, refers to structures and practices, particularly communicative ones, through which a society expresses and sustains its values. Finally, we defined communication as a dynamic, systemic process in which meanings are created and reflected in human interaction with symbols. Building on the foundations we've established in this chapter, other chapters will examine the range of ways in which gender, communication, and culture interact in our lives.

KEY TERMS

The following terms are defined in this chapter on the pages indicated as well as in alphabetical order in the book's glossary, which begins on page 261. The text's companion website also provides interactive flash cards to help you learn these terms and the concepts they represent. You can access the site at www.cengagebrain.com.

androgyny 23	*gender role 19*
cis 25	*intersex people 20*
communication 30	*mixed research methods 16*
content level of meaning 31	*patriarchal 29*
critical research methods 16	*qualitative research methods 16*
culture 28	*quantitative research methods 16*
essentializing 18	*relationship level of meaning 31*
gender 19	*sex 19*
gender expression 19	*sexual orientation 25*
gender identity 19	*transgender 26*

GENDER ONLINE

1. To learn more about intersex people and their activism, visit this website: **http://www.isna.org**. While at the isna.org site, read the FAQ section to inform yourself about different views of what counts as intersex.

2.   Scott Turner Schofield is a critically praised performance artist who defines himself as a "gender renegade" (Cooper, 2006). His theater pieces include *Debutante Balls* and *The Southern Gents Tour*. Schofield's TED talk is available at **https://www.youtube.com /watch?v=TWubtUnSfA0**

3.   Hit TV series, *Orange Is the New Black*, features Laverne Cox who portrays a transgender inmate and who is transgender in real life. If you did not see Katie Couric's insensitive interview with Cox, do a Google search to watch it. Would the questions Couric asked Cox have ever been imposed on a straight or cisgender actor? Google "Katie Couric, interview, Laverne Cox."

4.   Online search terms: *androgyny, cisgender, transgender*.

REFLECTION, DISCUSSION, AND ACTION

1.   If you have traveled to other countries and experienced other cultures, what differences from U.S. views of women and men and masculinity and femininity did you notice?

2.   How comfortable are you with current views of masculinity and femininity? Which ones, if any, do you find restrictive? Are you doing anything to change them in society's views or to resist them in how you personally embody gender?

3.   Talk with grandparents or with people of their generations. Ask them what it meant to be a woman or man when they were your age. Analyze how their views differ from yours.

4.   Conduct a survey on your campus:
   - Ask 10 people whom you know at least casually: How should the campus accommodate transgender students in housing and restroom facilities? (Be prepared to define transgender.)
   - Combine the results of your survey with those of classmates' surveys. What do the data tell you about attitudes on your campus?

RECOMMENDED RESOURCES

1.   *Boys Don't Cry*. (1999). Directed by Kimberly Pierce. Distributed by Fox. Although this film is dated, it offers a stunning portrait of how social linkage of sex, gender, and sexual orientation can oppress individuals.

2.   Molly Haskell's 2013 book, *My Brother My Sister*, tells the story of her 59-year-old sibling's journey to becoming a woman.

3.   *Trans Bodies, Trans Selves: A Resource for the Transgender Community*. (2015). Titled the "most comprehensive trans resource ever published" by *The Advocate* magazine, this extensive resource covers a range of issues, from trans history and health to gender theory and contemporary sociopolitical concerns.

2

Theoretical Approaches to Gender Development

Knowledge Challenge:

- At what age do most children realize that their sex is not going to change?
- Are males or females likely to be diagnosed with autism?
- Who performs gender?
- What is the relationship between social location and standpoint?

Some of our students have told us that they don't see the value of studying theory because it has nothing to do with "real life." Actually, theories are very practical. They help us understand, explain, and predict what happens in our real lives and in the world around us.

Theoretical Approaches to Gender

A **theory** is a way to describe, explain, and predict relationships among phenomena. Each of us uses theories to make sense of our lives, to guide our attitudes and actions, and to predict others' behavior. Although we're not always conscious of the theories we hold, they still shape how we act, how we expect others to act, and how we explain, or make sense of, what we and others say and do. In this sense, theories are very practical.

In everyday life, we use theoretical frameworks to make sense of human behavior. For instance, assume that you know Kevin and Carlene, who are 11-year-old fraternal twins. In many ways, they are alike; yet they also differ. Carlene is more articulate than Kevin, and she tends to think in more integrative ways. Kevin is better at solving analytic problems, especially ones that involve spatial relations. He also has better-developed muscles, although he and Carlene spend equal time playing sports. How you explain the differences between these twins reflects your implicit theory of gender.

If you trust biological theory, you might think that different cognitive strengths result from hemispheric specialization in male and female brains. You might also assume that Kevin's greater muscle development results from testosterone, which boosts musculature, whereas estrogen programs the body to develop less muscle and more fat.

Then again, if you rely on social learning theory, you might explain the differences by assuming their parents reward Kevin for athletics and Carlene for language skill. These are only two of many ways we could explain the differences between Kevin and Carlene. Each explanation comes out of a particular theoretical viewpoint—a way of understanding the relationship between sex, gender, behaviors, and abilities. Each viewpoint makes sense, yet each is limited, which suggests that a full understanding of gender relies on multiple theories.

Our theories about sex and gender affect how we think and act. If you think the differences in language skill are determined by biology, then you probably would not push Kevin to spend more time reading and working with words in order to develop his language skills. On the other hand, if you think differences result from socialization, you might encourage Kevin to spend more time writing, reading, and speaking.

There are many theories about gender. Because each theory attempts to explain only selected dimensions of gender, different theories are not competing to be the definitive explanation of how gender develops and what it means. Instead, theories often complement one another by sharpening our awareness of multiple ways in which communication, sex, gender, and culture interact. Thus, instead of trying to pick the "best" theory, try to appreciate the strengths of each one and realize how multiple theories can work together to provide a richly layered account of how we become gendered.

Theories of gender development and behavior can be classified into four broad types: (1) biological, (2) interpersonal, (3) cultural, and (4) critical.

Within these broad categories, a number of specific theories focus on particular factors and processes that contribute to the gendering of individuals. As we discuss these, notice both how they differ in focus and how they work together to create an overall understanding of gender.

Biological Theories of Gender

Biological theory maintains that biological characteristics such as chromosomes, hormonal activities, and brain specialization account for gender differences.

One focus of biological theories is sex chromosomes. As we saw in Chapter 1, most males have XY sex chromosomes. Most females have an XX chromosomal structure, because they inherit an X chromosome from each parent. Men are more prone to a number of hereditary conditions such as muscular dystrophy, hemophilia, and Hunter syndrome because males' single X chromosome may have a faulty gene that is not overridden by a second X chromosome. Some scientists think males' single X may also explain why they are four to seven times more likely than females to be diagnosed with autism and attention disorders (Wang, 2013; Why It's Not, 2014).

X and Y chromosomes are distinct. The X holds 1,100 genes whereas the Y holds only about 50 genes (Angier, 2007a, 2007b; Richardson, 2013). In part because of the larger number of genes carried on the X chromosome, it is more of a multitasker than the Y. Yet, the Y chromosome is evolving faster than any other human chromosome (Borenstein, 2010). The Y chromosome's primary function is determining that a fertilized egg will evolve into a male. The X chromosome, however, controls a lot more than sex determination; it influences intelligence, some hereditary conditions, and sociability (Angier, 2007a).

EXPLORING GENDERED LIVES

Chromosomal Variations

Although most humans have either XX or XY sex chromosomes, there are variations.

- About 1 in 2,500 females has Turner's syndrome, in which there is a single X chromosome in most cells, although some cells may have a Y chromosome. Girls with Turner's syndrome tend to be shorter than average, do not undergo the usual changes at puberty, and are usually unable to have children.
- About 1 in 700 males has Klinefelter syndrome, which is determined by the presence of two or more X chromosomes instead of a single X. Boys with Klinefelter syndrome tend to be taller

than average, usually produce less testosterone, and are often infertile.

- Approximately 1 in 1,500 females is born with three X chromosomes. Triple X girls tend to be taller than XX girls, otherwise, they look and act like other females. Without genetic testing, triple X girls are unlikely to be identified.
- Males with XYY chromosomes, also called Jacobs syndrome, tend to be very tall and have higher than usual testosterone levels. Otherwise, they look and act like other males and do not have compromised fertility. Many XYY males are unaware of their unusual chromosomal structure.

TAKE A STAND: If people with XX chromosomes are classified female, and people with XY chromosomes are classified male, should people with other sex chromosomal structures be classified as other sexes?

A second focus of biological theories is hormonal activity. For instance, estrogen, the primary female hormone, causes bodies to produce "good" cholesterol and to make blood vessels flexible (Ferraro, 2001). Estrogen strengthens the immune system, so that people with high amounts of estrogen are generally less susceptible to immune disorders, infections, and viruses. Estrogen causes fat tissue to form around the hips, which provides cushioning for a fetus during pregnancy. And estrogen seems to inhibit liver functioning so people with high estrogen supplies eliminate alcohol more slowly than people with lower supplies and thus may react more quickly to alcohol consumption (Lang, 1991).

Like females, males have hormonal cycles that affect their behavior (Federman & Walford, 2007). Research shows that males at the peak of their testosterone cycle are more likely to use drugs and engage in violence and abuse. A 2011 study reported that testosterone levels tend to decrease markedly when a cisgender man becomes a father. Scientists think this may be an evolutionary pattern aimed to lessen men's aggression and interest in other mates while increasing their tendencies to nurture (Belluck, 2011).

Beginning around the age of 30, men's testosterone level gradually declines, with testosterone levels dropping about 1% a year after age 30 (Federman & Walford, 2007; LaPuma, 2014). Researchers estimate that about 10 million U.S. men over the age of 50 have testosterone levels sufficiently low to decrease muscle, bone strength, and interest in sex and to increase body fat, moodiness, and depression (Federman & Walford, 2007).

Hormones influence some tendencies that we associate with gender. Research shows that some girls favor trucks over dolls if their mothers had atypically high levels of testosterone during pregnancy and that males who are given estrogen experience declines in normally strong spatial skills and increases in usually less strong verbal skills (Gurian & Stevens, 2007;

Tyre, 2006). Males who are given a spray of oxytocin, known as the "cuddle" hormone, show more empathy and sensitivity to others' feelings (Hurlemann et al., 2010).

A third focus of biological theories is brain structure and development. Some studies indicate that although both sexes use both lobes of the brain, each sex tends to specialize in one (Andersen, 2006; Vive la Différence, 2013). Males tend to have more developed left lobes, which control linear thinking, sequential information, spatial skills, and abstract reasoning. Females tend to have more developed right lobes, which control imaginative and artistic activity, holistic and intuitive thinking, and some visual tasks. In females, the prefrontal cortex, which restrains aggression, is larger and develops earlier than in males (Brizendine, 2007; Tyre, 2006), and the insula, which affects intuition and empathy, is larger (Brizendine, 2007). In males, the amygdala, which is the center of emotions such as anger and fear, is larger (Brizendine, 2007).

A bundle of nerves and connecting tissues called the corpus callosum links the two lobes of the brain. Females generally have greater ability to use this structure, which allows crossing from one lobe to the other (Fausto-Sterling, 2000; Vive, 2013). Males generally have more within-hemisphere connections, which may aid their ability to focus attention on one thing at a time.

Interestingly, most of the differences in the sexes' brains are absent or very small at birth. They tend to increase as individuals age, usually becoming most noticeable around the age of 17 (Hotz, 2013). We do not yet know whether these differences result from biological factors or social influences or a combination of the two.

EXPLORING GENDERED LIVES

The Claims of Sociobiology

One of the more controversial theories of sex and gender differences is sociobiology (also called evolutionary psychology, Barash, 2002; Wilson, 1975). According to sociobiology, differences between women and men result from genetic factors that aim to ensure survival of the fittest.

A key claim of sociobiology is that women and men follow distinct reproductive strategies in an effort to maximize the chance that their genetic lines will continue (Barash & Lipton, 2002; Buss, 1995, 1996, 1999; Buss & Kenrick, 1998). For men, the best strategy is to have sex with as many women as possible in order to father many children who continue their genetic line. Because men produce millions of sperm, they risk little by impregnating multiple women. Women,

however, usually produce only one egg during each menstrual cycle during their fertile years, so the best evolutionary strategy for them is to be highly selective in choosing sex partners and potential fathers of their children.

Sociobiology has at least as many critics as proponents. One criticism is that the theory fails to account for sexual behavior that occurs without the goal of reproduction—and sometimes actively tries to avoid that outcome! Another criticism is that sociobiology ignores the ways in which social influences mitigate biological drives (Newcombe, 2002).

Behavioral ecology advances a less extreme view. According to behavioral ecology, factors in the environment influence—but do not determine—sexual behaviors and preferences (Begley, 2009).

TAKE A STAND: To what extent do you think that men and women in the United States currently follow the reproductive strategies claimed by sociobiology?

Although our discussion suggests that biological influences are moderated by socialization, it would be a mistake to dismiss biology's power to affect our lives. The force of biology is evident in cases where doctors try to change a child's biological sex, perhaps most famously in the case of David Reimer (Butler, 2004; Colapinto, 2006; McClelland, 2004). When David was eight months old, a doctor mistakenly amputated his penis during a surgery to correct phimosis, a condition in which the foreskin of the penis interferes with urination. Following doctors' advice, the parents authorized "normalizing surgery" so David's testicles were removed he was given hormones to induce female characteristics and was renamed Brenda.

Brenda did not take to being a girl. Her preferred toys were trucks and guns; she routinely ripped off the dresses her parents made her wear; and, despite not having a penis, Brenda preferred to stand to urinate. Even hormonal treatments and therapists could not convince Brenda to identify as a girl. Finally, when Brenda was about 15, her father told her that she had been born male. For Brenda/David, things now made sense. David had his breasts removed and a penis constructed using muscle tissue and cartilage, took male hormone shots, and began to live as a man. At age 25, David married a woman with children, and he helped raise his three stepchildren.

LUANNE

When I was in high school, I wanted to play football. My folks were really cool about it, since they'd always told me being a girl didn't mean I couldn't do anything I wanted to. But the school coach vetoed the idea. I appealed his decision to the principal as sex discrimination (my mother's a lawyer), and we had a meeting. The coach said girls couldn't play football as well as guys because girls are less muscular, weigh less, and have less dense bodies to absorb the force of momentum. He said this means girls can be hurt more than guys by tackles and stuff. He also said that girls have smaller heads and necks, which is a problem in head-to-head contact on the field. My dad said the coach was talking in generalizations, and he should judge my ability by me as an individual. But the coach's arguments convinced the principal, and I didn't get to play, just because women's bodies are generally less equipped for contact sports.

Before leaving our discussion of biology, we should note that biological classification into male or female is not as clear-cut as many people think. The term **gender binary** refers to the division of humans into two sexes that are presumed to be opposite, distinct, natural, and enduring. The gender binary assumes that a person's sex, gender, and sexuality align in socially prescribed ways. Thus, males are assumed to identify as boys/men, adopt masculine attitudes and behaviors, and be heterosexual; females are assumed to identify as girls/women, adopt feminine attitudes and behaviors, and be heterosexual.

One of the earliest challenges to the gender binary came from a professor of medical sciences who specialized in molecular and cell biology. Fausto-Sterling's (1982, 1989, 1992) laboratory research showed that intersex people have both male and female genitalia, which means they cannot be classified as only male or only female. She also recognized that some people have identities that do not align with social expectations for their anatomy. Fausto-Sterling (1993) claimed there are actually five distinct sexes based on biological differences in human beings.

Other scientists challenged the gender binary for a different reason. They noted that research consistently showed there is more variation within each socially defined sex than between the two (Lorber, 2012). In other words, there are more differences among females than between

---

EXPLORING GENDERED LIVES

Biological Differences That Make a Difference

Although males and females are alike in many respects, there are some significant biological sex differences (Belluck, 2015; Duenwald, 2005; Fisher, 2000; Richardson, 2013; Wartik, 2002). These sex differences are based on studies of cisgender people; additional research is needed to understand how sex hormones impact the lives of trans and queer people during/after hormonal transition.

- Women are more likely than men to suffer from migraine headaches; men are more likely than women to suffer from cluster headaches.
- On average, women's brains are smaller than men's; women's brains are also more densely packed with neurons than men's.
- Men's livers metabolize most drugs, including alcohol, more quickly than women's.
- Women's resting metabolic rate is an average of 20 to 32% lower than men's, which explains why women are often cold in temperatures that men find comfortable.
- Daily use of low-dose aspirin is helpful in preventing first heart attacks in men but not in women; low-dosage

aspirin does seem to offer women some protection against stroke, which is not a benefit that has been demonstrated for men.
- Men tend to experience heart disease 10 to 15 years earlier than women.
- Women and men typically have different symptoms of heart attack. Women's symptoms include shortness of breath, jaw pain, backache, and extreme fatigue. Men's primary symptom is usually chest or arm pain.
- Women are more likely to develop melanoma, but men are more likely to die from this cancer.
- Ambien, a widely prescribed sleeping medication, was recently found to be metabolized differently by males and females. As a result, the FDA cut its recommended dosage for females in half, making it the only drug currently on the U.S. market with different dosage recommendations for the sexes.

In part as a result of sex differences such as these, in 2014, the National Institutes of Health announced that all future government-funded health research must include both male and female subjects (Sex Matters, 2014).

TAKE A STAND: How can you use knowledge of biological sex differences to understand yourself and guide your behaviors?

---

females and males; there are more differences among males than between males and females. If that is the case, the dichotomy between male and female seems untenable, they reasoned.

By the 1990s, an increasing number of scholars argued that there is far more variety in human beings than is accommodated by two rigid categories (Butler, 1990, 1993a; Fausto-Sterling, 1992, 1993; Sedgwick, 1990). These scholarly breakthroughs encouraged people who had never felt comfortable with the gender binary to define themselves in a range of ways beyond the two traditional categories. The term *genderqueer* was coined to signify identities that resist the gender binary. In 1994, Kate Bornstein published *Gender Outlaws: Men, Women, and the Rest of Us*, in which she described how she had transitioned from being a heterosexual male to a lesbian. In summary, biological theories focus on the ways that chromosomes, hormones, and brain structure affect physiology, thinking, and behavior. Biological theory is valuable in informing us about genetic and biological factors that may influence our abilities and options. Yet, biological theories tell us only about physiological and genetic qualities of males and females. They don't necessarily describe individual men and women (Carothers & Reis, 2013; Fine, 2011; Richardson, 2013). Some men may be holistic, creative thinkers, whereas some women, like Luanne, may excel at football.

Increasing evidence indicates that biological differences other than reproductive ones do not explain most differences between women and men. That's why a majority of researchers believe that biology is substantially edited by social factors (Kolata, 2012; Rivers & Barnett, 2011). Further, an increasing number of scholars believe the gender binary is socially constructed and perhaps not accurate or adequate as a model for thinking about human identity.

Interpersonal Theories of Gender

Three theories focus on interpersonal influences on the development of masculinity and femininity. Psychodynamic theory emphasizes interpersonal relationships within the family. Two psychological theories, social learning and cognitive development, stress learning and role modeling between children and a variety of other people.

Psychodynamic Theories of Gender Development

Psychodynamic theories claim that the first relationship we have fundamentally influences how we define our identity, including gender. Most infants are cared for by women, often mothers. Because the mother or mothering figure herself is gendered and may subscribe to social views of girls and boys, she may act differently toward male and female infants.

Psychodynamic theories assert that between mother and daughter, there is a fundamental likeness that encourages close identification (Chodorow, 1989). Mothers generally interact more with daughters, keeping them physically and psychologically closer than sons. In addition, mothers tend to be more nurturing and to talk more about emotions and relationships with daughters than with sons. This intimate bond allows girls to grow into their gender identity in relation to their mothers.

Theorists suggest that infant boys recognize in a primitive way that they differ from their mothers (Chodorow, 1978, 1999). More importantly, mothers realize the difference, and they may reflect it in their interactions with sons. In general, mothers encourage more and earlier independence in sons than in daughters, and they talk less with sons about emotional and relationship matters (Galvin, 2006).

ABE

I remember something that happened when I was a little kid. Mom had taken me to the playground, and we were playing together. Some other boys started teasing me, calling me "Mama's boy." I remember thinking I had to stop playing with Mom if I wanted those other boys to accept me.

To establish his independent identity, a boy must distinguish himself from his mother or other female caregiver—he must define himself as distinct from her. Whether he rejects his caregiver or merely differentiates himself from her, defining himself as different from her is central to most boys' initial development of a masculine identity (Kaschak, 1992).

Identity, of course, is not fixed in the early years of life. We continue to change throughout life. Yet, psychodynamic theorists maintain that, for most people, the identity formed in infancy remains core to the self. Thus, as infants mature, they carry with them the basic identity formed in the pivotal first relationship. As girls become women, many tend to elaborate their identities in connection with others, giving relationships high priority in their lives. As boys grow into men, many build on the basic identity formed in infancy, making independence central to how they live and work. Thus, for someone who identifies as feminine, intimate relationships may be a source of security and comfort, and they may affirm the view of self as connected with others. In contrast, someone who identifies as masculine may feel that really close relationships threaten the autonomy needed for a strong identity.

Psychological Theories of Gender Development

Psychological theories focus on the interpersonal bases of gender, but they do not emphasize intrapsychic processes at the center of psychodynamic explanations. Instead, psychological theories of gender highlight the influence of interaction within families and social contexts.

Social Learning Theory

Developed by Walter Mischel (1966) and others (Bandura, 2002; Bandura & Walters, 1963; Burn, 1996), **social learning theory** claims that individuals learn to be masculine and feminine by imitating others and getting responses from others to their behaviors. Children imitate the communication they see on television, online, and in videos as well as the communication of people around them. At first, young children are likely to mimic almost anything. However, others reward only some of children's behaviors, and the behaviors that are rewarded tend to be repeated. Thus, social learning suggests that rewards from others teach boys and girls which behaviors are appropriate for them (Kunkel, Hummert, & Dennis, 2006; Wood, 2013).

Children imitate role models in the process of building gender identity.

Parents and others who reward girls for behaviors and attitudes that are considered feminine and discourage ones perceived as masculine shape girls into femininity. Similarly, parents and others who communicate approval to boys for behaving in masculine ways and curb them for acting feminine influence boys to become masculine. Even people who claim to treat all children the same often have unconscious gender biases. When told a female infant is a boy, adults describe the infant as angry. When told a male infant is a girl, adults describe the same infant as happy and socially engaged (Elliott, 2009). In each case, adults perceive the child according to their own gender stereotypes.

VICTORIA

When I was little—like four or five maybe—if I got dirty or was too loud, Mama would say, "That's no way for a lady to act." When I was quiet and nice, she'd say, "Now, you're being a lady." I remember wanting Mama to approve of me and trying to act like a lady. But sometimes it was hard to figure out what was and wasn't ladylike in her book. I had to just keep doing things and seeing how she responded until I learned the rules.

DERRICK

Over break, I was visiting my sister's family, and her little boy attached himself to me. Wherever I went, he was my shadow. Whatever I did, he copied. At one point, I was dribbling a basketball out in the driveway, and he got it and started dribbling. I egged him on, saying, "Attaboy! What a star!" and stuff like that, and he just grinned real big. The more I praised him for playing with the ball, the harder he played. It was really weird to see how much influence I had over him.

Media also play a role in teaching children what activities and roles are rewarded for each sex. If children watch TV programs that show only women caring for children, traditional gender roles are reinforced. However, if children watch TV programs that show men caring for children, children learn that it's appropriate for men to engage in caregiving.

Likewise, if parents and others encourage children to explore a range of behaviors and roles, the children are likely to develop interests, skills, and goals that are not rigidly gendered.

MARICRUZ

Growing up I never had to worry about playing with "gender-approved" toys. I preferred playing with Legos instead of Barbies and my parents never scolded or "corrected" me. Instead they bought me Lego Harry Potter toys and encouraged me to play whatever game I wanted.

Cognitive Development Theory   Unlike social learning theory, **cognitive development theory** assumes that children play *active* roles in developing their gender identities. They do this by picking models of competent masculine or feminine behavior.

From birth until about 24 to 30 months, children notice the ways others label and describe them (Gilligan & Pollack, 1988; Kohlberg, 1958; Piaget, 1932/1965). When they hear others call them a "girl" or "boy," they learn the labels for themselves. "My sweet little lady" and "my strong man" are distinct gendered descriptions that children may hear.

A key point in the process of developing gender identity is **gender constancy**, which is a person's understanding that his/her/their assigned sex is stable or permanent and that it is accompanied by gendered expectations. Gender constancy generally occurs by age three (Hanish & Fabes, 2014; Miller-Day & Fisher, 2006; Rivers & Barnett, 2011). Once gender constancy is established, most children are motivated to learn how to be competent at being boys or girls. Same-sex models become critical as young children try to identify and become skilled in the behaviors, attitudes, and feelings that are prescribed for their gender. Many young girls see their mothers and key women in their lives as models of femininity, whereas little boys often study their fathers and men in their lives as models of masculinity (Tyre, 2006).

LINDSAY

The gender constancy that we read about doesn't happen so easily or "naturally" for everyone. Long before I started kindergarten I knew that I was a boy, but I also knew that I wasn't. Everyone called me a boy, and I knew I had boy genitals, but I also knew that I identified more with girls and women and with girl things like dolls and dresses. So, for me, gender constancy didn't happen—I was caught on a fence between how everyone else saw me and how I saw myself.

Gender constancy can be more challenging for children who do not identify with their assigned sex and its gender expectations. However, recent research suggests that it is possible to minimize this stress. A study by the American Academy of Pediatrics suggests that transgender children who are socially transitioned—supported in their gender identity and not forced to live as their biological sex—exhibit far less depression and anxiety than trans children living as their biological sex. In fact, trans children who are socially transitioned achieve levels of mental health wellness almost equal to that of their cisgender peers (Olson, Durwood, DeMeules, & McLaughlin, 2016).

Related to cognitive development theory is **gender schema theory** (Frawley, 2008). According to gender schema theory, even before reaching the first birthday, an infant distinguishes between male and female faces and voices. By the age of two, gender schema theorists claim that children begin to organize their understandings of gender into coherent wholes. A **gender schema** is an internal mental framework that organizes perceptions and directs behavior related to gender. Using gender schemata, children organize clothes, activities, toys, traits, and roles into those appropriate for boys and men and those appropriate for girls and women. They use gender schemata to guide their choices of activities, roles, clothes, and so forth.

Reliance on role models doesn't end with childhood. As people mature, they continue to seek role models to guide them in how to be masculine and feminine at different ages and in diverse contexts. We learn it's feminine to squeal or scream at the sight of bugs and mice, but boys who do so are labeled sissies. It's acceptable—if not pleasant to everyone—for adolescent boys to belch, but a teenage girl who belches would most likely be criticized. Seeing women and men in the workplace gives us models of how professionals embody femininity and masculinity.

Cultural Theories of Gender

Cultural theorists assume that biological and interpersonal influences on gender reflect larger cultural contexts.

Of the many cultural contributions to knowledge about gender, we will focus on two. First, we'll look at findings from anthropology to appreciate the range of ways that societies define gender. Second, we will explore symbolic interactionism, which explains how individuals acquire their culture's views of gender in the process of interaction.

Anthropology

Many societies have views of gender that differ from those currently prevalent in the United States (Brettell & Sargent, 2012). Australian Aboriginal fathers have no say in their daughters' marriages; mothers have that authority. In the United States, women have only recently been allowed to serve in combat roles, but in other countries such as Israel, women have long been part of armed combat. Germany, New Zealand, Nepal, and Australia legally recognize more than two genders. And on Orango Island on the western shore of Africa, women choose mates and a man cannot refuse without dishonoring his family (Callimachi, 2007).

Another example of how cultural attitudes vary comes from a group of villages in the Dominican Republic where it is common for males to be born with undescended testes and underdeveloped penises. Because this condition is not rare, the society doesn't regard it as abnormal. Instead, boys born with this condition are raised as "conditional girls," who wear dresses and are treated as girls during the early years of life. At puberty, a secondary tide of androgens causes the testes to descend, the penis to grow, and muscle and hair typical of

---

EXPLORING GENDERED LIVES

Cultural Variation in Fathering

Many countries have done more than the United States to link parenting to manhood. In 1990, only 4% of Swedish men took any time off when a child was born. The Swedish government decided to use public policy to encourage men to be more involved in fathering. In 1995, the Swedish government set aside 30 leave days for fathers only; if fathers didn't take them, their families lost the leave. In 2002, the state added a second month of leave that new fathers could either take or lose. Now more than 80% of fathers take months of leave for the birth of a child (Romano & Dokoupil, 2010).

Or consider Germany. In 2007, the country passed a law that new fathers were entitled to leave. The percentage of new fathers who take family leave soared 700%. Japan also provides paid leave to new fathers and honors men who devote themselves to child care as "stars of ikumen" (men who rear children; Romano & Dokoupil, 2010).

How much time fathers spend with children also varies across cultures. Hazda fathers in Tanzania spend about 5% of their time holding infants; Aka fathers in the Congo Basin hold their children for as much as 22% of the time; Indian fathers are typically near their children three to five hours a day; and Japanese fathers spend an average of 20 minutes near children each day (Gray, 2010).

TAKE A STAND: To what extent do you support laws and policies that allow or require fathers and mothers to take time off work when a child is born or adopted?

males to appear. At that point, the child is considered a boy—his dresses are discarded, and he is treated as a male (Henig, 2017).

> **SHENG**
>
> *Growing up, when guests came to our home, my mother and I served them drinks, then went to the kitchen to fix food while the men talked. If another woman was a guest, she came to the kitchen with us. Men ate at their own table. The women either stay in the kitchen or at a separate table.*

Symbolic Interactionism

Symbolic interactionism emphasizes the pivotal role of communication in gender development. According to symbolic interactionism, communication with others is the primary way we develop identity, including gender identity. Because communication reflects the values and meanings of society, parents often echo cultural views of gender in the words they use to describe children—big or little, dainty or hardy, strong or demure, and so on. With each label, others define children, and children internalize many of the definitions that others provide.

Cultural views of gender are also communicated through play activities with peers (Hanish & Fabes, 2014; Maccoby, 1998) and through teachers' interactions with students (Sander, 2004). Teachers may reprimand young girls for roughhousing but accept the same behavior in boys. When a young girl tries to tell a boy what to do, she may be told, "You can't boss me around. You're just a girl." Girls who fail to share their toys or show consideration to others may be told, "You're not being nice," yet this is less likely to be said to young boys. Reponses from others, including teachers and peers, not only reflect broad cultural values but also provide positive and negative rewards, consistent with social learning theory.

An important contribution to a cultural theory of gender is the concept of **role**— specifically, gendered roles. A role is a set of expected behaviors and the values associated with them. In a classic book, Elizabeth Janeway (1971) identified two dimensions of roles. First, roles are external to individuals because a society defines roles in general ways that transcend particular individuals. Thus, for each of us there are certain roles that society expects us to fulfill and others that society deems inappropriate for us.

Within our culture, gender roles assume that women are caretakers and should provide most of the care for infants, elderly relatives, and others who need help. In the paid labor market, women remain disproportionately represented in service and clerical jobs, whereas men are moved into executive positions in for-profit sectors of the economy. Women are still asked to take care of social activities on the job, but men in equivalent positions are seldom expected to do this.

Men are still regarded by many as the primary breadwinners. Thus, it is seen as acceptable for a woman not to have an income-producing job, but a man must earn a living to fulfill the masculine role. Postpartum depression, which is feelings of profound sadness following the birth of a child, has been associated with women. However, 10.4% of men suffer from depression three to six months after the birth of a child (Ostrow, 2010). The symptoms of men's depression have been evident, but social views of men may have prevented us from recognizing postpartum depression in them.

RACHEL

My father is in the Air Force, so he's away a lot of the time. Mom has had to become the head of our family. She does everything from work and take care of us to pay bills and cook. Normally, she sits at the head of the table for meals. But when Dad comes home, he sits at the head of the table. Mom still does everything—he says he's on vacation—but they both seem to think the man should be at the head of the table when he's home.

Not only does society assign roles, but it also assigns value to the roles. Western culture teaches women to accept the role of supporting, caring for, and responding to others. Yet that is a role clearly devalued in the United States. Competing and succeeding in work life and public affairs are primary roles assigned to men, and to those roles prestige is attached.

A second important dimension of role is that it is internalized. As we internalize our culture's gender roles, we learn not only that there are different roles for men and women but also that unequal values are assigned to them. This can be very frustrating for those who are encouraged to conform to roles that are less esteemed or that don't fit their identity.

Critical Theories of Gender

The theories we have discussed so far provide description, explanation, and prediction. Critical theories do something else—they direct our attention to structures and practices by which societies accord more or less privilege and power to different groups. Critical theorists show how the interests and perspectives of dominant groups are privileged. At the same time, critical theorists identify ways that oppressed groups challenge and sometimes change dominant ideologies. In this sense, critical theories have a political edge. We will discuss two critical theories that are particularly relevant to gender.

Standpoint Theory

Standpoint theory complements symbolic interactionism by noting that societies are made up of different groups that have different amounts of power and privilege. Standpoint theory focuses on how membership in groups, such as those designated by gender, race, class, ability, and gender identity, shapes what individuals experience, know, feel, and do as well as how individuals understand social life as a whole (Collins, 1986; Harding, 1991, 1998; McClish & Bacon, 2002; Wood, 2005). Standpoint theory makes three significant claims: (1) all perspectives on social life are partial; (2) some perspectives are more partial than others; and (3) a standpoint is earned by developing a political awareness of power differences among social groups.

Standpoint theory dates back to the writings of nineteenth-century German philosopher Georg Wilhelm Friedrich Hegel (1770–1831) and Karl Marx (1818–1883). Hegel (1807) noted that society as a whole recognized the existence of slavery but that the meaning of slavery was quite different depending on whether one's social location was that of master or slave. From this insight, Hegel reasoned that, in any society where power relationships exist, there can be no single perspective on social life. Marx's (1867/1975, 1977) contribution to standpoint theory was to emphasize that social location regulates our activities and labor, both of which shape consciousness, knowledge, and identity.

A social location is a group to which an individual belongs. But social location is *not* standpoint. A standpoint is earned through critical reflection on power relations and through engaging in the struggle required to construct a stance that challenges the dominant one in a culture. Being a woman (social location) does not necessarily confer a feminist standpoint, and being black, Asian, and/or Latino/a (social location) does not necessarily lead to a politically charged standpoint on race. Because social location and standpoint are so frequently conflated, let us emphasize the distinction one more time: A standpoint can grow out of the social location of group members' lives. Thus, a feminist standpoint can, *but does not necessarily,* arise from the conditions that shape women's lives.

Standpoint theory claims that marginalized standpoints can generate unique insights into how society works. When women, people of color, gays and lesbians, working-class people, intersex individuals, trans people, and others who are outside the cultural center who recognize and reflect on the power relationships of society may see the society in ways that are less biased than the ways of people in more privileged social locations. María Lugones and Elizabeth Spelman (1983) point out that dominant groups don't need to understand the perspective of less privileged groups in order to survive.

TIFFANY

I attended a predominantly white middle school. My mother made me check my homework twice before I turned it in. I asked her why I had to do that when most of the other kids in the school didn't. She said, "the number of times you check your homework is the same as the number of limitations set up against you—one for being black and two for being a girl." I said that was unfair and she said fairness had nothing to do with succeeding if you're black. I think that was my first lesson in standpoint.

Patricia Hill Collins (1986, 1998) uses standpoint theory to show that some black women scholars have special insights into Western culture because of their dual standpoints as "outsiders within," that is, as members of a minority group (African Americans) who are also members of majority institutions (higher education). Similarly, in his *Autobiography of an Ex-Coloured Man,* James Weldon Johnson (1912/1989) reflected, "I believe it to be a fact that the coloured people [*sic*] of this country know and understand the white people better than the white people know and understand them" (p. 22).

An intriguing application of standpoint logic came from Sara Ruddick's (1989) study of mothers. Ruddick concluded that the social location of mothers facilitates the development of "maternal thinking," which is values, priorities, and understandings that grow out of taking care of children. Ruddick argues that we often assume women are naturally nurturing ("maternal instinct"), but actually women learn to be compassionate and empathic as a result of being frequently located in caregiving roles.

The impact of social location on nurturing is further demonstrated in Barbara Risman's (1989) study of male caregivers. She found that men who are primary parents are more nurturing, attentive to others' needs, patient, and emotionally expressive than men in general and as much so as most women. Armin Brott, an ex-Marine and business consultant, is widely known as "Mr. Dad," the author of eight books for men like him who are stay-at-home dads. According to Brott, women are not born knowing how to take care of babies and children. They learn how to do it by doing it. The same goes for men, says Brott: They learn how to nurture, comfort, and guide children by engaging in the labor of doing so (Lelchuk, 2007). That's standpoint theory's argument: Social location shapes identities and skills, including parenting ability.

Each of us occupies multiple social locations that overlap and interact. For example, a heterosexual, middle-class, Asian-American man's social locations are different from those of a gay, working-class, European-American man.

Standpoint theory's major contribution to understanding gender is calling our attention to how membership in groups defined by sex, gender, and gender identity shapes individuals' experiences, perspectives, identities, and abilities. Our different social locations provide the possibility of developing standpoints that reflect a political awareness of social hierarchy, privilege, and oppression.

Queer Performative Theory

Perhaps the best way to introduce **queer performative theory** is with three examples.

1. Munroe identifies as "the hottest and coolest drag queen in town." Before going out, Munroe shaves twice to remove all stubble, spends an hour applying makeup, chooses one of four wigs, and selects an ensemble from the closet, hoping to hook up with an interesting man.

   - What is Munroe's sex?
   - What is Munroe's gender?
   - What is Munroe's sexual orientation?
   - Are men who hook up with Munroe straight or gay?

2. Two years ago, Aimee began hormone therapy to stimulate growth of facial hair, increase muscle mass, and decrease breast size. Over the summer, Aimee had chest surgery and decided to go by Andy. Andy has set up an appointment with the coach for the men's track team at the university in the hope of joining the team. Later over dinner, Andy will talk with his boyfriend about joining the track team.

   - Is Andy male or female?
   - Is Andy masculine or feminine?
   - Is Andy gay or straight?
   - Is Andy's boyfriend gay or straight?

3. Jada, who was born with a penis, testes, and a prostate gland, identifies as trans. Since the age of 15, Jada has had several romantic and sexual relationships, all with women.

   - How would you characterize Jada's sex?
   - How would you characterize Jada's gender?
   - How would you characterize Jada's sexual orientation?
   - Are Jada's girlfriends gay or straight?

Munroe, Andy, and Jada illustrate the focus and value of queer performative theory. Each of them defies conventional identity categories. Each challenges binary views of identity as male or female, masculine or feminine, gay or straight. The identities that they claim and perform don't fit neatly with conventional understandings of sex, gender, and sexual identity. According to queer performative theories, Munroe, Andy, and Jada trouble our thinking, and the trouble they provoke is very productive.

Queer theory and performative theory are distinct, yet closely allied. We'll define each theory and then explore how they interact and how, working together, they offer unique insights into gender, sex, sexual orientation, gender identity, and cultural life.

Queer theory is a critique of conventional categories of identity and cultural views of "normal" and "abnormal," particularly in relation to sexuality. Extending criticism of the gender binary that we discussed earlier in this chapter, queer theory argues that identities are not fixed, but somewhat fluid (Lorber, 2012; Wilchens, 2014). In our first example, Munroe invests significant effort in creating and performing femininity. In our second example, Aimee becomes Andy, thereby illustrating the fluidity of gender identity. In the third example, Jada identifies as trans, despite having biological features that fit society's category of male.

Queer theory arose in the context of gay and lesbian studies (Butler, 1990, 1993a, 1993b, 2004; Foucault, 1978; Sedgwick, 1990). The initial focus of queer theory was **heteronormativity**, which is the assumption that heterosexuality is normal and all other sexual orientations are abnormal. Yet, it would be a mistake to think queer theory is relevant only to gays and lesbians. Almost as soon as queer theory emerged, scholars realized that it has important implications for our understanding of many aspects of identity (Sloop, 2006; Wilchens, 2014; Zimmerman & Geist-Martin, 2006). Within the context of queer theory, the word *queer* does not refer only or necessarily to gays and lesbians, but to anything that departs from what society considers normal (Halperin, 2007). Queer theory challenges the ways that a culture defines and polices what is considered normal and abnormal.

Two ideas are central to queer theory. First, queer theory claims that terms such as *women, men, gay, and straight* are not useful, as they cannot tell us much about any individual person. Identities are shaped by numerous factors, so labeling someone according to any one factor is unavoidably misleading. As well, such terms erase variation among those who are placed into broad categories. Queer theorists point out that there are many different ways of being a woman or man, various ways to express masculinity and femininity, and multiple ways of being gay, straight, or trans. Using the single term *man* to refer to Barack Obama, CeeLo Green, and Mark Zuckerberg or the single term *woman* to refer to Laverne Cox, Adele, and Sonia Sotomayor obscures the distinct ways that these people enact their identities as men and women, respectively.

Second, queer theory assumes that identities are not fixed but are relatively fluid. Any of us may claim one identity in this moment and context and another in a different moment and context. As with Jada, Munroe, and Andy, features such as sex organs don't determine our identities. Rather, according to queer theory, identities arise from decisions about who we are and how we want to enact our identities.

Fluidity of identity means more than being able to transition from one sex or gender to the other or to claim a genderqueer identity. It can also mean refusing to accept any stable identity. Some people refuse labels altogether when it comes to sex, gender, and sexual orientation. For these individuals, defining themselves in terms of the existing categories (woman, straight, trans, bisexual, etc.) would simply reinforce those unhelpful categories (Valentine, 2007).

Performative theory argues that humans generate identities, including gender, through performance or expression. A key theorist, Judith Butler (1990, 2004), explains that gender comes into being only as it is expressed, or performed. The performance, she says, is the thing we call gender. Butler's point is that gender is not a thing we have but rather something that we do at specific times and in specific circumstances. In other words, for Butler and other performative theorists, gender is more appropriately regarded as a verb than a noun. Gender is doing. Without doing—without performance—there is no gender.

According to performative theorists, all of us perform gender, although we do so in diverse ways (Butler, 1990, 1993a, 1993b, 2004; Halberstam, 2012). We express, or perform, conventional gender through everyday practices such as dominating or deferring in conversations and crossing our legs so that one ankle rests on the knee of our other leg or so that one knee rests over the other knee. Conversely, we resist conventional views of gender if we act in ways that are inconsistent with the sex and gender society assigns to us. Some researchers suggest that gender performances shed light on why women generally do more housework than men. It is possible that women perform domestic labor as a way of demonstrating their femininity, while men refuse to perform household labor as a way to demonstrate masculinity (De Ruijter, Treas, & Cohen, 2005; Natalier, 2003).

But—and this is the second key claim of performative theory—our performances are not solo acts. They are always collaborative, because however we express gender, we do so in a context of social meanings. For instance, a woman who defers to men and tilts her head when talking to men (two behaviors more often exhibited by women than men) is acting individually, but her individual actions are stylized performances of femininity that are coded into cultural life.

Queer performative theory integrates queer and performative theories. The result is a view of queer (remember, in this context that means anything other than what is considered "normal") performances as means of challenging and destabilizing cultural categories and the values attached to them. As communication scholar John Sloop (2006) explains, "Queer scholarship works against the ways in which gender/sexuality is disciplined ideologically and

---

■ EXPLORING GENDERED LIVES ■

Ga Ga for Lady Gaga

Which of the following is true of Lady Gaga?

A. When asked if she was intersex, she said, "I think this is society's reaction to a strong woman" (Williams, 2010).

B. She has appeared as ultrafeminine and as entirely unfeminine.

C. In 2010, she told an audience, "If anyone ever tells you you're not good enough, not pretty enough, not smart enough, you tell them, 'Fuck you! I'm gonna be a star!'" (Gray, 2012, p. 3).

D. She is a self-described humanitarian who is an outspoken advocate for LGBTQ rights and mental health and sexual assault awareness.

E. All of the above.

If you selected E, you're correct. Lady Gaga, who says her art is her performance (Gray, 2012), defies gender categorization and does so quite deliberately.

Lady Gaga has often been compared to Madonna who presented herself as a material girl, traditionally feminine, erotically charged, a submissive victim of male power, a dominatrix, and a devoted mother. Both Madonna and Lady Gaga have performed traditional femininity and also parodied it; they have performed heterosexuality and homosexuality. They have courted the male gaze, disrupted it, and used it to examine gender.

Both Lady Gaga's and Madonna's performances subvert any stable notion of femininity. In so doing, they insist that a person can be both dominating and docile, both masculine and feminine, both gay and straight, both "good girl" and "bad girl."

TAKE A STAND: Identify other current cultural figures who perform different sex and gender identities.

institutionally and works toward a culture in which a wider variety of genders/sexualities might be performed" (p. 320).

To disrupt social categories and valuations, performances aim to queer normal. Notice that *queer* is working as a verb, which is consistent with queer performative theory's view that gender is performance. For instance, a person who wears a lace blouse, necktie, and combat fatigues cannot be reduced to simply feminine or masculine. This choice of dress is a performance that challenges and undermines conventional gender categories. Two women who perform disagreement with fist fights queer normative views of femininity. A heterosexual man who holds hands with male friends queers cultural views of heterosexuality and—by extension—of homosexuality. As Issac West (2013) points out, gays and lesbians who perform the rights and responsibilities of spouses queer heterosexual models of marriage. Everyday performances such as these become political tools that unsettle taken-for-granted categories of identity and social views of "normal" and "abnormal."

In sum, queer performative theories allow us to understand transgressive presentations of self as political acts that point out the insufficiency of binary categories of male/female, masculine/feminine, gay/straight, and normal/abnormal.

Theories Working Together

We've discussed seven theories discretely: biological, psychodynamic, social learning, cognitive development, anthropological, standpoint, and queer performative. Yet often these different theories work together to shed light on how we develop and enact gendered identities. For instance, women basketball players are nearly three times as likely to suffer anterior cruciate ligament (ACL) injuries as men. For soccer players, the risk for females can be eight times greater than for men (Jacobson, 2001; Miller, 2012; Scelfo, 2002). The fact that women suffer more ACL injuries than men suggests that there may be a sex difference—a biologically based difference between women's and men's knees. However, socialization may also be a factor.

Dr. William Garrett (personal communication, 2001), a sports medicine surgeon, notes that women and men athletes hold their bodies differently. Men, he says, are looser and tend to move and stand with their knees slightly bent. Women are more likely to keep their legs and knees straight and to maintain more rigid posture. Loose posture and bent knees reduce stress on the knee and thus reduce the risk of ACL injury. In addition, early socialization teaches girls and boys how to sit, run, and so forth. Thus, what seems a purely biological effect may also reflect interpersonal and social influences.

Let's consider another example that shows how theories we've discussed work together in complementary ways. In 2009, Sonia Sotomayor was confirmed to the U.S. Supreme Court; she is the first Latino/a and the third woman to hold this position. Despite her humble beginnings as a child of Puerto Rican immigrants growing up in a housing project in the Bronx, Sotomayor graduated from Princeton University and Yale Law School, excelled in a legal career, and served as a federal judge for 17 years. How do we explain Sonia Sotomayor's exceptional accomplishments?

Social learning and cognitive development theories shed light on Sotomayor's interests and related successes. As a child, she was rewarded for learning, ambition, living by her faith, and contributing to her community. Her mother stressed the importance of education, purchasing an *Encyclopaedia Britannica* for her children and working six days a week to send her children to Catholic schools. Growing up in a community of immigrants and working-class families while attending a high school with kids from privileged backgrounds, Sotomayor's social circles were diverse and eclectic. She also witnessed sexism and racism firsthand. The insights culled from these experiences, combined with analysis of them, shaped her oppositional standpoint that led her to challenge institutional discrimination. As this example shows, multiple theories often work together to give us a more complete understanding of gendered phenomena than any single theory could.

SUMMARY

In this chapter, we have discussed theories of relationships among communication, gender, and culture. Rather than asking which is the right theory, we have tried to discover how each viewpoint contributes to an overall understanding of how we develop, embody, and sometimes change gender. By weaving different theories together, we gain a powerful appreciation of the complex individual, interpersonal, and cultural origins of gender. Adding to this, critical theories invite us to be critical of constructed categories of identity, normalcy, and privilege.

The next two chapters build on this one by exploring how communication within rhetorical movements has challenged and changed social views of gender and gendered identities.

KEY TERMS

The following terms are defined in this chapter on the pages indicated as well as in alphabetical order in the book's glossary, which begins on page 261. The text's companion website also provides interactive flash cards to help you learn these terms and the concepts they represent. You can access the site at www.cengagebrain.com.

biological theory 35	*psychodynamic theories 40*
cognitive development theory 42	*queer performative theory 48*
gender binary 38	*queer theory 49*
gender constancy 43	*role 45*
gender schema 43	*social learning theory 41*
gender schema theory 43	*standpoint theory 46*
heteronormativity 49	*symbolic interactionism 45*
performative theory 49	*theory 34*

GENDER ONLINE

1. The Urban Dictionary offers definitions of many terms related to gender, communication, and culture. Visit the site and look up terms such as *cis, genderqueer, and ze:* **http://www.urbandictionary.com/**

2. Online search terms: *brain, sex differences, queer*

REFLECTION, DISCUSSION, AND ACTION

1. Distinguished anthropologist Ruth Benedict said that "the purpose of anthropology is to make the world safe for difference." Having read this chapter, how would you explain Benedict's statement?

2. Think about your relationship with your parents. How were your connections to your father and mother similar and different? If you have siblings of a different sex, how were their relationships with your parents different from yours?

3. Engage in an act that aims to queer gender in some way. Pick one action that challenges conventional understandings of sex and gender and the "normal" or "abnormal" judgments that are attached to them. Notice how you feel as you engage in queering gender and how others respond.

4. Now that you've read about a range of theories that describe and explain gender, how much weight do you put on nature and how much on nurture in the development and performance of gender?

RECOMMENDED RESOURCES

1. John Colapinto. (2006). *As Nature Made Him*. New York: Harper Perennial. This is a very readable account of the life of David/Brenda, who was born male and then medically altered and socialized as a female.

2. Caryl Rivers and Rosalind Barnett. (2011). *The Truth about Girls and Boys: Challenging Toxic Stereotypes about Our Children*. New York: Columbia University Press. Coauthored by a journalist and a scientist, this well-written book shows that many claims of sex difference are wildly exaggerated and undermined by looking closely at research.

3. bell hooks. (1990). The Politics of Radical Black Subjectivity. In *Yearning: Race, Gender, and Cultural Politics*. Boston: South End Press. This seven-page chapter provides an example of how some blacks move from black social location to a political standpoint.

3

Citizenship must be practiced to be realized.
—Spano

The Rhetorical Shaping of Gender: Competing Images of Women

Knowledge Challenge:

- To what extent have women's movements in the United States fought for the rights of all women?
- Is legal birth control liberatory for all women?
- To what extent do we live in a postfeminist era?

What are your dreams for the future? Do you imagine working with an NGO, playing professional sports, practicing law, being a professor, or running your own business? Do you intend to accumulate some savings? Do you plan to have children? Perhaps more immediately, have you taken out loans or credit cards in your name? Whom do you plan to vote for in the next election? Have you considered running for office yourself?

Entertaining the foregoing questions would have been impossible for a U.S. woman in the 1800s, and many of them would have been improbable even in the 1950s. Until 1920, women could not vote, attend college, or pursue training for most professions. Until the latter part of the twentieth century, women found it extremely difficult to get loans or credit in their own names; they had no legal control over their reproductive health; they were routinely and *legally* discriminated against in the workplace and elsewhere; and they had no hope of winning athletic scholarships. Changes in the status and rights of women didn't just happen. They came about because some citizens thought the status quo was wrong and took active roles in challenging and changing it.

This and the next chapter allow us to appreciate the profound ways that individuals and groups have transformed cultural views of gender and sex. We will explore rhetorical, or persuasive, efforts to challenge and change attitudes, laws, and policies that affect how women and men are understood and are treated. In this chapter, we will consider women's movements that have advanced distinct views of women's nature and rights in the United States. In Chapter 4, we'll explore men's efforts to safeguard or change the images and rights of men in the United States.

As we discuss these rhetorical movements, you'll discover that they are anything but uniform. They advocate diverse images of gender and pursue a range of goals, not all of which are compatible. Knowledge of activism about gender will enhance your understanding of the dynamism of U.S. culture and may allow you to clarify your own ideas about gender and how you personally express it. What you learn may also inspire you to become involved in issues related to gender within your community.

The Three Waves of Women's Movements in the United States

Many people think women's movements first emerged in the 1960s. This, however, disregards more than a century of intense activism about women's rights. It also implies that there is a single women's movement, while actually there have been and are multiple women's movements.

Rhetorical movements to define women's nature and rights have occurred in three waves. During each wave, two distinct ideologies have informed movement goals and efforts for change. One ideology, **liberal feminism**, holds that women and men are alike and equal in most respects. Therefore, goes the reasoning, they should have equal rights, roles, and opportunities. A second, quite different ideology, **cultural feminism**, holds that women and men are fundamentally different and, therefore, should have different rights, roles, and opportunities. These two ideologies coexist, reflecting different views of women and their rights. Also, as you will discover in reading this chapter, a number of women's movements challenge the assumption that there are two and only two distinct sexes and genders.

The wave metaphor for women's movements has limits (Hewitt, 2010). Movements don't necessarily fit neatly into generational compartments. Many themes that were in the first wave—reproductive rights, for example—were also in the second wave and are now part of the third wave. Likewise, some of the goals and tactics of third-wave feminists echo ones common in the second wave (Dow & Wood, 2014; Fixmer & Wood, 2005). As you read about three waves of women's movements, know that specific concerns and ideologies are not restricted to any single chronological point.

The First Wave of Women's Movements in the United States

From approximately 1840 to 1925, the first wave of women's movements included both liberal and cultural branches. Ironically, the conflicting views of these two movements worked together to change the status and rights of women in U.S. society.

Liberal Ideology: The Women's Rights Movement

The most well-known women's activism during the first wave endorsed a decisively liberal ideology. The **women's rights movement** arose to gain basic civil rights for women. Scholars date the start of this movement as 1840, when Lucretia Coffin Mott and Elizabeth Cady Stanton met at an international antislavery convention and were both denied entry based on their sex (Campbell, 1989a). Mott and Stanton realized that they could not work to end slavery if they were denied political voice as women. Thus, they helped organize the first women's rights convention, the Seneca Falls Convention, held in New York in 1848. The keynote address, entitled "Declaration of Sentiments," was ingeniously modeled on the Declaration of Independence (Campbell, 1989b, p. 34). It began with these words:

> We hold these truths to be self-evident: that all men and women are created equal; that they are endowed by their Creator with certain inalienable rights, that among these are life, liberty, and the pursuit of happiness.

The Declaration of Sentiments cataloged specific grievances women had suffered, including not being allowed to vote, exclusion from most forms of higher education, restrictions on employment, and loss of property rights upon marriage. At Seneca Falls, 32 men and 68 women signed a petition supporting women's rights. Instrumental to passage of the petition was the support of the former slave Frederick Douglass (Campbell, 1989).

Douglass' support of women's rights does not signify widespread participation of black men and women in the women's rights movement. Initially, there were strong links between abolitionist, or antislavery, efforts and women's rights (Beck, 2008). However, this alliance was strained when the U.S. Constitution was amended, in 1874, to extend suffrage to black men, but not to women. Additionally, many black women were disenchanted with the women's rights movement's focus on white women's circumstances and its lack of attention to grievous differences caused by race (Breines, 2006). Thus, the early women's rights movement became predominantly white in its membership and interests.

Women of different sexual orientations and gender expressions and identities were involved in the early women's rights movement. A number of first-wave feminists, including Susan B. Anthony and Alice Stone Blackwell, were in "Boston marriages"—committed, long-term, intimate relationships with other women. Frances Willard, the founder of the Women's Christian Temperance Union, was remarkably gender fluid—publicly lauded for embodying "true womanhood" (Campbell, 1989a; Dow, 1991)—but in intimate relationships with women, was referred to as "Frank," and adopted masculine behavior and dress (Faderman, 1999). According to historian Lillian Faderman (1999), lesbians' involvement in first-wave women's rights struggles is due to two significant factors. First, women who did not rely on men for protection were particularly vulnerable to the many gendered inequities of that era, including the inability to vote and to pursue education and most careers. Thus, obtaining political rights was linked to survival for these women. Second, women who did not have intimate relationships with men were less constrained by marriage and child rearing and therefore had more time to commit to the women's rights movement.

Women's rights activists marched and spoke at rallies and engaged in peaceful nonviolent protests and hunger strikes. They were jailed, assaulted, and violently force fed. Their struggles are dramatically chronicled in the HBO film *Iron Jawed Angels*. A long 72 years after the Seneca Falls Convention, women won the right to vote with the passage of the Nineteenth Amendment in 1920.

Cultural Ideology: The Cult of Domesticity

Although the Women's Rights Movement is often assumed to represent the interests of most white women in the 1800s, many women of the time did not believe that women and men were fundamentally alike and equal. Instead, they thought that women were suited to the

---

EXPLORING GENDERED LIVES

Aren't I a Woman?

Isabella Van Wagenen was born as a slave in New York in the late 1700s. After she was emancipated, Van Wagenen moved to New York City and became a Pentecostal preacher. She preached throughout the Northern states, using a new name: Sojourner of God's Truth. She preached in favor of temperance, women's rights, and the abolition of slavery.

On May 28, 1851, Truth attended a women's rights meeting in Akron, Ohio. Throughout the morning, she listened to speeches that focused on white women's concerns. Moved to point out what was missing, Truth rose and gave her own speech, "Aren't I a Woman?" which pointed out the ways in which white women's oppression differed

from that of black women (Campbell, 2005). The following excerpt from the speech is edited by Karlyn Kohrs Campbell and includes Frances Dana Gage's commentary (Ritchie & Ronald, 2001).

> That man over there says that women need to be helped into carriages, and lifted over ditches, and to have the best place everywhere. Nobody ever helps me into carriages, or over mud puddles or gives me any best place (*and raising herself to her full height and her voice to a pitch like rolling thunder, she asked*), and aren't I a woman? That man over there says that … I have borne thirteen children and seen them almost all sold off into slavery, and when I cried out with a mother's grief, none but Jesus heard—and aren't I a woman?

TAKE A STAND: To what extent do you think Sojourner Truth's claim that white women's oppression differs from black women's oppression is still true today?

---

domestic sphere because they were more moral and nurturing than men. These women belonged to what has been called the **cult of domesticity** (Welter, 1966).

Yet some women who were devoted to domestic life felt a need to represent their views in public. They worked for abolition because slavery destroyed families, lobbied for temperance because alcohol contributed to violence against women and children (Fields, 2003; Million, 2003), and fought for labor laws to protect children. Their advocacy required a public voice and the right to vote. Thus, for quite different reasons than those motivating women's rights activists, some women in the cult of domesticity also worked for women's enfranchisement (Baker, 2006; Sarkela, Ross, & Lowe, 2003).

After passage of the Nineteenth Amendment in 1920, women's movements in the United States were relatively quiet due to several factors. First, public energy was funneled into two world wars. While men were at war, women joined the labor force in record numbers to maintain the economy and support the war effort (Kiernan, 2013). Between 1940 and 1944, six million women went to work—a 500% increase in the number of women in paid labor—and the federal government funded childcare centers that, in some cases, also provided medical care and meal preparation (Douglas & Michaels, 2004; Harrison, 1988). Women's participation in paid labor fell sharply when soldiers came home. More than two million women employed during the wars were fired, and their positions were given to male veterans (Barnett & Rivers, 1996). With limited career options, the average woman in the 1940s married at 20 and had three children before turning 30. By the time she was 50, the children had left home (Collins, 2009b). The lack of opportunities beyond home and family sowed the seeds for the second wave of U.S. feminism.

▌ EXPLORING GENDERED LIVES ▌

Reproductive Rights

Birth control was and is a priority in many women's movements. In the nineteenth century, Elizabeth Cady Stanton insisted that "voluntary motherhood" was requisite to women's freedom (Gordon, 1976; Schiff, 2006). Margaret Sanger's work as a nurse made her painfully aware that many women, particularly immigrants and poor women, died in childbirth or as a result of illegal abortions (Chesler, 1992). She insisted that a woman's body belongs to herself, not the church or government.

During the second wave of feminism in the United States, feminists again protested for safe, accessible birth control and abortion. In 1973, the landmark case *Roe v. Wade* established abortion as a woman's right. Yet, abortion is still not available to all women in the United States.

Reproductive rights are also a focus of the third wave. The March for Women's Lives, held on April 25, 2004, on the Capitol Mall in Washington, DC, drew 1.15 million demonstrators to advocate for reproductive justice (Hayden, 2009).

Feminist thought about reproductive rights is nuanced in recognizing that birth control is not liberatory for all women. In reality, efforts to control reproduction have been liberatory only for some women, and they have been disempowering for other women (Fixmer-Oraiz, 2013; Gordon, 2007; Solinger, 2005). For instance, throughout much of the twentieth century in the United States, many women who were black, immigrant, poor, lesbian, mentally challenged, incarcerated, or otherwise considered "unfit" as mothers were sterilized without their consent.

TAKE A STAND: What does "reproductive justice" mean? How are reproductive rights connected to other issues such as environmental justice, a living wage, and access to health care and education?

The Second Wave of Women's Movements in the United States

Starting in 1963, a second wave of women's movements emerged in the United States. As in the first wave of U.S. women's movements, the second wave included liberal feminists and cultural feminists.

Liberal Ideology

The second wave of U.S. feminism included many groups that endorsed a liberal ideology (Cobble, Gordon, & Henry, 2015). The first feminist activism to emerge during the second wave was **radical feminism**, also called the **women's liberation movement.** Not surprisingly, college campuses provided fertile ground for the emergence of radical feminism. It grew out of New Left politics that protested the Vietnam War and fought for civil rights. Women in the New Left movement did the same work as their male peers—including risking arrest and physical assault—men in the New Left treated women as subordinates, telling them to make coffee, type news releases, and be ever available for sex. Outraged by men's refusal to treat women in the movement as equals, many women withdrew from the New Left and formed their own organizations (Stansell, 2010; Tong, 2013).

Radical feminists relied on "rap" or consciousness-raising groups, in which women gathered to talk informally about personal experiences with sexism and to link those personal experiences to larger social and political structures. Radical feminists' commitment to equality and their deep suspicion of hierarchy led them to insist on leaderless discussions so that participants would have equal power.

Radical feminists relied on revolutionary analysis and politics along with high-profile public events to call attention to the oppression of women and to demand changes (Barry, 1998; Freeman, 2002; Tong, 2013). Examples of public events they staged include the following:

- Occupation of the *Ladies' Home Journal* office
- Speak-outs about silenced issues such as rape and abortion
- Protests against the Miss America pageants in 1968 and 1969
- Guerrilla theater to dramatize public issues

JES

My grandmother was a radical feminist. I grew up hearing stories about how badly the guys treated her and other women who were working for civil rights. It's totally weird that the guys couldn't see women were their equals when they were all about blacks being equal and that's why they were in the Civil Rights movement. Grandma has told me about her rap groups and stuff like that. She says they changed her life.

Some women involved in radical movements of the 1960s formed organizations to represent concerns of women of color. The Third World Women's Alliance grew out of the Civil Rights Movement in 1968 and focused on ending imperialism, sexism, and racism (Thompson, 2002). The first national Chicana conference in 1971 drew over 600 women. They advocated free and autonomous reproductive health care, 24-hour community child care, and the "educational, political, social and economic advancement" of Chicanas (Vidal, 1971). Native women formed organizations such as Women of All Red Nations (WARN) and Northwest Indian Women's Circle to confront involuntary sterilization, infant mortality, land tenure, and systemic racism in foster care and adoption (Langston, 2003). Similarly, Asian-American feminists formed grassroots organizations that reflected gender, ethnic, and class concerns, including the Filipino American Women Network, the Organization of Chinese American Women, the Vietnamese Women's Association, and Asian American Women United (Chow, 1989).

Radical feminism also fostered the activism of many lesbian, bisexual, trans, and gender nonconforming women. Many of these activists had been involved with women's rights, civil rights, and gay liberation movements. However, issues specific to their experiences were not always included in the political agendas of other movements, and some straight, cisgendered feminists and gay men were openly hostile to them. As a result, some LGBTQ feminists focused their activism on lesbian and queer issues. Like other forms of radical feminism, their organizing focused on revolutionary analysis and transforming systems of oppression, which led them to form organizations such as the Radicalesbians, the Furies Collective, and groups that worked at the intersections of sexuality, race, class, and gender such as the Combahee River Collective and the Street Transgender Action Revolutionaries.

EXPLORING GENDERED LIVES

The Famous Bra Burning (That Never Happened!)

One of the most widespread misperceptions is that feminists burned bras in 1968 to protest the Miss America pageant. That never happened. Here's what did. In planning a response to the pageant, protesters considered a number of strategies to dramatize their disapproval of what the pageant stood for and how it portrayed women. They decided to protest by throwing false eyelashes, bras, and girdles into what they called the Freedom Trash Can.

They also put a crown on an animal labeled Miss America and led it around the pageant. In early planning for the protest, some members suggested burning bras, but this idea was abandoned (Collins, 2009a; Hanisch, 1970). However, a reporter heard of the plan and reported it as fact on national media. Millions of Americans accepted the report as accurate, and even today many people refer to feminists as "bra burners."

TAKE A STAND: How do you think the belief that feminists burned bras in 1968 has affected perceptions of feminists?

An important outcome of radical feminism was identification of the structural basis of women's oppression. The connection between individual women's situations and social structures and practices was captured in radical feminists' declaration that "the personal is political."

Another branch of second-wave feminism emerged from the U.S. middle-class suburbs in the early 1960s. **Mainstream second wave feminism**, which advocates women's social, economic, educational, and political equality, was ignited in 1963 with publication of *The Feminine Mystique* by Betty Friedan. The book's title was Friedan's way of naming "the problem that has no name," which was the discontent that many white, middle-class American women felt because they had limited opportunities beyond home and family. Echoing radical feminists, Friedan declared that this seemingly personal problem was actually also a political issue. She pointed out that women were not able to pursue personal and professional development because American institutions, especially laws, kept many women confined to domestic roles. Although most suburban stay-at-home moms loved their families and homes, they also longed for an identity outside of home, particularly in the 30 to 50 years of life after children left home (Collins, 2009b). Liberal feminism is embodied in NOW, the National Organization for Women. Founded in 1966, NOW works to secure social, political, professional, and educational equality for women and has become one of the most influential public voices for women's rights.

Although second-wave liberal feminism was characterized by more focus on and leadership by white, middle-class women, it would be a mistake to accept the stereotype that second-wave liberal feminism was "lily white." As scholars (Dow, 2014; Lumsden, 2009; McDonald, 2012) have pointed out, the truth is more nuanced. From the start, concerns about race and racism were negotiated alongside concerns about sex and sexism. Most liberal feminists as well as radical feminists fought for civil rights, and second-wave liberal feminism benefited from strong voices of nonwhite women, such as Flo Kennedy, Pauli Murray, Shirley Chisholm, and bell hooks (Gallagher, 2012). In 1970, Jamaican-American Aileen Hernandez became NOW's second president. Liberal feminism today is inclusive of diverse women and the issues in their lives.

EXPLORING GENDERED LIVES

About NOW

NOW was established in 1966. Betty Friedan and the Reverend Pauli Murray, an African-American attorney and poet, coauthored NOW's original mission statement, which states: "The purpose of NOW is to take action to bring women into full participation in the mainstream of American society now, exercising all privileges and responsibilities thereof in truly equal partnership with men." NOW's achievements include the following:

- Executive Order 11375, which prohibits sex discrimination by federal contractors
- Amending the Civil Rights Act of 1965 to include sex, along with race, religion, and nationality, as an illegal basis for employment discrimination

- Support of federally financed childcare centers to enable women to work outside the home
- Documenting sexism in media
- Identification of and publicity about sexism in children's books and programs
- Reform of credit and banking practices that disadvantage women
- Enlargement of women's opportunities to participate in sports
- The Equal Employment Opportunity Commission's adoption of a rule that sex-segregated want ads are discriminatory
- Support for women who seek elective and appointive public office
- Highlighting gender inequities worldwide, particularly in poorer countries

TAKE A STAND: To what extent do you agree with and support NOW's mission?

Liberal feminism is not confined to the United States. Feminist groups around the world are committed to equal rights for women.

- Feminist NGOs (nongovernmental organizations) have contributed substantially to global awareness of particular forms of oppression of women, such as sex trafficking (Coalition against Trafficking in Women).
- In 2013, thousands of women in over 50 cities across Turkey marched to promote state recognition of women's educational and reproductive rights and to end violence against women ("Global Short Takes," 2013).
- In response to growing awareness of violence against women worldwide, the online International Feminist Network was launched in 2013 by feminists in 30 countries, creating a platform for global activism and demonstrating solidarity among women across borders (Chemaly, 2013).

CASS

I really like what NOW is about and how it works. It's not as cool as some of the radical groups, but it makes change happen by working within the system. NOW has changed laws and policies. It's given a national platform for fighting racism and women's self-hatred. It's gotten women elected to office. You can't have that kind of impact unless you get inside the system and figure out how to change it from the inside.

Although many liberal feminists of different races in the 1960s and 1970s grappled with issues of race, black feminism or **womanism** is explicitly dedicated to foregrounding issues of race and class as they are related to gender. Highlighting how oppressions intersect, womanists work to shape a political movement specific to the concerns of black women. Womanists point out that, compared to white women, black women as a group are more often single, bear more children, are paid less, and assume more financial responsibility for families (Parks, 2010; Walker, 1992). In addition to focusing on race, womanists attend to ways in which class intersects race and sex to create inequality. Womanist organizations often include working-class women and address issues that keenly affect lower-class African-American women. Their goals include reforming social services to be more responsive to poor women and increasing training and job opportunities so that women of color can improve the material conditions of their lives.

In 1997, African-American women held a **Million Woman March** in Philadelphia. Powered by grassroots volunteers who built support in their localities, the steering committee of the Million Woman March was made up not of celebrities but of average women who worked at unglamorous jobs and lived outside the spotlight.

EXPLORING GENDERED LIVES

To Be Womanish, To Be a Womanist

Alice Walker is credited with coining the term *womanism* as a label for black women who believe in women's rights and opportunities. According to Walker, Southern black women often said to their daughters, "You acting womanish," which meant the daughters were being bold, courageous, and willful. To be womanish is to demand to know more than others say is good for you—to stretch beyond what is prescribed for a woman or girl (Collins, 1998). In her 1983 book *In Search of Our Mothers' Gardens,* Walker writes, "Womanist is to feminist as purple is to lavender" (p. xii).

TAKE A STAND: What does Walker's analogy tell you about womanism and feminism?

After the Million Woman March, many African-American women began building a movement focused on racial oppression. As we will see in Chapter 4, this evolution in activism brought men and women of color together in important ways. In 2013, three Black women—Alicia Garza, Opal Tometi, and Patrisse Cullors—created **#BlackLivesMatter,** igniting Twitter feeds and moving quickly from the Internet to the streets. Alicia Garza notes in the "herstory" of the movement: "Black Lives Matter is an ideological and political intervention in a world where Black lives are systematically and intentionally targeted for demise. It is an affirmation of Black folks' contributions to this society, our humanity, and our resilience in the face of deadly oppression" (Garza, n.d.). Inspired by the founders, two of whom identify as queer and one of whom comes from an immigrant family, #BlackLivesMatter organizers have been diligent in ensuring that *all* black voices—including trans voices, girls' and women's voices—are heard, forging an intersectional movement against racist violence that attends to black people of all gender identities, sexualities, abilities, immigration statuses, and classes.

In 1981, Cherríe Moraga and Gloria Anzaldúa edited and published the groundbreaking book, *This Bridge Called My Back: Writings by Radical Women of Color.* This marked the entrance of **multiracial feminism**—a liberation movement characterized by global perspective, coalition-building, and emphasis on multiple systems of domination that shape women's lives (Anzaldúa, 2002; Anzaldúa & Keating, 2002; Collins, 1998; Ryan, 2004; Thompson, 2002; Tong, 2013). Drawing on the work of earlier radical women of color, as well as womanism's focus on black women's lives, multiracial feminists work to dismantle the various forms of oppression that impact women's lives. Although race is especially important in multiracial feminism, race is understood to be intertwined with other systems of domination. Multiracial feminists insist that gender does not have universal meaning—instead, what gender means and how it affects our lives varies as a result of race, economic class, sexual orientation, gender identity, and so forth. While some feminist historians cite a decline in feminist activism in the early 1980s, the 80s and 90s were decades in which multiracial feminism flourished. Also, feminism during the 1980s and 1990s was increasingly attentive to sexual orientation and gender identity, issues that provided the foundation for grappling with the gender binary that we discussed in Chapter 2.

KATIE

I like the ideas of the multiracial feminists. I agree that race cuts across everything else. I'm middle-class, but my life isn't the same as a white, middle-class girl's, because I'm Asian American. It's like the issues in my life aren't just about my sex; they're also about my race. I can talk to black or Hispanic girls, and we have a lot in common—more than I have in common with most white girls. You just can't get away from the issue of race unless you're white.

Central to both womanism and multiracial feminism is emphasis on women's agency. Despite the constraints imposed by systems of domination, many women of color have resisted their oppressions. Even when they operated within abhorrent systems of domination such as slavery, women of color found ways to care for themselves and their families and to contribute to their communities (hooks, 1990; Walker, 1983). In recognizing that women of color have resisted oppression, multiracial feminists highlight the strengths of women.

A final strand in liberal feminism is **ecofeminism**. Ecofeminists assert there is a connection between the effort to control and subordinate women and the struggle to dominate nature (perhaps not coincidentally called "Mother Earth"). Rosemary Radford Reuther (1974, 1983, 2001), a theological scholar, argues that the lust to dominate has brought the world to the brink of a moral and ecological crisis in which there can be no winners. Ecofeminists believe that, as long as oppression is culturally valued, it will be imposed on anyone and anything that is unable or unwilling to resist.

Ecofeminists understand women's oppression as a specific example of an overarching cultural ideology that esteems oppression. Believing in humans' profound interdependence with all other life forms, ecofeminists argue that exploitation, domination, and aggression oppress women, men, children, animals, and the planet itself. While some early ecofeminist writings tended to essentialize women (and men), ecofeminism is increasingly intersectional. In *Sistah Vegan*, A. Breeze Harper (2010) says that all forms of oppression are linked and must be addressed through activism that connects feminism, decoloniality, environmental justice, and animal liberation.

STEPHANIE

Some of my strongest values involve ending the oppression of animals and living a sustainable lifestyle. Until I read about ecofeminism, I never saw the connection between those beliefs and feminism. But it makes sense, once you think about it, that if it's wrong to oppress animals and the earth, it's wrong to oppress women ... or anyone ... or anything.

Cultural Ideology

Just as in the first wave, the second wave also includes groups that believe that women and men are different in important ways and, thus, should have different rights and roles.

Separatism was developed to provide communities for women to live independently of men. Finding that feminine values of life, equality, harmony, nurturance, and peace gain little hearing in a patriarchal, capitalist society, separatists formed all-women communities in

EXPLORING GENDERED LIVES

The Text of the Equal Rights Amendment

Equality of the rights under the law shall not be denied or abridged by the United States or by any state on account of sex.

TAKE A STAND: Should the United States pass the Equal Rights Amendment? Why or why not?

which feminine values can flourish without the aggressive, individualistic, oppressive values these women associate with Western masculinity.

Because separatists did not assume a public voice to critique the values they found objectionable, they exercised little political influence. Yet, their very existence defines an alternative vision of how we might live—one that speaks of harmony, cooperation, and peaceful coexistence of all life forms.

REGINA

I don't see much to be gained by having equal rights to participate in institutions that are themselves all wrong. I don't believe dog-eat-dog ethics are right. I don't want to be part of a system where I can advance only if I slit somebody else's throat or step on him or her. I don't want to prostitute myself for bits of power in a business. I would rather work for different ways of living, ones that are more cooperative, like win-win strategies. Maybe that means I'm a dreamer, but I just can't motivate myself to work at gaining status in a system that I don't respect.

Revalorism highlights women's traditional activities and contributions to society. The broad goal of revalorists is to increase the value that society places on women and their traditional roles.

MADELINE

It saddens me that so few young women knit or crochet or even sew. Nearly all women of my generation knew how to sew, and many of us knew how to knit or weave or quilt. Historically, women have made beautiful clothing and linens for their families—the kind you can't buy in a store. Women today seem so focused on career that they are cutting off their links to their own histories. Does it have to be either or?

Drawing on standpoint theory, which we discussed in Chapter 2, revalorists believe that women's traditional involvement in homemaking and caregiving makes most women more nurturing, supportive, and cooperative than most men. In documenting women's contributions, revalorists aim to render a more complete history of the United States and its people.

LYLE

I'm a lot older than most students. I've had a career, and my wife and I raised four kids. I should say she raised them because that was her job. Mine was to earn an income for the family. That system worked for us, and our kids turned out just fine. I don't understand why so many young people don't want to follow traditional roles. We approve of division of labor in business and government; what's wrong with division of labor (he makes the money, she takes care of family) in our personal lives?

EXPLORING GENDERED LIVES

Antifeminism

Women's rights were not achieved without dissent. Beginning with the first wave, there have been intense antifeminist efforts, also called the **backlash** against feminism (Superson & Cudd, 2002). **Antifeminism** opposes changes in women's roles, status, rights, or opportunities.

The first example of antifeminism was the **antisuffrage movement**, which argued that women's rights to vote, pursue education, or hold property conflicted with women's natural roles as wives and mothers, and that women's suffrage would weaken the nation (Palczewski, 2005). Antisuffrage activism reached its apex between 1911 and 1916 and disbanded after women won the right to vote.

Antifeminist activism resurged in the 1970s in books that advocated women's return to traditional attitudes, values, and roles (Andelin, 1975; Morgan, 1973) and the STOP ERA movement, which opposed the 1972–1973 campaign to ratify the Equal

Rights Amendment (ERA). The most vocal proponent of STOP ERA, Phyllis Schlafly, traveled around the nation announcing that feminism was destroying femininity by encouraging women to leave traditional roles. Ironically, although Schlafly argued that women's place was in the home, her speaking schedule kept her away from her own home and family. The STOP ERA movement was successful in blocking passage of the bill. To this day, the United States has not passed the ERA.

Antifeminism also exists in the twenty-first century. The 2001 book *The Surrendered Wife: A Practical Guide for Finding Intimacy, Passion, and Peace with a Man* (L. Doyle) counsels women to abandon the quest for equality if they want happy marriages (Clinton, 2001). Another book, *The War against Men* (Hise, 2004), claims that women have gained power at the expense of men and that this is contrary to God's commandments.

TAKE A STAND: Do you see evidence of antifeminism in your community?

Contemporary Feminism

Many branches of second-wave feminism continue to be active today (Cobble et al., 2015). Alongside them, a new generation of feminist activism began emerging in the late 1980s. Sometimes referred to as the third wave, younger feminists are distinct from earlier generations because they are the beneficiaries of the second wave. They inherit a world partially transformed by the gains of the twentieth century, such as the right to vote, laws barring sexual harassment and discrimination, and increased professional and educational opportunities for women.

As was the case with previous waves of feminism, as the third wave has evolved, it has become less monolithic. Different branches have emerged and additional ones are likely to appear in the years ahead.

Riot Grrrl

Riot Grrrl was an underground feminist movement that began in the late 1980s and was aligned with punk music, radical politics, and Do-It-Yourself (DIY) ethics (Marcus, 2010). Angered to find that the lessons of second-wave struggles had not been fully absorbed by U.S. culture, Riot Grrrls formed feminist collectives across the country. They created and self-published music, art, and magazines ("zines") in order to tell women's stories and build a "Revolution, Girl Style Now." Zines such as *Girl Germs, Jigsaw,* and *Bamboo Girl* tackled a range of feminist issues, from rape culture and eating disorders to homophobia and racism (Alcantara-Tan, 2000). Riot Grrrl bands like *Bikini Kill* and *Bratmobile* wrote songs to rage against sexism and celebrate grrrls' independence and sexuality. Consider the lyrics from the song "Rebel Girl," commonly celebrated as a Riot Grrrl anthem: "That girl thinks she's the queen of the neighborhood/She's got the hottest trike in town/That girl, she holds her head up so high/I think I wanna be her best friend/Rebel girl, rebel girl/Rebel girl you are the queen of my world" (Hanna, 1991).

Many scholars consider Riot Grrrl to signal the beginning of third-wave feminism as a whole. Before we turn to other branches of the third wave, however, we must examine another, and very different, movement emerging around the same time.

Power Feminism

Power feminism emerged in the early 90s. Power feminists assume that society does not oppress women because women have the power to control what happens to them. Naomi Wolf (1993) tells women that the only thing holding them back from equality is their own belief that they are victims. Similarly, power feminist Katie Roiphe (1993) claimed that Take Back the Night marches, annual nonviolent protests to speak out against rape, are self-defeating because "proclaiming victim-hood" does not project strength.

EXPLORING GENDERED LIVES

Riot Grrrl Day

In 2015, the mayor of Boston proclaimed April 9 Riot Grrrl Day to honor Kathleen Hanna and others in the Riot Grrrl movement (Boston Proclaims, 2015). The proclamation included this excerpt from the Riot Grrrl Manifesto:

> The Riot Grrrl philosophy has never felt more relevant, with misogyny still rampant

in many cultural spaces…. Riot grrrls redefine the language used against them and continue to fight the newest incarnations of patriarchy. In doing so, they ironically confirm one ex-congressman's accidental wisdom: "the female body has ways to try to shut that down." It sure does: women's voices telling their stories can shut that down.

TAKE A STAND: Do you think the excerpt from the Riot Grrrls' manifesto is still rele
today?

> **FOLANA**
>
> *The only people I know who talk the power feminist talk have never been raped and never been slapped in the face with discrimination. They think their success and safety is a result of their own efforts and that any woman or minority person who hasn't achieved what they have just didn't try. I'll bet a lot of them would drop the power feminist line if they got raped. That might make them see that women and minorities don't have as much power as people like Wolf and Roiphe. As for me, I don't think of myself as a victim, but I know I'm vulnerable just because I'm black and a woman.*

Power feminism ignores the difference between being a victim in a particular moment, on the one hand, and adopting victim as an identity, on the other hand. Power feminism may appeal to women who are financially comfortable, successful, well educated, and living in safe neighborhoods. It is less persuasive to women who do not enjoy those privileges. Perhaps that is why power feminism is embraced mainly by white, heterosexual, middle- and upper-class ciswomen who have little or no personal experience with discrimination and violence. As a result, power feminists tend to have less in common with Riot Grrrls, transfeminists, and other branches of contemporary feminism.

Transfeminism

Transfeminism is a movement by and for trans and gender nonconforming people that advances an intersectional view of liberation (Stryker & Bettcher, 2016). It is worth noting that trans and gender nonconforming people were active participants in both first- and second-wave feminism, and that transfeminist perspectives have informed intersectional feminisms for decades—evidenced, for example, in the work of Frances Willard, Dr. Pauli Murray, and Sylvia Rivera (Faderman, 1999; Feinberg, 2006; Stone, 1992; Stryker & Bettcher, 2016). However, the term *transfeminism* is more recent—coined in the early 1990s when transfeminism and transfeminists became increasingly visible.

One of the signal achievements of the second wave was separating gender from sex and emphasizing that gender is socially constructed. Transfeminism goes a step further and asserts that sex is also socially constructed (Koyama, 2003). In other words, society has created expectations regarding how males and females should look, behave, and feel. But these expectations are just as arbitrary as views of masculinity and femininity. If there is no single, "real" essence of male or female, then people should be free to define their sexed and gendered identities in a range of ways.

According to Emi Koyama (2003), transfeminism is based on three primary beliefs:

1. People have the right to define and express their own identities.
2. People have the right to expect society to respect the identities they claim and express.
3. People have the right to bodily autonomy without fear of discrimination or violations from anyone, including religious, political, or medical authorities.

Transfeminists believe that the issues they face are familiar to many feminists—for example, gendered expectations for appearance and behavior that restrict individual agency, or gendered forms of violence used to police gender identity and expression. For this reason, transfeminists believe that their liberation is directly linked to the liberation of all women, as well as gays, lesbians, people with disabilities, people of color, poor and working class people, and men. As Emi Koyama explains, "Every time a group of women previously silenced begins to speak out, other feminists are challenged to rethink their idea of whom they represent and what they stand for" (2003, p. 244). Thus, this movement invites all people to reflect on the extent to which they have internalized gender stereotypes and the heterosexist and patriarchal perspectives upon which they are based.

In building coalitions and respecting people's "conscious, informed choices about the best way to live their embodied lives" (Stryker & Bettcher, 2016, p. 7), transfeminism contributes to intersectional feminist analysis and theorizing that challenges the gender binary.

Mainstream Third-Wave Feminism

Emerging from Riot Grrrl and influenced by multiple branches of second-wave feminism, especially radical and multiracial feminism, **mainstream third-wave feminism** includes women of different ethnicities, abilities and disabilities, classes, appearances, sexual orientations, and gender identities. Although third wavers draw on earlier movements, third-wave feminism is not simply an extension of the second wave (Fixmer, 2003; Fixmer & Wood, 2005; Johnson, 2007). We'll discuss features that characterize third-wave feminism in its first two decades.

First, third-wave feminism is focused on intersectionality. Drawing on the insights of multiracial feminists, third-wave feminists recognize that women differ in ways that significantly shape their experiences and opportunities. They focus on the intersectionality of oppression, pointing out that race, class, sex, sexual orientation, and gender identity are intricately woven together and must be addressed holistically. They work to speak about and for women as a group while simultaneously recognizing differences among women (Adichie, 2015; Fixmer, 2003; Zack, 2005). Eve Ensler's latest book, *I Am an Emotional Creature* (2011), includes monologues from girls all over the world, showing both how they are different and how they have commonalities.

Second, because third-wave feminists recognize the intersectionality of oppression, they are committed to building alliances with other groups that work against various kinds of oppression. As early third-wave writer, Mocha Jean Herrup (1995) explained, "To fight AIDS we must fight homophobia, and to fight homophobia we must fight racism, and so on.... Oppression is interrelated" (p. 247).

KATY

I really appreciate what the sixties women's movement did to make my life better, but I can't identify with it. My life is different than my mother's, and so are the issues that matter to me. Mom fought to get a job. I want a job that pays well and lets me advance. Mom worked really hard to find day care for her children. I want to have a marriage and a job that allow me not to have to rely on day care. Her generation fought to make it okay for women not to marry. My generation wants to figure out how to make marriages work better, more fairly. Different generations. Different issues.

Another feature of third-wave feminism is everyday resistance. Third-wave feminists note that many of the reforms won by the second wave have not been woven into everyday life. Sexism is often more subtle today than in 1960 or 1980, but it still exists; in fact, its subtlety is what makes it so challenging (Bennett, Ellison, & Ball, 2010). This motivates third wavers to embrace grassroots organizing, to challenge racist comments in social or professional settings, to confront homophobic attitudes, and be willing to reject class privileges. Third-wavers Jennifer Baumgardner and Amy Richards (2000) declare that third-wave feminists' "politics emerge from our everyday lives" (p. 18). Personal acts in local contexts are seen as a key way to instigate change (Bates, 2016; Fixmer & Wood, 2005; Sheridan-Rabideau, 2009).

Third-wave feminists insist that their politics must be rooted in personal, bodily resistance to oppressive ideologies (Babel & Kwan, 2011). In a stunning essay that explicitly links social constructions of female beauty to eating disorders that jeopardize millions of women's health, Abra Fortune Chernik (1995) wrote, "Gazing in the mirror at my emaciated body, I observed a woman held up by her culture as the physical ideal because she was starving, self-obsessed and powerless, a woman called beautiful because she threatened no one except herself" (p. 81). After recognizing the connection between cultural codes for femininity and her own body, Chernik responded in a way that was both personal and political: "Gaining weight and getting my head out of the toilet bowl was the most political act I have ever committed" (p. 81).

Third-wave feminism is also media savvy and engaged. Like others of their generation, third-wave feminists tend to be digitally networked so that they gain information from numerous sources and also create media of their own (Kearney, 2006). Third-wave feminists are likely to learn immediately of new developments from blogs and social media and often post their own videos of rallies and other events on YouTube and other websites. They also organize online as was the case when The Komen Foundation, which fights against breast cancer, announced it would no longer provide support to Planned Parenthood. Using social media, feminists got the word out, fueled outrage toward Komen's announced action, and forced Komen to reverse its position and continue funding Planned Parenthood.

Some, but not all, women who identify as third-wave feminists embrace consumption, individualism, and traditional "girl culture" by placing a premium on being feminine and fashionable. Yet, while being sexy and being feminist aren't mutually exclusive, embodying society's ideal of womanhood is not equally possible for all women. Beauty ideals tend to privilege youth and whiteness, and meeting those ideals requires energy and money. Thus, feminists who have sufficient time and money can embrace consumerism—spending money to be seen at trendy restaurants and bars and to acquire designer clothes, products, and cosmetic procedures (Chaudhry, 2005).

The third wave's focus on individual choice is attractive to many because it suggests that our personal choices determine our lives. Many women in our classes believe that if they do well in school and work hard, they will succeed in any career they choose. Yet, we worry that these young women may confront obstacles such as lower pay than male peers and discrimination against mothers (Hayden & O'Brien Hallstein, 2010). Obstacles such as these cannot be overcome by individual effort. They require structural change, and structural change grows out of collective political action.

━━━━━ **EXPLORING GENDERED LIVES** ━━━━━

"Don't Tell Us How to Dress. Tell Men Not to Rape."

In January 2011, Toronto Police constable Michael Sanguinetti spoke about crime prevention to a group of women at York University. He advised them to "avoid dressing like sluts" if they wished to prevent sexual assault (Stampler, 2011). Some women who heard Sanguinetti's comment were angry about what they perceived as yet another instance of blaming victims and excusing perpetrators of sexual violence. In response, two women organized the first SlutWalk protest, which took place on April 3, 2011, at Queen's Park in Toronto.

Although the organizers asked participants to dress in their everyday clothing to symbolize the fact that women in ordinary dress are assaulted, some participants chose to wear lingerie, stilettos, and other provocative clothing to symbolize their right to dress "like sluts" without being becoming victims of sexual violence. Some of the marchers scrawled messages on their bodies or carried signs reading "My dress is not a yes" and "Don't tell us how to dress. Tell men not to rape" (Valenti, 2011). Since the movement's inception, SlutWalk protests have emerged organically in over 200 countries as well as in cities across the United States (SlutWalk Toronto).

Opinions of SlutWalks vary widely (see Dow & Wood, 2014). One social critic cheers, "Here at last is that bold, original, do-it-yourself protest movement we've been waiting for, a rock-hard wall of female solidarity ... presented as media-savvy street theater that connects the personal and the political" (Pollitt, 2011). But another social critic sees SlutWalks as "narcissistic stunts" that are a "frivolous distraction by those who take advantage of the unprecedented freedoms won by others as they wrap themselves in the mantle of victim" (Phillips. 2011).

TAKE A STAND: Go online to learn more about SlutWalks. After doing so, what do you think of these protests?

Hip-Hop Feminism

In the late 1990s, another branch of younger feminist activism announced itself (Morgan, 1999). **Hip-hop feminism** is a movement rooted in black feminism and responsive to the concerns of the post–civil rights or hip-hop generation. Not unlike other branches of third-wave, hip-hop feminists "recognize culture as a pivotal site for political intervention to challenge, resist, and mobilize collectives to dismantle systems of exploitation" (Durham, Cooper, & Morris, 2013).

Hip-hop feminism is, however, distinct from other branches of third-wave feminism in significant ways. It is centered on the needs and experiences of younger black women and draws explicitly on hip-hop as a subculture committed to challenging the status quo. According to hip-hop feminist scholars, "Hip-hop feminism is concerned with the ways the conservative backlash of the 1980s and 1990s, deindustrialization, the slashing of the welfare state, and the attendant gutting of social programs and affirmative action, along with the increasing racial wealth gap, have affected the lifeworlds and worldviews of the hip-hop generation" (Durham et al., 2013). In the decades following the height of the Civil Rights Movement, the hip-hop generation of black youth find themselves in a difficult bind—some forms of racist discrimination have been prohibited through law, but systemic racism persists. Black culture is popularized in music and film, but black communities are disproportionately subject to police brutality, violence, incarceration, and institutionalized poverty. Hip-hop feminists took center stage at the 2016 HipHop Literacies Conference, which named as its theme: "Black Women and Girls' Lives Matter" (Hiphop Literacies Conference, n.d.).

Of course, not all hip-hop and rap music is feminist. As hip-hop became popular, some artists abandoned the genre's social justice roots. Mainstream, male-dominated hip-hop and rap has been critiqued for its misogyny and glorification of violence (Ofori-Atta, 2011).

TIFFANY

It makes black guys angry when I say it, but I think gangsta rap is totally sexist and destructive. Some of my girlfriends say they like rap and don't take the anti-woman lyrics personally. The way I see it, though, calling women bitches and whores is as hateful as you can get. It totally disses women. If black men talk that way about black women, how can we respect ourselves or expect others to?

But hip-hop feminists are meeting the challenge head-on. "I love hip-hop, but it upsets me that young boys treat girls like objects. I feel like I don't have a voice," said 17-year-old Tempestt Young (Dawson, 2005, p. 18). So she became a key organizer for the 2005 Feminism and Hip-Hop Conference, which was attended by more than 2,000 people, including music industry professionals. Young is just one of many activists building a strong and vibrant community of hip-hop feminists—a movement that includes men and women, artists and activists, writers and scholars and has long advocated for gender and racial justice (Durham et al., 2013; Pough, Richardson, Raimist, & Durham, 2007).

EXPLORING GENDERED LIVES

A Postfeminist Era?

Perhaps you have seen or heard the term *postfeminism* used to describe our era (Dubriwny, 2013; McRobbie, 2009). Claiming we live in a **postfeminist era** assumes that feminism is no longer relevant or needed because sexism has been fully eradicated (Bates, 2016). Postfeminism adopts the language of feminism—using words such as *choice* and *empowerment*—to advance an agenda that undermines feminist commitments to gender justice. Postfeminism's emphasis on individual choice confuses personal decision-making with freedom and gender equality (Ferguson, 2010). Consider the way pursuing an education is often thought of as a "choice" that individuals freely pursue. Although personal choice is important, it alone doesn't lead to an education. The decision to attend a university or college is often determined by finances. Full merit scholarships are hard to come by, and financial aid is difficult to secure if you or your parent(s) do not have credit. If you are a parent, the decision to pursue education is made more complex by limited childcare options. And class status often determines the quality of K–12 education and thus whether an individual can get into a good college. Placing emphasis on personal choices above all else, postfeminism depoliticizes women's lives and struggles—reducing structural conditions such as lack of societal support for child care and unequal pay to individual challenges, which individual women are personally responsible for resolving.

TAKE A STAND: What factors other than personal choice led to your enrolling at your college or university?

Hip-hop feminism is also expressed in music. It is embodied in the work of artists like Queen Latifah and Lauryn Hill, and more recently, Beyoncé, Andra Day, Nicki Minaj, and Erykah Badu, who challenge gender norms and misogyny in their lyrics and performance. As Marcyliena Morgan, renowned hip-hop scholar and director of the Hip-Hop Archive at Harvard University, notes: "Hip-hop feminists have been consistent in championing women's rights, which encompasses everything from sexuality to abuse.... And that has always been irrespective of what men in hip-hop were doing" (quoted in Ofori-Atta, 2011).

Like earlier waves of feminism, the contemporary wave is dynamic and continually evolving. Some of the current branches will become stronger, some will wane, and new branches will emerge in the years to come. Various forms of activism will shape the future of feminism.

The first stirrings of a new stage in feminist activism were evident on January 21, 2017, as women across the world marched with their allies in over 650 cities. Estimates of the number of marchers range from 3.3 to 4.6 million marchers in the United States, and between 250,000 and 300,000 more globally ("We Marched Everywhere," 2017). Drawing on intersectional feminist traditions, marchers emphasized reproductive justice, environmental justice, education, immigrant rights, LGBTQ rights, and the value of free speech.

Millions of people of all ages, sexes, genders, sexual orientations, and ethnicities participated in the historic Women's March on January 21, 2017.

SUMMARY

This chapter demonstrates that there are competing images of women that circulate in society. Through activist efforts, people argue for the images they think are most true, right, fair, or useful. And others argue back in an ongoing dialogue about who women are and what that means for their rights, roles, and opportunities.

The issue of whether a person is a feminist is considerably more complicated than it first appears. The "women's movement" is really a collage of many movements that span more than 170 years and include diverse ideologies. Whether or not you define yourself as a feminist, you have some views about women's identities, rights, and nature. The analysis provided by women's movements should inform your thinking about women's roles and lives.

KEY TERMS

The following terms are defined in this chapter on the pages indicated as well as in alphabetical order in the book's glossary, which begins on page 261. The text's companion website also provides interactive flash cards to help you learn these terms and the concepts they represent. You can access the site at www.cengagebrain.com.

antifeminism 65

antisuffrage movement 65

backlash 65

#BlackLivesMatter 63

cult of domesticity 57

cultural feminism 55

ecofeminism 64

hip-hop feminism 71

liberal feminism 55

mainstream second wave feminism 60

mainstream third-wave feminism 69

Million Woman March 62

multiracial feminism 63

postfeminist era 72

power feminism 67

radical feminism 58

revalorism 66

Riot Grrrl 67

separatism 64

transfeminism 68

womanism 62

women's liberation movement 58

women's rights movement 55

GENDER ONLINE

1.   Visit the Lesbian Herstory Archives online. What kinds of materials are included in the collection? What do they tell us about lesbian lives? How do you perceive their connection to feminist history?

2.   Visit NOW at: **http://www.now.org**

3.   To learn more about the third wave and differences and commonalities between it and earlier waves, visit this website: **http://www.thirdwavefoundation.org/**

4.   Online search terms: *ecofeminism, A. Breeze Harper, postfeminism, third-wave feminism.*

REFLECTION, DISCUSSION, AND ACTION

1. How have your views of feminism changed as a result of reading this chapter?

2. With which of the women's movements discussed in this chapter do you most identify? Compose a statement that outlines your vision for the future of women's movements.

3. Write or act out a discussion about whether women should serve in combat roles, which takes place between three feminists: an ecofeminist, a power feminist, and a separatist.

4. To what extent do you think it is possible for women to be both politically engaged feminists and sexy and conventionally feminine?

RECOMMENDED RESOURCES

1. Michael Kaufman & Michael Kimmell. (2011). *The Guy's Guide to Feminism*. Berkeley, CA: Seal Press. In this short, accessible book, Kaufman and Kimmel explain why, in their own words, "in spite of all the garbage jokes and media stereotypes, feminism is also an amazing gift to us guys" (p. 9).

2. *Iron Jawed Angels*. (2004). Directed by Katja von Garnier. Distributed by HBO. This film dramatizes the final stage of the fight for women's right to vote.

3. *The Punk Singer*. (2013). Directed by Sini Anderson. Distributed by Sundance Selects. This film documents the Riot Grrrl movement through the life and activism of Kathleen Hanna, lead singer for *Bikini Kill, Le Tigre*, and the *Julie Ruin*.

4. Sue Monk Kidd. (2014). *The Invention of Wings*. New York: Viking. This novel provides a rich narrative account of women's struggles in the nineteenth century through the lives of Sarah Grimke and her servant, Hetty "Handful" Grimke.

4

The Rhetorical Shaping of Gender: Competing Images of Men

Knowledge Challenge:

- What does it mean to perform traitorous identity?
- Which men's groups ally themselves with feminism?
- What is the Good Men Project?

In the summer of 2014, National Public Radio aired a series on what it means to be a man in the United States today (NPR, 2014). Consider the following statements made by men who were interviewed:

- *Being honest, responsible, respectful, and hardworking.*
- *Strong and stoic.*
- *Kind, caring, dedicated.*
- *Something that you're always learning on the job, and you don't have an instruction manual.*
- *Being a dad is absolutely the best part of being a man.*
- *My father gave me all the wrong concepts about being a man. If you're going to be a man in this world, you better learn how to dominate and control people and circumstances.*
- *A manicure…. It's manly. You got to be well groomed. Sometimes I get pedicures, too.*

Perhaps some of these statements resonated with you more than others. Perhaps you found yourself considering your own beliefs about what it means to be a man. Competing images of manhood are not new; they've existed throughout history. Images of men as strong and stoic coexist with views of men as engaged fathers and family cooks. Although particular images tend to dominate at any given time, alternative images are always in the mix and often serve as catalysts for changing how we understand manhood and masculinity. That is why Professor Michael Kimmel chose the name Center for the Study of Men and Masculinities for his program at Stony Brook. He wants to emphasize that there is "more than one way to be a man" (S. Bennett, 2015, p. ST7).

Historically, American men have been less involved than women in organized efforts to challenge gender norms. Although many men have not given sustained thought to their identity as men, some men have. In this chapter, we examine those men's efforts to define what manhood and masculinity mean. Like women's activism, men's activism has reflected diverse, sometimes deeply conflicting, political and personal values and goals. Some men's groups aim to usher in new images of masculinity, whereas others want to reinvigorate traditional images of masculinity and safeguard or increase men's privileges. Also like women's activism, men's activism is evolving, with new groups arising as once-prominent groups fade.

Men's efforts to define manhood are not independent of women's activism. As we will see in this chapter, some men's groups ally themselves with feminist organizations. Other men's groups fiercely reject feminism and feminists, and they work to bolster traditionally masculine roles, status, and privilege.

Profeminist Men's Groups

Profeminist men's groups, also called *progressive men* and **male feminists**, emerged in the 1960s. Although many men in New Left social movement organizations ignored women who accused them of sexism, other men thought women's criticism was on target and wanted to change their attitudes and behavior to be consistent with the egalitarian ideology they espoused. They joined forces with women to work for women's rights. Profeminist men's close relationship with liberal feminism generated two distinct foci, one related to women and the other to men.

BILL

I can't remember when I wasn't a feminist. It's as much a part of me as being a man or a Christian. My parents both work, Mom as a lawyer and Dad as an accountant. I grew up seeing my mother as strong and achieving and loving, just as Dad was. I grew up seeing my mother express her ideas articulately and seeing my father respect what she said and did. She listened when he talked; he listened when she did. When I was a kid, sometimes Mom worked late, and Dad was in charge of fixing dinner for me and my brother. Other times, Dad worked late, and Mom was in charge. Both of them took care of us. Both of them were successful outside of the home. I grew up seeing that women and men are equal. How could I not be a feminist?

Because they believe in the equality of the sexes, male feminists support women's battles for equitable treatment and participate in efforts to increase women's rights. For instance, during the 1972 campaign to ratify the Equal Rights Amendment (ERA), many men gave time, effort, and money to the battle for legal recognition of women's equality. Today, most male feminists support ending men's violence, rights for LGBTQ people, men's greater involvement with family, and working for social justice (National Organization for Men against Sexism, 2014). Profeminist men's movements increasingly have members of different races, ethnicities, sexual orientations, and gender identities. Also, they are visible on a global scale, with profeminist activism occurring in Australia, Brazil, India, Mexico, Nepal, New Zealand, and South Africa, among other countries (Okun, 2014).

One strategy used by some profeminist men is performing a **traitorous identity**. In performing a traitorous identity, a group member criticizes attitudes or actions that are common and accepted among members of that group. One example comes from a former student and football player, Trevor, who writes: "When I call out others on sexist language and behavior, many are shocked to see a hypermasculine male like me levy such criticism." Women who object to sexist comments are often dismissed, but men find it more difficult to ignore these objections when they come from "one of the guys." Trevor finds enacting a traitorous identity to be empowering: "I was creating positive social change, as micro as it was. Even if I could not wholly correct the behaviors of those around me, I believed I was at least generating conscious-ness with former football teammates, fraternity brothers, and coworkers." People who perform traitorous identity are not really "traitors" to their group. Rather, by questioning certain behav-iors, they are challenging the group to become better. As another one of our students observed, they act as "privilege punks"—allies that leverage their power on behalf of those with less.

Male feminists also engage in persuasion to convince friends and coworkers to alter dis-criminatory attitudes and practices. For instance, Scott Straus (2004) wrote an article in which he criticized men in the fraternity to which he had belonged for practices such as bragging about who had sex with whom and rating females' attractiveness.

RAYMOND

When one guy isn't playing well, others on the team will say he's playing like a girl. I don't know where that started, but you hear it a lot when a guy's game is off. My girlfriend gets really ticked off about that. She's in sports, too, and she says it's really disrespectful to talk like girls aren't any good at sports. So, last week I was off my game, and one of the other guys shouted that I was playing like a girl; I said "Like Venus Williams? Thanks, bro."

Another interest of male feminists is challenging society's prescriptions for masculinity. Endorsing the liberal belief that men and women are alike in most ways, male feminists want to develop the emotional capacities that society approves in women but discourages in men. Whereas social codes have restricted women's professional development and civic rights, they have tended to push men to repress many emotions. Male feminists encourage men to be more caring, open, and comfortable engaging in close relationships with women and other men. In her study of black men who define themselves as feminist, Aaronette White (2008) showed how these men's feminism enriches their parenting, friendships, and self-identity.

In 1975, the first Men and Masculinity Conference was held in Tennessee. This continu-ing conference explores the meaning of masculinity and provides a support network for men who want to talk about problems and frustrations inherent in cultural views of masculin-ity and the roles and activities appropriate for men (Doyle, 1997; Messner, 2001). We will look more closely at the National Organization for Men against Sexism (NOMAS), the AIDS Coalition to Unleash Power (ACT UP), and men's antiviolence groups as prototypes of the profeminist movement.

NOMAS

One of the most prominent and long-lasting male feminist organizations is **NOMAS**. NOMAS sponsors workshops to expand men's awareness of ways in which their emotional development has been hindered by restrictive social views of masculinity and to guide men in becoming more feeling and expressive. Often, these groups serve as safe testing grounds in which men experiment with talking about their feelings, needs, and problems.

━━━━━━━━ **EXPLORING GENDERED LIVES** ━━━━━━━━

The Scariest Phrase?

"Be a man." This is the scariest phrase boys and men hear in their lives, according to Joe Ehrmann, former NFL star, winning coach, and cofounder of Coach for America. Ehrmann thinks society does a terrible job of helping boys become men: "Our young boys are taught from a very early age that in order to be a man they have to separate their hearts from their heads … so we have this massive repression of the very thing that makes us human" (Ehrmann, 2013).

Our culture teaches three flawed criteria for manhood: athletic ability, sexual conquest, and economic success. When boys are taught to strive for these three things, they wind up constantly competing with each other, feeling isolated and without community. In place of what he calls "false masculinity," Ehrmann advocates for "strategic masculinity," which is defined by relationships with others and having a cause beyond yourself.

TAKE A STAND: Do you see evidence of false masculinity on your campus? How might you or others challenge or replace it with strategic masculinity?

Although members of NOMAS believe that some qualities traditionally associated with masculinity, such as courage and ambition, are valuable in men, NOMAS condemns other conventionally masculine qualities, such as aggression, violence, and emotional insensitivity. One of the major achievements of NOMAS is its Fathering Task Group. This group issues a newsletter called *Brother*, which promotes strong, supportive ties between men.

At NOMAS conferences on men and masculinity, four issues consistently arise as priorities. The first is recognizing and resisting the power and privilege that accompany being men. The second is ending violence against women by analyzing how cultural codes for masculinity legitimize men's violence against women. A third issue is working to end men's homophobic attitudes and the resulting cruel, sometimes deadly, attacks on gay and trans people. The fourth issue is developing men's studies at colleges and universities.

Modeled on the consciousness-raising groups popular with many second-wave feminists, NOMAS discussion groups encourage men to talk about what our society expects of men and the problems these expectations create. In this supportive context, men learn to talk openly with other men about feelings, fears, personal problems, and ways to change attitudes and behaviors they find unworthy in themselves.

NOMAS members are often involved in educational outreach programs that aim to raise other men's awareness of the constraints of traditional masculinity. Finally, members of NOMAS often enact traitorous identities to challenge everyday incidents of homophobia, sexism, and devaluation of women.

ACT UP: The AIDS Coalition to Unleash Power

The AIDS Coalition to Unleash Power was a grassroots movement that used street-based direct action and civil disobedience to advocate for people living with HIV and AIDS (Rimmerman, 2001). The group fought for medical treatment and changes in social attitudes toward those disproportionately impacted by HIV/AIDS, including but not limited to gay men. Their activism and legacy inspired changes in health policy, social attitudes toward gay men, and cultural expectations for men.

■■■■■■■■ EXPLORING GENDERED LIVES ■■■■■■■■

Men's Studies

You've heard of women's studies, but have you ever heard of men's studies? Although not widespread, courses in men and masculinity have been around for more than 25 years. The American Men's Studies Association was founded in 1991 (Bennett, 2015).

The profound changes in women's identities and rights have been paralleled by changes in men's identities and rights. A recent Shriver report found that about 44% of men think it's more difficult to be a man today than it was for their fathers (Bennett, 2015). Courses in men's studies provide opportunities for men to reflect on cultural changes and trends that affect them, to question why men have higher suicide rates than women, and to contemplate alternative ways to design work and family life (Reiner, 2016). Yet, skeptics point out that men's lives and experiences have always been central to academic curricula and do not need special attention.

TAKE A STAND: For what reasons would you support or not support men's studies at your school?

ACT UP was originally founded in 1987 in New York, at the height of the U.S. AIDS crisis. At that time, HIV and AIDS were erroneously assumed to affect gay men exclusively and were therefore largely ignored by a homophobic culture. Elected officials and medical professionals refused to invest in HIV/AIDS research, so we understood little about the disease, its transmission, and how it could be managed (France, 2012). ACT UP challenged political leaders, medical professionals, religious authorities, pharmaceutical companies, and the public to respond to the health crisis with research, education, and awareness to stop the spread of HIV/AIDS.

Recalling tactics of civil rights movements and radical feminists of the 1960s, ACT UP groups were intentionally leaderless and democratic in order to encourage participation. ACT UP often used direct action politics, leading visible and effective demonstrations against Wall Street, the New York Stock Exchange, the Food and Drug Administration, Northwest Airlines, CBS Evening News, and other organizations that discriminated against people living with HIV/AIDS. Some of ACT UP activism, and the work of the group it inspired, Queer Nation, used the street to highlight the fluid and performative aspects of gender and sexuality.

Although ACT UP was largely led by white, middle-class men and worked primarily to challenge and change discrimination against men, women were also involved. ACT UP women led a highly publicized action in the New York Mets' Shea Stadium in 1988, protested *Cosmopolitan* magazine for printing misleading and inaccurate information about HIV transmission, and did direct action education for teenage girls in New York high schools (Juhasz, 2012; Timmer,Rimmerman 2001). ACT UP also drew inspiration from the women's health movement and created underground networks of self-educated health care providers to get HIV/AIDS patients the care they desperately needed. ACT UP activism piqued in the late 80s and early 90s as discrimination against people with HIV/AIDS began declining, in part because of ACT UP's work. The movement is thoughtfully captured in the 2012 documentary *How to Survive a Plague*.

> ### KEVIN
>
> *If someone had told me five years ago I would say I'm a feminist, I wouldn't have believed it. Four years ago, my little sister was raped. I was enraged, and I felt totally powerless to help her, which was hard for me to deal with. I thought I was supposed to solve the problem, make things right, get the guy who did it.*
>
> *But I couldn't. I went with my sister to the rape crisis center and began to learn how bad the problem is. I began to see that the problem wasn't just the guy who raped her. It's the way that most men are socialized, including me—my wanting to be in control and get the guy who raped her. Gradually, I got more involved with others who want to end violence against women. Ending it has to start with men.*

Men's Antiviolence Groups

As we saw in our discussion of NOMAS, profeminists are committed to ending violence against women. Like Kevin, whose commentary appears above, profeminists believe that violence against women is not just a "woman's issue." These men reason that it's a men's issue since most violence against women (as well as men) is enacted by men. Three specific men's antiviolence programs deserve our attention.

The White Ribbon Campaign   Perhaps you've noticed that some men wear white ribbons between November 25 and December 6. Those who do are stating that they identify with the **White Ribbon Campaign (WRC)**, an international organization working to end men's violence against women. Formed in 1991, the WRC is the largest men's antiviolence group in the world.

The WRC began when a group of Canadian men responded to an appalling incidence of violence against women. On December 6, 1991, 14 women were slaughtered in what came to be called the Montreal Massacre. They were students in the Engineering School at the Université de Montreal. The murderer, who had failed to be admitted to the engineering school (Kaufman & Kimmel, 2011), felt that engineering was a man's field in which women had no rightful place, so he removed the women students from the school—and from life. Some male students at the Université de Montreal felt compelled to speak out and make it clear that not all men hate women, and not all men condone violence against women.

At first, only a handful of men met about the issue, but the group grew. Members defined their mission as taking the responsibility as men to speak out against men's violence against women. Designating a white ribbon as the symbol of men's opposition to men's violence against women, within six weeks, this small group convinced more than 100,000 Canadian men to wear white ribbons. According to the White Ribbon website, "Wearing a white ribbon is a symbol of a personal pledge never to commit, condone, nor remain silent about violence against women" (White Ribbon, n.d.).

Since the WRC was founded in Canada in 1991, it has spread to many other countries. Many college campuses have local WRC groups. Although seldom in the limelight, the WRC continues its efforts to persuade men to take responsibility for ending men's violence against women.

Wearing a white ribbon for one or two weeks a year is not the WRC's only rhetorical strategy. Members also present antiviolence workshops in schools, communities, and places of employment. In the workshops, WRC members encourage men to become part of the solution

---

EXPLORING GENDERED LIVES

Men Can Stop Rape

Men Can Stop Rape is a group that focuses primarily on raising college-age men's awareness of rape culture, encouraging them to resist it and to stop sexual assault by other men. The group's mission is to mobilize men to create cultures free from violence, especially men's violence against women. The group's website that explains its mission and provides videos and texts of interviews on a range of topics related to rape and, more generally, gendered violence: **http://www.mencanstoprape.org/**

TAKE A STAND: To what extent do you believe men should be involved in efforts to end rape? If you believe that men should be involved, what form might that involvement take?

---

by speaking out against men's violence and by talking with other men about the issue. The workshops focus not only on physical violence such as battering and rape but also on emotional violence, sexual harassment, sexist humor, and other practices that devalue and harm women.

WRC emphasizes that it is not "bashing men." On its website, this statement appears:

> The majority of men are not violent. At the same time … many men have come to believe that violence against a woman, child, or another man is an acceptable way to control another person. By remaining silent about these things, we allow other men to poison our working and learning environments.

Walk a Mile in Her Shoes   Complementing the efforts of the WRC, **Walk a Mile in Her Shoes** relies on community awareness and fundraising to end men's violence against women. Licensed therapist and educator Frank Baird founded the organization in 2001 in California to increase men's involvement with local antiviolence work. Each year in cities across the world, men involved with Walk a Mile in Her Shoes establish teams, don high heels, and participate in a one-mile march through local streets to cultivate men's compassion for women's experiences, generate community awareness, and raise money for local violence prevention programs. The marches have grown steadily in popularity, and an average of 300 walks are organized each year (**www.walkamileinhershoes.org**, 2016).

Across the country, many men participate in Walk A Mile in Her Shoes marches.

As the organization's website proclaims, "First you walk the walk ... then you talk the talk," explaining that the march involves men in antiviolence work on a grassroots, street performance level and afterward generates dialogue about gendered violence. Walk a Mile in Her Shoes aims for multiple levels of impact, stating: "For preventive education, it helps men better understand and appreciate women's experiences, thus changing perspectives, helping improve gender relationships and decreasing the potential for violence. For healing, it informs the community that services are available for recovery. It demonstrates that men are willing and able to be courageous partners with women in making the world a safer place" (Walk a Mile in Her Shoes, n.d.).

One criticism of both the WRC and Walk a Mile in Her Shoes is that they don't go far enough in their analysis of men's violence. This criticism maintains that the problem is not a few men who are violent, but rather that violence is intimately woven into how society defines men and masculinity.

Mentors in Violence Prevention   Jackson Katz is one of the leaders in men's effort to end male violence against women. The program he developed, **Mentors in Violence Prevention (MVP)**, aims to educate men about socialization that links masculinity to violence and to motivate men to reject violence in themselves and other men as "empowered bystanders" (Katz, n.d.).

In Michael Kaufman and Michael Kimmel's (Kaufman & Kimmel, 2011) words, "Men look to other guys to define what it means to be a man" (p. 167). Men are more likely to be violent toward dates if they associate with peers who verbally endorse or actually engage in violence against female partners (Williamson & Silverman, 2001). And men are more likely to be involved with antiviolence work if their peers are supportive and/or also engaged in this work (Casey & Smith, 2010).

The MVP program instills antiviolence attitudes in men who then teach their male peers not to be violent. The program has two foci. The first is to teach men that aggression and violence are closely linked to cultural views of masculinity and thus part of routine masculine socialization. In other words, the MVP program focuses on normative masculinity—on the ways in which violence is seen as a normal part of manhood in our society (Katz, 2013; Katz & Jhally, 2000). From sports to the military, masculine socialization teaches boys that violence is an appropriate means of gaining and maintaining control over others and winning—whether it's winning on the football field or the bedroom. Becoming aware of normative masculine socialization is the first step in challenging and changing it.

The second focus of the MVP program is to call attention to the role of bystanders in preventing violence. Jackson and other MVP trainers reject the idea that only those who actually commit violence are blameworthy. In many cases, for violence to be committed there must be bystanders who approve, encourage, condone, or just remain silent, Katz (n.d.) insists. MVP encourages men to take responsibility not only for refraining from violence themselves but also for refusing to allow, condone, or be silent in the face of other men's violence.

As the foregoing pages demonstrate, profeminist men's groups are distinct. Some prioritize ending sexist views that restrict men and women, while others focus on the rights of particular groups such as gay men and others living with HIV/AIDS. What they have in common is the belief that conventional views of sex, gender, and sexual orientation are limiting for all of us. In stark contrast are masculinist groups. We turn now to those.

■ **EXPLORING GENDERED LIVES** ■

Bystanders Who Don't Just Stand By

Have you ever felt uncomfortable listening to a rape joke? Have you ever been offended by a racist or sexist comment? What do you do in such situations? If you are like many people, you do nothing not because you don't care, but because you don't know how to intervene or are afraid of ruining your relationship with the person speaking offensively.

But "doing nothing" is actually doing something—it is allowing the offensive behavior to go unchecked, which amounts to passively approving it. Sharon Potter, who codirects the Prevention Innovations Research Center, says, "When we hear this egregious, uncomfortable talk and we don't speak up, the person speaking is getting a green light. It encourages them" (Carey & Hoffman, 2016, p. A18).

There are alternatives to doing nothing. In fact, there are lots of options and many of them are not confrontational. Recent years have brought great attention to ways that bystanders can intervene to curb offensive language and the attitudes it reflects (Banyard, 2015; Wooten

& Mitchell, 2016). Here are some of the ways bystanders can respond to offensive comments:

- Change the subject abruptly.
- Distract by spraying water (in a locker room) or cranking up the music.
- Be honest without sounding holier than thou: "That comment bothers me because a good friend of mine was assaulted."
- Act as if you think the speaker must be joking. Say, "I love your humor" or "I know you're joking, but it's not funny."
- Walk out.
- Use nonverbal communication: Shake your head or roll your eyes.
- Disagree using a tone that is friendly: "I wouldn't use the word 'pushy' to describe Anika. I see her as assertive like anyone with ambition."

The National Sexual Violence Resource Center provides information about and links to a range of intervention programs, including the one used by MVP: **http://www.nsvrc.org/bystander-intervention-campaigns-and-programs**

TAKE A STAND: Are you willing to try one or more of the listed means of intervening?

Masculinist Men's Groups

A number of men's groups embrace cultural ideology, which holds that women and men are fundamentally different and, therefore, should have different roles and rights. Men's groups that believe this are called **masculinist** (Fiebert, 1987), or *promasculine*. They assert that men suffer from discrimination and that men need to reclaim their rightful status as men (Kimmel, 2013; Roy, 2014).

Masculinists also differ from profeminist men in attitudes toward gay men. The issue of gay rights is not a primary concern for most masculinist men, who tend to either ignore or denounce gay men.

Men's Rights

Among the most conservative men's groups are **men's rights activists**, whose goal is to restore the traditional roles of men and women and, with that, the privileges men historically enjoyed (Roy 2014; Timm, 2014). Men's rights groups include A Voice for Men, Men

Achieving Liberation and Equality (MALE); Men's Rights, Incorporated (MR, Inc.); the National Coalition for Free Men; and the National Organization of Men (NOM).

One of the more extreme men's rights groups is **Free Men**, a small group that aims to restore men's pride in being "real men," who are tough, rugged, invulnerable, and self-reliant. Free Men regard male feminists as soft and unmanly. According to Free Men, the primary burden of masculinity is the provider role, which makes men little more than meal tickets whose worth is measured by the size of their paychecks.

Free Men want men to regain their rightful places as heads of families. At the same time, they think their status should not be tied to the breadwinner role. Free Men oppose affirmative action and believe men should not have to pay alimony and child support (Kimmel, 2013).

> **SAM**
>
> *I know it's not politically correct these days to say it, but I agree with a lot of what masculinist men believe. I think families were stronger when the man was the head and the woman knew to follow. Families can't work if both spouses want to lead. There can be only one leader. I think the country was a lot stronger, too, before women started getting into business and government. I think women and men have different abilities. They're equal, but they're different. As far as gays go, I'm not homophobic or anything, but I don't see protecting their rights as a priority.*

Men's rights groups think that discrimination against men is a greater problem than discrimination against women. To support their claim that men are oppressed, men's rights groups point to issues such as the military draft, shorter life spans, more health problems, and child custody laws that favor women (Kimmel, 2013). The group's website, **http://mensrights.com**, offers advice and recommends books to help men win child custody battles and negotiate favorable divorce settlements (**http://mensrights.com**, 2016).

Father's Rights Groups

Fathers' rights groups are angry and hurt that men don't have at least 50% custody of their children after divorce. They claim that courts discriminate against men by assuming that women should be the primary parents.

The highest-profile fathers' rights group is in England. **Fathers 4 Justice** works to initiate public dialogue around fathers' rights. Fathers 4 Justice sometimes perform dramatic stunts to generate publicity around fathers' rights issues. These performances often involve dressing up as iconic figures such as Spiderman, Batman, and Father Christmas and protesting in places like Buckingham Palace or Tower Bridge. More recently, Fathers 4 Justice has also embraced political dialogue to bring about social change ("Our Story," n.d.).

Fathers 4 Justice isn't the only group fighting for fathers' rights. In the United States, there are dozens, including the American Coalition for Fathers, Fathers and Families, and Children and Dads against Discrimination. These groups file class-action custody suits to argue that a father has a constitutional right to be a parent, and thus he is guaranteed nothing less than 50% of the time with his children. The key questions fathers' rights groups ask are the following:

- Can fathers love their children as much as mothers?
- Do children need their fathers as much as they need their mothers?
- Is it sex discrimination to give mothers an advantage when it comes to custody rights?

Many of us would answer "yes" to these questions. However, the issues are a bit more complicated than these questions suggest. Not all fathers make the legally required child-support payments, and a number of fathers don't contact children following a divorce. This makes it difficult for judges and family-service agencies to be confident that all or most fathers will accept the responsibilities that accompany the rights they seek.

Mythopoetic Men

Another men's group that gained attention in the late 1980s and early 1990s was the **mythopoetic movement**, founded by poet Robert Bly. The mythopoetic movement aimed to foster men's personal growth, wholeness, and bonding in all-male gatherings (Bonnett, 1996; Silverstein, Auerbach, Grieco, & Dunkel, 1999).

Mythopoetics claimed that men's formerly profound connections to the earth and to other men were destroyed by modernization. When men began to work outside the home, young boys lost role models for manhood and how to relate to other men. Mythopoetics think ideal manhood existed prior to and during the Middle Ages, when men were self-confident, strong, emotionally alive, and sensitive. As exemplars of ideal manhood, mythopoetics cited the Knights of the Round Table, Henry David Thoreau, Walt Whitman, and Johnny Appleseed (Gross, 1990).

Like Free Men, mythopoetics have no use for feminists, saying "feminists have been busy castrating American males. They poured this country's testosterone out the window in the 1960s" (Allis, 1990, p. 80).

Mythopoetics urge men to reclaim courage, aggression, and virility as masculine birthrights and as qualities that can be put to the service of bold and worthy goals, as they were when knights and soldiers fought for grand causes.

Central to modern man's emotional emptiness, argued Bly, is **father hunger**, a grief born of yearning to be close both to actual fathers and to other men. To help men who experience

---

EXPLORING GENDERED LIVES

Rites of Manhood

Men's rites may be as important as men's rights. Prior to the Industrial Revolution, most American fathers worked at or near their homes, so they spent a great deal of time with their sons, teaching them what it means to be a man. The same sort of mentoring of young boys existed in African tribes. When a boy reached a certain age, the men of the tribe—not just the father—would take the boy away from the village and teach him the tribe's values. When the boy returned to the village, he was recognized as a man.

Building on traditions of mentoring boys into manhood, Rites of Passage is a program that pairs African-American boys with male elders in the community, who serve as a mentors and role models (McDonald, 2005). The elder teaches the boy to take responsibility for caring for himself and his community, to eschew violence, drugs, and other things that weaken self and community, and to keep promises to himself and others. When the elder is satisfied that the boy understands what it means to be a man, he gives the boy an African name, which symbolizes that he has become a man.

TAKE A STAND: Do you think all boys would benefit from rites to mark the passage into manhood? Why or why not?

father hunger, Bly and other movement leaders held workshops and nature retreats where men gathered in the woods to beat drums, chant, and listen to poetry and mythic stories, all designed to resolve father hunger and establish positive traditional masculinity.

The mythopoetic movement received both praise and blame. Naming father hunger highlights the anguish many men feel because they have or had distant relationships with their fathers or other men (Chethik, 2001; Schwalbe, 1996). At the same time, mythopoetics have been charged with unwillingness to confront issues of gender inequality and with participation in sustaining that inequality (Schwalbe, 1996). In addition, some think that the mythopoetics were elitist, as the membership was largely white and middle class.

You may have noticed that the majority of references in our discussion of mythopoetics were published in the early 1990s. Although they still host retreats, the group is attracting few new members. It is possible that mythopoetics' focus on personal growth wasn't enough to sustain a movement. Without a political agenda, it's difficult to keep a movement charged and vital. Even so, the mythopoetic movement contributed to the dialogue about masculinity by naming father hunger.

Promise Keepers

In 1990, Bill McCartney and Dave Wardell conceived the idea of filling a stadium with Christian men. Later that year, McCartney and Wardell motivated 72 men to pray and fast about the idea of men coming together in Christian fellowship. The first **Promise Keepers** event in 1991 drew 4,200 men. Two years later, McCartney achieved his goal of filling the 50,000-seat Folsom Field. In 1994, the Promise Keepers spread out to seven sites, at which more than 278,000 men came together to pray and commit themselves to a Christ-centered life. Promise Keeper events, such as "Stand in the Gap," "Storm the Gates," and "The Challenge," drew thousands of men each year (Shimron, 1997, 2002; Wagenheim, 1996).

SOPHIA

A few years ago my dad went to a Promise Keepers event, and it changed him and our whole family. Before he went, he was the stereotype of the absent or uninvolved husband and father. After he went, he totally turned around—he was there for mom and for me and my brother. He started making the family the center of his life. For us, Promise Keepers has been a good thing.

Whereas mythopoetics saw reconnecting with nature as the way for men to regain their wholeness, Promise Keepers see reconnection to God's commandments as the path. The movement urges men to be the leaders of their families because Promise Keepers believe that it reflects the God's view of the proper relationship between husbands and wives. Following the Christian path requires men to be good husbands, fathers, and members of communities; each Promise Keeper makes seven promises that reflect these commitments (Shimron, 1997).

Supporters of Promise Keepers believe that the movement promotes values that build strong families and strong communities (Whitehead, 1997). Furthermore, a number of women who are married to Promise Keepers say their marriages have improved since their husbands joined the movement (Cose, 1997; Griffith, 1997; Shimron, 2002; Whitehead, 1997).

Others voice reservations about the Promise Keepers. They question the prohibition on women's attendance at Promise Keepers' meetings. The Promise Keepers' answer is to quote Proverbs 27:17: "Iron sharpens iron, and one man sharpens another." This reflects Promise Keepers' belief that men should lean on each other, not on women (Shimron, 2002). Similarly, some ask, "Why can't husbands and wives be equals?" (Ingraham, 1997). McCartney responded, "When there is a final decision that needs to be made and they can't arrive at one, the man needs to take responsibility" ("Promise Keepers," 1997, p. 14A). Critics charge that "taking responsibility" is a code term for denying women's equality, voices, and rights.

KATHY

I really don't know what to think of the Promise Keepers. I like what they say about men committing to family values and strong spirituality. I'm Christian, so I agree with a lot of what they stand for. But I don't like the idea that men have to be the leader in relationships. I won't be led by a man, and I don't want to lead a man, either. I want a relationship where we're equal in all respects. This makes me identify with only parts of what the Promise Keepers stand for.

Another frequently expressed criticism is that Promise Keepers are elitist. The great majority of Promise Keepers are white and economically middle or upper class (Heath, 2003). In response to criticism, Promise Keepers tried to broaden its membership to include men of different races and to soften its rhetoric about husbands leading wives. In a move to symbolize the group's racial diversity, when McCartney retired from the presidency in 2003, the group chose Thomas Fortson, an African American, to head Promise Keepers (Gorski, 2003).

But racial inclusiveness didn't help Promise Keepers respond to charges of another kind of exclusion. Promise Keepers assert that homosexuality is a sin, promote literature on "leaving homosexuality" on their website, and offer advice on how to challenge LGBTQ-positive branches of Christianity. Naturally, this makes gays and their allies uncomfortable with the movement. A final criticism is that Promise Keepers is more a conservative political movement than a social and spiritual movement.

The Promise Keepers reached its peak in 1997, with a budget of $117 million and a well-attended "Stand in the Gap" rally at the National Mall in Washington, DC. Six years later, the budget was $27 million, reflecting a steep decline in membership (Gorski, 2003).

TONY

The PKs really frustrate me. I am a born-again Christian. I'm also gay. I believe everything that PKs stand for except their condemnation of gays. I'll put my Christian values up against those of any PK, but there's no room for me in the organization.

Whether Promise Keepers reinvigorates itself or not, its impact continues. Some men who were involved with Promise Keepers in the 1990s have used the movement as a model for building grassroots men's ministries in churches around the United States (Murphy, 2005).

Men's ministries work to make local churches relevant to men, because some male Christian leaders believe that the church has been "feminized" (Caughlin & Caughlin, 2005; Pinsky, 2007).

The Millions More Movement

Just as many African-American women think that feminism doesn't speak to or for them, many African-American men believe that most of the men's movements don't fit their histories and lives (Hammer, 2001). In the fall of 1995, Minister Louis Farrakhan, leader of the Nation of Islam, and the Reverend Benjamin Chavis Jr., organized the first **Million Man March**. Their goal was for black men to fill the mall of the nation's capital. The goals of the 1995 meeting were for black men to atone for sins and reconcile with one another. Spike Lee's film *Get on the Bus* (Lee, 1997) offers a dramatic documentation of this first march.

At the march, organizers encouraged men to pledge themselves to spiritual transformation and political action. Specifically, organizers called for the men to register to vote, to fight drugs in their lives and communities, and to stand against unemployment and violence. Men were asked to recommit themselves to their wives and families and to active involvement in their churches and communities.

MICHAEL

I attended a Million Man March years ago, and it was the most important event of my life. It was wonderful to see so many black men in one place—all there to unite with one another and to change our world. The whole mood was one of total brotherhood. It strengthened my pride in being a black man and my feeling that I can build a life around strong spiritual values.

EXPLORING GENDERED LIVES

Grassroots Men's Ministries

Would you like to learn more about grassroots men's ministries? Would you like to start one in your community? Two model groups are the Washington Area Coalition of Men's Ministries and the National Coalition of Men's Ministries. On its website, the Washington Area Coalition of Men's Ministries offers this description of itself:

We join together as men from local churches and organizations in the Washington D.C. Metro area to encourage every man within the sphere of our influence to pursue a vital relationship with God and with one another, to equip them for servant leadership in the home,

workplace, community and world, and to enable them to gather for corporate celebration and edification.

Now including more than 100 grassroots groups, the National Coalition of Men's Ministries states the following mission:

The National Coalition of Men's Ministries welcomes inquiries from people who are interested in starting a men's ministry in their community. Contact the group at 180 Wilshire Blvd., Casselberry, FL 32707. Phone Number: (407) 332-7703. Toll Free: (877) MAN-NCMM (626-6266). E-mail: office@ncmm.org.

TAKE A STAND: How do you think ministries should be involved in profeminist and/or masculinist men's movements?

Glenn Loury (1996), an African-American professor of economics, expressed concern that Million Man encouraged black men to base their rage on the racial identity of those who suffer rather than to rage against suffering and inequity no matter who is the victim. The Million Man March was also criticized for being antifeminist and antigay and for holding overly conservative views of families and women.

The inaugural Million Man March in 1995 became a model for other groups. Since that march, America has seen a Million Woman March in Philadelphia, a Million Youth March in Harlem, a Million Mom March in Washington, a Million Family March ("Million Family March," 2000), and the Millions More Movement was launched in the nation's capital. Conceived by Minister Louis Farrakhan, who also led the Million Man March, the Millions More Movement learned from criticisms of Millions marches. From the start, it was defined as an ongoing movement rather than a march. The mission statement focuses on educational, political, spiritual, social, and economic aspects of community development. Also, unlike the Million Man March, the Millions More Movement is inclusive of all sexes, races, and sexualities, although its focus remains on racial disparities that continue to affect black people and communities negatively (Muwakkil, 2005).

By 2015, the movement evolved further. An event called the Justice or Else Rally was headlined by Louis Farrakhan, the co-organizer of the initial march, who said he was passing the torch to the new generation (Nakamura, 2015). The new generation that Farrakhan recognized has been galvanized by #BlackLivesMatter, which we discussed in Chapter 3 and noted for its radical intersectionality (Garza, n.d).

The evolution of this movement exemplifies the fluidity of activism surrounding race, gender, and sexual orientation. What was originally a male-focused march has become a decisively inclusive movement. The initial Million Man March was largely masculinist in ideology, but the contemporary #BlackLivesMatter movement is profeminist.

Contemporary Men's Movements

Does the traditional script for masculinity still work in contemporary America? The recession that began in 2008 resulted in massive job losses. The losses, however, were not evenly distributed. Initially, the hardest hit sectors were manufacturing and construction, two of the sectors that remain heavily male dominated. And many of those jobs aren't coming back. Over the next 10 years, more than 15 million new jobs will be created, and a majority of them will be ones that women have traditionally held—nursing, primary and secondary teachers, and home health assistants (Romano & Dokoupil, 2010).

JENNA

When my dad got laid off in 2009, it hit him like a ton of bricks. At first, he was sure he'd get another great job. Didn't happen. After a year, he really hit bottom. Some days, he didn't even get up. Mom said he was depressed, but he refused to see a doctor or even talk to us. The most he says is that he feels like nobody because he can't support his family. He could do a lot to support us that doesn't have anything to do with making money, but he doesn't see that.

Jenna's father is not alone. Many men have struggled in the wake of the great recession, but men's responses to the recession have varied significantly.

The economic downturn is one of three recent and large social changes that have fueled contemporary masculinist movements (Kimmel, 2013). A second change fueling masculinist movements is that U.S. family laws have not kept pace with changing family dynamics. Thus, Kimmel states that even though fathers' rights groups overlook significant gendered patterns in parenting responsibilities that have shaped divorce and custody resolutions, they also offer some important perspectives on cultural biases against fathers. Finally, the Internet has made it possible for masculinist men to connect with one another. The anonymity of virtual space also facilitates vitriolic speech on men's rights websites (Kimmel, 2013; Potok, 2014). For example, Paul Elam, founder of men's rights website A Voice for Men, targeted feminists by publishing their personal information online; several feminists have faced threats and verbal attacks as a result.

■ EXPLORING GENDERED LIVES ■

Misogyny

Paul Elam is "the best-known men's rights activist in the United States" (Potok, 2014), so it's not surprising that he organized an international men's rights conference in 2014 that attracted over 250 attendees (A Voice for Men, n.d.). The conference was held in Detroit because organizers believed such an industrial city exemplified masculinity.

Elam once declared the month of October as "Bash a Violent Bitch Month" and elaborated by saying "I mean literally to grab them by the hair and smack their face against the wall" (Elam, 2014). Elam posts photos of women with black eyes and battered faces with captions such as "Maybe she DID have it coming" and "you mess with the bull, you get the horn" (Elam, 2014). Elam has also repeatedly said that women who are raped bring the violence on themselves: "THEY ARE NOT ASKING TO GET RAPED. They are freaking

begging for it. Damn near demanding it" (Elam, 2010). Elaborating his opinion, Elam writes, "A lot of women get pummeled and pumped because they are stupid (and often arrogant) enough to walk through life with the equivalent of a I'M A STUPID, CONNIVING BITCH—PLEASE RAPE ME neon sign glowing above their empty little narcissistic heads" (Elam, 2010).

The attitude that Elam expresses has a name: **misogyny**, which is hatred of women. Misogyny is more than sexism or even disliking some women. It is hatred of women as a group.

The Internet provides a home for people who hate women. The manosphere is the name given to blogs and other online forums that refer to women as "whores" and "social cancers" and make comments such as "if you were allowed to beat your wife we wouldn't be dealing with this" (Bellafante, 2016).

TAKE A STAND: Do you think people who espouse hatred of women and encourage violence toward women should be protected by freedom of speech?

Masculinist responses to the economic downturn are not the only responses, however. Research suggests that younger men are redefining masculinity beyond the traditional breadwinner role. In 2012, the Pew Research Center reported that for the first time in America's history, more 18- to 34-year-old women (66%) than men (59%) say succeeding in a high-paying career is one of the most important things in life (Blow, 2012). Men of this era may find it useful to do what many women did during the second wave—consider new ways of defining their identities, figure how to balance paid labor and contributions to home and family, think outside of the conventional boxes about careers, and reinvent themselves to fit changing constraints and opportunities.

A recently organized men's movement takes up this invitation to rethink traditional roles for and expectations of gender and to craft a new definition of manhood in the twenty-first century.

The Good Men Project

By outside measures, Tom Matlack's life was a huge success. Barely 30, he was earning a large salary and was even featured in a story in the *Wall Street Journal*. He had a stunning home and a wife and children. But Matlack's outward success wasn't matched by inward happiness. His dependence on alcohol contributed to ending his marriage and almost cost him his life. When he reached his personal bottom, Matlack began asking how he could make a life that he respected.

That was the start of the **Good Men Project**, which is a multifaceted effort to stimulate a national conversation about what it means to be a good man today. Partnering with James Houghton and Larry Bean, Matlack published a book, *The Good Men Project* (Houghton, Bean, & Matlack, 2009), whose royalties are donated to groups that work with at-risk boys. The book is a collection of stories by men who are black and white, gay and straight, rich and poor, NFL Hall of Fame Linebackers, and ex-cons. Each man's story describes a defining moment in his life. Accompanying the book is a DVD (Gannon, 2009) in which men talk honestly about spiritual crises, watershed moments in fathering, turning points in relationships, and struggles with infidelity, alcohol, and drugs. According to Matlack, the stories are effective because "men are more open to listening to issues in male ways, like being in the locker room. It's not talking about emotion directly but talking about emotion in terms of a story of a guy dying in combat" (Weigel, 2010).

Although the men featured in the book and DVD have widely varying life experiences and circumstances, what they have in common is that they are all trying to figure out what it means to be good men today. In introducing the book, Matlack states, "There is no definitive way to be 'good'" (Houghton et al., 2009, p. 8). But, he continues, reading other men's stories and thoughts can help each man formulate his own definition of what it means to be good. Not only has the book sold well and men are reading and talking about it, but it also has propelled creation of an online community for thinking about manhood today.

In 2010, the Good Men Foundation launched the *Good Men Project*, an online magazine, whose readers and contributors represent diverse ages, ethnicities, races, religions, economic classes, and sexualities. This online magazine features stories and columns that address issues that surface in men's lives: sex and relationships (Mark Greene, "Why I Hate Porn"), sports (open thread, "Should Penn State's Football Team Be Shut Down?"), dads, (Al Watts, "The Reality of Being an At-Home Dad"), and advice ("Dear John" responds to readers' questions on everything from wearing hairpieces to dealing with difficult neighbors). In addition, the magazine facilitates an ongoing conversation about what masculinity does and might mean. Perry Glasser, prizewinning author, says the magazine is

---

EXPLORING GENDERED LIVES

"If You Don't Like What's Being Said, Change the Conversation."

Tom Matlack knows something about being at risk. More than once, his drinking endangered his life, including time when a rollover car accident threw him through windows. Looking back on that time, Matlack says he had "this perfect, superficial picture—two kids, a big house, a wife. I had everything and yet I was ashamed of my behavior—drinking, cheating. At 31, I was a professional success and personal failure all at once" (Weigel, 2010).

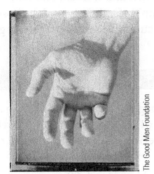

The Good Men Foundation

Matlack's efforts to come to grips with his life led him to realize he wasn't alone—there are lots of men trying to figure out how to live lives of integrity. With James Houghton, Matlack set up The Good Men Foundation, which has two goals: funding organizations that help at-risk boys and launching a national discussion about what it means to be a good man. Proceeds from the book and a portion of proceeds from the media arm of the foundation go to organizations that help at-risk boys.

The *Good Men Project*'s online site magazine encourages participation— comment on others' ideas, initiate your own, and help shape the dialogue. As the site says, "If you don't like what's being said, change the conversation."

Tumblr: **http://goodmenproject.tumblr .com/**

Facebook: **www.facebook.com /thegoodmenproject**

Twitter: @GoodMenProject

TAKE A STAND: How would you define a "good man"?

---

an alternative to "media images of masculinity that are dangerously repellent and full of rage" (Bergeron, 2009).

The magazine tells readers, "Guys today are neither the mindless, sex-obsessed buffoons nor the stoic automatons our culture so often makes them out to be.... We explore the world of men and manhood in a way that no media company ever has, tackling the issues and questions that are most relevant to men's lives. We write about fatherhood, family, sex, ethics, war, gender, politics, sports, pornography, and aging. We shy away from nothing" (**http:// goodmenproject.com**). The magazine steers clear of prescriptions and proselytizing. It doesn't tell men *how* to be good; it simply provides a forum for discussing issues so that each man can figure out his own definition of good.

Men aren't the only readers of *The Good Men Project* magazine. A third of the readers are women who want to understand men's perspectives and who find the magazine offers something more real and more interesting than the superficial stereotypes in *Sports Illustrated*, *Maxim*, and *GQ*. Senior Editor Henry Belanger says that men today "are trying to do more things than their fathers did." As men try to figure out how to do that, many of them find it helpful to be part of a community of other men who are struggling with similar issues.

SUMMARY

Men's efforts to define gender are diverse and even contradictory. Some men consider themselves feminists, work with women for gender equality in society, and attempt to become more comfortable expressing their feelings. Other men think feminism has destroyed families, twisted women, and diminished men. As this chapter has shown, men's activism varies greatly in its foci and relationship to women's activism. Historically and today, men's groups are important in the cultural conversation about gender and its effects on individual men and women.

In this chapter and the preceding one, we discussed a wide range of groups that give voice to diverse images of women and men. As the conversation evolves, some of the current voices will fade out and new voices will emerge. Some people will tune out the conversation. Others will reflect thoughtfully on what different groups say about men and women. Still others will join the conversation and take active roles in defining masculinity, femininity, and the host of issues linked to gender. It's up to you to define your role in the cultural conversation about gender.

KEY TERMS

The following terms are defined in this chapter on the pages indicated, as well as in alphabetical order in the book's glossary, which begins on page 261. The text's companion website also provides interactive flash cards to help you learn these terms and the concepts they represent. You can access the site at www.cengagebrain.com.

ACT UP 80	*Million Man March 89*
father hunger 86	*misogyny 91*
Fathers 4 Justice 85	*mythopoetic movement 86*
Free Men 85	*NOMAS 78*
Good Men Project 92	*Promise Keepers 87*
male feminists 77	*traitorous identity 77*
masculinists 84	*Walk a Mile in Her Shoes 82*
Mentors in Violence Prevention (MVP) 83	*White Ribbon Campaign (WRC) 81*
men's rights activists 84	

GENDER ONLINE

1. To learn about the range of men's movements and issues and resources on all of them, visit the Voice of the Shuttle's directory online.

2. If you wish to learn more about a specific men's movement (NOMAS, Free Men, Promise Keepers, the Good Men Project), visit their websites. Check out each mission statement, current projects, and recommended resources.

3. Check out the Good Men Project's magazine, which is available on the Good Men Project's home page.

4. Online search terms: *fathers' rights, male feminist, mentors in violence prevention.*

REFLECTION, DISCUSSION, AND ACTION

1.   Before you read this chapter, did you know that there were so many men's groups with such diverse goals? What does limited knowledge of men's groups imply about biases in media and education in America?

2.   Which of the men's groups are most and least consistent with your values and your views of masculinity?

3.   Write or act out a discussion of whether men should pay alimony and child support as that discussion might transpire between a Free Man, a mythopoetic, and a Promise Keeper.

4.   Compose a letter to a significant man in your life. Drawing on the knowledge you have gained in reading this chapter, you might offer your own definition of what it means to be a good man or invite this man into a dialogue with you about issues related to men and masculinity.

RECOMMENDED RESOURCES

1.   *How to Survive a Plague*. Directed by David France. (2012). Distributed by Sundance Selects. This moving documentary chronicles the activism of ACT UP, which brought the HIV/AIDS crisis to the attention of people around the world.

2.   *Get on the Bus*. Directed by Spike Lee. (1996). Distributed by Sony. This award-winning film provides a dramatic representation of the first Million Man March and what it meant to black men.

3.   Michael Kimmel. (2008). *Guyland: The Perilous World Where Boys Become Men*. New York: Harper. Long-standing feminist Michael Kimmel examines the pressures, fears, and anxieties facing many young men today.

4.   The Good Men Project DVD. This is available with the book of the same title or separately from the Good Men Project website.

5.   Rob Okun. (2014). *Voice Male: The Untold Story of the Profeminist Men's Movement*. Northhampton, MA: Interlink Publishing Group. An acclaimed collection of essays written by men currently engaged in profeminist men's movements.

5

Gendered Verbal Communication

Knowledge Challenge:

- Do women or men generally talk more?
- Why are more people killed by hurricanes with feminine names?
- What is *conversational maintenance work* and who generally does it?

Consider these four statements:

> *The woman judge cast the deciding vote.*
> *Jason babysat his son while his wife attended a meeting.*
> *Freshmen find it difficult to adjust to college life.*
> *Every student should sign his or her paper.*

What do these sentences tell us about Western culture's views of women and men? The first sentence highlights the sex of the judge, reflecting an assumption that it is odd for women to be judges. In the second sentence, the word *babysat* implies that the father was performing a special service, one for which we usually pay people who are not related to the children. Have you ever heard someone say that a mother babysat her children? Unless the third sentence refers to first-year students at an all-male school, the word *freshmen* erases first-year female students. The final statement assumes that all students identify as either male or female; trans and genderqueer students may not identify with either pronoun.

In this chapter and the one that follows, we look closely at relationships between communication and gender. This chapter focuses on verbal communication and Chapter 6 concentrates on nonverbal communication. We will explore how communication reflects cultural views of sex and gender. We will also consider how individuals' communication embodies or challenges cultural prescriptions for femininity and masculinity.

Verbal Communication Expresses Cultural Views of Gender

Our language both reflects and reinforces cultural views and values, including those about gender. We'll discuss six ways that language and gender are connected.

Gendered Language Excludes

Our vocabularies—the very words we speak and the tools for our thoughts—are marked by gender in at least two ways. First, **generic language** purports to include everyone, yet literally refers only to men. Examples of generic language are nouns such as *congressman*, *spokesman*, *mailman*, and *mankind* and pronouns such as *he* and *his* used to refer to everyone.

Research makes it clear that inclusive language has impact. In a classic study (Schneider & Hacker, 1973), children were asked to select photographs for a textbook with chapters entitled "Urban Man" and "Urban Life." Children almost always chose pictures of men when the titles included male generic language. When the titles did not refer only to men, children chose more photographs that portrayed men and women. The language of the titles shaped what the children thought chapters would discuss.

Later research confirmed the finding that generic language leads many people to assume that only males are included (Gastil, 1990; Hamilton, 1991; Switzer, 1990). In one study, students from first grade through college were asked to make up a story about an average student. When the instructions referred to the average student as *he*, only 12% of students composed a story about a girl or woman. However, when the instructions defined the average student as *he* or *she*, 42% of the stories were about girls and women (Hyde, 1984).

Because there is convincing evidence that generic language is not perceived as including everyone, dictionaries and national newspapers now have policies requiring inclusive language, and writing style manuals caution against using generic language.

Second, gendered language is apparent in traditional pronouns, which erase people who do not fit into conventional categories. For instance, Rocko Gieselman was born female and embodies a feminine style, yet Rocko doesn't identify as a woman. Instead, Rocko uses the terms *trans* and *genderqueer*. Like many trans people, Rocko also prefers the pronoun *they* to *he* or *she*. *They* is increasingly accepted as a singular pronoun that substitutes for *he* or *she*. Some universities, such as the University of Vermont, have agreed to use *they* to refer to individual students as well as more than one student (Scelfo, 2015). The *Washington Post*, one of the premiere U.S. newspapers, has approved the singular *they* in its style guidelines (Hess, 2016). Online sites such as OKCupid and Facebook allow people to designate their identity (Scelfo, 2015), and users of Tumblr often pin the pronouns they prefer to their pages (Hess, 2016).

Language Defines Gender as Binary

Recent studies have found that hurricanes with feminine names are more deadly than those with masculine names (Jung et al., 2014; Yan, 2016). Due to gender stereotypes that link masculinity with greater risk and strength, people were more likely to discount warnings for hurricanes with feminine names. For high-damage storms with masculine names, people heeded warnings and there were an average of only 11 deaths. Storms with feminine names were not taken as seriously and there were 59 deaths on average.

EXPLORING GENDERED LIVES

Nobel Prize for British Wife

That was the headline of the *New York Times'* obituary for Dorothy Crowfoot Hodgkin who figured out the crystal structure of vitamin B12 (Swaby, 2015). Wouldn't you think that having won the highest honor in science merited a headline? Similarly, a 2013 obituary for

Yvonne Brill noted that she was the world's best mom and that she followed her husband from one job to the next. It even mentioned her recipe for beef stroganoff. All of this information appeared before stating that Brill was a rocket scientist (Swaby, 2015).

TAKE A STAND: Why do you think relatively recent obituaries might reflect traditional gender biases?

Women are frequently defined by appearance and by relationships with others, whereas men are more typically defined by activities, accomplishments, and positions. Throughout the 2008 Democratic primary contest, commentators discussed Hillary Clinton's appearance—she was being suggestive when she wore a V-necked top; her pantsuits were dowdy; and she had crow's feet (Mandziuk, 2008). Similarly, in the early stages of the 2016 presidential primaries, candidate Donald Trump said of candidate Carly Fiorina, "Look at that face! Would anyone vote for that?" (Miller, 2016c). Can you imagine such derogatory comments about male candidates' appearance?

ANDY

For a long time, it seemed really clear to me that a word like mankind obviously includes women or that chairman can refer to a girl or a guy who chairs something. I thought it was pretty stupid to hassle about this. Then, last semester I had a woman teacher who taught the whole class using she or her or women whenever she was referring to people, as well as when she meant just women. I realized how confusing it is. I had to figure out each time whether she meant women only or women and men. And when she meant women to be general, I guess you'd say generic for all people, it still made me feel left out. A lot of the guys in the class got pretty hostile about what she was doing, but I kind of think it was a good way to make the point.

Coverage of women's sports focuses more on appearance of female athletes than male athletes. Commentators describe women athletes' outfits, bodies, and hairstyles, whereas their descriptions of male athletes more typically focus on athletic skills. For example, during the 2014 Sochi Winter Olympics, news commentators regularly referred to professional female athletes as "girls"; one analyst stated that women skiers were highly skilled in managing extreme courses "while in a Lycra suit, maybe a little bit of makeup—now that is grace under pressure" (Feeney, 2014). The 2016 Olympics may take the prize for sexist references to women athletes. When Corey Cogdell won two bronze medals, a *Chicago Tribune* reporter tweeted that the wife of a Bears' lineman won the medals. After beating her own record in the 400-meter freestyle, an NBC reporter said, Katie Ledecky "swims like a man." The Associated Press carried this headline: "Phelps Ties for Silver in 100 Fly." The subtitle for the article was: "Ledecky Sets World Record in Women's 800 Freestyle." When BBC reporter

---

■ EXPLORING GENDERED LIVES ■

Parallel Language?

Parallel language means equivalent terms. For instance, male and female are equivalent, or parallel. But what about some other allegedly parallel terms?

Masculine Term	Feminine Term
Master	Mistress
Wizard	Witch
Patron	Matron
Bachelor	Spinster
Name/Name	Birth Name/ Married Name
Player	?

TAKE A STAND: What other terms can you think of that do not have equivalent masculine and feminine forms?

John Inverdale congratulated Andy Murray on being the first person to win two Olympic medals in tennis, Murray noted that Venus and Serena Williams had won about four each.

Language also reflects social views of women as passive and men as active participants in sexual activity. Consider common phrases like: "He laid her," "He balled her," "He screwed her," and "She got knocked up." Perhaps because men are expected to be sexual initiators, inappropriate sexual initiative by men is sometimes described in language that makes it seem acceptable. For instance, during the 2016 election season, then-candidate Donald Trump excused his vulgar comments about grabbing women's genitalia as "locker room talk," despite the fact that his actions fit the legal definition of sexual assault.

Our language also reflects society's view of women as more defined by relationships than men are. On prime-time television, even professional women are often depicted primarily in interpersonal contexts, and their appearance is highlighted (Dow & Wood, 2006). Historically, women who don't marry have been referred to in negative ways such as *spinsters* or *old maids* (contrast this with the nonpejorative term *bachelors* for men). Similar attitudes are expressed in other cultures. For example, journalist and sociologist Leta Hong Fincher (2014) examined a recent state-sponsored campaign in China that negatively depicts single, professional women over the age of 27. Referred to as *leftover women*, they are described this way: "Girls with an average or ugly appearance … hope to further their education in order to increase their competitiveness. The tragedy is that they don't realise that, as women age, they are worth less and less, so by the time they get their M.A. or Ph.D., they are already old, like yellowed pearls" (quoted in Lovell, 2014).

BRIAN

I never considered whether my wife would take my name. I just assumed she would. I'm proud of my family, and I feel tied to who we are, and my family name represents that. I always thought it would be a great honor for a woman to have my family name. But my fiancé doesn't feel the same way. She says she's proud of her name, too, that it's who she is, too. I can understand that in a way, but still it seems like she should want to take my name. She turned the tables on me by asking if I would take her name.

EXPLORING GENDERED LIVES

What's in a Name?

U.S. laws concerning marriage and naming have undergone significant transformation. Prior to 1975, U.S. states insisted that a woman assume her husband's last name on marrying in order to vote, drive, or participate in basic forms of public life (Emens, 2007). The law was resolved when a Hawaiian statute requiring women to give up their birth names on marriage was ruled unconstitutional in 1975 (Schroeder, 1986).

Research demonstrates that a great number of heterosexual men prefer that their partners change their names upon marriage, and some indicate disappointment or a feeling of loss if their partners refuse (Emens, 2007). Currently, approximately

20% of U.S. women who marry choose to keep their birth names (Foss, Edson & Linde, 2015; Nagem, 2015).

Like heterosexual couples, lesbians who place high priority on social recognition of their relationship prefer that one or both partners change their names. For lesbians who keep their names, individual identity is a higher priority (Suter & Oswald, 2003).

Like many traditions, those related to naming are culturally variable. In China, women keep their birth names when they marry, and Quebec has laws requiring both spouses to keep their birth names upon marrying (Ingber, 2016).

TAKE A STAND: Do you have different perceptions of women who choose to keep their birth names and women who choose to take their partners' names on marrying?

A majority of heterosexual women take their husbands' names upon marrying, but there are alternatives to the traditional ways of naming ourselves (Foss, Edson, & Linde, 2015). Some women choose to retain their birth names when they marry. Some adopt hyphenated names, such as Johnson-Pham, to symbolize the family heritage of both partners. In some countries, such as Spain, both the mother's and father's family names are used to construct children's family names. Other alternatives, although less often practiced so far, are choosing a new surname together (Moore, 2015) or renaming oneself to reflect **matriarchal** rather than patriarchal lineage, which involves changing a last name from that of the father's family to that of the mother's. (The term *matriarchy* means "rule by the mothers" and generally refers to systems of ideology, social structures, and practices that are created by women and reflect the values, priorities, and views of women as a group.) Because a mother's last name still reflects male lineage—that of the mother's father—some women use their mothers' first names to create a matrilineal last name: For example, Lynn Franklin's daughter, Bailey, might rename herself Bailey Lynnschild.

Language Shapes Awareness of Gendered Issues

Naming is important. We name things that matter to us and don't name what doesn't matter (Spender, 1984a, 1984b). The power of naming is clear with sexual harassment and date rape (Harris, 2011a; Wood, 2008, 2009a). For most of history, sexual harassment occurred frequently but was unnamed. Because it wasn't named, sexual harassment was difficult to recognize or stop. If sexual harassment was discussed at all, it was described as *making advances, getting out of line,* or *being pushy.* None of these phrases conveys the abusiveness of sexual harassment. Only when the term *sexual harassment* was coined was it recognized as a form of violence in need of redress.

━━━━━ **EXPLORING GENDERED LIVES** ━━━━━

Reversal versus A Flower's Opening

Like other languages, American Sign Language (ASL) is dynamic and fluid. New signs are added for new words that emerge; other signs are changed to reflect changing social perspectives. A good example of this is the sign for trans. For many years, ASL's sign for the word *trans* or *transgender* was the sign for the word sex, followed by a finger rotating 180 degrees to indicate reverse sex. As social understandings of trans people have matured, many people realize that they are not simply reverse sex people. In response to changing perspectives, ASL created a new sign. Today, transgender is signed by holding the fingers of the hand facing downward over the heart like a closed flower bud, followed by the rotating the fingers upward and spreading them open over the heart to suggest a flower opening (Boylan, 2016).

TAKE A STAND: Can you think of examples in which English words for a person or activity have been changed to reflect contemporary perspectives?

Similarly, for years women who were raped by their dates had no recognized way to name what had happened. Until we coined the term *date rape*, women had to deal with their experiences without the language to define grievous violations that often had lifelong repercussions. Even today, not all women are comfortable using the term *date rape* to refer to nonconsensual sex with friends and dates. For them, rape is violent assault by a stranger (Harris, 2011a).

As our discussion shows, language is not static. We continually change language to reflect our changing understandings of ourselves and our world. We reject terms we find objectionable (generic language), and we create new terms to define realities we think are important (*they* as a singular pronoun, *sexual harassment, Ms., trans*). As we modify language, we change how we see ourselves and our world. Further, we shape meanings of our culture.

━━━━━ **EXPLORING GENDERED LIVES** ━━━━━

Seeing the Unseen/Naming the Unnamed

Naming helps us notice things we otherwise don't see. Scholars from the United States and Germany collaborated to see whether people became less tolerant of sexist behavior when they were given names that allowed them to detect it. Results showed that learning to name sexism made women, but not men, less tolerant of the behavior. Of particular interest to the researchers was participants' learned ability to detect **benevolent sexism**, which is a paternalistic attitude that describes women affectionately but assumes they aren't competent to do particular tasks. For instance, "that sweet little thing can't change a tire" is benevolent sexism (Swim & Becker, 2011).

TAKE A STAND: Can you think of communication strategies for responding to a benevolent sexist comment?

Language Organizes Perceptions of Gender

Two ways in which language organizes perceptions of gender are through stereotyping and encouraging polarized perceptions of sex and gender.

A **stereotype** is a generalization about an entire class of phenomena based on perceptions of some members of the class. For example, if most women you know aren't interested in sports, you might stereotype women as uninterested in sports. This stereotype could keep you from noticing that many women engage in sports and enjoy attending athletic events. Relying on stereotypes can lead us to overlook important qualities of individuals and to perceive them only in terms of what we consider common to a general category.

Many people stereotype women as emotional and men as rational. Stereotypes such as these can distort our perceptions. For instance, women's arguments are sometimes dismissed as emotional when, in fact, they involve evidence and reasoning (Mapstone, 1998). Women who use assertive speech are frequently described as rude or bitchy (O'Neill & O'Reilly, 2011; Sandberg & Grant, 2015b), whereas men who employ emotional language may be described to be wimps or weak (Rasmussen & Moley, 1986).

The English language may also encourage **polarized thinking**, which is conceiving of things as absolute opposites. Something is right or wrong; a person is male or female or masculine or feminine. Our commonly used vocabulary emphasizes all-or-none terms and thus all-or-none thinking. As we saw in Chapter 2, queer performative theory challenges polarized language for sex, gender, and sexual orientation, claiming that polarized terms—or gender binaries—obscure the range of identities that humans express. Also, the categories of men and women erase transgender and intersex people.

Language Evaluates Gender

Language reflects cultural values and is a powerful influence on our perceptions. Trivializing language is sometimes applied to women to define them as immature or juvenile (*honey, girl, darling*). A stunning example of infantalizing women came in the presidential campaign in 2016. On January 8, Senator Ted Cruz chided Secretary Hillary Clinton saying she deserved a "spanking" like his five-year-old daughter.

Other common terms equate girls and women with food (*sugar, sweet thing, cupcake*) and animals (*chick, pig, dog, cow, bitch*). Diminutive suffixes designate women as reduced forms of the standard (male) form of the word: *actress, waitress*. Women who are sexually active may be called derogatory names such as *slut*, whereas men who are equally sexually active are described with terms such as *player*, which our students say is a compliment. In addition, feminine terms are used to degrade boys and men (*sissy, momma's boy, bitch, girly-man*).

ANTHONY

Until we talked about language in class, I hadn't really thought about the double standard for sexually active girls and guys. Or if I had thought about it, I probably would have said that the double standard doesn't exist anymore. Our discussion got me thinking, and that's not really true. Guys who have sex with a lot of girls are studs or players. Girls who have sex with a lot of guys are sluts or easy. It's not as bad as it used to be, but I guess there still is kind of a double standard.

EXPLORING GENDERED LIVES

Fat Talk

"I'm fat.""You're not half as fat as I am. Look at my big butt.""I need to give up eating." Fat talk is common. In fact, it's almost obsessive among some people, both male and female (Martz, Petroff, Curtin, & Bazzini, 2009). Almost always fat talk is negative, self-critical comments about how the speakers' bodies don't measure up to ideals advanced by media.

Fat talk isn't harmless. Engaging in fat talk predicts lower body satisfaction and greater depression and increases perceived pressure to be thinner (Arroyo & Harwood, 2012). At the same time, people who have lower satisfaction with their bodies are more likely to engage in fat talk. In other words, fat talk and body dissatisfaction make up a self-defeating cycle (Arroyo & Harwood, 2012).

TAKE A STAND: Have you encountered or engaged in fat talk? What are some steps you could take to avoid or challenge fat talk when you hear it?

Language Allows Self-Reflection

We also use language, inflected with social values, to reflect on and evaluate ourselves. In the 1950s, a 5-foot 5-inch woman who weighed 140 pounds would have considered herself slender. In 2010, a 5-foot 5-inch woman who weighs 140 pounds might view herself as overweight. In 1950, a man would not feel pressure to be as muscular as is the current masculine ideal. We live in a celebrity culture (Lamb & Brown, 2006; Newsom, 2011), which makes it tempting to define ourselves in comparison to celebrities—or airbrushed, digitally manipulated images of them. According to Michael Rich (2008), director of the Center on Media and Child Health, "Exposure to body ideals of impossibly thin women and unrealistically muscular men can contribute to negative self-images and viewers' attempts to alter their bodies through restrictive eating, exercise, drugs, or surgery" (p. 90).

If we find the existing language inadequate, we can move beyond it. For instance, we can label ourselves androgynous, a concept we first mentioned in Chapter 1. Likewise, we can define ourselves as genderqueer or gender nonconforming. By coining new language to describe our identities, we nudge culture to recognize us on our own terms.

Gendered Styles of Verbal Communication

In addition to expressing cultural views of gender, language is a primary means by which we express our gendered identities. In the pages that follow, we'll explore the ways we use verbal communication to perform masculinity and femininity. Keep in mind that we're looking at *gendered* styles of communicating, not necessarily sex-based styles. In other words, although most girls are socialized to communicate primarily in feminine ways, some girls learn masculine modes of communicating; although most boys are encouraged to cultivate primarily masculine styles of communicating, some boys learn feminine modes. Also, some people work to become fluent in both masculine and feminine modes of communication, and some people perform identities that are beyond the conventional gender binary.

Gendered Speech Communities

Philosopher Suzanne Langer (1953, 1979) asserted that culture, or collective life, is possible only to the extent that a group of people share a symbol system and the meanings encapsulated in it. William Labov (1972) extended Langer's ideas by defining a *speech community* as a group of people who share norms about communication. By this, he meant that a **speech community** exists when people share understandings about goals of communication, strategies for enacting those goals, and ways of interpreting communication.

It's obvious that we have entered a different speech community when we are in countries whose languages differ from our own. Distinct speech communities are less apparent when they rely on the same language but use it in different ways and attach different meanings to it. Yet, as standpoint theory points out, belonging to a particular race-ethnicity, gender identity, economic class, and gender influences what we know and how we communicate.

Children are typically socialized into gendered speech communities. To understand these different communities, we will consider how we are socialized into feminine and masculine speech communities as well as divergence within feminine and masculine speech communities. Please note the importance of the words such as *typically* that indicate we are discussing general differences, not absolute ones.

The Lessons of Children's Play

A classic study by Daniel Maltz and Ruth Borker (1982) gave initial insight into the importance of children's play in shaping patterns of communication. Watching young children playing, researchers observed two phenomena: Young children usually played in sex-segregated groups, and girls and boys tended to play different kinds of games. Maltz and Borker found that boys' typical games (football, baseball, war) and girls' typical games (school, house, tea party) cultivate distinct communication styles.

Recent research confirms that sex-segregated groups and forms of play remain the norm for children (Barbu, Cabanes, & Le Maner-Idrissi, 2011; Hanish & Fabes, 2014; Rudman & Glick, 2010). Even children as young as two or three years old (about the time that gender constancy develops) show a preference for same-sex playmates, and this preference has been found in multiple cultures ranging from the United States to India and Kenya (Fouts, Hallam, & Purandare, 2013).

Boys' Games   Boys' games usually involve fairly large groups—nine individuals for each baseball team, for instance. Most boys' games are competitive, have clear goals, involve physically rough play in large spaces, and are organized by rules and roles that specify who does what and how to play (Hanish & Fabes, 2014; Rudman & Glick, 2010).

Because the games boys typically play are structured by goals and roles, there is limited need to discuss how to play, although there may be talk about strategies. In playing games, boys learn to communicate to accomplish goals, compete for and maintain status, exert control over others, get attention, and stand out. Specifically, boys' games cultivate four communication rules:

1. Use communication to assert your ideas, opinions, and identity.
2. Use talk to achieve something, such as solving problems or developing strategies.
3. Use communication to attract and maintain others' attention.
4. Use communication to compete for the "talk stage." Make yourself stand out, take attention away from others, and get others to pay attention to you.

Paolo Bona/Shutterstock.com

Many favored boys' games have a large number of players.

Consistent with other aspects of masculine socialization, these rules focus on individuality, competition, and achievement. Finally, we see the undercurrent of masculinity's emphasis on invulnerability: If your goal is to control and to be better than others, you need to show only your strengths.

Girls' Games   Many girls today also play competitive games. In addition, most girls play some games that few boys play. The games played primarily by girls cultivate distinct ways of communicating. Girls tend to play in pairs or in small groups rather than large ones (Benenson, Del Bianco, Philippoussis, & Apostoleris, 1997; Hanish & Fabes, 2014). Games such as house and school do not have preset, clear-cut goals and roles. There is no touchdown in playing school, and the roles of teacher or student aren't fixed like the roles of guard and forward. Because traditional girls' games are not highly structured by external goals and roles, players have to talk among themselves to decide what to do and what roles to play.

When playing, young girls spend more time talking than doing anything else—a pattern that is not true of young boys' play (Goodwin, 2006; Hanish & Fabes, 2014). Playing house, for instance, typically begins with a discussion about who is going to be a parent and who is going to be a child. The lack of preset goals for the games requires girls to develop interpersonal communication skills. The games generally played by girls teach four basic rules for communication:

1. Use communication to create and maintain relationships. The process of communication, not its content, is the heart of relationships.
2. Use communication to establish egalitarian relations with others. Don't outdo, criticize, or put down others. If you have to criticize, be gentle.
3. Use communication to include others—bring them into conversations, respond to their ideas.
4. Use communication to show sensitivity to others and relationships.

EXPLORING GENDERED LIVES

Gender and Gaming Culture

Contrary to popular belief, girls and women are no less interested in video games than boys and men. Gendered differences do exist, however, in how video games are played and for what reasons. Studying these differences can teach us something about gendered speech communities. Consider the following findings (Terlecki et al., 2011):

- Of all adolescents, 90% describe technology as "cool," and the vast majority of adolescent boys and girls play video games.
- Approximately 43% of online gamers are female.

- Girls and women often seek games that privilege real-life simulation, puzzles, and strategy; boys and men often prefer sporting, action, and combat games.
- Female gamers aim to build relationships and make connections with others through gaming; male gamers tend to play video games for individual achievement.
- On average, men tend to purchase games with more violence and higher ratings from the Entertainment Software Rating Board than do women.

TAKE A STAND: Can you identify connections among traditional childhood games, video games, and gendered communication patterns?

The typically small size of girls' groups fosters prosocial, cooperative play (Rudman & Glick, 2010), whereas the larger groups in which boys usually play encourage competition (Barbu et al., 2011; Hanish & Fabes, 2014). In a study of preschoolers, boys gave orders and attempted to control others, whereas girls were more likely to make requests and cooperate with others (Weiss & Sachs, 1991). In another investigation, 9- to 14-year-old African-American girls typically used inclusive and nondirective language, whereas African-American boys tended to issue commands and compete for status in their groups (Goodwin, 1990).

ERIN

I played house and school, but I also played softball and soccer. Most of my friends did too. We learned to compete and work with external rules and be goal oriented just as much as boys did. The games children play aren't sex segregated anymore.

Erin is correct that young girls today often play competitive sports and that doing so allows them to learn and use the rules of masculine speech communities. This is consistent with standpoint theory's premise that members of subordinated groups are motivated to learn the standpoint of dominant groups. Note that although many girls now play games that were once associated primarily with boys, boys are less likely to play games associated with girls, such as house and school.

Gendered Communication Practices

We will consider features of feminine and masculine speech that have been identified by researchers. We'll also explore some of the complications that arise when people of different genders operate by different rules in conversations with each other.

Feminine Communication   People who are socialized in feminine speech communities—most women and some men—tend to regard communication as a primary way to establish and maintain relationships with others. They use language to foster connections and support closeness and mutual understanding (Ye & Palomares, 2013).

Establishing equality between people is a second important feature of feminine communication. To achieve symmetry, communicators often match experiences to indicate "You're not alone in how you feel." Typical ways to communicate equality would be saying "I've felt just like that" or "I totally know what you mean." Growing out of the quest for equality is a participatory mode of interacting in which communicators respond to and build on each other's ideas in the process of conversing. Rather than a rigid "You tell your ideas, then I'll tell mine" sequence, feminine speech more characteristically follows an interactive pattern for the collaborative creation of conversation.

A third characteristic of feminine speech is support for others. To demonstrate support, communicators often express emotions (Guerrero, Jones, & Boburka, 2006; Mulac, 2006; Ye & Palomares, 2013) to show understanding of another's situation or feelings. "Oh, you must feel terrible" communicates that we understand and support how another feels. Related to these first two features is attention to the relationship level of communication (Eisenberg, 2002; MacGeorge, Gillihan, Samter, & Clark, 2003). You will recall that the relationship level of talk focuses on feelings and on the relationship between communicators rather than on the content of messages. Conversations between feminine people tend to be characterized by intensive adverbs ("That's *really* exciting") (Mulac, 2006) and questions that probe for greater understanding of feelings and perceptions surrounding the subject of talk. "How did you feel when it occurred?" "How does this fit into the overall relationship?" are probes that help a listener understand a speaker's perspective.

YOLANDA

With my boyfriend, I am always asking, "How was your day? Your class? Your jam session? Did you get such and such done? Did you talk to so-and-so?" He answers my questions, usually with just a few words, but he almost never asks questions about my day and my life. When I do talk about myself, he often interrupts and sometimes listens, but he doesn't say much in response. I'm tired of doing all the work to keep a conversation going in our relationship.

A fourth feature of feminine speech style is conversational "maintenance work" (Fishman, 1978; Taylor, 2002). This involves efforts to sustain conversation by inviting others to speak and by prompting them to elaborate their ideas. Questions are often used to include others: "How was your day?" "Did anything interesting happen on your trip?" "Do you have anything to add?" (Mulac, 2006). Communication of this sort maintains interaction and opens the conversational door to others.

A fifth quality of feminine speech is responsiveness. A feminine person might make eye contact, nod, or say, "Tell me more" or "That's interesting." Responsiveness affirms the other person and encourages elaboration by showing interest in what was said.

A sixth quality of feminine talk is personal, concrete style. Typical of feminine talk are details, personal disclosures, and concrete reasoning. These features cultivate a personal tone, and they facilitate feelings of closeness by connecting communicators' lives.

A final feature of feminine speech is tentativeness (Mulac, 2006; Ye & Palomares, 2013). This may be expressed in a number of forms. Sometimes people use verbal hedges, such as "I kind of feel you may be overreacting." In other situations, they qualify statements by saying "I'm not sure if this is right, but…." Another way to keep talk provisional is to tag a question onto a statement in a way that invites another to respond: "*Scandal* is a pretty good show, isn't it?" Tentative communication opens the door for others to respond and express their opinions.

There is controversy about tentativeness associated with feminine speech. Robin Lakoff (1975), who first reported that women use more hedges, qualifiers, and tag questions than men, claimed that these indicate uncertainty and lack of confidence. Calling women's speech "powerless," Lakoff argued that it reflects women's insecurity. It's important to note that Lakoff's judgment that feminine speech is powerless was based on her assumption that masculine speech is the standard. If we use feminine speech as the standard, the use of hedges, qualifiers, and tag questions may reflect not powerlessness but the desire to keep conversations open and to include others. You should realize, however, that people outside feminine speech communities—for example, in professional settings—may use masculine standards, as Lakoff did, to interpret tentative speech.

Masculine Communication   Masculine speech communities tend to regard talk as a way to accomplish concrete goals, exert control, preserve independence, entertain, and enhance status. Conversation is often seen as an arena for proving oneself and negotiating prestige.

The first feature of masculine speech is the effort to establish status and control. Masculine speakers do this by asserting their ideas and authority, telling jokes and stories, or challenging others. Also, men maintain both control and independence by disclosing less than women. Men and boys typically use more I-references ("I have a plan," "I had a good game") than women and girls (Mulac, 2006). One way to exhibit knowledge and control is to give advice. For example, a person might say, "The way you should handle that is …," or "Don't let your boss get to you." On the relationship level of meaning, people socialized in feminine speech communities may interpret advice as the speaker saying she or he is superior—smarter, more experienced, and so on—in comparison to the other person.

A second prominent feature of masculine speech is instrumentality—the use of face-to-face or computer-mediated communication (CMC) to accomplish instrumental objectives (Kimbrough, Guadagno, Muscanell, & Dill, 2013). Particularly when men think they are knowledgeable about a topic, they may want to show their knowledge to others (Leaper & Ayres, 2007). In conversation, this is often expressed through problem-solving efforts to get information, discover facts, and suggest solutions. Conversations between feminine and masculine communicators are often derailed by the lack of agreement on the meaning of this informational, instrumental focus. When a man focuses on the content level of meaning after a woman has disclosed a problem, she may feel that he is disregarding her emotions. He, on the other hand, thinks he is supporting her in the way that he has learned to show support—suggesting how to solve the problem.

JOANNE

My boyfriend is the worst at throwing solutions in my face when I try to talk to him about a problem. I know he cares about me; if he didn't, he wouldn't use up all that energy thinking up solutions for me. But I'm the kind of person who prefers a good ear (and maybe a shoulder) when I have a problem. I would like it so much better if he would forget about solutions and just listen and let me know he hears what's bothering me.

A third feature of masculine communication is conversational command. Despite jokes about women's talkativeness, research indicates that, in most contexts, men tend to talk more often and at greater length than women (Mulac, 2006). Further, masculine speakers may reroute conversations by using what another says as a jumping-off point for their own topics, or they may interrupt. Although all genders interrupt, most research suggests that men do it more frequently (Farley, Ashcraft, Stasson, & Nusbaum, 2010; West & Zimmerman, 1983).

Not only do men generally interrupt more than women, they may do so for different reasons. Research indicates that men are more likely to interrupt to control conversation by challenging other speakers or wresting the talk stage from them, whereas women interrupt to indicate interest and respond to others. A different explanation is that men generally interrupt more than women because interruptions are considered normal and good-natured within the norms of masculine speech communities. Whereas interruptions that reroute conversation might be viewed as impolite and intrusive in feminine speech communities, the outgoing, give-and-take character of masculine speech may render interruptions just part of normal conversation.

Fourth, masculine speech tends to be direct and assertive. Compared with women's language, men's language is typically more forceful and authoritative (Mulac, 2006). An exception to this pattern is when men talk with someone of high status. In this situation, men with lower status may be less assertive and commanding (O'Neill & Colley, 2006; Palomares, 2008, 2010).

Fifth, masculine speech tends to be more abstract than feminine speech. Men frequently speak in general or conceptual terms that are removed from concrete experiences and personal feelings. Within public environments, norms for speaking call for theoretical, conceptual, and general thought and communication. Yet, within more personal relationships, abstract talk sometimes creates barriers to intimacy.

CHRIS

Once I decided to live as a woman, I had to learn a whole different way of communicating. Even though I've always identified as female, I've always hung out with guys and I learned pretty much what our textbook describes as masculine speech patterns. To be accepted as a woman, I've had to relearn how to communicate—ask more questions about others, express more feelings, describe my experiences with a lot more detail, be more indirect like saying "Maybe we need to do such and such" instead of "Do such and such."

Finally, masculine speech tends to be less emotionally responsive than feminine speech, especially on the relationship level of meaning (Guerrero et al., 2006). Men, more than women, give what are called **minimal response cues** (Parlee, 1979), which are verbalizations such as "yeah" or "um hmm." Studies suggest that this verbal communication pattern is reflected in CMC as well, with men using fewer references to emotions in email than do women (Ye & Palomares, 2013). People socialized into feminine speech communities may perceive minimal response cues as indicating lack of involvement (Fishman, 1978). Men's conversation also often lacks self-disclosure as well as expressed sympathy and understanding (Eisenberg, 2002), although men report feeling more comfortable with higher levels of disclosure to romantic partners when communicating via CMC (Walton & Rice, 2013). Within the rules of masculine speech communities, sympathy is a sign of condescension, and the revealing of personal problems is seen as making one vulnerable. Yet, within feminine speech communities, sympathy and disclosure are understood as demonstrations of equality and support. This creates potential for misunderstanding between people who express themselves in different ways.

As you many have noticed, gendered patterns in online communication often reflect gendered speech communities. Research indicates that men and women tend to differ in their motivation and use of the Internet, with men emphasizing instrumentality and task completion and women emphasizing connectivity to others. While men were quicker to adopt computer technologies, women now use digital technologies more than do men due to the rise in social media networks (Kimbrough et al., 2013).

The Gender-Linked Language Effect   We've discussed some gendered tendencies in communication. However, these are not as hard and fast as they may seem. Recent study identifies the **gender-linked language effect** (Palomares, 2008; Ye & Palomares, 2013), which notes that language differences between women and men are influenced by a variety of factors, including topics, speaker status, salience of gender in a communication situation, and other people present. One study (Palomares, 2008) found that women tend to speak more tentatively when talking about masculine topics (sports and automotive matters were the topics in the study), but men speak more tentatively than women when talking about feminine topics (shopping and fashion in the study). Another study showed that women communicate in more typically feminine ways when they're assigned feminine avatars than when they're assigned masculine avatars. The same is true of men: They communicate in more typically masculine ways when assigned masculine avatars. Research on the gender-linked language effect reminds us that our gender expression varies according to context and other factors.

Gender-Based Misinterpretations in Communication

In this final section, we explore what happens when gendered communication styles meet in conversations. We'll consider five communication misunderstandings that can arise.

Showing Support   Maddie tells her coworker Jorge that she is worried about Angelina, who has been late to work several days recently. Jorge gives a minimal response cue, saying only "Oh." To Maddie, this suggests that he isn't interested. Yet, operating by norms of masculine speech communities, Jorge assumes that if Maddie wants to say anything further or ask his opinion, she will assert her ideas.

Even without much perceived encouragement, Maddie continues by saying she knows Angelina has a teenage daughter who has been causing some worries lately. Maddie says, "I feel so bad for Angelina, and I want to help her, but I don't know what to do." Jorge then says, "It's her problem, not yours. Just butt out." At this, Maddie explodes: "Who asked for your advice?" Jorge is now completely confused. He thought Maddie wanted advice, so he gave it. She is hurt that Jorge didn't tune into her feelings. Both are frustrated.

The problem is not so much what Jorge and Maddie say and don't say. Rather, it's how they interpret each other's communication—actually, how they *misinterpret* each other, because they fail to understand that they are operating by different rules of communication. Jorge is respecting Maddie's independence by not pushing her to talk. When he thinks she wants advice, he offers it in an effort to help. Maddie, on the other hand, wants comfort and a connection with Jorge—that's her primary purpose in talking with him. To her, Jorge's advice seems to dismiss her feelings. He doesn't offer sympathy, because masculine rules for communication define this as condescending. Yet, the feminine speech community in which Maddie was socialized taught her that giving sympathy is a way to show support.

EXPLORING GENDERED LIVES

Caution: Woman Speaking

In 2015, Jennifer Lawrence penned an essay on her experiences being a woman in Hollywood: "A few weeks ago at work … I spoke my mind and gave my opinion in a clear and no-[BS] way; no aggression, just blunt. The man I was working with (actually, he was working for me) said, 'Whoa! We're all on the same team here!' As if I was yelling at him. I was so shocked because nothing that I said was personal, offensive, or, to be honest, wrong. All I hear and see all day are men speaking their opinions, and I give mine in the same exact manner, and you would have thought I had said something offensive" (quoted in Petri, 2015).

Lawrence's observation is supported by research. What's the difference between being outspoken and being shrill? Between voicing opinions and hogging the stage? It turns out much of the difference may be the speaker's sex. Yale psychologist Victoria Brescoll (2012) reports that male executives who speak more often than peers are perceived as more competent, whereas female executives who speak more often than peers are rated as less competent.

When women speak up in professional contexts, they face a tough balancing act: To be perceived positively, they need to conform enough to feminine style to be perceived as acting appropriately while also being firm and forceful enough to be perceived as competent (Sandberg & Grant, 2015b). Speak as assertively as many men and you're perceived as angry or shrill; speak as quietly as women are expected to and you're perceived as incompetent.

Washington Post columnist Alexandra Petri (2015) offered this humorous example to make a not-so-humorous point. Rewriting famous quotes "the way a woman would have to say them in a meeting," Patrick Henry's "Give me liberty or give me death" became "Dave, if I could, I could just—I just really feel like if we had liberty it would be terrific, and the alternative would just be awful, you know? That's just how it strikes me. I don't know." Instead of Martin Luther King Jr.'s powerful "I have a dream today," Petri wrote: "I'm sorry, I just had this idea—it's probably crazy, but—look, just as long as we're throwing things out here—I had sort of an idea or vision about maybe the future?"

TAKE A STAND: How do you perceive women who speak assertively, voice their opinions, and speak frequently in professional settings?

Troubles Talk   Talk about troubles, or personal problems, is a kind of interaction in which hurt feelings may result from differences between masculine and feminine styles of communicating. Carmen tells her partner, Caleb, that she is feeling down because she didn't get a job she wanted. In an effort to be supportive, Caleb responds by saying "You shouldn't feel bad. Lots of people don't get jobs they want." To Carmen, this seems to dismiss her feelings—to belittle them by saying lots of people experience her situation. Yet within masculine speech communities, you show respect by assuming that others don't need sympathy.

Now, let's turn the tables and see what happens when Caleb feels troubled. When he meets Carmen, Caleb is unusually quiet because he feels down about not getting a job offer. Sensing that something is wrong, Carmen tries to show interest by asking "Are you okay? What's bothering you?" Caleb feels she is imposing and pushing him to expose his vulnerability. Carmen probes further to show she cares. As a result, he feels intruded on and withdraws further. Then Carmen feels shut out.

But perhaps Caleb does tell Carmen why he feels down. After hearing about his rejection letter, Carmen says, "I know how you feel. I was so bummed when I didn't get that position at DataNet." She is matching experiences to show Caleb that she understands his feelings and that he's not alone (Basow & Rubenfeld, 2003). According to a masculine speech community, however, Carmen's comment about her own experience is an effort to steal the center stage from him and focus the conversation on herself.

JAY

Finally, I understand this thing that keeps happening between my girlfriend and me. She is always worrying about something or feeling bad about what's happening with one of her friends. I've been trying to be supportive by telling her things like she shouldn't worry, or not to let it get her down, or not to obsess about other people's problems. I was trying to help her feel better. That's what guys do for each other—kind of distract our attention from problems. But Teresa just gets all huffy and angry when I do that. She tells me to stuff my advice and says if I cared about her I would show more concern. Finally, it makes sense. Well, sort of.

CATE

When I broke up with Tommy, my dad tried so hard to help me through it. He took me to games and movies, offered to pay for it if I wanted to take horseback riding lessons. He just kept trying to DO something to make me feel better. That's how he's always been. If Mom's down about something, he takes her out or buys her flowers or something. It used to really bother me that he won't talk to me about what I'm feeling, but now I understand better what he's doing. I get it that this is his way of showing love and support for me.

The Point of the Story   Another instance in which feminine and masculine communication rules often clash is in relating experiences. Masculine speech tends to follow a linear pattern, in which major points in a story are presented sequentially to get to the climax. Talk tends to be straightforward without much detail. The rules of feminine speech, however, call for more detailed, less linear storytelling. Whereas men are more likely to provide rather bare information about what happened, women are more likely to embed the information within a larger context of the people involved and other events (Wood, 1998, 2011a). Women tend to include details because they matter at the relationship level of meaning. Recounting details is meant to increase involvement between people and to invite a conversational partner to be fully engaged in the situation being described.

Because feminine and masculine rules about story telling differ, men may find feminine accounts wandering and tedious. Conversely, the masculine style of storytelling may strike women as leaving out all the interesting particulars. Many a discussion between women and men has ended either with his exasperated demand, "Can't you get to the point?" or with her frustrated question, "Why don't you tell me how you were feeling and what else was going on?"

Relationship Talk   "Can we talk about us?" is the opening of innumerable conversations that end in misunderstanding and hurt. In general, people who are socialized into masculine style are interested in discussing relationships only if there is a problem to be

addressed. However, people socialized into feminine style generally find it pleasurable to talk about important relationships even—or perhaps especially—when there are no problems (Acitelli, 1988).

Masculine speech communities view communication as a means to doing things and solving problems, whereas feminine speech communities regard the *process* of communicating as a primary way to create and sustain relationships. No wonder many men duck when their partners want to "discuss the relationship," and women often feel a relationship is in trouble when their partners don't want to talk about it.

Public Speaking   Differences in feminine and masculine communication patterns also surface in public contexts. Historically, men have dominated politics. Thus, it's not surprising that the assertive, dominant, confident masculine style is the standard for public speaking. Women who are effective in politics tend to manage a fine balance in which they are sufficiently feminine to be perceived as acting appropriately for women and sufficiently masculine to be perceived as acting appropriately for politicians (Sheeler & Anderson, 2013). Women running for political office must be perceived not only as qualified but also as likeable. Voters will elect men they don't like if they perceive the men as qualified; they will not elect women they perceive as unlikeable (Collins, 2015).

These are only five of many situations in which gendered differences in communication style may lead to misunderstandings. Many people find they can improve their relationships by understanding and adopting both masculine and feminine speech. When partners understand how to interpret each other's rules, they are less likely to misread motives. Thus, greater fluidity and fluency in gendered communicative norms can empower us to become more gratifying conversational partners and enhance the quality of our relationships.

SUMMARY

In this chapter, we have explored relationships among verbal communication, gender, and culture. We first looked at how language reflects and sustains cultural views of masculinity and femininity. By defining, organizing, and evaluating gender, language reinforces social views of sex and gender. From generic male terms to language that demeans and diminishes women, verbal communication is a powerful agent of cultural expression. We also saw, however, that symbolic abilities allow us to be self-reflective about our definitions of masculinity and femininity in general and our own gender identities in particular.

The second theme of this chapter is that we express gendered identities through our communication. Because males and females are often socialized in different gender communities, they learn different rules for expressing support, interest, and involvement. This can lead to misunderstanding, frustration, hurt, and tension. Appreciation of and respect for the distinctive validity of each style of communication are foundations for better understanding between people. Further, learning to use different styles of communication allows all of us to be more flexible and effective in our interactions with a range of people.

KEY TERMS

The following terms are defined in this chapter on the pages indicated as well as in alphabetical order in the book's glossary, which begins on page 261. The text's companion website also provides interactive flash cards to help you learn these terms and the concepts they represent. You can access the site at www.cengagebrain.com.

benevolent sexism 101   *minimal response cues 109*
gender-linked language effect 110   *polarized thinking 102*
generic language 97   *speech community 104*
matriarchal 100   *stereotype 102*

GENDER ONLINE

1. Visit this site to learn what sexist language is and why it matters: **http://www.bbc.com/news/world-34962113**

2. Online search terms: *gender-linked language effect, generic language, speech community.*

REFLECTION, DISCUSSION, AND ACTION

1. Think about naming—specifically, about naming yourself. If you marry, do you expect to take your partner's name, or do you expect (or want) your partner to take yours? How important is it to you to keep your birth name? Have you or would you consider changing or hyphenating your own name?

2. Think back to your childhood games. What games did you play? Do you think the games you played affected your style of verbal communication?

3. Read several newspapers. To what extent are women and men represented differently in stories, including obituaries? Are women described by appearance, marital status, and family life more often than men? Are men described in terms of accomplishments and action more than women?

4. Apply what you have learned in this chapter to improve your communication. The next time you have a conversation in which you feel that gendered rules of talk are creating misunderstandings, try to clarify your expectations. For instance, if you are a feminine communicator talking with a masculine communicator about a problem, you may be

offered advice. Instead of becoming frustrated for the lack of focus on your feelings, say, "I appreciate your suggestions, but I'm not ready to think about how to fix things yet. Right now, I wish you would help me work through my feelings about this issue." Discuss what happens when you explain what you want from others.

RECOMMENDED RESOURCES

1. Susan Ehrlich, Miriam Meyerhoff, and Janet Holmes (Eds.). (2014). *The Handbook of Language, Gender, and Sexuality*. Chichester, UK: Wiley-Blackwell. This is a useful book for those who want more in-depth coverage of relationships between language and gender.

2. Jessica Valenti. (2008). *He's a Stud, She's a Slut, and 49 Other Double Standards Every Woman Should Know*. New York: Seal Press. This is a somewhat humorous look at a serious issue—double standards in how behaviors are named for women and men.

6

We first make our habits, and then our habits
make us.
—John Dryden

Gendered Nonverbal Communication

Knowledge Challenge:

- How do women and men differ in their typical use of nonverbal communication to regulate conversation?
- To what extent does physiology explain men's generally lower vocal pitch?
- Are there any female action figures?

Lego is one of the most successful toys in history. With Legos, you can build a castle, a skyscraper, a military tank, a robot, or a spaceship. Using Legos to build things that allow them to take on the world is what children do, at least what many male children do. Since Legos debuted in 1949, the plastic bricks and gears have attracted predominantly boys.

In 2011, the giant toymaker decided to increase its market share by going after the girl market with a new line of Legos called Friends. In place of the strong primary colors on its regular Legos, Friends were pastels. Suggestions for what to build changed too: Instead of machines, castles, and such, girls were encouraged to build and decorate homes, patios, and beauty parlors.

What's the harm in toys, right? Toys are not as innocent as we might first think. They are among the many "small" ways that culture socializes children into gender. In playing with regular Legos, boys are encouraged to build things that give them power and expand the space they command—spaceships and tanks, for instance. Friends, in contrast, encourage girls to build and decorate domestic spaces, and their adventures consist of makeovers in salons. The toys encourage boys and girls to see themselves and their options in distinctly unequal ways.

Parents who don't want their children hemmed in by sex stereotypes resent toys that reproduce rigid gender roles. Teachers too note the influence of sex-typed toys in narrowing children's perceptions of who they can be and what they can do. And many children don't like sex-typed toys. Working together, people formed Let Toys Be Toys (**www.lettoysbetoys.org.uk**) to challenge toymakers and the stores that sell sex-typed toys. In 2013, huge toy retailer Toys "R" Us responded to the group's pressure by agreeing to have gender-inclusive photographs in its U.K. holiday toy catalog, so consumers see boys and girls in play houses, spaceships, kitchens, and fire trucks. Other major retailers such as Target and Amazon have recently abandoned sex-specific labels for toys (Tabuchi, 2015). In 2016, Mattel announced that Barbie will no longer be a single

---

EXPLORING GENDERED LIVES

I Am Elemental

Two moms, Dawn Nadeau and Julie Kerwin, wanted to get empowering action figures for their daughters, but they could find none in stores or online. Not easily discouraged, they raised funds on Kickstarter, which they used to create I Am Elemental, a series of action figures that portray women as strong, physically fit heroes.

Each figure in the I Am Elemental series embodies a specific element of heroism: energy, bravery, industry, enthusiasm, persistence, honesty. The motto of the series is "If you give a girl a different toy, she will tell a different story" (**iamelemental.com**).

TAKE A STAND: To what extent do you think specifically gendered action figures make a difference in children's socialization?

---

size: There are now tall, petite, and curvy Barbies as well as Barbies of different ethnicities (Ziobro, 2016).

Toys provide an introduction to the nonverbal dimension of communication. Nonverbal communication is important, constituting between 65% (Birdwhistell, 1970) and 93% (Mehrabian, 1981) of the total meaning of communication. That's not surprising when we realize that **nonverbal communication** includes all elements of communication other than words themselves. Nonverbal communication is not only limited to gestures and movement but also includes inflection, volume, physical appearance, environmental factors, and artifacts such as toys.

Like language, nonverbal communication is learned through interaction with others. Also like language, nonverbal communication is closely related to gender and culture. When we conform to cultural prescriptions for gendered nonverbal communication, we reflect and reinforce cultural views of the sexes (Butler, 1990, 2004). On the other hand, we can use nonverbals to challenge existing perceptions of the sexes. In other words, nonverbal communication continually reproduces or contests cultural meanings for femininity and masculinity.

Functions of Nonverbal Communication

The three primary functions of nonverbal communication are to (1) supplement verbal communication, (2) regulate interaction, and (3) convey the bulk of the relationship level of meaning.

Supplement Verbal Communication

Nonverbal behavior supplements, or adds to, verbal messages in five ways (Knapp, Hall, & Horgan, 2013).

1. Nonverbal communication may *repeat* words, as when you say, "Right!" while pointing to the right.
2. Nonverbal communication may *contradict* verbal messages. For example, you say, "I'm fine" while weeping.

3. Nonverbal behavior may *complement* verbal communication by underlining a verbal message. The statement "I never want to see you again" is more forceful if accompanied by a threatening glare.

4. Nonverbal behavior may *replace* verbal messages. Rather than saying "I don't know," you might shrug your shoulders.

5. Nonverbal communication may *accent* verbal messages, telling us which parts are important. "I love *you*" means something different from "*I* love you" or "I *love* you."

Regulate Interaction

Nonverbal communication can also regulate interaction (Knapp et al., 2013). We use body posture, eye contact, and vocal inflection to signal others that we wish to speak or that we are done speaking. Similarly, we rely on eye contact to signal others that they have spoken long enough or that we want to hear more from them.

There are some gendered patterns of regulating interaction. Women frequently use nonverbal communication to invite others into conversation—looking at someone who hasn't spoken, smiling when a new person sits down in a group. Men are more likely to use nonverbal communication to hold onto the talk stage—for instance, by avoiding eye contact to maintain conversational command. This pattern reflects norms that encourage women to include others and men to stand out.

Establish the Relationship Level of Meaning

A final and particularly important function of nonverbal communication is to convey the relationship level of meaning that expresses relationships between communicators. The three primary dimensions of relationship-level meaning are *responsiveness*, *liking*, and *power*, each of which is linked to gender.

Responsiveness   The first dimension of the relationship level of meaning is **responsiveness**, which indicates interest in and attentiveness to others. Nonverbal cues of responsiveness include inflection, eye contact, and attentive body posture. Lack of responsiveness may be signaled by yawns or averted eyes.

Research shows that women generally are more responsive communicators than men. If you recall the lessons learned in gender speech communities, you'll realize that greater responsiveness is cultivated in feminine speech communities. Socialized to be affiliative, many women use nonverbal behaviors to indicate engagement with others, emotional involvement, and empathy. Women tend to smile and maintain eye contact, whereas men lean forward and adopt postures congruent with those of the persons speaking (Hall, 2006; Miller, 2011).

Liking   A second dimension of the relationship level of meaning is **liking**. We use nonverbal behaviors to signal that we like or dislike others. Nonverbal cues of liking include vocal warmth, standing or sitting close to others, touching, and holding eye contact. Girls and women are typically socialized to be nice to others and to maintain relationships, so it is not surprising that they are more likely than men to employ more nonverbal communication that signals liking, acceptance, and friendliness (Miller, 2011).

We can also use nonverbal behaviors to signal that we do not like others. A frown, glare, or turning away communicates dislike.

Power or Control   The third aspect of the relationship level of meaning is **power**, or control. Power refers to the degree to which people are equal to, dominant over, or deferential to others. Control is exerted in conversations by defining topics, directing conversation, and interrupting, all of which may involve both verbal and nonverbal communication. Although many nonverbal behaviors convey control messages, three are especially important: vocal qualities, touch, and use of space. In all three categories, men generally exceed women in engaging in control (Knapp et al., 2013). For instance, men tend to use greater volume and inflection, which add force to their words and allow them to be heard over others.

Nonverbal behaviors may also express power through uses of personal space. Women are more likely than men to surrender their personal space and less likely to enter others' personal space except to express liking. You can confirm this by watching people on campus and elsewhere. Notice what men and women do when walking toward each other on a sidewalk. Usually, women move to one side and they often do so well in advance.

Now that we have seen how nonverbal communication functions to supplement verbal communication, to regulate interaction, and to define the relationship level of meaning, we are ready to explore how it reflects and expresses gender.

Forms of Nonverbal Communication

We'll consider six forms of gendered nonverbal communication.

Artifacts

An **artifact** is a personal object that can both express identity and influence how we see ourselves. Beginning with pink and blue blankets for newborns, personal objects are used to assign gender to children. Parents send artifactual messages through the toys they give to sons and daughters. Play weapons, toy soldiers, and miniature race cars invite competition and active, rough play, whereas dolls, play houses, and makeup kits encourage nurturing, domestic activities, and attention to appearance.

Toy catalogues offer clear messages about cultural meanings attached to the sexes. In opening this chapter, we noted that the U.K. Toys "R" Us franchise agreed to have less sex-typed photos in toy catalogs and that other major retailers are following suit. However, while many retailers have removed sex-specific signs, critics note that the divisions remain apparent to any shopper strolling the aisles (Tabuchi, 2015). At the writing of this book in 2016, Toys "R" Us continues to segregate toys according to sex on its website, featuring pastel pictures of girls playing with kitchen appliances, makeup, hair accessories, and pink tutus. Pages with bolder colors show boys playing with soldiers, science equipment, swords, shields, and building sets. And it's not just that vehicles, weapons, and construction sets are presented as "for boys" while toys of domesticity and beautification are "for girls." Toys presented as for boys facilitate competition, control, agency, and dominance; those presented as for girls promote cooperation and nurturance. All of these are worthy qualities that can enrich the lives of all children, regardless of sex or gender.

Highly gendered toys have not always been the norm. In the early 1900s, toys were seldom designated for boys or girls. A quarter of a century later, in 1975, the majority of toys—nearly 70%—were not gender marked. In fact, many 1970s ads for toys showed girls building airplanes and boys working in kitchens (Abadi, 2013; Sweet, 2011, 2012, 2013; Tabuchi, 2015).

Toys are not the only artifacts that are gendered. As sociologist Elizabeth Sweet noted wryly in an interview with the *New York Times*: "Practically everything is gendered … school supplies. Toothbrushes. Snacks with bunnies or princesses on them, and snacks with Superman. And boy is the gender-neutral default. For girls, they 'shrink it and pink it'" (quoted in Tabuchi, 2015). Gendering persists into adulthood. If you look at wallets on the market, note that those marketed to women are more often pastel than those marketed to men. The same is true of razors, shoes, smartphones, and lots of other products. Pay attention to the colors on packaging and marketing for products—you will notice clear and patterned differences.

Although clothing is less gender segregated than in former eras, fashions for women and men still differ, especially in the professional world. Men's clothes generally are not as colorful or bright as women's and are designed for function. Pockets in jackets and trousers allow men to carry wallets, change, keys, and phones. The relatively loose fit of men's clothes and the design of men's shoes enable them to move quickly and with assurance. Thus, men's clothing facilitates comfort and freedom of movement.

Women's clothing is quite different. Reflecting social expectations of femininity, women's clothing is designed to call attention to women's bodies and to make them attractive to viewers. Form-fitting styles, clingy materials, and revealing cuts encourage women to perform femininity and sexuality. Women's professional clothing often has no pockets, emphasizing form at the expense of function. Further, most women's shoes are designed to flatter legs at the cost of health, comfort, and safety—how fast can you run in stilettos?

■ EXPLORING GENDERED LIVES ■

Guns Are for Girls; Tea Parties Are for Boys

Even at very young ages, boys are more likely than girls to want to play with guns and girls are more likely than boys to want to play with tea sets.

BUT

Research suggests there's nothing about guns or tea sets themselves that makes them differently attractive to boys and girls. Researchers created a gun that was purple and covered with rhinestones and a tea set that was dark and covered with spikes. Guess what happened? Boys went for the spiked tea set and girls went for the sparkling gun. Researchers concluded that the children had learned from others that "boy stuff" is dark and angular and "girl stuff" is glittery (Rivers & Barnett, 2011).

For years, *Dora the Explorer* was the top commercial television program for girls and boys aged two to five. But then Dora started getting more, well, girly. Dora moved to town so she doesn't go on adventures in nature. Dora replaced her shorts and shirts with miniskirts. Products to go with the new Dora included a magic kitchen, a shopping cart, younger siblings to care for, jewelry, and flower lip gloss. Boys, who had loved *Dora the Explorer* as much as girls, lost interest (Wade, 2009).

TAKE A STAND: When you were a child, what were your favorite toys and what do you think they taught you?

EXPLORING GENDERED LIVES

Banning Swimwear for Women

France got pushback when it banned burkinis, which are swimwear that covers the full body. According to designer Aheda Zanetti, the burkini is "a garment to suit a modest person, or someone who has skin cancer, or a new mother who doesn't want to wear a bikini" (quoted in Fishwick, 2016). Supporters of the burkini like not being subject to lewd stares and unwanted sexual comments on public beaches. Some commentators have noted that banning the burkini seems Islamophobic since nobody bans nuns from wearing their robes when they go swimming.

Nonetheless, French mayors in over 30 resort communities have banned the swimwear for its alleged allegiance to Islam. While the French high court recently declared the ban unconstitutional, many mayors have refused to yield (Chrisafis, 2016).

TAKE A STAND: Who should decide what forms of dress are appropriate, indecent, and legal?

Selecting clothing is particularly challenging for trans and gender nonconforming people. Laura Jane Grace, who fronts the punk band *Against Me!* says transgender women like her find shopping for clothes "terrifying." They are sometimes asked to leave stores or refused access to dressing rooms. Further, even if they are allowed to try on clothes, the clothes may not fit well. Women's tops may not have enough shoulder room for trans women, and men's shirts are often too tight in the chest for masculine-presenting women or trans men. Clothing designed specifically for LGBTQ and gender nonconforming people is growing in popularity and offered by retailers such as Sharpe Suiting, Wildfang, Androgyny, and Saint Harridan, started by Lea Delaria from *Orange Is the New Black* (Italie, 2014).

Artifacts and what they mean depend on cultural context. This point is well made by Zainab, an international student in California, who emailed us her thoughts on wearing a hijab.

ZAINAB

Most Americans I have met think that the hijab [head covering] worn by Muslim women is oppressive. I must disagree with that. Muslim women who choose to wear the hijab are liberated from the stereotypes of women as sex objects. We are not oppressed by the standards of our culture, which are the standards that we should be judged by.

Consider how women are encouraged to consume products to meet current cultural ideals of femininity. In the United States alone, cosmetics is a multimillion-dollar industry that profits by persuading girls and women that they need various products to be considered attractive or acceptable. Ads urge women to buy products to straighten curly hair and curl straight hair, extend short hair and style long hair, lighten dark hair and add depth to light hair, and remove hair on legs, under arms, and at bikini lines. Cosmetic companies claim that using their merchandise allows girls and women to create a "natural look" by concealing blemishes, coloring skin, hair, and lips, and thickening and curling lashes.

RAQUEL

As a Puerto Rican I often felt like I was always different as a child. My skin was darker and there seemed to be no Puerto Ricans in the media to make me feel more pride in my ethnicity as a child.

I think it's very sad the things we do to conform to the ideal beauty. I have a friend who is Vietnamese who hates her eyes. She is very beautiful but she would rather have the Western eyes. I have another friend who is Italian and had the large Roman nose but right after high school she had rhinoplasty to "fix" it. When I was younger I wanted lighter skin even though all of my white friends said they were jealous of my "tan."

RIANNE

I've never really noticed how females are pressured to upkeep and maintain their appearances. It makes sense now since there are tools to apply makeup, change your hairdo, shape your eyebrows, change your lip color, add blusher to enhance your cheekbones. I'm tempted to stop shaving my legs and applying makeup in an effort to accept my natural state. If men can be regarded as handsome without having to work as hard, women should too.

Some people use artifacts to challenge existing perceptions of gender. For example, some men wear skinny jeans or one or more earrings; women might don military boots or other articles of clothing that defy conventional femininity.

Proximity and Personal Space

Proxemics refers to space and our use of it. Space is an index of power, a primary way to designate who is important and privileged. In strongly patriarchal societies, women are not allowed to own property; thus, they are denied the right to literal, physical space that is their own.

Consider who gets more and less space in our society. Executives have large offices, although there is little functional need for so much room. Executive assistants, however, are often crowded into cubicles that overflow with file cabinets and computers. Generally, there is a close correlation between status and the size of a person's home, car, office, and so forth. Who gets space and how much space they get indicate power.

Think about the home in which you grew up. Who sat at the head of the table—the place typically associated with being head of the household? Did one or more of your parent(s) have their own room, space, or chair? If so, which parent(s)? Many fathers have private studies, workshops, or other spaces, but fewer mothers have such spaces. Some of our students initially disagreed with this observation; but when we discussed the topic, it turned out that many of their mothers' spaces were kitchens and sewing rooms—places where mothers do things for other family members. Students whose mothers had spaces for their own work in the home often reported their mothers used parts of other rooms (a corner in the living room) or temporary spaces (using the dining room table as a desk when the table is not needed for meals).

Territoriality is personal space. Yet, not everyone's territory is equally respected. People with power tend to enter the spaces of those with less power, but the converse is not true. In general, men go into women's spaces more than women enter men's spaces and more than men enter other men's spaces. Also, men are more likely than women to challenge those who enter their territory (Knapp et al., 2013; LePoire, Burgoon, & Parrott, 1992).

Haptics (Touch)

Haptics, or touch, from parents and other adults communicates different messages to boys and girls. Parents tend to touch daughters more often and more gently than they touch sons, which teaches girls to expect touching from others and to view touching as an affiliative behavior. Boys are more likely to learn to associate touching with control and power.

ROSEANNE

A few months ago, I was out with this guy I'd been seeing for a while. We weren't serious or anything, but we had gone out a few times. Well, we were at his place listening to music when he started coming on to me. After a while, I told him to stop because I didn't want to go any further. He grinned and pinned my arms back and asked what I was going to do to stop him. Well, I didn't have to, thank goodness, because he didn't really push, but just the same I had to think there really wasn't anything I could have done if he had. That's always there when I'm with a guy—he could overpower me if he wanted to.

Because men are generally taller and often stronger than women, they tend to have more physical confidence and to be more willing to use bodily force than women. Some men are unaware of how imposing their size strength is, especially to others who are smaller or less physically strong.

Kinesics (Facial and Body Motion)

Kinesics are face and body movements. Feminine kinesic behaviors include tilting heads, smiling, and condensing their bodies to take up less space. Masculine kinesic behaviors include using large gestures, taking up space, and entering others' territories. These gender-differentiated patterns suggest that women's facial and body motions generally signal that they are approachable, friendly, and unassuming. Men's facial and body communications, in contrast, tend to indicate that they are emotionally reserved and in control.

ELAINE

I never thought it would be so hard not to smile. When you challenged us in class to go one day without smiling except when we really felt happy, I thought that would be easy. I couldn't do it. I smile when I meet people; I smile when I purchase things; I even smile when someone bumps into me. I never realized how much I smile. What was most interesting about the experiment was how my boyfriend reacted. We got together last night, and I was still working on not smiling. He asked me what was wrong. I told him, "Nothing." I was being perfectly nice and talkative and everything, but I wasn't smiling all the time like I usually do. He kept asking what was wrong, was I unhappy, had something happened—even was I mad. I pointed out that I was being as friendly as usual. Then he said, yeah, but I wasn't smiling. I told him that I just didn't see anything particular to smile about, and he said it wasn't like me. I talked with several other women in our class, and they had the same experience. I just never realized how automatic smiling is for me.

DUNCAN

When I was in high school, I played on the football team. On the day we were taking the team photograph, one of the seniors on the team yelled out before the photo, "if anyone smiles, I'm going to beat your ass." Football is a tough, aggressive game, so you're not supposed to smile when you're playing or having a photo in your uniform.

Called by poets the "windows to the soul," eyes can express love, anger, fear, interest, challenge—a great range of emotions. Many women have learned to signal interest and involvement by sustaining eye contact, whereas men are less likely to sustain eye contact during conversations. An exception to this rule is using eye contact to meet a perceived challenge. Men in our classes tell us that they would risk losing face if they didn't return a stare.

RANDALL

It sounds kind of stupid when we talk about it, but it's true that a guy has to return another guy's stare if he wants to hold his own. It's like a staring contest. Sometimes, on a street another guy will meet my eyes. When I notice, then he's locked into holding the stare, and that means that I have to, too. It's like that old joke about the first one to blink loses. It's kind of dumb, but I'd feel strange not returning another guy's gaze. Like a wimp or something.

Paralanguage

Vocal cues that accompany verbal communication are called **paralanguage**. Paralanguage includes inflection, tone, volume, accent, pitch, and rhythm. Although there are physiological differences in male and female vocal organs (the larynx and pharynx), these do not account fully for gender differences in paralanguage. For instance, the larger, thicker vocal folds typical of male larynxes do result in lower pitch, but the difference between the average pitch of male speakers and female speakers exceeds that explained by physiology.

To understand why women and men tend to have divergent paralanguage, we must once again consider socialization. What vocal cues would you expect of someone taught to be deferential and caring? What would you expect of someone taught to be assertive, emotionally reserved, and independent? Your expectations probably closely match identified differences in male and female paralanguage. In general, women use higher pitch, softer volume, and more inflection. Men tend to use lower pitch and greater volume in order to assert themselves and command the conversational stage. Also consider the impact of smiling—vocal pitch tends to rise when we smile because of the way lips are positioned.

Physical Appearance

Western culture places high priority on physical appearance. Although striving to meet physical ideals is typically associated with girls and women, men are not immune. Members of both sexes often feel pressured to meet current cultural criteria for being physically attractive.

An increasing number of men feel pressure to embody social prescriptions for ideal masculinity. For them, the goal tends to be having buff, muscular bodies rather than losing weight (Roosevelt, 2010), and recent research suggests that the more men conform to rigid

▮▮▮ EXPLORING GENDERED LIVES ▮▮▮

Beauty for Sale

Q: Isn't it mainly women who have cosmetic surgery?

A: Today, both sexes have cosmetic surgery. Of more than 15 million cosmetic surgeries in 2015, women constituted 92% of all cosmetic procedures and most often had breast augmentation, liposuction, eyelid surgery, nose reshaping, and tummy tuck (American Society of Plastic Surgeons, 2016). The most popular surgeries for men are nose reshaping, eyelid surgery, breast reduction, liposuction, and face lifts (American Society of Plastic Surgeons, 2016). Both sexes also increasingly rely on less invasive treatments such as soft tissue filler, chemical peels, and laser hair removal—14.2 million of these procedures were performed in the United States in 2015 (American Society of Plastic Surgeons, 2016).

Q: Isn't cosmetic surgery for people with lots of discretionary income?

A: Cosmetic surgeries and procedures have become popular among all economic classes in the United States. One in three people having cosmetic surgery makes less than $30,000 a year, and fewer than one in three make over $70,000 a year (Dana, 2011). Even when the United States was in a deep recession and many people were unemployed, the cosmetic surgery industry grew. While Americans spent approximately 4% less on food and 7% less on entertainment, they spent 5% more on liposuction, 8% more on eyelid surgery, and 24% more on butt lifts.

Q: But adults are entitled to make their own choices, right?

A: Yes, but cosmetic surgery is not restricted to adults. Increasingly Americans between 13 and 19 years old are having injections of botulinum toxin, which goes by the brand names Botox and Dysport. Consider Charice Pempengco, a Filipino singer. Before her

appearance on Glee in 2010, Pempengco, who was 18 at the time, had Botox injections and a skin-firming treatment "to look fresh" (Louis, 2010b).

Q: So what's the big deal? Maybe appearance shouldn't matter so much; but if you can afford to have cosmetic surgery, why not do it?

A: All of us care about our looks. However, too many people seeking cosmetic surgery have unrealistic expectations that breast augmentation or a face-lift will make others like them more. That's unlikely.

Cosmetic surgery also entails possible complications. Injections to remove wrinkles can distort the face. Skin resurfacing can cause inflammation and discoloration of skin. Eyelift surgeries can make it difficult or even impossible to close the eyes completely. Breast implants decrease breasts' sensitivity to touch. Scarring, chronic pain, and nerve damage are other possible complications. Botox and Dysport injections in facial areas can result in facial nerve paralysis and speech impairments (Louis, 2010b).

Another reason to think carefully about surgery that changes your appearance is that body ideals change. Years ago, when small-breasted Twiggy was a supermodel, women had breast-reduction surgeries in record numbers. Larger breasts are part of the current physical ideal for women, which goes a long way toward explaining why breast augmentation was the leading cosmetic surgery procedure in 2015 (279,000 procedures performed). And it's probably no coincidence that record numbers of women had lip augmentation when Angelina Jolie became a superstar (Louis, 2010a). When ideals for breast and lip size change, fashion-conscious people may need more procedures to reverse the earlier ones.

TAKE A STAND: To what extent do you think cosmetic procedures, such as liposuction and Botox injections, are different than wearing makeup or having body piercings or tattoos?

definitions of masculinity, the more likely they are to struggle with muscular dissatisfaction (Giraldi, 2016; Griffiths et al., 2015). Rob Lazebnik (2013) notes that male heroes in earlier eras (Johnny Weissmuller, Kirk Douglas, Cary Grant) did not have the super pumped bodies we see in today's male heroes (Hugh Jackman, Ryan Gosling, Liam Hemsworth). Even male news reporters such as Anderson Cooper and Jason Carroll and expert consultants such as Dr. Sanjay Gupta increasingly have toned bodies (Trebay, 2010).

Men who don't have personal trainers and hours for working out may find today's masculine body ideals unattainable (Kunitz, 2016). The extreme nature of current masculine ideals was highlighted in *Crazy Stupid Love* when Ryan Gosling removed his shirt and Emma Stone's response was "Seriously? It's like you're photoshopped" (Lazebnik, 2013).

Action figures socialize boys at an early age to understand that being ripped is the current ideal for masculinity. As with other toys, action figures are more gender-typed today than in earlier eras. Consider one example: The 1973 G.I. Joe action figure, if a real man, would be 5 foot 10 inches tall and have a 31.7-inch waist, a 44.4-inch chest, and 12.2-inch biceps, but the more recent G.I. Joe Extreme, if a real man, would be 5 foot 10 inches tall and have a 36.5-inch waist, a 54.8-inch chest, and 26.8-inch biceps (Harrison, 2008).

EXPLORING GENDERED LIVES

Too Feminine to Be a Scientist?

When 22-year-old engineer Isis Wenger agreed to appear in an ad campaign for her San Francisco-based tech firm in 2015, she never dreamed it would ignite such fierce criticism. Wenger is a self-described introvert who began building websites at age eight. Her appearance in the ad became fodder for public debate, as Wenger ran into gendered expectations of physical appearance: Scientists are usually male so they can't look too feminine, and Wenger was accused of being "too attractive" to be an engineer. Appalled, Wenger fought back. Her Twitter hashtag "ILookLikeAnEngineer" went viral, as engineers of various genders and backgrounds rallied in response (Banchefsky et al., 2016; O'Brien, 2015). Wenger is currently working to extend the Twitter campaign into a larger platform for discussing issues of gender and diversity in engineering (Anchalee, 2015).

Unfortunately, Wenger is not alone in her experience. Eileen Pollock (2015), another woman in the sciences, recalls that when she first became interested in sciences, she worried "about being perceived as unfeminine or uncool" (p. xiii). Later, when she had earned her medical degree, she reports that she "needed to minimize my femininity to be regarded seriously" (p. 240). Gender bias continues to shape attitudes about who is best able to excel in science, technology, engineering, and math (STEM), and at least some of it has to do with nonverbal communication. A 2016 study set out to understand how subtle variations in gender expression might shape perceptions of an individual's likely profession (Banchefsky et al., 2016). Participants in the study were given professional photographs of faculty—half women, half men—in STEM fields at prominent U.S. research universities and asked to evaluate each photo according to first impressions. The faculty pictured were all in professional, semiconservative attire. When prompted to consider the likelihood that the individuals pictured were scientists, participants consistently ranked women with longer hair, subtle jewelry, and makeup less likely to be scientists (Banchefsky et al., 2016).

TAKE A STAND: When you imagine a scientist, what image or images come to mind? If you imagine a specifically female scientist, what images do you have?

Girls and women are more likely than boys and men to feel pressure to look good not just for special occasions, but all the time. Lynn O'Brien Hallstein notes that body work has recently been integrated into cultural prescriptions for "good" mothering, increasing the pressures that mothers already face (Hallstein, 2015). As one new mom put it, when Kate Middleton appears with gorgeous hair and makeup right after delivery, "how are you, brand-new mom, supposed to leave the hospital with your own locks untended?" (Weiner, 2015). Given this, it is unsurprising that, for many women, concerns about appearance affect their overall sense of self-worth (Bulik, 2011; Davies-Popelka, 2015). Many women, particularly young ones, find it nearly impossible to resist the pervasive pressure to be thin (Davies-Popelka, 2015; Rhode, 2010; Weitz & Kwan, 2013). Although many young women say they know that models are digitally altered and not "real," they still dislike their own bodies for not measuring up to the manufactured image (Rhode, 2010).

EMILY

Why do girls have to look nice all the time? My boyfriend rolls out of bed and goes to class or the mall or wherever. He doesn't have to shampoo and blow his hair or dress in clean, ironed clothes. His clothes are rumpled and his hair isn't even combed some days. Once when I had a really bad cold, I felt so bad I didn't do what I usually do before going out. I showered, but I didn't do my hair or put on blusher and eye shadow, and I wore workout clothes. My boyfriend told me I looked like a slob just because for once I looked like he did.

For many girls and women, concern about weight starts early. By third grade, 50–80% of girls say they want to lose weight (Rhode, 2010), and by the fourth grade, 40% of girls diet (Kilbourne, 2007, 2010; Weitz & Kwan, 2013). Today, 30 million people in the United States suffer from eating disorders and even more have unhealthy attitudes and behaviors regarding food (National Association of Anorexia Nervosa and Associated Disorders, 2016). Women make up between 85% and 95% of people with eating disorders, and 25% of college-aged women engage in binging and purging as a weight-management technique (National Association of Anorexia Nervosa and Associated Disorders, 2014).

The consequences of eating disorders are substantial. Almost half of people who have eating disorders meet the criteria for a diagnosis of clinical depression. Further, roughly 20% of people suffering from anorexia will prematurely die, primarily from suicide and heart problems (National Association of Anorexia Nervosa and Associated Disorders, 2014).

NIKKI

When I was growing up, my mother and grandmother were always on diets. They think being ultrathin is essential. Four years ago, when I came to college, I gained the "freshman 15." When I went home for the summer, my mother and grandmother commented on how much weight I'd gained and how bad I looked. Mother got her doctor to put me on FenPhen, the diet pill. I'd heard it could be dangerous (you've probably read about the lawsuits against it), but I took the pills for two months and lost a lot of weight—more than the 15 pounds I'd gained. Then, I started having echoing sounds in my ears. I went to a doctor, and he said it was the result of taking FenPhen. The ringing is with me all the time, even though I've quit taking that pill. Being thin is fine, but it's not worth risking your health. I actually feel sorry for my mother and grandmother because they obsess over their weight and never enjoy eating food.

Women who focus so intensely on their bodies have less attention to devote to other things. For many young women in Western culture, the body has become an all-consuming project that takes precedence over developing character, intelligence, and engaging with the world (Barash, 2006; Davies-Popelka, 2015; Whitefield-Madrano, 2016).

In general, African-American women tend to be less prone to eating disorders and less likely to pursue unrealistic physical ideals (Berry, 2014; Bruns & Carter, 2015; Walker, 2007). African-American women who identify strongly with their ethnic heritage may be less vulnerable to obsession with thinness than African-American women who do not. In a letter to us, Daneen, a black student from a northern college, described the ideology behind the views of physical beauty that she and other black women in her community learned:

> My family and my African American culture instilled pride in me. I was told that my full lips, round body, and rough hair encompassed the beauty and pride of my history. To want to be skinny or have straight hair or thin lips would be to deny my identity as a Black woman.

KarlProuse/Catwalking/GettyImages

Many current models are anorexic.

Because our culture is increasingly emphasizing men's bodies, more and more men report body dissatisfaction related to masculinity and are exercising, working out with weights, taking fitness supplements, and using potentially lethal steroids to develop muscularity (Griffiths, Murray & Touyz, 2015; Roosevelt, 2010). In addition, some men develop eating disorders in an effort to stay slim. One eating disorder, binge eating, seems to be increasing among men. Approximately 7.5% of men between 18 and 65 report binging (Ellen, 2012). Male model Ron Saxen (2007) details his battle with binge eating in his book, *The Good Eater*. In addition, gay men are more likely to be concerned about appearance and to develop eating disorders because physical appearance is linked more closely to self-worth and attractiveness to possible partners for gay than straight men (Lanzieri & Hildebrandt, 2011). Lesbian, gay, and bisexual youth report higher rates of disordered eating than their straight peers, which some scholars attribute to the social stress that accompanies growing up LGB (Watson et al., 2016).

KYLE

For me, the issue of physical appearance is really complicated because I'm transgender. Biologically, I am female, but psychologically and spiritually I am male. Every time I see my naked body or have my period, it's totally unsettling because I'm really a man and shouldn't have breasts or periods. Surgery scares me, but I may have it one day so that my body matches my self-concept.

Interpreting Nonverbal Behavior

There are also gendered differences in decoding others' nonverbal behaviors. Research indicates that women are generally more skilled than men at interpreting others' nonverbal communication (Hall, 2006; Miller, 2011). There is one exception to this generalization. Although overall women exceed men in their ability to decipher facial cues, men recognize angry faces more quickly than women (Bakalar, 2006). One explanation for this is that historically men's survival depended on having a keen ability to detect anger and other signs of possible aggression.

Although researchers agree that women are generally more skilled than men at interpreting nonverbal behavior, they disagree on why this is so. One explanation is sex-related brain differences—females' right brain specialization may make them more adept at interpreting emotions. A second explanation is that, from childhood on, most females are encouraged to be sensitive to others, which requires being able to decipher others' nonverbal cues. Related to this is a third explanation: Women's social location encourages them to learn to read their feelings and needs. For example, a mother who is her child's primary caregiver learns to interpret her baby's subtly different nonverbal behaviors (crying, hand motions, etc.) as signaling the baby is hungry, needs a diaper changed, needs to be burped, or wants company.

A fourth explanation comes from standpoint theory, which suggests that women's decoding skill results from their location as subordinate members of society. In order to survive, people who have little power learn to interpret others with greater power. Women's decoding skills probably result from a combination of biology, socialization, and persisting power discrepancies between the sexes. You might think about your experiences and observations of others and ask which explanation makes most sense to you.

KRISTA

I buy the power explanation for women's decoding skill. I know that I learned to do this from my mother. My father is very moody, and you have to know how to read him, or there's trouble ahead. I remember, when I was a little girl, my mother would tell me not to ask Daddy for something or not to tell him about things at certain times because he was in a bad mood. I asked her how she knew, and she gave me a blueprint for reading him. She told me, when he was mad he fidgeted and mumbled more and that he got real quiet when he was upset. Later, she taught me other things, like how to tell when he's getting angry about something—his eyebrows twitch. She made it seem like a science, and I guess it was in a way. But she sure knew how to read his moods, and that's how we stayed out of his way when he was on the warpath.

EXPLORING GENDERED LIVES

A New Model for Models?

For years, European-American features have been represented as the only standard of female beauty. Tyra Banks, Naomi Campbell, and other women of color who are successful models have skin color, hair, and features that are more like those of European-Americans than like members of their own ethnic groups. Women of color who have darker skin are often photoshopped so that they appear more light skinned as was Gabourey Sidibe, who starred in *Precious*, for the cover of *Elle* magazine. In 2013, black models accounted for only 6% of the models in Fashion Week's runway show (Wilson, 2013). But there is some evidence of change. In 2016, Zac Posen attracted attention for casting models of color almost exclusively in his lineup for New York Fashion Week. While Posen did not comment on this decision, others noted his as a powerful statement in an industry dominated by white models (Mau, 2016).

For the past several decades, models have also been stick-thin—so thin that many are anorexic and suffer serious health conditions, including severe dehydration,

immunodeficiency, osteoporosis, and kidney and heart failure. According to the World Health Organization's standards, the average international runway model has a body mass index (BMI) low enough to indicate starvation (Rancaño, 2015).

This too has begun to change. Researchers have advocated for worker protection standards in the industry, and French model Isabelle Caro famously appeared in an ad campaign against anorexia prior to her death from the illness at age 28. The public has also participated in demanding models of varying sizes like the women who buy the clothes being modeled. Many fashion magazines and designers now feature models of different body shapes and sizes. Israel has banned underweight models, and the French Parliament is considering a BMI standard that excludes underweight models—a 5-foot 7-inches model would need to weigh at least 120 pounds (Rubin, 2015). Most recently, London's mayor banned ads that promote "an unhealthy body image" ("No Skinny Models," 2016, p. 10).

TAKE A STAND: To what extent do you think the fashion industry should employ models whose features reflect diverse sizes, races, and ethnicities?

Respecting Gendered Styles of Nonverbal Communication

What we've discussed in this chapter empowers you to be more effective in your communication and in your interpretation of others' communication. People who have been socialized in conventionally masculine speech communities may perceive a woman who defers as less confident of her ideas than a man who advances his views assertively. Similarly, someone socialized in conventionally feminine speech communities might view a man as insensitive and domineering if he looks impassive, offers little response to her talk, and promotes his agenda. And some people make negative judgments of anyone who defies conventional expectations of gender and performs outside of the usual identity categories. Yet, such judgments reflect the communication rules we have learned, and our rules may not pertain to others' ways of communicating. It's insensitive to impose our values on behaviors that emanate from alternative social locations and the rules learned in those locations.

Once we realize that people have different rules for communicating, we are more likely to interpret others on their own terms, not ours. This might lead you to ask for clarification of intent from conversational partners whose nonverbal communication patterns diverge from yours. For example, it might be constructive to say to someone less facially expressive than you, "I don't know how you're feeling about what I just said, because your face doesn't show any reaction. Could you tell me what you feel?" Conversely, understanding may be enhanced when someone with a masculine, assertive, nonverbal style says to his/her/their more deferential partner, "I'm not sure where you stand, because you seem to be responding to my ideas rather than expressing your own. I'm interested in your opinion." Communicative techniques such as these allow you to minimize the potential for misunderstandings that grow out of gendered communication styles.

There's another benefit to learning to understand and respect alternative styles of nonverbal communication. It enhances your personal effectiveness by increasing the range of options you have for communicating with different people in diverse contexts and for varied reasons. Now that you are aware of gendered patterns in nonverbal communication, reflect on your own behaviors. Which of the patterns typical of your gender describe your nonverbal communication? Are you comfortable with your style and its effects, or would you like to alter your nonverbal behavior in some respects? By reflecting on your own nonverbal communication, you empower yourself to consciously create a style that reflects the identity you assign to yourself.

SUMMARY

Nonverbal communication expresses cultural views of gender and reflects our personal gendered identities. Social definitions of women as deferential, decorative, and relationship-centered are reinforced through nonverbal communication that emphasizes their appearance and limits their space. Views of men as independent, powerful, and in control are reflected in nonverbal behaviors that grant them larger territories and more permission to touch others, particularly women, and to invade their space. Differences in women's and men's nonverbal behaviors often reflect these social definitions. Whereas many women embody femininity by speaking softly, condensing themselves, yielding territory, and displaying responsive facial expressions, men are likely to command space and volume, defend their turf, and display little facial expression to keep feelings camouflaged.

Recognizing the value a range of communication styles, both verbal and nonverbal, enables you to reflect critically on the patterns assigned by society. In turn, this empowers you to revise your own nonverbal communication to reflect the identity you want, practice greater fluency in communicating with others, and resist those social expectations that you find unconstructive or limiting. In doing this, you participate in the processes of constructing gender and the values assigned to different forms of communication.

KEY TERMS

The following terms are defined in this chapter on the pages indicated as well as in alphabetical order in the book's glossary, which begins on page 261. The text's companion website also provides interactive flash cards to help you learn these terms and the concepts they represent. You can access the site at www.cengagebrain.com.

artifact 119	*paralanguage 124*
haptics 123	*power 119*
kinesics 123	*proxemics 122*
liking 118	*responsiveness 118*
nonverbal communication 117	*territoriality 122*

GENDER ONLINE

1. To learn more about race and cultural representations of female beauty visit this site: **http://misrepresentationofwomen.weebly.com/standards-of-beauty.html**

2. Online search terms: *cosmetic surgery, Let Toys Be Toys,* and *I Am Elemental, BMI.*

3. Tatyana Fazlalizadeh is an artist whose work includes public art to challenge street harassment. Learn about her "Stop Telling Women to Smile" public art by visiting this site: **http://stoptellingwomentosmile.com/**

REFLECTION DISCUSSION, AND ACTION

1. Look at the ads in magazines you enjoy reading. Describe the gendered ideals that are reflected in them.

2. Observe people in your classes, in restaurants and stores, and walking around campus. To what extent do you see gendered patterns of nonverbal communication that were identified in this chapter?

3. Visit a store and study the packaging on products marketed to men and women. What differences do you notice?

4. Violate an expectation for nonverbal communication for your sex. Analyze how people respond both verbally and nonverbally.

5. Conduct an informal survey to learn how students on your campus define the physical ideals for women and men:

    - Ask five men and five women to describe their physical ideal for women and men. Did you notice any differences that reflect gender, race, and/or sexuality?
    - Record their answers, and share your findings with those of classmates.
    - Compare physical ideals stated by people of different races and gender expressions and identities.
    - To what extent are your findings consistent with those reported in this chapter?

RECOMMENDED RESOURCES

1. *Transamerica* draws attention to the ways in which people perform gender even when they do not realize they are "performing."

2. Standards for male attractiveness have gotten more difficult to attain. The Good Men Project has an article that offers a critical perspective on images of six-pack men with no fat are used to sell men's underwear: **https://goodmenproject.com/featured-content/not-typical-underwear-models-jvinc/**

7

The most radical step you can take is your next one.
—James Baldwin

Becoming Gendered

Knowledge Challenge:

- To what extent do mothers and fathers interact differently with children?
- How do ego boundaries affect approaches to relationships?
- What does it mean to grow up masculine or feminine in the twenty-first century?

"Mommy, when is the good fairy going to come with her magic wand and change my penis into a vagina?" (My Secret Self, 2009). That's the question that two-year-old Jazz Jennings posed to her mother. Born with male genitalia, Jazz says she knew from the start that she was a girl. Explaining it in an interview, she said, "I have a girl brain and a boy body" (My Secret Self, 2009). At first Jazz's parents, particularly her father, resisted Jazz's declaration of gender identity. They thought their youngest was just going through a phase. But, no: Liking dresses and dolls was not a phase that Jazz would grow out of. Instead of asking Jazz to change, her family—mother, father, twin brothers, and older sister—changed to recognize Jazz as a daughter and sister rather than a son and brother.

Jazz and her family made the decision to be not just open but public about Jazz's identity and the challenges that she and the family faced. Sometimes joined by her family, Jazz has appeared on *20/20, 60 Minutes*, the *Rosie Show*, and a documentary on Oprah's network. By the time she was an adolescent, Jazz had started the Transkids Purple Rainbow Foundation as a resource for other transkids and their families. Jazz also designs and sells silicone mermaid tails to raise money to support trans people because "mermaids are not judged on body parts" so you "don't have to worry what's around the private area," says Jazz (My Secret Self, 2009).

Now a teenager, Jazz continues to work for trans awareness and rights. After winning a long battle with the U.S. Soccer Federation that granted trans students access to team sports, she coauthored a book about transkids for four- to eight-year-olds (Herthel, Jennings, & McNicholas, 2014). Her efforts have earned accolades and recognition from *Time, Advocate,* Human Rights Campaign, and LogoTV. Her memoir, *Being Jazz: My Life as a (Transgender) Teen*, was published in 2016.

KevinWinter/GettyImages

Jazz Jennings: "I have a girl brain and a boy body."

From Chapter 2, recall that children usually achieve gender constancy by age three, often earlier. Society and families are organized to help cisgender children achieve gender constancy, but trans children often struggle to define themselves in a world that often doesn't understand or accept their identities. For them, the challenges of claiming a gender and learning how to perform it competently are even greater than those faced by cisgender children.

Before reading further, write one or two paragraphs describing what it means to you personally to be the sex and gender that you are. Later in this chapter, we'll return to what you've written.

This chapter focuses on the important early years of our lives. Our experiences as infants, children, and adolescents profoundly influence who we are. Although we continue to evolve throughout our lives, the foundations of our identities, including gender, are keenly shaped by the first few years of life.

Because much of the scholarship on child development focuses on traditional families, our discussion is necessarily weighted toward those families. When research is available, we integrate information on more diverse family forms. The research on diverse families suggests that traditional families tend to enforce conventional gender roles more rigidly than single parents and lesbian and gay families.

Because parents are such a key influence on most people's identities, we will examine at length how parental communication teaches children cultural codes related to gender. We will also consider contemporary college students' views of what it means to be a man, woman, cisgender, transgender, lesbian, gay, bisexual, or straight in the United States today. Their descriptions give rich insight into current prescriptions for gender—and some of the difficulties those prescriptions pose.

Gendering Communication in the Family

To understand how families contribute to gendering children, we will first elaborate on the largely unconscious dynamics at work in gender development, which we discussed briefly in Chapter 2. Second, we will draw on social learning, cognitive development, and symbolic interaction theories to examine more overt ways in which children learn gender in families.

Unconscious Processes

The conscious realm of human experience does not fully explain human development. Insight into unconscious dynamics comes primarily from psychoanalytic theories, which claim that core identity, including **gender identity**, is shaped in the early years of life.

> ### GABBY
> *Growing up was not a piece of cake for me. My father was in the Army and he embraced a very rigid code of masculinity. Since I was five, I liked to dress up in my sister's clothes. By the time I was 12, I was stuffing tissues in my shirt so I looked like I had breasts— always in the privacy of my own room, of course. Dad expected me to be a fullback and I wanted to be a ballerina. As I said, not easy.*

Gender Identity   As children, each of us develops a gender identity, which is a person's subjective sense of his/her/their gender. Traditional psychoanalytic theory asserted that biology, particularly the genitals, determines with which parent a child will identify and, thus, how the child's psyche will develop. Freud believed that children of both sexes focus on the penis as a symbol of power. Boys identify with their fathers, who have penises, whereas girls recognize their similarity to their mothers, who do not have penises. Freud theorized that girls regard their mothers as responsible for their "lack" of penises, whereas boys view their fathers as having the power to castrate them.

> ### MAYA
>
> *I don't buy this stuff about penis envy. I've never envied my brother, his penis. I remember, when we were both little, we took baths together sometimes, and I saw that he was made differently than I was. I thought it looked strange, but I didn't want it myself. But I do remember being jealous of him, or of the freedoms my parents allowed him but not me. They let him go off all day long to play, but I had to stay in the yard unless my mother was with me. He could play rough and get dirty, but I'd get a real fussin' if I did. I remember wishing I were a boy so that I could do all of the fun things, but I didn't wish I had a penis. Definitely not.*

As interesting as Freud's theory is, there is limited empirical support for his beliefs that girls envy penises and boys fear castration. Despite rejecting some of Freud's ideas, current psycho-analytic theorists agree with the basic claim that families play a critical role in the formation of gender identity. In infancy, children of both sexes tend to depend on and identify with the person who takes care of them. Usually, this is a woman, as mothers are more likely to take time off from work when a child is born or adopted. Although many fathers in our era are committed to active involvement in their children's lives and most millennials of all genders anticipate equal partnerships, mothers still spend more time with children than fathers (Medved, 2016; Parker & Wang, 2013). In fact, mothers who work outside of the home spend more time caring for children and homes (3.4 hours a day) than men who do not work outside of the home (3 hours a day) (Shulevitz, 2015). Thus, most infants, regardless of sex, form their first identification with a woman.

Common identification with a woman does not mean that boys and girls pursue similar paths to develop gender identity. Around the age of three, boys' and girls' developmental paths diverge dramatically. You'll recall from cognitive development theory that this is the age at which gender constancy is usually secured, such that children realize that their sex is an unchanging, continuous part of their identity. For most girls, concrete, daily interactions with mothers or other female caregivers crystallize a sense of self within a relationship.

To develop masculine gender identity, however, many boys feel the need to identify with a male. Boys who have close relationships with fathers or other adult males have role models to help them define their own masculine identity. However, the process of defining personal masculinity can be complicated for boys who do not have close relationships with their fathers or other adult men. Sons of single mothers may lack adult male role models if there are no uncles, grandfathers, or other adult males in their lives (Miller, 2015a).

> ### ADRIENNE
>
> *I remember watching my mother fix her hair and makeup in the morning. I thought she was the most beautiful woman in the world, and I wanted to be just like her. Many days, I went into her dressing room when she was busy downstairs and practiced putting on makeup and fixing my hair just like she did.*

For boys who lack a strong, personal relationship with an adult male, masculine gender can be elusive and difficult to grasp (Miller, 2015a). This may help explain why many boys define their masculinity predominantly in negative terms—as not feminine, not female, not like mother. By extension, young boys' vigorous contempt for anything feminine may be a way to assure themselves that they are truly masculine.

NOAH

My father left us before I was even a year old, so I didn't know him at all. My mom worked all day and was too tired to date or anything else, so there wasn't a man around. I tried to help Mom, but she'd tell me I didn't have to do this stuff, because I was "her little man." I used to watch Mom doing stuff around the house, and I'd think, "That's not what I'm supposed to do," but I had a lot of trouble figuring out what it was that I was supposed to do. I just knew it wasn't girl stuff. Then, I got a Big Brother through a program at school. He was 17, and he spent most every Saturday with me and sometimes a while after school during the week. Michael was great. He'd let me hang out with him, and he'd show me how to do stuff like play ball and use tools to make things. Finally, I had a sense of what I was supposed to be like and what I should do. Michael really helped me figure out who I was.

Although boys and girls engage in many of the same activities, there are also patterned differences in what they are encouraged to do. Young girls are often praised for being "Mommy's helper" and interacting with their mothers and younger siblings. Boys, on the other hand, are more likely to be praised for being independent and engaging in competitive play. Boys' social development typically occurs in larger groups with temporary and changing memberships, whereas for many girls identity develops within ongoing, personal relationships with family members and regular playmates. These different paths of social development encourage boys to see themselves as independent and able to meet physical challenges and girls to see themselves as involved in continuing relationships with others.

Building on this foundation, many girls and women continue to prioritize close relationships throughout their lives. Because most boys develop masculine identities that require separating from their initial relationship with their mothers, and because they tend to interact in activity-specific groups with changing members, many of them grow into men who define themselves relatively independently of others.

Much of the research on children's development that we have discussed thus far is based on heterosexual, two-parent families. Today, however, families are increasingly diverse. Traditional families headed by a husband and wife represent less than half of all families today (Suter, Kellas, Webb, & Allen, 2016). Families headed by LGBT parents as well as parents who are single are growing in number and cultural visibility. While children in nontraditional families may face social stigma or, in some cases, have difficulty finding available models of both sexes (Raeburn, 2014), family diversity often fosters new ways of thinking about and performing gender and is positively linked with healthy child development in a variety of ways (Coles, 2015; Suter et al., 2016).

Today, approximately two million children are being raised with one or more gay or lesbian parents, and this number is expected to rise as more same-sex couples decide to parent (Suter et al., 2016). Children raised by same-sex parents tend to have more expansive views of gender roles because they have seen their parent(s) perform all of the duties—those considered masculine and feminine—of running a household. In comparison to heterosexual fathers, gay dads are more likely to reject hegemonic masculinity, prioritize family over work, and encourage greater empathy and open-mindedness in their children. Lesbian moms tend to model greater egalitarianism in romantic relationships than their heterosexual peers and encourage economic and emotional self-sufficiency in their children, particularly daughters (Schulevitz, 2015; Suter, 2014). Interestingly, some studies suggest that children raised

---

EXPLORING GENDERED LIVES

Superheroes and Slackers

When searching for role models, boys are not limited to the men who are actually in their lives. They also have media, which offer images of men. But how diverse are these images? Both traditional and social media offer boys pretty limited role models (Halberstam, 2012; Kimmel, 2013). Interviews with nearly 700 boys aged 4 to 18 revealed two primary media characters with

which young males most identify (Lamb, Brown, & Tappan, 2009):

The superhero, who is aggressive and often violent, has high-powered weapons and is disrespectful, if not exploitive, of women.

The slacker, who is amusing, doesn't like school or responsibility and has no plans for his life.

TAKE A STAND: To what extent do your experiences confirm or challenge these as dominant media images of men today?

---

by same-sex parents who share equally in wage earning and child care tend to hold more egalitarian views of gender, but that their views of gender adhere more strongly to gendered stereotypes when same-sex parents divide labor between a primary caregiver and a primary wage earner (Leaper, 2014).

There has been less research on what happens when heterosexual men are single dads or stay-at-home parents, perhaps because only 16% of stay-at-home parents are fathers (Livingston, 2014). Preliminary research indicates that single-father families can be highly cohesive and that father–child discussions are more elaborate and less competitive than discussions between fathers and children in families with mothers as well as fathers (Coles, 2015; Galvin, 2006).

Ego Boundaries   At the same time that most children construct gender identity, they simultaneously form **ego boundaries** (Chodorow, 1989; Surrey, 1983). An ego boundary is the point at which an individual stops and the rest of the world begins. It distinguishes the self—more or less distinctly—from everyone and everything else. Because ego boundaries are linked to gender identity and evolve concurrently with it, masculine and feminine ego boundaries tend to differ. Individuals who develop feminine gender identities, which emphasize interrelatedness with others, tend to have relatively permeable ego boundaries that do not entail rigid separation from others.

VINCE

My girlfriend is so strange about her friends. Like, the other night I went by her apartment, and she was all upset and crying. When I asked her what was wrong, she told me Mai, her best friend, had just been dumped by her boyfriend. I said she acted like it was her who'd broken up, not Mai, and she didn't need to be so upset. She got even more upset and said it felt like her problem too; couldn't I understand what Mai was going through? I said I could, but that she wasn't going through it; Mai was. She told me it was the same thing because when you're really close to somebody else you hurt when they hurt. It didn't make sense to me, but maybe this concept of ego boundaries is what that's all about.

The relatively permeable ego boundaries associated with femininity may partially explain why many girls and women tend to experience the feelings of those close to them almost as their own (Hall, 2006; Hartman, 1993; Wood, 2013). It may also explain why some women become so involved in helping others that they neglect their own needs. Finally, this may shed light on the tendency of many women to feel responsible for others and for situations that they do not create or control. When the lines between self and others are blurry, it's hard to make a clear distinction between your own responsibilities and needs and those of others.

Conventional masculine gender identity is premised on differentiating from a female caregiver and forming fluid alliances with others. It makes sense, then, that masculine individuals tend to have relatively firm ego boundaries. They generally have a clear sense of where they stop and others begin; they may sympathize with others but not experience others' feelings as their own. People with masculine gender identities and firm ego boundaries tend to feel secure when autonomy is high, and they may feel smothered in relationships that are extremely close. The firmer ego boundaries that usually accompany a masculine gender identity explain why many men have fewer emotionally intimate relationships than women typically do.

Parental Communication about Gender

From Chapter 2, recall that one way children learn gender roles is by receiving positive and negative reinforcements for various behaviors (social learning theory) and through observing and emulating others whom they see as models (cognitive development theory). Typically, girls are rewarded for being cooperative, helpful, nurturing, friendly, and polite. Parents may also reward—or at least not punish—girls for being sensitive, athletic, and smart. For boys, rewards are more likely to come for behaving competitively, independently, and assertively.

While some parents' attitudes and communication about gender are becoming more egalitarian, much evidence of traditional stereotyping still exists (Leaper, 2014; Ryle, 2015). A classic study showed that in just 24 hours of birth, parents responded to their babies in terms of gender stereotypes (Rubin, Provenzano, & Luria, 1974). Although male and female babies were matched for size, weight, and level of activity, parents described boys as *strong*, *big*, *active*, and *alert* and described the equally large, active girls as *small*, *dainty*, *quiet*, and *delicate*. These findings have been replicated in more recent studies (Elliott, 2009). In another recent study, despite the absence of sex differences in babies' vocal pitch, adults erroneously attributed the higher-pitched cries to girls and the lower-pitched cries to boys (Reby, Levréro, Gustafsson, & Mathevon, 2016). These studies suggest the powerful influence of gendered stereotypes on parental attitudes and beliefs.

NADIA

In my family, I learned that thinking about boys was not a high priority. If I told my mama that I liked a boy or that I was afraid a boy I was dating was going to break up with me, she'd say "Get your mind off boys and on books." Mama made it very clear that I was supposed to get my education and learn to take care of myself. Period.

EXPLORING GENDERED LIVES

#StillABoy

In 2012, Sam selected his favorite pair of shoes—pink, zebra-striped ballet flats—for the first day of preschool. When his mom posted a picture of him on Facebook, a number of friends and family responded with concern—describing the shoe selection as "wrong" and warning that the shoes might "turn him gay" (Warner, 2012).

Sam's story went viral, generating public controversy as to the role of parents in gendering their children. But it has also inspired much more. After hearing Sam's story, Martine Zoer founded Quirkie Kids as a mom of two boys who believed that children should be able to express themselves free from societal pressure or scorn. Quirkie Kids is a gender-neutral line of t-shirts designed to challenge stereotypes. Unlike most "gender neutral" clothing lines, many of Zoer's designs feature pink. When her business was accused of "robbing kids of their gender,"

Zoer launched the hashtag #StillABoy on Instagram to challenge the narrow spectrum of behaviors, interests, and abilities expected of boys (Bologna, 2016). #StillABoy features photos of boys holding hands, caring for siblings and baby dolls, and wearing butterfly wings, nail polish, and sparkly sunglasses.

Actions such as those by Zoer make a difference. Just four years later, in 2016, something very different happened when 10-year-old Charlie's mom posted a photo of him in clothes he selected at a girls' clothing store. Her post was shared 25,000 times, and she received a flood of supportive messages from people who applauded her openness to her child's gender expression (Iszler, 2016). Diane Ehrensaft (2016) calls such children *gender creative* because they step outside of the tight boxes—boy or girl—and experiment with different ways of being who they are.

TAKE A STAND: To what extent would you support your child if they were gender creative?

Some parents convey distinct messages about assertiveness and aggressiveness to sons and daughters. Parents, particularly white middle-class parents, reward verbal and physical activity, including aggression, in sons more than daughters and reward interpersonal and social skills in daughters more than sons (Helgeson, 2016; Reiner, 2016). Because many girls are discouraged from direct, overt aggression yet still feel aggressive at times, they develop other, less direct ways of expressing aggression, which we will discuss in later chapters.

Recent research also shows that parents of young adolescents place greater importance on leadership activities and accomplishments for sons than daughters (Sandberg & Chávez, 2014). Heterosexual fathers are particularly likely to encourage sons to be heterosexual (Solebello & Elliott, 2011). Gay fathers, however, are more likely to resist normative expectations for fathers, embracing greater nurturance and non-gender-specific parenting than that of their heterosexual peers (Berkowitz, 2011).

Mothers tend to communicate with children more than heterosexual fathers (Bianchi, Robinson, & Milkie, 2006; Coles, 2015). Mothers use talk to build connections with children and to give information, advice, encouragement, and emotional support to children (Segrin & Flora, 2005; Shulevitz, 2015). Mothers surpass heterosexual fathers in talking with children, particularly daughters, about feelings and relationships, guiding them in how to build relationships and interact socially (Galvin, 2006; Segrin & Flora, 2005). Even when children are less than two years old, mothers call sons' attention to numbers and talk with sons about numbers more than they talk with daughters (Chang, Sandhofer, & Brown, 2012).

TREVOR

My father took me hunting and coached me in football. He taught me to be strong around other men and to treat any woman with respect. He taught me that a real man is tough when he needs to be, loyal to friends, and protective of women.

When interacting with children, mothers typically focus on providing comfort, security, and emotional development. They engage in more eye contact and face-to-face interaction with children than do fathers, and they are more likely than fathers to hug children and tell children they love them (Blow, 2014a). More than fathers, mothers tend to play with children at the children's level, which develops children's confidence and security in play.

Although heterosexual fathers spend less time than mothers in one-on-one communication with children, today's fathers talk more with children than did fathers in previous generations (Pruett & Pruett, 2009; Tarkan, 2009). Fathers tend to engage in play that is physically stimulating and exciting, and they encourage children, especially sons, to develop skills and meet challenges (Raeburn, 2014). Fathers, more than mothers, stretch children by urging them to compete, achieve, take risks, act independently, and move beyond their current levels of ability (Luster & Okagaki, 2005; Popenoe, 1996; Raeburn, 2014; Stacey, 1996).

Another notable difference between communication typical of mothers and fathers concerns talk about sexual activity. Mothers are much more likely than fathers to discuss sex topics with children, particularly daughters, and mothers' communication with teens about sex is especially linked to safer sex behaviors (Dennis & Wood, 2012; Widman, Choukas-Bradley, Noar, Nesi, & Garrett, 2016; Wilson & Koo, 2010). When mothers talk with daughters about sex, the daughters are more likely to delay sexual activity and to engage in safer sex when they decide to be sexually active (Wilson & Koo, 2010).

Parents also communicate gender expectations through encouraging particular toys and activities for sons and daughters. Although many parents encourage their children to play with a range of toys, some parents actively discourage their children's interest in toys and games that are associated with the other sex. For instance, boys may be persuaded not to play with dolls (other than action figures), and girls may be dissuaded from engaging in physically aggressive sports.

As we noted in Chapter 6, childhood toys and activities affect how we see ourselves and the possibilities for our lives. Toys typically marketed for girls, such as dolls, encourage gentle, nurturing interaction with others, physical closeness, and verbal communication. Toys that are marketed to boys, such as sports equipment and train sets, promote independent or competitive activities and less verbal interaction. Parents who don't want to limit their children to sex-typed toys may encounter challenges. Many stores sell girls' bikes in pink and other pastels and boys' bikes in darker colors (Abadi, 2013; Orenstein, 2011a, 2011b; Rivers & Barnett, 2011). Even animals that appear on children's clothing and toys are gendered—kittens are marketed to girls and dinosaurs to boys. Halloween costumes are also very sex-typed. Typical costumes for boys are based on characters who have supernatural powers, strength, and bravado, whereas costumes for girls are based on characters who are brides, princesses, sex objects, and witches.

Another way parents communicate gender expectations is through household chores that they assign to sons and daughters. Like toys, various tasks cultivate particular ways of seeing ourselves. Domestic chores, which are more often assigned to girls, emphasize taking care of others, whereas outdoor work and repair jobs, more typically assigned to boys, encourage independent activity.

In general, gender socialization is more rigid for boys than for girls (Helgeson, 2016), and heterosexual fathers are especially insistent on gender-stereotyped toys and activities, especially for sons (Leaper, 2014). It's more acceptable for girls to play baseball or football than for boys to play house or to cuddle dolls (Halberstam, 2012). Similarly, it's considered more suitable for girls to be strong than for boys to cry and more acceptable for girls to act independently than for boys to need others. Overall, boys are more intensively and rigidly pushed to be masculine than girls are pushed to be feminine.

> **TAYLOR**
>
> *My father always tried to encourage me to be strong, play sports, and do things that girls were not supposedly good at doing, like working on carpentry, for example. I tried my best to meet my father's expectations, but I often failed. Peers often teased me and called me names like "wuss" because I was never good at playing sports and because of my size. I really enjoyed watching sports, but I was afraid to even try to get on teams in middle school because I was setting myself up for failure.*

Parental Modeling

Another way parents communicate gender is through modeling masculinity, femininity, and, for heterosexual parents, male–female relationships. As you will recall from Chapter 2, cognitive development theory tells us that, once children have gender constancy, they actively look for role models of their sex and use those models to develop masculine or feminine qualities, behaviors, and so forth. For most children, parents are the single most visible and available models of gender. By observing parents, children often learn the roles socially prescribed for women and men.

As noted earlier in this chapter, however, not all families adopt traditional gender roles, and families in our era are highly diverse in membership and roles (Halberstam, 2012; Suter et al., 2016). In addition to LGBTQ families and single-parent families, another departure from tradition has to do with the breadwinner role. In 1970, approximately 50% of married women worked outside the home (Pew Research Center, 2015). Today, approximately 70% of children in the United States live in households in which all adults work (Pew Research Center, 2015), and 40% of American women who are in the paid labor force and are in two-earner marriages earn more money than their male partners (Langfield, 2013; Reeves & Sawhill, 2015). Parents who remarry create blended families. Being part of more than one family and observing multiple models of gender give these children more diverse ideas about how families can work and how gender can be embodied.

In sum, parents are major messengers about gender. For most people, parents provide gender with their modeling, descriptions of children, and chores and activities they encourage. Yet, gender is not just about learning society's rules. Gender is also deeply personal. Let's now translate the research we've considered into personal portraits of becoming gendered in contemporary Western society.

The Personal Side of the Gender Drama

At the beginning of this chapter, we asked you to write a paragraph or two about what it means to be the sex and gender that you are. In the pages that follow, you'll learn how other college students answer that question. As you read their responses, consider how their ideas harmonize with and depart from your own.

Growing Up Masculine

What does it mean to identify as a man in America in the twenty-first century? Although there is a dominant model of masculinity, there are also many variations on and challenges to that (Jackson & Murali, 2011; Reeser, 2010). To understand the advantages, challenges, and issues of various masculinities, let's consider what five college men have to say. In their commentaries, Mark, Aaron, Steve, Devon, and Chris focus as much on the pressures, expectations, and constraints of manhood as its prerogatives and privileges. What these five men tell us is consistent with research (Coontz, 2013; Kimmel, 2013; Kimmel & Messner, 2012; Lindgren & Lélièvre, 2009; Reeves & Sawhill, 2015). We'll discuss six themes of manhood in America today. Five of these were first identified by Doyle (1997).

Don't Be Feminine   For many men, the most fundamental requirement for manhood is not to be feminine. One man recalls his high school football coach goading injured players by asking, "You a football player or are you a little girl" (Sexton, 2016). To be accepted by peers, boys become less verbally expressive of feelings other than ones considered appropriate for men—anger, for example. A male who shows sensitivity or vulnerability is likely to be called sissy, girl, or wimp. Peer groups pressure males to be tough, aggressive, and not feminine. The antifemale directive is at least as strong for men of color as for white men (Katz, 2013; Messner, 2007; Sander & Taylor, 2012). As Jackson Katz, a leading researcher on men and masculinity, explains, "in a lot of ways that pressure to conform is more acute among men whose power and identity are under threat in the real world from things like racism and growing economic inequality" (quoted in Katz, 2013).

Not being like a girl means learning to "suck it up." Youths of both sexes engage in sports and sustain injuries, yet males are less likely than females to report pain or symptoms of injuries, including life-threatening brain injuries (Katz, 2013; Lindgren & Lélièvre, 2009; Reiner, 2016).

> **MARK**
>
> *Being a man means being strong and able to take care of yourself without whining or asking for help. Guys learn early not to be sissies. A kid who cries when the ball hits him will be called a girl. You learn or you don't have friends. It's not a big deal, just how it is.*

Be Successful   This is the second requirement for men. From boyhood through the teen years, boys are expected to be successful at sports and other competitive activities. Sports train boys to compete and be aggressive in an effort to win (Kimmel, 2013; Messner, 2007; Messner & Sabo, 2006). As adults, men are expected to compete to achieve status in their professions, to "make it."

The theme of success translates into not just being good at what you do but being better than others, being most valuable player (MVP) rather than just another player, being more powerful than your friends, pulling in a bigger salary than your colleagues, and having a more expensive home and car than your neighbors. Many men today, like Aaron, say that being a good provider is the primary requirement for manhood—an internalized requirement that appears to cut across lines of race and economic class.

Yet supporting a family financially may not be a realistic goal for all men in the present era. In 2009, the height of the recent recession in the United States, one in five men didn't have jobs. Seven years later in 2016, while 10% of college-educated white men are not working, almost 25% of white men without a college degree are unemployed (Luhby, 2016). These hardships are compounded for some men by racial inequality, as African-American and Latino men continue to face higher rates of unemployment than white men (Blackwell, 2014; Miller, 2015a).

Men who are not in the paid labor force have to find other ways of focusing their lives and defining themselves. A record number of out-of-work fathers are caring for children: 32% regularly care for children under 15 years of age and 16% are primary caregivers for preschool children (Livingston, 2014; Stonington, 2011). In his commentary, Steve expresses some anger about the breadwinner expectation.

AARON

The one thing I know for sure is that a man takes care of his family. My dad had no respect—zero—for his cousin who had to go on unemployment and then got a job but didn't earn enough to support his family. My dad called him "lazy," "no 'count," and "freeloader." The whole reason I'm majoring in business is because students who graduate from the business school have higher starting salaries and higher salaries down the line.

STEVE

I am sick of hearing about "male privilege." Where is it? That's what I'd like to know. I'm expected to pay for dates; girls get a free ride. I have to pay a cover charge to get into a bar; ladies' nights are freebies for girls. If the draft comes back, I could be drafted and shipped to a war; women aren't subject to the draft. I have to get a job and make money; a woman can do that, but she doesn't have to. So tell me where male privilege is in all of this.

Be Aggressive   A third injunction for masculinity is to be aggressive. Boys and men are expected to take stands, be tough, and not run from confrontations. Many boys first learn this lesson in sports as coaches psych teams up with demands that they "make the other team hurt, hurt, hurt" or "make them bleed." Of course, sometimes the other team makes you hurt, and here again, sports teach masculinity by telling boys they have to "be tough" and they have to "play through the pain."

Media fuel ideals of extreme masculinity such as the oversized, muscled male figures in video games and the TV characters who are dropped into wilderness locales and must forage and rely on survival techniques. These images of "real men" lead many young boys to decide they have to toughen up to make it (Brown, Lamb, & Tappan, 2009). A recent study (Vokey, Tefft, & Tysianczny, 2013) of advertising images in magazines targeted at men, such as *Fortune*, *Field & Stream*, *Playboy*, and *Game Informer*, found that men are most often portrayed as "hyper-masculine"—violent, tough, sexually aggressive, and dangerous.

Be Sexual   The fourth element of masculinity is to be interested in sex—all the time, any time. The more partners a man has and the more casually he treats them, the more of a stud he is. Cornell West (2007) notes that for black males, sexuality is particularly associated with a masculine identity and with being powerful. A man who doesn't want a lot of sex with a lot of women may find his manhood questioned by other men (Kimmel, 2008, 2013).

The pressure to be highly sexual with women is problematic for many men. Those who identify as gay, bisexual, or trans may not be interested in sex with women, and a number of younger men report that they do not want constant casual sex. National surveys (Schalet, 2011, 2012) report that romantic relationships matter to many young men, and that 40% of men between 15 and 19 have not had sex because they are waiting for the right relationship. For men who aren't into hooking up, peer pressure to measure up to the stud image can be very uncomfortable.

Be Self-Reliant   Many men feel that a "real man" depends on himself, not others. Both physically and emotionally, men are expected to be self-sufficient.

DEVON

Black men face their own issues with masculinity. You have to present yourself as manly and powerful. If you don't get that down, you won't be seen as a man by any other black men. For black men, being a man also means knowing that you're expected to be violent, not to support your family, and to know everything about music and sports. That's what whites expect, and they put that on me all the time. But black women are looking for men who will stand true—be strong and be there for them all the time. So what it means to be a black man depends on whether you look from a white or black perspective.

Embody and Transcend Traditional Views of Masculinity

The sixth theme highlights the confusing messages about masculinity that confront many boys and men today. In his commentary, Chris expresses his frustration with the paradoxical expectations to be a "real man" in traditional ways and simultaneously to defy traditional views of men.

CHRIS

It's really frustrating to be a man today. My girlfriend wants me to open up and show my feelings and talk about them and stuff like that. But the guys on the team get on my case whenever I show any feelings other than about winning a game. I'm supposed to be sensitive and not. I'm supposed to keep my feelings to myself and not. I'm supposed to open doors for girls and pay for dates but then respect them as equals. A lot of times it feels like a no-win situation.

For many males, a primary source of pressure to be conventionally masculine is other boys and, later, men who enforce the masculine code (Kimmel, 2013; Messner, 2005; Sexton, 2016). At the same time, many men feel other pressures—often from romantic partners, female friends, sisters, and mothers—to be sensitive and emotionally open and to be full partners in relationships. It's daunting to try to be both traditionally masculine and not traditionally masculine.

Some counselors believe that men's struggles to live up to social ideals of masculinity have produced an epidemic of male depression, substance abuse, and stress (The Toll of Toxic Sexism, 2016). Because masculine socialization emphasizes emotional control and self-reliance, many men who are depressed or stressed are unwilling to seek help (Freed & Freed, 2012, p. 36). Men are four times more likely to take their own lives than women and account for nearly 80% of suicides in the United States (Centers for Disease Control and Prevention, 2015).

The first five themes of masculinity clearly reflect gender socialization in early life and form a blueprint for being a man. Yet, the sixth theme points out the contradictions between traditional and emerging views of masculinity. Individual men have options for how they define and embody masculinity in an era where gender is in flux.

Growing Up Feminine

What does it mean to be a woman in America in the twenty-first century? Two quite different narratives of femininity coexist today. One suggests that women are liberated from traditional roles to have careers, enjoy egalitarian marriages with partners who share in homemaking and child care, and raise amazing children; in short, they can "have it all" (Sandberg, 2013; Wood, 2010).

Simultaneously, a very different narrative tells women they may be able to get jobs, but fewer than one in five women will be given opportunities to advance to the highest levels of professional life. The 2016 *Fortune 500* list has fewer companies headed by female CEOs than in preceding years; women currently hold a mere 4.2% of the top positions in the largest U.S. corporations (Zarya, 2016). Additionally, most women continue to be paid less than their male counterparts, a trend that is consistent across occupations (American Association of University Women, 2016). When compared to white men's earnings, Asian-American women average 85%, white women average 76%, African-American women average 64%, and Latinas average 54%.

Not only do women earn less than men doing comparable work, but women's professional success is often additionally undermined by workplace policies that don't accommodate their family responsibilities. The gender pay gap grows if women become mothers and continues to grow as women age (American Association of University Women, 2016; Slaughter, 2013; Williams & Dempsey, 2014). Moreover, the gender pay gap is wider in particular industries—for example, in 2015, female financial managers' earnings averaged just 65% of that of their male counterparts (American Association of University Women, 2016).

Prevailing images of women are conflicting and confusing, as the commentaries by Jessica, Anika, Bonita, Emily, Kimberly, and Maria demonstrate. We can identify five themes in current views of femininity and womanhood.

JESSICA

Hungry. That's what being a woman means to me. I am hungry all of the time. Either I'm dieting, or I'm throwing up because I ate too much. I am scared to death of being fat, and I'm just not made to be thin. I gain weight just by smelling food. I think about food all the time—wanting it but being afraid to eat, eating but feeling guilty. It's a no-win situation. I'm obsessed, and I know it, but I can't help it. How can I not think about my weight all the time, when every magazine, every movie, every television show I see screams at me that I have to be thin to be desirable?

Appearance Still Counts   This is the first theme. As Jessica notes in her commentary, women are still judged by their looks. To be desirable is to be pretty, slim, and well dressed. The focus on appearance begins in the early years of life with gift catalogs for children that feature makeup kits, adornments for hair, and even wigs, so girls learn early to spend time and effort on looking good. Teen magazines for girls are saturated with ads for makeup, diet aids, and hair products. Romance novels send the message that popularity depends on being rich, thin, fashionable, and sexy (Afful & Ricciardelli, 2015; Johnson, 2010, 2011; Wolf, 2006). In stores, women see clothes they are encouraged to buy on mannequins that are size 4, 2, or 0. Given the relentless pressure to be thin and beautiful, it's not surprising that disorders related to body image have become so common that they are considered customary in young women (McRobbie, 2009; Spar, 2013). The makeover genre of television programs features a person, most often a woman, who looks ordinary when viewers first see her and who is then made over to be physically stunning. To maintain the new "improved" image, she must become an active consumer, spending her time and money on products and services that make her acceptable. Consumption is unending and never sufficient to secure lasting success (Johnson, 2011; Spar, 2013). Women athletes may feel special pressure to look and act feminine. Women athletes in our classes tell us that, if they don't look feminine, others assume they are lesbians simply because they are strong and athletically skilled. To assert their femininity, female Olympic competitors increasingly pose nude or nearly nude in *Sports Illustrated*, *FHM* (*For Him Magazine*), and *Playboy* (Gilenstam, Karp, & Henriksson-Larsen, 2008; Meân & Kassing, 2008; Padawer, 2016).

Be Sensitive and Caring   A majority of women feel they are expected to be nice, deferential, and helpful and to care about and for others. From assuming primary responsibility for young children to taking care of elderly, sick, and disabled relatives, women do the preponderance of hands-on caring.

In addition, many girls learn that being outspoken and smart does not win them prizes in the quest to be seen as feminine. Males who take charge are praised and admired, but females who take charge risk being called the new b-word: bossy (Sandberg & Chávez, 2014). Girls are encouraged to soften their opinions and not to stand up to boys at school because they fear being perceived as a bitch (Bennett, Ellison, & Ball, 2010; Helgeson, 2016). The bottom line is that, for many girls, adolescence is the start of shifting attention from developing and asserting identity to pleasing others.

ANIKA

Males are favored over females in Indian culture. It is custom for a girl's family to give a dowry to a man who marries the girl to make it worth his while. As a result, many poor families in India kill a newborn baby if it is female and rejoice if the baby is male. When my third sister was born, my great grandmother expressed her disappointment that we had no boys and so many girls.

Negative Treatment by Others   This is a third persistent theme of femininity for women. Male students in our classes sometimes challenge this as a theme of femininity. They say women are treated better than men. They point out that women—but not men—get free drinks at "Ladies' Night," they get their meals paid for by dates, and they can cry their way out of speeding tickets. However, these minor advantages don't compensate for significant disadvantages such as being more likely to be sexually assaulted, live in poverty, and face job and salary discrimination.

Devaluation and mistreatment of females is pervasive in Western cultures. The Web teems with sites that feature sexual assaults on women. Popular music refers to women as "bitches" and "hos" and routinely shows men abusing them. Mainstream video games allow players to earn points by assaulting or killing women. Candidates running for office openly describe women—female candidates, news anchors, winners of beauty contests, the wives of other candidates—are unattractive, overweight, or pushy. Fat jokes and derogatory remarks about women's appearance in popular culture are common, reinforcing the value placed on women's appearance and normalizing negative treatment of them (Afful & Ricciardelli, 2016).

Devaluation of femininity is not only built into cultural views but typically is internalized by individuals, including women. Negative treatment of females begins early and can be especially intense in girls' peer groups (Wilier, 2011). Girls can be highly critical of other girls who are not pretty, thin, and otherwise feminine, as Emily's comment and the Exploring Gendered Lives feature on page 136 demonstrate.

Emily is right when she says that sugar and spice is not a full description of girls. Research shows that many young girls engage in relational aggression toward other girls (Simmons, 2011). As the term implies, *relational aggression* involves attacking others using social, rather than physical, strategies. It takes forms such as spreading hurtful rumors, excluding a peer from groups, and encouraging others to turn against a particular girl. Social media provide abundant new ways to express social aggression. For instance, girls can post photos of their parties on Instagram or Facebook so that those who were not invited are aware of their exclusion (Simmons, 2011).

Relational aggression is not exclusive to girls—boys also engage in relational aggression—and additional factors such as popularity, confidence, and social competence can encourage this form of aggression (Loflin & Barry, 2016; McQuade, Achufusi, Shoulberg, & Murray-Close, 2014). However, studies suggest that girls are more likely to aggress indirectly than their male peers. One reason appears to be that, even at young ages, girls understand that

---

■ EXPLORING GENDERED LIVES ■

Sisterhood?

Sororities claim to be sisterhoods—communities in which unrelated women become caring sisters to one another. Catherine Mitchell disagrees. In an article penned for the *Atlantic*, she writes about being shamed and excluded because of her weight. Citing research that correlates poor self-esteem and disordered eating with Greek life, Mitchell writes that sororities, which "claim to have been formed for the specific purpose of empowering university women are sometimes having the opposite effect. Instead of being retreats from a patriarchal and sexist world, they can

propagate the outdated hierarchies of the past" (Mitchell, 2013, n.p.).

And Mitchell is not alone. In 2007, 23 members of DePauw University's chapter of Delta Zeta were dropped from the sorority for failing to meet standards of "social image, appearance, and weight" (Adler, 2007, p. 47). The only black member of the sorority was ousted, as were two of the three Asian members, and all members who wore a size larger than eight. Only 12 of the original 35 members were allowed to stay. However, only half of those—six women—chose to stay. The other six left to show solidarity with their ousted sisters.

TAKE A STAND: Do you think sororities have a right to exclude girls who don't meet a specific physical ideal?

---

they are supposed to be nice to everyone, so they fear that being overtly mean or competitive would lead to disapproval or punishment (McQuade et al., 2014; Simmons, 2004). Instead of learning how to work through feelings of anger, dislike, and so forth, young girls learn to express those feelings only indirectly.

Be Superwoman   This is a fourth theme emerging in cultural expectations of women (Sandberg, 2013; Slaughter, 2015; Spar, 2013). Kimberly's exhilaration (see box below) over the choices open to her is tempered by Maria's impression that women feel they are required to try to have it all. It's not enough to be just a homemaker and mother or just a career woman. Many young women today seem to feel they are expected to do it all.

KIMBERLY

My mother and I talk about women, and she tells me that she's glad she didn't have so many options. She says it was easier for her than it is for me because she knew what she was supposed to do—marry and raise a family—and she didn't have to go through the identity crisis that I do. I see her point, yet I kind of like having alternatives. I know I wouldn't be happy investing my total self in a home and family. I just have to be out doing things in the world. But my best friend really wants to do that. She's marrying a guy who wants that, too, so as soon as they've saved enough to be secure, they plan for her to quit work to raise a family. I know someone else who says she just flat out doesn't want to marry. She wants to be a doctor, and she doesn't think she can do that plus take care of a home and family, so she wants to stay single. I don't really know yet if I will or won't have kids, but it's nice to know I can choose to go either way. My mother couldn't.

| MARIA |

Women are expected to want to climb the business ladder, yet they are also expected to pick up the kids after school, make dinner, help with homework, and be a loving wife. I do not want a career that will ruin my family life or a family life that will ruin my career. How am I supposed to pick between my personal life and my career goals? Why is it that women are expected to sacrifice their careers or be superwomen who do it all but men don't have to be that way?

Female students talk with us frequently about the tension they feel trying to figure out how to have a rich family life and a successful career. The physical and psychological toll on women who try to do it all is well documented, and it shows no signs of abating (Coontz, 2013; Kantor, 2012; Spar, 2013; Traister, 2012; Williams & Dempsey, 2014). Anne-Marie Slaughter, law professor and leader of a major think tank, has recently labeled this problem *unfinished business*, which refers to the need to balance career and family demands in ways that make gender equality a reality (Slaughter, 2015).

There Is No Single Meaning of Feminine Anymore   This is the final theme of femininity in the current era. This theme reflects all the others and the contradictions inherent in them. A woman who is assertive and ambitious in a career is likely to meet with approval, disapproval, anger, and curiosity from some people and to be applauded by others. At the same time, a woman who chooses to stay home while her children are young will be criticized by some women and men, envied by others, and respected by still others. Perhaps, as Kimberly suggests in her commentary, there are many ways to be feminine, and we can respect all of them.

Prevailing themes of femininity in Western culture reveal both constancy and change. Traditional expectations of attractiveness and caring for others persist, as does the greater likelihood of negative treatment by others. Yet, today there are options that allow women with different talents, interests, and identities to define themselves in diverse ways and to chart life courses that suit them as individuals.

EXPLORING GENDERED LIVES

Careers for Women: Gendered, Raced, and Classed

What do gender, race, and class have to do with expectations about working? In-depth interviews revealed that expectations about who works full-time are shaped by gender, race, and socioeconomic class (Damaske, 2011). Roughly half of women who grew up in working-class white or Latino families expected to work, whereas nearly all working-class black women expected to work in the paid labor market. The clear majority of middle-class white, Asian, African-American, and Latina families expect to work continually.

TAKE A STAND: In what ways do you think your race and ethnicity shape your expectations regarding working outside of the home?

Growing Up outside Conventional Genders

Not every person grows up identifying with socially prescribed gender, sex, and sexual orientation. For people who do not identify with and perform normative gender identity and heterosexuality, growing up can be particularly difficult. Homophobia is often used to police gender—pressuring girls to conform to femininity and boys to masculinity, and threatening discrimination or violence if they do not (Ehrensaft, 2016; Iszler, 2016; Nutt, 2015).

Social isolation also greets many people who are gender nonconforming or trans (Boylan, 2013a, 2013b). They find themselves trapped in a society that conflates male, men, and masculinity, as well as female, women, and femininity. It's difficult to find in-between spaces, ways to blur rigid lines, and options to the binary choices of male/female, man/woman, masculine/feminine, and straight/gay. Consider this blog post from a 17-year-old (Kellerman, 2012):

> I'm CJ, formerly known as Chana. I'm also "genderqueer," which, in my case, means that I feel part-female and part-male. I'm not sure yet whether I will transition or not.... My mother requested to list me on Facebook as her daughter, but I didn't feel that that was totally right, but neither was "son." But there was no other choice. I either have to be a brother or a sister to my sisters on Facebook. And that's not me. It's troubling that I can't be Facebook friends with my family and correctly identify my relationships with them, because according to Facebook those relationships don't exist. Or maybe I don't exist. How strange is that?

For people who do not fit neatly into conventional sex and gender categories, it's hard to find role models and equally difficult to find acceptance from family, peers, and society. Trans people also may be frustrated by others who hold wildly inaccurate assumptions about their identities. Of the students who have studied gender and communication with us over the years, a few have volunteered commentaries on growing up outside of conventional gender roles. Ben, Zena, and Mike's commentaries appear on this page and the next.

BEN

What it means to be a man depends totally on whether you're gay or straight. I'm gay— knew that since I was 9 or 10. And being gay is hell for a teenager. Other guys, the straight ones, called me names all through middle school and high school—fag, queer, girlie. It didn't matter that I was big and toned and good at baseball. They totally excluded me because I was gay.

Until very recently, transgender and intersex people seldom made their identities or struggles public. That's changing as more and more people who don't fit conventional categories demand to be recognized and accepted on their own terms. One sign of changing attitudes toward transgender people is evolving school policies and laws. Some states and local districts have passed explicit antidiscrimination policies to ensure trans students' access to school facilities, including locker rooms and bathrooms. Many colleges have added gender identity and expression to their nondiscrimination policies and passed gender-neutral housing policies. While federal law has not yet recognized gender identity and expression as a protected category, existing laws banning sex discrimination have been interpreted by the courts to protect trans and gender-nonconforming students (National Center for Transgender Equality, 2015).

> ## ZENA
>
> *I wear a tie always and a dress never. If I go to a doctor, I'm labeled "female," but in everyday life, most people think I'm a "male." The problem is, neither of those labels is right. Neither fits me. I'm both or neither or maybe something that is totally different than those stupid categories. Sexually, I'm attracted to both "males" and "females," although more often to "females." I have no interest in girlie things, but I'm sensitive to others and a very caring person. All I can say is that I'm Zena, and that's a name I gave myself.*

Individuals who don't fit into conventional categories for sex, gender, and sexual orientation face challenges that most gender-conforming people can't imagine. For those of you who fit comfortably in the conventional gender system, imagine this: You visit a doctor and learn that you are actually a different sex than you have believed yourself to be and than you identify with. If you identify as a woman, you discover that genetically you are male. If you identify as a man, you learn that genetically you are female. Your physiology and/or anatomy doesn't match your self-concept. Everything from how you dress to whom you date to which bathroom you can use suddenly becomes an issue that you have to negotiate.

> ## MIKE
>
> *I have no idea what it means to be a man. I've never felt I was one, never identified with men. As a kid, I liked to dress in my mother's clothes until my dad caught me and beat the—out of me! I still identify more with women, and I think that I was meant to be a woman. Growing up looking like a male but feeling like a female meant that I didn't belong anywhere, didn't fit with anyone. It's better now that I'm in college and have found some people like me, but there was nobody in my rural Southern hometown!*

Stay with this hypothetical situation. Would you want to have hormone treatments and surgery so that your body was more consistent with your gender identity? The surgery is expensive and painful and hormonal treatments can have side effects. Or would you continue living as you have, looking and acting in accordance with your gender identity while knowing that by medical criteria you are actually a different sex? Or would you choose, instead, to change how you dress, style your hair, move, speak, and so forth in order to perform the gender that traditionally aligns with your genetic sex?

SUMMARY

Young children get first ideas about identity as they interact with parents and siblings who often see them and treat them as gendered. Additional messages about gender come as children watch boy characters on television engaging in more adventurous, rugged play than girl characters. They see cereal boxes that feature girls with dolls and boys with guns. They play with peers who, because of their own socialization, exert pressure to conform to gender norms.

But socialization is not as deterministic as it may seem. Clearly, we are influenced by the expectations of our culture, family, and peers. Yet these expectations endure only to the extent that individuals and institutions sustain them. Through our own communication and the ways we act, we reinforce or challenge existing views of gender. As we do so, we contribute to forming social views that affect the extent to which each of us can define ourselves and live our lives on our own terms.

KEY TERMS

The following terms are defined in this chapter on the pages indicated, as well as in alphabetical order in the book's glossary, which begins on page 261. The text's companion website also provides interactive flash cards to help you learn these terms and the concepts they represent. You can access the site at www.cengagebrain.com.

ego boundaries 139   *gender identity 136*

GENDER ONLINE

1. Visit Jazz Jenning's Purple Rainbow Foundation at **http://www.transkidspurplerainbow .org.** Statistics about diverse family forms are available from the Census Bureau at **http://www.census.gov/**

2. Check out the #StillABoy Instagram campaign, available at **https://www.instagram .com/stillaboy_/**

3. Online search terms: *father role, feminine socialization, masculine socialization, trans identity.*

REFLECTION, DISCUSSION, AND ACTION

1. How did your parents and/or stepparents model gender? Does your own embodiment of gender reflect their influences?

2. Analyze how your ego boundaries work in one particular relationship in your life. How do your ego boundaries both enhance and constrain that relationship?

3. We opened this chapter by asking you to write what it means to you to be the sex and gender that you are today in the United States. How does your response echo or differ from themes in the responses of student commentaries presented in this chapter? How does your response differ from or contradict themes in the commentaries presented in this chapter?

RECOMMENDED RESOURCES

1. *Tough Guise, 2* (Katz, 2013). Media Education Foundation, 26 Center Street, Northampton, MA. This film offers a critical perspective on socialization that links traditional masculinity with aggression and violence. It is a disturbing video and an important one.

2. Laura Bates, (2016). *Girl Up*. Praised as "hard-hitting," "hilarious," and "bold," Bates tackles body image, media representations, sexual harassment, and other issues related to young women and contemporary feminism.

3. Michael Messner is a scholar who studies gender, particularly as it relates to athletics. Visit his blog at *Huffington Post*: **http://www.huffingtonpost.com**

8

Education is the most powerful weapon which you can use to change the world.
—NELSON MANDELA

Gendered Education: Communication in Schools

Knowledge Challenge:

- What gendered challenges do students face in schools?
- How has Title IX affected college athletics?
- How influential are gender and economic standing on students' academic success?
- What is invisible hand discrimination?

America's schools are failing boys. Fewer men than women graduate from high school, college, or graduate school because schools are hostile environments for boys and men.	America's schools are failing girls. Despite higher grades and graduation rates, they get less prestigious jobs and make less money than men because schools don't prepare them to succeed.

Which of the above claims seems more accurate to you? If you believe schools are biased against boys, there's evidence to support your belief. Particularly in the early grades, the demands of school—sit in your seat, be quiet and still, focus on lessons—frustrate many young boys whose developmental stage makes it difficult for them to be calm and to concentrate.

Or perhaps you think that schools discriminate against girls. If so, there's evidence to support that belief too. Persisting biases discourage women from studying science, math, and technology, and there is less support for female athletes than male athletes. It's also the case that education confers greater economic benefit on men than on women.

The two claims advance a false dichotomy by pitting boys against girls and suggesting one is better or worse off in an absolute sense. In actuality, students of all genders—including gender-nonconforming students—face challenges in schools starting with kindergarten and going through professional degree programs.

In this chapter, we will explore how schools support—or fail to support—students of all sexes and genders. We will consider expectations and pressures that are based in academic structures and practices, athletics, and peer cultures.

Second, we will more briefly discuss gendered expectations and pressures that faculty face. As we will see, although schools in the United States no longer discriminate blatantly based on sex, gendered biases and issues continue to infuse educational institutions.

As you read this chapter, keep in mind that a great deal is at stake. Schools do more than instruct us in various subjects. They are also powerful agents of gender socialization. They teach us what each sex is expected to be and to do and which careers are appropriate for women and men.

Gendered Expectations and Pressures Facing Students

To understand the range of gendered dynamics facing students today, we'll examine academics, athletics, and peer cultures.

Academics

All students encounter gendered expectations and pressures in schools from kindergarten through graduate and professional school. We'll consider gendered expectations affecting boys and men, girls and women, who are both cisgender and trans. We will also note the ways in which economic standing affects academic success.

Boys and Men   Compared to girls, young boys tend to be more restless, have more physical energy, and have less impulse control. In addition, boys' verbal skills mature later than those of girls, so young boys may be understandably frustrated by the strong emphasis on reading and writing in the early years of school.

These developmental differences make it difficult for many young boys to adjust to school contexts where they are supposed to sit quietly, follow instructions, and focus on teachers' lesson plans (Garloch, 2009; Sax, 2016a; Whitmire, 2011). In other words, many elementary classrooms may not be boy friendly, which can render the early years of school a time of frustration and often of failure for boys (Sommers, 2013; Tyre, 2009). Elementary teachers may reward girl students for their good classroom manners by giving them higher grades than their test scores alone would justify (Cornwell, Mustard, & Van Parys, 2013).

The challenges boys face in elementary grades may affect their success later in school. More women than men attend college and pursue graduate study. Currently, women comprise 57% of undergraduate enrollment and earn 60% of master's and 52% of doctoral degrees in the United States (Mangan, 2012).

Personal choices also affect academic performance and success. From elementary school through college, boys and men spend less time preparing for classes and more time on leisure activities such as sports, video games, and watching television than female students (Sax, 2016b). Choices of how to spend time—studying or relaxing—influence academic accomplishment.

Girls and Women   Despite much effort to eliminate discrimination against women, not all barriers have disappeared. Women still face prejudice in particular fields such as technology and natural sciences. In addition, what enables girls' and women's success in school may not prepare them for success in professional life.

■ EXPLORING GENDERED LIVES ■

Single-Sex Educational Programs

Would single-sex schools or programs solve some of the problems we've discussed? If there were no girls in reading classes, teachers might be able to give young boys the help they need to develop reading skills. Might courses in science and computer technology be developed to tap into girls' and women's interests so that they are more likely to enter STEM fields? Would faculty be more likely to mentor female students at schools that don't admit male students?

From elementary school through college, heterosexual males and females are more likely to make academics a priority in single-sex schools. If students aren't focused on impressing members of the other sex, won't they study more without worrying about seeming like nerds? The facts on graduates of women's schools are persuasive: Although women's colleges produce only about 5% of all female college graduates, a disproportionate number of women in the U.S. Congress and running top businesses graduated from women's colleges (Salome, 2007; Scelfo, 2006; Spielhagen, 2013). When the citadel was all male, its graduation rate was 70%—much higher than the 48% national average (Citadel, 2017).

But critics of single-sex education argue that sex-segregated education isn't the answer to gender inequities in schools. They think a better solution is to make sure that schools support all students equally so that students of all sexes and genders have the same educational opportunities and support. Also, single-sex schools tend to be private, too expensive for most families, and often exclude trans and gender nonconforming students. Thus, although single-sex schools may benefit cisgender children from wealthy families, they are unlikely to help the majority of students (Rivers & Barnett, 2011; Spielhagen, 2013).

TAKE A STAND: What do you see as the advantages and disadvantages of single-sex schools? Would you want to attend one?

The long-standing belief that females have less innate ability in math and science erects barriers to women's study of science and math, not to mention barriers to careers in those fields. But the belief that girls are innately less gifted at science and math is not well supported. In fact, girls frequently outperform boys on a standard science test administered to students in developed countries. Girls outscore boys in a majority of countries, including China, Finland, Ireland, Sweden, Uruguay, Argentina, and Indonesia, whereas boys outperform girls in a minority of countries, including Canada, Chile, Peru, and the United States (Fairfield, 2013). The fact that girls in most countries score better than boys on science tests raises doubt about significant innate sex differences in scientific aptitude or ability.

Yet, in the United States, females progressively drop out of math and science curricula as they advance in school. One reason is persisting bias in the United States against female students in math and science (Riegle-Crumb & Humphries, 2012; Why STEM Fields Still Don't Draw More Women, 2012). This bias is manifest in various ways such as an advisor counseling a female not to take an advanced math course because it is very rigorous, a physics teacher who never calls on female students, and assigning female students to marketing and male students to engineering on Robotics teams (Why STEM Fields Still Don't Draw More Women, 2012).

There is also some faculty bias against female students in science. Researchers asked science professors to review applications from students seeking a lab assistant job (Moss-Racusin, Dovidio, Brescoll, Graham, & Handelsman, 2012). The applications were identical except that they were randomly attributed to either a male or a female student. Science professors who believed the applicant was male were more likely to hire the student, propose a higher salary, and offer mentoring than professors who believed the identical application was submitted by a female. In a similar study, researchers at the University of Pennsylvania emailed professors with identical requests for mentoring meetings, but the email authors were assigned different names, such as Brad Anderson, Lamar Washington, Juanita Martinez, Sonali Desai, and Mei Chen. There were large disparities in response rates. Women and minorities were significantly less likely to receive a response or a positive response, and women and minorities were least likely to get a positive response from professors at private schools in fields that led to lucrative positions (Vedantam, 2014).

SCARLETT

I always liked science. Right from the first grade, it was my favorite subject. The older I got, though, the more I felt odd in my science classes. Especially in college after the required courses, I felt odd. Sometimes, I was the only woman in a class. I was majoring in early education and just took science electives for fun. That changed when I had a woman professor in a course about unsolved problems in biology. She was really good, and so was the course, but to me the main thing was seeing a woman teaching science. That's when I decided to change my major and become a science teacher.

Another reason young women may drop out of math and science courses is stereotypes of both the fields and the sexes. There is a precipitous drop in the number of girls seeking training in computer science as they move from middle school to high school (Williams & Dempsey, 2014). It's not coincidental that this is precisely the time at which efforts to meet gender ideals peak. In other words, as they pass through puberty and become more aware of themselves as gendered and sexed beings, many young women shy away from being geeky or seeming overly smart. In addition, women place a higher priority than men on helping others and making the world better, which are not goals many associate with careers in technology and math (Sander, 2012). And yet the health and growth of society depend deeply on a work force skilled in sciences, math, and technology.

To address this problem, a number of schools have begun to revise curricula to emphasize the social goods that science serves, which makes the fields more attractive to women students ("Why STEM," 2012). In 2014, University of California, Berkeley, launched a new Ph.d. minor in engineering focused on designing cost-effective solutions to problems plaguing low-income communities. When that program was announced, 50% of the enrollees were women (Nilsson, 2015). Similarly, women make up 74% of students in MIT's D-Lab, which develops "technologies that improve the lives of people living in poverty" (Nilsson, 2015, p. A17), and Princeton's student chapter of Engineers Without Borders has a 70% female board (Nilsson, 2015). When engineering is tied to social goods, women are interested.

In addition to gendered biases in science, technology, engineering, and mathematics (STEM), girls and women face other challenges in academic environments. The very behaviors that facilitate girls' success in school, particularly the early grades, may work against them later in life. The praise girls earn for completing work, following directions, being neat, and minding the teacher don't teach girls to think and act independently, take risks, and consider when it might be useful to bend or break rules, all of which can facilitate career success.

ALLIE

My grandmother is really smart, but she wasn't able to go to college. Her father sent her four brothers to college, but he said girls didn't need an education. When she was 34, her husband died and she had three kids to support on her own. It surely would have been easier on her if she'd had a degree so she was qualified for a good job instead of the one she had to take.

Another form of academic gender bias is curricula that misrepresent or erase women and gender-nonconforming people. Consider how history is taught. Accounts of wars focus on battles and military leaders. Seldom noted are the contributions of women either on the battlefields or at home. Who kept families intact and food on the table while men fought? Who manufactured supplies for troops on the front? Chronicles of important events such as the civil rights movement focus on male leaders' speeches and press conferences and obscure the ways in which women contributed to the movements. We are taught about the leadership of Stokely Carmichael, Malcolm X, and the Reverend Martin Luther King Jr., but few of us learn about Ella Baker's pivotal work in organizing neighborhoods in support of civil rights (Parker, 2006; Ransby, 2003), Pauli Murray's courageous defiance of discrimination against women and people of color, or the activism that took place in African-American beauty shops during the Jim Crow era (Gill, 2010; Scott-Bell, 2016).

EXPLORING GENDERED LIVES

Name That (Wo)man

In the following columns, name 10 famous women and 10 famous men in U.S. history made significant contributions to economic, political, scientific, or social progress.

Write the names of 10 famous men:

_____

_____

_____

_____

_____

_____

_____

_____

_____

_____

Write the names of 10 famous women:

_____

_____

_____

_____

_____

_____

_____

_____

_____

_____

TAKE A STAND: Compare your experiences generating names for each column. What does this comparison tell you about gender bias in curricula?

If women are included in curricula, they tend to fall into two categories. First, there are women who fit traditional stereotypes of women. For example, most of us learned that Betsy Ross sewed the first American flag and Florence Nightingale nursed soldiers. A second group of women included in curricula distinguished themselves on men's terms and in masculine contexts. Mother Jones, for example, was a powerful union organizer, Amelia Earhart flew as well as men, and Annie Oakley could outshoot most men. Women in this category tend to be represented as exceptional cases—as atypical of women in general. Yet, throughout history, women have made extraordinary contributions to political, social, educational, and domestic life. Women such as Mary White Ovington, Jessie Daniel Ames, and Myrtilla Miner, who changed the world on their own terms, remain invisible in most history curricula (Arneson, 2014; Spitzack & Carter, 1987).

Similarly, gender-nonconforming people are rarely mentioned in curricula; if they are, their gender identities are generally obscured or erased. For example, Joan of Arc is generally remembered as a saint and military leader. Often overlooked is Joan of Arc's embrace of a masculine appearance, which was the primary charge for which she was sentenced to death (Feinberg, 1997). In another example, Pauli Murray is recognized for her contributions to civil rights and feminism, but her struggles as "a black gender-nonconforming woman who explored hormonal masculinization in the 1940s" (Stryker & Bettcher, 2016, p. 9) are seldom acknowledged.

Historical epochs tend to be taught in terms of their effects on men while neglecting their impact on women, people of color, and other historically disenfranchised communities. For instance, textbooks represent the Renaissance as a period of rebirth and progress in human life because it expanded men's options. The Renaissance is *not* taught in terms of its impact in reducing the status and opportunities of most women, nor its fueling European conquest and colonization of Africa, Asia, and the Americas. The Enlightenment is taught as a time when reason ascended as the surest route to truth and human progress. The Enlightenment is *not* taught as a time when women and people of color were considered inferior because they were assumed to have limited capacity to reason. The Industrial Revolution is taught as a time when mechanization of production systems enabled mass production, which propelled factories as the primary workplace for men. The Industrial Revolution is *not* represented in terms of how it changed women's lives, work, and relationships with their husbands and children.

Even science, which we might assume is a highly objective field, has gender stereotypes that can distort knowledge (Rosser, 2012). For instance, until recently science textbooks routinely misrepresented the process of human reproduction by describing *vigorous* sperm as *invading* the passively waiting egg. When research proved that the egg is actually quite active in controlling which sperm it allows to enter, many science books revised their description of the process (Hammonds, 1998). As this example shows, gender stereotypes can be corrected when people heed evidence that disproves them. For this reason, curricula, including those in science, are less gender biased than in the past.

As we have seen, sexism in education intersects with other forms of discrimination: racism, classism, and heterosexism. Not just any males are presented as the standard: White, heterosexual, able-bodied, and middle- and upper-class men continue to be depicted as the norm in textbooks. How often have you studied contributions of lesbians, gays, trans people, or people with disabilities? How frequently did you learn about the lives and contributions of economically disadvantaged people? Have you learned about African Americans in journalism, Asian and Asian-American writers, scientists of Central or Latin-American descent, or African economists? Women, people of color, people with disabilities, and LGBTQ people continue to be underrepresented in educational materials, where the reference point has been and remains white, cisgender, heterosexual, able-bodied, and middle- and upper-class males.

Gender-stereotyped curricular material diminishes education for all students. When schools teach primarily about straight, white, wealthy men and their experiences, perspectives, and accomplishments, students are deprived of understanding the perspectives and contributions of most of the population. On a more personal level, biases in instructional content encourage straight, white, able-bodied, middle-class men to see themselves as able to fulfill high ambitions and affect the course of events and discourage women and minorities from those self-perceptions (Smith, 2004b; "Why STEM," 2012).

LGBTQ Students   Students who identify as lesbian, gay, bisexual, transgender, intersex, or genderqueer also face challenges and discrimination in school settings. Despite some schools' efforts to eliminate barriers to LGBTQ students (Misner, 2014), many schools still have practices and policies that range from unintentionally inequitable to blatantly exclusionary or hostile.

Many of the challenges faced by LGBTQ students stem from the gender binary that infuses schools as well as society overall. The gender binary assumes that people fit neatly and completely into two sex and gender categories, but that isn't the case for everyone. How do gender-segregated bathrooms compromise the rights and safety of trans and genderqueer students? To what extent do women's colleges accommodate trans students? Given that most sports are divided by sex, on which teams should trans athletes compete? Which locker rooms should they use?

The assumption of cisgendered heterosexuality pervades schools as it does in other institutions. Books to teach reading in the first grade often involve a family of characters: Mama Bear, Papa Bear, and Baby Bear. Snow White falls for the cisman Prince Charming. In elementary school, children often make cards for Mother's Day and Father's Day, despite the fact that the traditional nuclear family is no longer the majority family form in the United States (Baxter, 2014). How do such heterosexual, nuclear family models make children with a single parent, or two mothers, or two fathers feel? Novels assigned in literature classes in more advanced grades usually feature heterosexual romances and traditional nuclear families, again proclaiming heterosexuality as normal and right.

The presumption of heterosexuality continues throughout education. The process of assigning roommates in single-sex dormitories assumes students are cisgender and heterosexual. For example, if a transman applies to a university and is required to use his legal name and sex, whether those match his gender identity or not, what are his options in applying for housing and a roommate? Given the persistence of homophobia on campuses, to what extent should gay and lesbian students feel safe in disclosing their sexual orientation to assigned roommates? Should gay or lesbian students be expected to disclose their sexual orientation when straight men and women aren't expected to announce their sexual orientation? Does the student health insurance plan cover the physical and psychological needs of LGBTQ students (DeSantis, 2013)? As these questions demonstrate, the personal experience and identity of students who are gay, lesbian, bisexual, or transgender are at odds with some campus cultures.

> ▼
>
> *Maybe I have just been chased out of too many bathrooms, but gender-segregated bathrooms are the worst! Why do you have to assign it a gender? Especially when so many bathrooms are just one stall. I always have a small amount of anxiety walking into a women's bathroom. It's that moment when I am walking to the stall, or just standing in line, that I find myself trying to make my chest stand out or avoiding eye contact to make it seem like I belong, even though I don't feel like I do. I think most people are concerned with what they do in the stalls, but for me it's what happens before and after that is stressful.*

The unspoken norms of the gender binary and heterosexuality aren't a problem for most students. In fact, most students don't even notice that those norms shape numerous school policies and practices. However, if you aren't a straight, cisgender man or woman, then the disconnect between your identity and the normative practices of educational settings can be a source of discomfort, alienation, and even danger.

Gender Isn't the Whole Story   Before ending this section of the chapter, we should note that academic challenges are not exclusively tied to gender or sexual orientation. The gap between female and male success in schools, while important, is eclipsed by the gap between rich and poor students (Duncan & Murane, 2011; Noah, 2012; Stiglitz, 2012). On standardized tests, the gap between low-income and affluent students' scores has grown by 40% since the 1980s (Tavernise, 2012).

The growing chasm between educational achievement by rich and poor students is due, in large measure, to the greater investments of time and other resources that economically well-off parents make in their children. Affluent parents have the luxury of spending more time reading and talking to children. It's no surprise that children who are immersed in language from birth develop strong language and conceptual skills. Affluent parents also provide their children with enrichments—summer camp, tutors, travel, and SAT preparation classes—that less wealthy parents cannot afford (Brooks, 2012; Noah, 2012). All of those investments in children pay off in schooling where affluent children tend to be more comfortable, better prepared, and, ultimately, more successful.

Athletics

Today's female students enjoy unprecedented opportunities to participate in athletics. In large part, that is due to **Title IX**. There are three basic parts of Title IX as it applies to athletics (Title IX Q & A, 2008; Ware, 2014):

1. Women must be provided an equitable opportunity to participate in sports (not necessarily identical sports but an equal opportunity to play).

2. Colleges must provide female athletes with athletic scholarship dollars proportional to their participation. For instance, if there are 100 male athletes and 50 female athletes at a school that has a $150,000 athletic scholarship budget, then female athletes must receive $50,000 in scholarships.

3. Equal treatment includes more than playing time and scholarship. Schools are also required to provide female and male athletes with equivalent equipment and supplies, practice times, travel and daily allowance, tutoring, coaching, locker rooms and facilities, publicity and promotions, recruitment programs, and support services.

■■■ **EXPLORING GENDERED LIVES** ■■■

Straddling Two Cultures

First-generation college students make up at least 20% (Housel, 2012) of undergraduates in the United States. In addition to negotiating all of the challenges that face other students, first-generation undergraduates often have the extra challenge of learning how to navigate the social context of college life. These students find themselves trying to straddle two cultures—the working-class culture in which they grew up and the middle- to upper-class culture of academic institutions. Consider these examples of disconnects experienced by first-generation college students (Housel, 2012; Stephens, Hamedani, & Destin, 2014):

• Listening to peers talk about upcoming summer vacations or study abroad opportunities, which their families could not afford.

• Going to symphonies and museums, neither of which they had ever attended.
• Going to restaurants that served international foods, which they had never encountered at home.
• Having to rely on advisors more than peers because parents cannot provide advice on other aspects of college life such as which classes to take.

When first-generation college students go home, they often experience a different and equally unsettling set of disconnects:

• Being accused of acting "stuck up" or "too good" for family members.
• Ridiculed for revealing what they have learned at college or for vocabulary that is unfamiliar to family members.
• Feeling resentment from family and friends from primary and secondary school.

TAKE A STAND: If you are a first-generation college student, which of the above experiences are familiar to you? Would you add anything to this list? If you are not a first-generation college student, which of the above experiences can you identify on your campus?

Despite Title IX, the playing field still is not exactly even. Girls who play fierce baseball in elementary school too often are told they can't be on the middle-school or high-school baseball team and are routed instead to softball (Ring, 2013). At the college level, male athletes and coaches of men's teams continue to have more support, financial and otherwise, than female athletes and coaches of women's teams. In addition, male athletes are more likely than female athletes to get academic tutoring and prime schedules and venues for practice.

The National Collegiate Athletic Association (NCAA) is not required to comply with Title IX guidelines. And it doesn't. For each NCAA game a team plays in the men's tournament, that team's conference is awarded over $250,000 plus the same amount each of the next five years. Women's teams get $0 for each game they win. Although some people think that men's teams deserve money because they are moneymakers, women's teams also earn revenue. They are broadcast on ESPN and many of their games sell out (Zimbalist, 2016). Some argue that an emphasis on revenue harms male athletes. Revenue-generating sports—namely, football and men's basketball—absorb 78% of the budget for men's athletics at Division I universities, forcing cuts or program elimination for nonrevenue men's sports like swimming, wrestling, and baseball (Fagan & Cyphers, 2012).

Hartford Courant/Tribune News Service/Getty Images

The NCAA provides substantial monetary awards for men's teams that play in the tournament but does not provide monetary awards for women's teams.

HEATHER

This school claims to go by Title IX, but the support for women athletes doesn't even come close to what men get. The school is fair about the number of women it recruits and funds with scholarships, but that's where the equity stops. The men have tutors who basically babysit them through their classes. We are expected to earn our own grades. They have the best practice times on the field; we get the leftover times. They get more travel allowance than we do, and they get a lot more publicity.

Some colleges and universities use deceptive practices to appear to comply with Title IX while actually undermining gender equity in athletics (Thomas, 2011; Zimbalist, 2016). Some schools require women who are cross-country runners to join the indoor and outdoor track teams, which allow the schools to count each runner three times in tallying up the number of women athletes it has. Some Division I schools count male players who practice with women as female athletes. Other schools pad the rosters of female athletes by adding players to teams when the numbers are counted and then cutting the players after the count is done.

Inequities in athletics have consequences beyond the school years. Girls and women who participate in sports are more likely to pursue additional education and have higher earning power in their 20s and 30s (the latest ages for which data are available). They are also more likely to be healthy on many measures, including weight (Parker-Pope, 2010a).

Gender Pressures from Peers

The power of peer pressure is no myth. To be accepted by peers, many students work hard to conform to prevailing expectations for their gender. Schools are a training ground for adulthood, and peers are primary agents of gender socialization.

■ **EXPLORING GENDERED LIVES** ■

Title IX: Fiction and Fact

Although Title IX has been around for more than 30 years, it is still widely misunderstood. Check your understanding of Title IX (Messner, 2002; Neinas, 2002; Suggs, 2005; Title IX Q & A, 2008; Zimbalist, 2016).

Fiction: Title IX focuses on athletics.

Fact: Although Title IX has become almost synonymous with athletics, it is a very small part of what the legislation addresses.

Fiction: Title IX is binding on all schools in the United States.

Fact: Title IX is binding only on schools that accept federal funds.

Fiction: Title IX bans sex discrimination only in athletics.

Fact: Title IX bans sex discrimination of all sorts in federally supported schools. This applies to academics as well as athletics.

Fiction: Title IX has reduced opportunities for male college athletes.

Fact: Since the passage of Title IX, college men's sports opportunities have actually increased. Some schools have cut specific men's teams, but overall male athletes have more opportunities. Further, in 2016 there are 53,317 more male athletes in colleges than there were in 2006.

Fiction: Title IX requires identical athletic programs for males and females.

Fact: Title IX does not require that men's and women's teams receive identical support. Instead, it requires that they receive comparable levels of service, supplies, and facilities. Variations between men's and women's programs are allowed.

Fiction: Because of Title IX, colleges that receive federal funds provide fully equal support to women's and men's sports.

Fact: Compared to male athletes, female athletes receive fewer scholarship dollars, and their teams get fewer dollars for recruiting and operating teams.

Fiction: Most Americans are opposed to Title IX.

Fact: In a recent poll, 82% of Americans said they support Title IX. The poll included all political parties and people with and without children.

TAKE A STAND: Are you satisfied with Title IX as it is currently implemented? If so, why? If not, how do you think it should be modified?

Pressures to Conform to Masculinity   As young boys grow into adolescence, male peer groups reinforce masculine identification. Cisgender men often engage in drinking and sexual activity to demonstrate their masculinity, and they encourage the same in peers (Bennett, 2015; Kimmel, 2008). To be accepted by their peers, some men do things as part of the group that they would never consider doing as individuals.

SCOTT

On this campus, Greeks are cool. It took me just a few weeks on campus to figure out that if I wanted to be popular in college, I had to join a fraternity. So I rushed and pledged my first year. I like being part of the group and being considered cool, but I'm still uncomfortable with some of what goes on in the house. Some of the brothers talk about girls like they're all sluts, and if you don't go along with that talk, you're a jerk. Same with drinking—you have to drink a lot to be in with the group.

Male students often enjoy athletic activities since the field and the court are primary social venues where male students find companionship and camaraderie. But male students who don't want to play sports or don't have time may perceive peer pressure to play sports either on school or club teams or intramural teams.

Students of color, especially black men, often encounter obstacles rarely faced by other students. Fewer black men graduate from high school, attend college, graduate from college, and receive advanced degrees than white men, white women, or black women (Patton, 2012). Financial circumstances make it difficult or impossible for some black men to attend college (Patton, 2012). In addition, black students, whether male or female, are more likely than white students to attend high schools that provide less rigorous coursework, offer fewer classes necessary for college admission, and have less experienced teachers (Toldson, 2014).

Pressures to Conform to Femininity   Female peer groups tend to encourage and reward compliance with feminine stereotypes. Girls often make fun of or exclude peers who don't wear popular brands of clothing or who weigh more than what is considered ideal (Spar, 2013).

SPENCER

Tuition is nothing compared to what you have to spend to dress well! At this school, it's almost like there is a competition among girls to dress in the latest styles. If you're not wearing the cool boots or not layering the way models do in Marie Claire, you're just out of it. It takes a lot of money to buy all of the clothes and pay for haircuts and manicures. It also takes huge amounts of time that I could spend other ways.

In addition, girls and women are particularly targeted for sexual harassment and assault. From the earliest years of school through college and graduate education, girls and women report that they experience jeering, lewd suggestions, and unwanted physical contact from other students (Paludi, Martin, Gruber, & Fineran, 2015). And boys are not exempt, as the Penn State scandal shows. Yet, while both sexes report being subjected to sexual comments, gestures, and jokes, harassment that includes touching or forced sexual activity is more commonly experienced by girls than boys.

Sexual discrimination and harassment are not confined to peer interactions. Faculty and coaches may harass and discriminate against women. Ranging from comments on appearance instead of on academic work to offers of higher grades for sexual favors, these actions make women students' sex more salient than their abilities and aspirations. In treating women as sexual objects, such actions tell women students that they are not taken seriously as members of an intellectual community.

BAILEY

It's so unfair how professors treat women. I'm a serious student, and I plan a business career, but my professors have never asked me about my career plans. Even when I bring the subject up, all I get is really superficial stuff—like they really don't want to talk to me. One of my boyfriend's teachers invited him to have coffee and talk about graduate school. My boyfriend didn't even have to ask! They spent over an hour just talking about what he would do after undergraduate school. And my grades are better than his!

■ EXPLORING GENDERED LIVES ■

Creating Victims or Protecting Victims?

Are women or men responsible for stopping rape? Should women be told that drinking alcohol increases their risk of being raped or is that blaming the victim? Do campus policies against sexual assault and harassment make it too difficult for students who are accused of misconduct to defend themselves? Do efforts to protect against sexual assault go too far in representing the dangers of sex and obscuring the pleasures of sex?

These questions are at the center of a heated and long-standing controversy about how feminists should negotiate issues related to rape and sex (Bazelon, 2015). Feminists such as Janet Halley, a Harvard law professor, believe that efforts to safeguard women from unwanted sex have gone too far in portraying women as vulnerable and in need of protection by others. For these feminists, overprotective

policies erase women's agency and—even worse—teach women to underestimate their own ability to take care of themselves by, for instance, learning self-defense and drinking safely. In short, they claim, overzealous protection policies create victims.

On the other side of the debate are feminists who argue that male dominance makes it difficult for women to be self-actualized agents who can assert their wills. According to these feminists, laws and policies are not creating victims. Rather, it is a fact that many women *are* victims who need tools like laws to resist violence and to seek remedies for harms that are done to them. They see laws and policies as empowering. Further, they see emphasizing women's self-defense and warning women about alcohol as saddling women with the responsibility to stop rape when that burden should be squarely on men who commit rape.

TAKE A STAND: To what extent should campuses protect women from unwanted sex and hold men responsible for sexual assaults?

An increasing problem for all students is **bullying**, which is behavior intended to hurt, embarrass, shame, or intimidate another person. Bullying behaviors include words, physical actions, and nonverbal behaviors that can cause emotional, sexual, or physical harm. Bullying is often directed at people who do not conform to gender prescriptions (Martocci, 2015).

For women, peer pressures often increase during the college years. Studies of women students at colleges and universities report that they feel two sets of pressures: to be successful as women—attractive and fun to be with—and to be academically successful. Women feel compelled to achieve **effortless perfection**: to be beautiful, fit, popular, smart, and accomplished without any visible effort (Dube, 2004; Hinshaw, 2009). Many undergraduate women say they feel enormous pressure to be perfect—to earn high grades, have leadership roles in campus groups, and excel in sports while also being nice, kind, caring, and pleasing to others (Girls Incorporated, 2006; Orenstein, 2011b). Amy Yao (2013) writes that "the race to become 'effortlessly perfect' is still a very significant, albeit unspoken, part of our reality."

JACQUIE

College is supposed to be a place for thinking and education, but the bottom line here is that you have to be really attractive if you want to be liked. Brains may get you good grades, but they won't get you friends or dates. Most of the girls I know spend as much time shopping for clothes and fixing their hair and nails as they do studying.

━━━━━━━━━━ **EXPLORING GENDERED LIVES** ━━━━━━━━━━

Schoolyard Bullying

When the term *schoolyard bullying* was coined, it referred almost exclusively to a belligerent male student who beat up other male students on school grounds. Today, bullying in schools comes in many forms including but not restricted to beating someone up. Anonymous apps such as Yik Yak and Secret allowed students to post comments and photos without revealing their identities (Williams, 2014). Yik Yak has been banned in 85% of high schools and Secret was shut down by the app developer in 2015 due in large part to their use in cyberbullying contexts. Anonymous apps designed to take their place such as Whisper and After School attempt to prevent bullying—Whisper bans the use of posts with names and After School staff review all posts before they are published (Purewal, 2015).

Following is a partial listing of common types of bullying; many of the types can be perpetrated face-to-face or via social media. You'll note that the types are not mutually exclusive. For instance, verbal, physical, or sexual bullying may also be emotional bullying, and most types of bullying may be perpetrated via social media at least as easily as through face-to-face interaction.

Physical Bullying

- Hitting
- Shoving
- Pushing
- Kicking
- Pinching
- Beating

Sexual Bullying

- Uninvited touching
- Forced stripping
- Rape, including group rape
- Circulating private, sexual images of another person via social media without the person's consent
- Any coerced or nonconsensual sexual activity

Emotional

- Spreading hurtful rumors
- Excluding individuals from groups
- Ignoring (the silent treatment)
- Degrading
- Teasing
- Ridiculing

Verbal

- Cursing at
- Name calling
- Making fun of appearance
- Insulting a person's race, ethnicity, or sexual orientation
- Slander (lies)
- Belittling

Nonverbal

- Circulating embarrassing photos that may be photoshopped
- Public displays of photos that disparage particular groups (ethnic, sexual orientation, etc.)

TAKE A STAND: What forms of peer bullying have you observed or experienced?

Peer groups on campus may also propel college women into a **culture of romance** (Holland & Eisenhart, 1992). Some women in college become discouraged by barriers to their academic achievement, such as lack of intellectual mentoring from professors and required readings and class discussions that emphasize men and men's achievements and give little or no attention to women and their achievements. The second factor propelling college women into a culture of romance is intense peer pressure that emphasizes attracting men as more important than anything else women can do.

> ### MARIA
>
> *My sorority is a great example of the culture of romance. When a girl gets engaged, we throw her in a cold shower and then give her the "warm shower," which is lots of gifts and good wishes. Our newsletter lists alums' marriages and births of children. What it doesn't list and what we don't celebrate is academic achievement or alums' career moves. Aren't those important too?*

Gay, lesbian, and trans students are not exempt from peer pressure. In fact, they are often subjected to more strenuous pressures to conform to conventionally gendered identities than are straight students. They are also more likely to be bullied for living outside of normative prescriptions for gender and sexuality. Bullying of LGBTQ students can be particularly vicious. In 2010, 18-year-old Tyler Clementi committed suicide after discovering that his roommate Dharun Ravi had sent out Twitter and text messages inviting others to watch a sexual encounter between Clementi and another man. Ravi was tried on 15 charges including hate crime; he was found guilty of a bias crime and using a webcam to spy on Clementi. His sentence was 30 days in jail, three years on probation, and 300 hours of community service (Zernike, 2012).

Clementi is not an isolated case. Estimates are that at least half of LGBTQ youth experience abuse and bullying, including cyberbullying (Goldblum, Espelage, Chu, & Bongar, 2014).

Gendered Expectations and Pressures Facing Faculty

In addition to being educational institutions, schools are also workplaces, so we want to examine gendered attitudes and practices that affect the faculty who work there. As you will discover, gender dynamics faced by faculty often affect students as well.

Women faculty members often experience some of the same pressures faced by women students. They may be stereotyped into traditionally feminine roles—for instance, appointed to the social committee—and perform considerably more service than their male peers regardless of race/ethnicity, rank, or field (Guarino & Borden, 2017). In addition, many women faculty have to deal with sexual harassment and sometimes sexual assault. In a recent survey (Aschwanden, 2014), a majority of women faculty in the sciences reported having been sexually harassed. Most frequently men in supervisory positions perpetrated the harassment.

The more advanced the educational level, the greater the ratio of male to female faculty members. In elementary schools, the vast majority of teachers are female, but most superintendents and assistant superintendents are male. In high schools, female teachers still outnumber male teachers, but the imbalance is less pronounced. On faculties at colleges and universities, men significantly outnumber women, especially at the higher faculty ranks (Curtis, 2011; Differences between Male and Female Full-Time Professors, 2014; Hill, 2016; Misra, Hickes, Holmes, & Agiomavritis, 2011). In addition, male faculty still earn more than female faculty, regardless of professional achievement (Curtis, 2010; Hill, 2016). At doctoral universities, men outnumber women three to one, and women average 90 cents per dollar earned by male faculty (Differences between Male and Female Full-Time Professors, 2014). At two-year colleges where the salaries are lower overall, female faculty outnumber men. Only 26.4% of chief administrators of colleges are female and only 12.6% are members of minority groups (Stripling, 2012).

Limited numbers of female faculty and faculty of color mean that women and racial/ethnic minority students have fewer role models among faculty. Recall cognitive development theory, which we discussed in Chapter 2. This theory notes that we look for models—preferably ones like us in gender, race, and so forth—to emulate as we develop identities. If more men than women are principals and full professors, then students may infer that it's normal for men (but not for women) to rise to high levels in education.

MORGAN

With so many male professors, I think it is difficult for some students to feel comfortable getting to know their professors and asking for help. Women are more likely to connect with a female teacher, minorities are more likely to connect with a teacher of their race, and so on. Colleges always make a big deal about having a diverse campus, but what about the professors? Where are the female professors? Where are the LGBTQ professors? Where are the professors from other cultures and races? If colleges want to have a diverse student body, they should also have a diverse faculty that correlates with the students.

Researchers have identified three major sources of gender bias hiring and promotion of faculty. First, women's performance tends to be more closely scrutinized and judged by stricter standards than men's. Second, men have to give more convincing demonstrations of incompetence to be judged by others as incompetent. Third, male candidates tend to be judged on whether they show promise, whereas female candidates tend to be judged on accomplishments. All in all, different standards are used to evaluate men and women, and the way in which those standards are applied results in men being judged as more competent.

The subtlety of gender bias in evaluation of faculty explains why it is called *invisible hand discrimination* (Haag, 2005). **Invisible hand discrimination** is unwitting discrimination in applying policies that are not inherently biased (Haag, 2005). It does not happen because a person consciously intends to discriminate or because a policy or practice is inherently discriminatory. The largely unconscious nature of invisible hand discrimination makes it particularly difficult to eliminate.

Consider a few examples of how invisible hand discrimination works. Collegiality is a criterion many universities use when deciding whether to promote faculty members. There is nothing inherently biased about the criterion, as it is reasonable to expect all faculty members to be courteous and reasonably easy to work with. So, how might a tenure committee evaluate the collegiality of Professor Smith, who is known to be very assertive? Assertiveness in male faculty is likely to be taken as a sign of confidence and intelligence, whereas assertiveness in female faculty is often regarded as confrontational and non-collegial (Haag, 2005). That's invisible hand discrimination.

Another example is gender-typed assignment of service work. All faculty members are expected to perform service work to maintain the intellectual and social culture of their academic units and schools. A department chair might ask a female faculty member to organize a reception without realizing that he or she is acting on the unconscious assumption that women should take charge of social events. More substantive service assignments are given to male faculty also without conscious intention to be biased (McMurtrie, 2013). That's invisible hand discrimination. During the early years of an academic appointment, faculty members have probationary status—they must earn tenure to become permanent faculty. Thus, the early years require particularly long hours and heavy investments. For women, those years usually coincide with the ideal years for bearing children, a pressure that affects women faculty in ways it does not affect male faculty. The tenure schedule is at odds with the biological clock, which creates tensions for faculty who are also parents (Hayden & O'Brien Hallstein, 2010; O'Brien Hallstein & O'Reilly, 2012). The small number of female faculty and faculty of color generates another problem: excessive responsibilities for service and mentoring. Faculty committees are ubiquitous at universities, and committees are expected to reflect gender and racial diversity. Because they are underrepresented, women and people of color are routinely asked to serve on more committees than their white male peers. The same goes for advising students, particularly for women and minority students. If there is only one woman of color on the faculty of a department, she's likely to be besieged by requests from the majority of graduate and undergraduate students who are also women of color.

SUMMARY

Today both sexes face gender-based issues, expectations, and biases in educational institutions. Males, especially boys in the early years of schooling, are disadvantaged by a system that doesn't accommodate their developmental status. As males progress through school, they are more likely than women students to attract faculty mentors, particularly in graduate and professional school. For female students, the reverse sequence is more common. They tend to be quite successful through high school and perhaps college, but they often hit barriers when they enter graduate and professional school, particularly in math and sciences.

Peer culture on college campuses further encourages male and female students to conform to particular gender ideals, which can limit personal and professional development. Male peer cultures tend to link masculinity with drinking, aggression, and sexual activity. Female peer cultures too often encourage campus women to participate in a culture of romance and to attempt to meet the impossible ideal of effortless perfection. And while all students may be bullied by peers, gender-nonconforming students are more likely to be harassed and have greater difficulty locating peers and mentors supportive of their gender identity. These factors may make gender-nonconforming students more likely to fall behind in academic coursework as a result.

Faculty also experience gender biases and pressures. Discrimination in hiring, promotion, and pay continues to be a problem at colleges and universities across the nation, as does the disparate expectations for service that women and men faculty members face. Further, invisible hand discrimination affects women faculty, typically in ways that are both subtle and insidious.

Our examination warrants a mixed report card for schools in the United States. Discrimination and disadvantage based on sex, gender, sexual orientation, and gender identity have been greatly reduced for students, but gendered dynamics persist at all grade levels. The same is true for faculty.

Yet we should keep in mind that as social views of gender have changed, so have educational opportunities for women and men. As social views continue to change in the years ahead, so will educational practices.

KEY TERMS

The following terms are defined in this chapter on the pages indicated, as well as in alphabetical order in the book's glossary, which begins on page 261. The text's companion website also provides interactive flash cards to help you learn these terms and the concepts they represent. You can access the site at www.cengagebrain.com.

bullying 167

culture of romance 168

effortless perfection 167

invisible hand discrimination 170

Title IX 162

GENDER ONLINE

1. Learn more about Title IX by visiting **http://www.titleix.info**

2. Information about the United Nations' education initiative for girls can be found at **http://www.ungei.org/**

3. Online search terms: *effortless perfection, peer pressure, single-sex education.*

4. Learn about the National Center for Faculty Development and Diversity, an organization dedicated to the mentoring and success of underrepresented faculty, at **http://www .facultydiversity.org/**

REFLECTION, DISCUSSION, AND ACTION

1. Talk with male and female athletes on your campus to find out the extent to which they perceive that your school complies with Title IX.

2. If you could make three changes in elementary schools, with the goal of making them work better for all children regardless of sex and gender, what changes would you make?

3. Follow up on the Exploring Gendered Lives box on page 159 by asking students on your campus to name 10 people who have had substantial impact on U.S. culture. How many of these people were men? Women? Trans? Of color?

4. What is your opinion on the desirability of single-sex schools? What do you see as the advantages and disadvantages both for students in the schools and for the society?

RECOMMENDED RESOURCES

1. Peg Tyre (2008). *The Trouble with Boys: A Surprising Report Card on Our Sons, Their Problems at School, and What Parents and Educators Must Do.* New York: Crown. This book, which was a reference for the chapter, gives a thoughtful summary of barriers boys and men face in educational institutions. The book is written for general audiences.

2. Jennifer Ring (2013). *Stolen Bases: Why American Girls Don't Play Baseball.* Urbana: University of Illinois Press. This well-written book provides an interesting history of women's involvement in baseball and also shows how young women today are discouraged from playing hardball once they enter middle school.

9

The doors we open and close each day decide the lives we live.
—Flora Whixttenmore

Gendered Close Relationships

Knowledge Challenge:

- To what extent are talking and sharing activities important for creating and sustaining intimacy?
- Which gender(s) typically fall in love faster?
- On average, are straight, gay, or lesbian relationships more equitable?

Perhaps you have found yourself in situations such as those that Mark and Paige describe on the next page. For Mark, as for most people socialized into masculinity, communicating is important when you need to address an issue or solve a problem, but he doesn't see the point in talking extensively about small stuff. For Paige, it's incomprehensible that Mark can work on his paper when there is tension between them. If Paige and Mark do not figure out that their gendered viewpoints are creating misunderstandings, they will continue to experience frustration in their relationships.

In this chapter, we will focus on gender dynamics in close relationships. To begin our discussion, we will clarify what personal relationships are. We will then consider typically masculine and feminine ways of experiencing and expressing closeness and how Western culture views each of those ways. Finally, we'll explore gendered patterns in friendships and romantic relationships to appreciate different ways that people create closeness.

The Meaning of Personal Relationships

Of the many relationships we form, only a few become really personal, occupying a special place in our lives and affecting us deeply. **Personal relationships** are those in which close friends and romantic partners depend on each other for various things from affection to material assistance. In personal relationships, we expect trust, honesty, affection, respect, companionship, time, energy, and assistance with the large and small issues in life. Also, close friends and romantic partners regard each other as unique individuals who cannot be replaced. If a casual friend moves, we can find a replacement; if a business associate goes to another company, we can work with a new colleague. When a personal partner leaves or dies, however, the relationship ends, although we may continue to feel connected to the person who is no longer physically with us.

Research demonstrates that people often choose friends and romantic partners who are similar to themselves in terms of age, gender, race, sexual orientation, and socioeconomic status. Close friendships are often particularly salient for those with minority identities—for example, LGBTQ individuals are more likely to refer to their friends as "family" and may depend on these relationships to meet needs neglected by the larger culture (Galupo & Gonzalez, 2013; Galupo, Bauerband, Gonzalez, Hagen, Hether, & Krum, 2014).

MARK

Sometimes I just don't know what goes on in Paige's head. We can have a minor problem—like an issue between us, and it's really not serious stuff. But can we let it go? No way with Paige. She wants "to talk about it." And I mean talk and talk and talk and talk. There's no end to how long she can talk about stuff that really doesn't matter. I tell her that she's analyzing the relationship to death, and I don't want to do that. She insists that we need "to talk things through." Why can't we just have a relationship, instead of always having to talk about it?

PAIGE

Honestly, I almost left my boyfriend when we had our first fight after moving in together. It was really a big one about how to be committed to our relationship and also do all the other stuff that we have to do. It was major. And after we'd yelled for a while, there seemed to be nothing else to do—we were just at a stalemate in terms of conflict between what each of us wanted. So Mark walked away, and I sat fuming in the living room. When I finally left the living room, I found him working away on a paper for one of his courses, and I was furious. I couldn't understand how he could concentrate on work when we were so messed up. How in the world could he just put us aside and get on with his work? I felt like it was a really clear message that he wasn't very committed.

Models of Personal Relationships

People often, but not always, approach close relationships in ways that reflect gender. Some scholars argue that masculine approaches are inferior to feminine ones, while others think that the two styles are different yet equally valid. We'll consider each of these viewpoints.

The Male Deficit Model   Because our society views women as interpersonally sensitive, feminine ways of interacting are often assumed to be "the right ways." Thus, a number of researchers maintain that a masculine style of building and maintaining relationships is inadequate. This view, the **male deficit model**, asserts that men are less skilled than women in developing and sustaining personal relationships.

The fundamental assumption of the male deficit model is that personal, emotional talk is the hallmark of intimacy. A classic investigation (Caldwell & Peplau, 1982) measured the intimacy of same-sex friendships by the amount of intimate information disclosed between friends. As women generally self-disclose more than men, it is not surprising that the researchers concluded that women were more intimate than men. Based on this line of research, men were advised to learn to express their feelings more openly.

> **CARLOS**
>
> *I don't have any problem being emotionally sensitive or expressing my feelings. I may not go on forever about my feelings, but I know what they are, and I can express them fine. It's just that the way I express my feelings is different from the way most girls I know express their feelings. I'm not dramatic or sentimental or gushy, but I have ways of showing how I feel.*

Even today, many assume that women are the experts at building intimacy and support-ive relationships (Burleson, Hanasono, Bodie, Holmstrom, McCllough, Rack, & Rosier, 2011; Burleson, Holmstrom, & Gilstrap, 2005). Films, television programs and print, TV, self-help literature, and online ads often represent men as emotionally lacking and women as naturally adept at relationships. But some researchers question the male deficit model, offering a sec-ond interpretation of different ways people create and express closeness.

The Alternate Paths Model
The **alternate paths model** claims that there are dif-ferent and equally valid paths to closeness. This model agrees with the male deficit model that gendered socialization is the root of differences between feminine and masculine styles of relating. It departs from the deficit model, however, in two important ways. First, the alternate paths model does not presume that masculine people lack feelings or emo-tional depth. Rather, it suggests that masculine socialization limits men's opportunities to practice emotional talk, which leads them to be less comfortable engaging in emotional communication.

Second, the alternate paths model argues that masculine people do express closeness but in an alternate way than feminine people. According to this model, masculine and feminine ways of expressing closeness are different, and the two ways are equally valid.

The alternate paths model points out that Western culture relies on a **feminine ruler** to define and measure closeness and supportive communication (Cancian, 1987, 1989; High & Solomon, 2014; Wood, 2011). Using a specifically feminine ruler (emotional talk) falsely measures masculine modes of caring in the same way that using male standards to assess women's speech misinterprets women's communication.

Influenced by this viewpoint, Scott Swain (1989) studied men's close friendships in a clas-sic study. He discovered that many men develop closeness by doing things together. Follow-ing Swain's lead, other studies showed that closeness between men generally doesn't grow primarily out of emotional talk and self-disclosure, and it is not primarily expressed in those ways (Clark, 1998; Sherrod, 1989). Research has also shown that father–son relationships are built largely on doing things together (Morman & Floyd, 2006). For many men, like Paige's boyfriend, talking about problems may be less effective than diversionary activities to relieve stress (Metts, 2006a).

Yet, it would be a mistake to think that women don't do things with friends and men don't talk with friends. Women friends enjoy doing things together and helping each other out just as most men talk with their friends (Chapman & Hendler, 1999). Further, as Paul Wright (2006) notes, many of the activities in which men engage enhance emotional closeness. Camp-ing, for instance, provides a rich opportunity to share experiences, thoughts, and feelings.

Expectations and behavior in close relationships can also vary in response to a friend's gender. For example, recent research indicates that the more information a man shares on a social networking site, the more likely a viewer is to pursue social interactions with that individual, but for women, the opposite is true (Baruh, Chisik, Bisson, & Şenova, 2014). Both women and men judge a friend more harshly for betraying a confidence if that friend is female (Felmlee, Sweet, & Sinclair, 2012). Additionally, all people, regardless of gender, tend to be more sensitive when trying to comfort women than when trying to comfort men.

From this research, we may conclude that masculine individuals less often express their feelings in feminine ways, just as feminine individuals less frequently express theirs in masculine ways, while also noting that these tendencies are influenced by the context in which they unfold (Frey, Beesley, Hurst, Saldana, & Licuanan, 2016).

Gendered Styles of Friendship

Before discussing gendered differences in relationships, let's note that there are many similarities. Regardless of sex or gender, most individuals value close friends and invest in them. Also, people of all gender identities and expressions engage in instrumental and expressive modes of building and expressing closeness, although gendered differences exist with regard to the frequency and extent of using each mode (Felmlee et al., 2012; Frey et al., 2016; Grayling, 2013; Monsour, 2006). Against the backdrop of commonalities in approaches to friendship, there are gendered differences in how individuals typically—but not invariably—build friendships and interact within them. As you read about these different styles, keep in mind that most of us use both styles, although women tend to favor feminine style and men tend to favor masculine style. Research that includes LGBTQ experiences and identities in the context of friendships is unfortunately limited, but where it exists, greatly enhances our understanding of how gender shapes relationships.

As early as 1982, Paul Wright noted that women tend to engage each other face-to-face, whereas men usually interact side by side. By this, Wright meant that women are more likely than men to communicate face-to-face with each other. Men more typically engage in activities that do not involve facing each other. Wright's observation gives us a foundation for exploring how gender shapes friendships.

Feminine Friendships: Closeness in Dialogue

Regardless of race, ethnicity, sexual orientation, or economic status, a majority of women regard talk as the primary way to build and enrich friendships (Tannen, 2017; Wood, 2015; Wright, 2006). Consequently, many women share their personal feelings, experiences, fears, and problems in order to know and be known by each other (Bane, Cornish, Erspamer, & Kampman, 2010; Yalom, 2015). To capture the quality of women's friendships, Caroline Becker (1987) described them as "an evolving dialogue" through which initially separate worlds are woven together.

EXPLORING GENDERED LIVES

Passionate Friendships

Researchers have coined the term ***passionate friendship*** to refer to unique interpersonal relationship, typically between women, that blends aspects of romance and friendship (Diamond, 2000; Glover, Galliher, & Crowell, 2015). While these relationships exclude sexual desire or activity, they exceed conventional friendship in emotional intensity, physical intimacy, disclosure, and exclusivity. This is not a new phenomenon. During the sixteenth century, many women believed that they and their best friend shared a single soul (Yalom, 2015).

Both heterosexual and LGBTQ-identified women engage in passionate friendships,

and these friendships share similar features and developmental paths regardless of sexual orientation (Glover et al., 2015). However, some women's descriptions of passionate friendships differed based on sexual orientation, as LGBTQ-identified women are more likely to describe passionate friendships as a place to explore same-sex attraction and connection, while heterosexual women describe passionate friendships as important to identity development more generally (Glover et al., 2015). The scholarship on passionate friendships suggests that the lines between friendship, romance, and sexual identity are less rigid for women than previously believed.

TAKE A STAND: To what extent does naming the concept of *passionate friendship* change how you think about romance, friendship, and sexuality?

To know each other in depth, women friends typically confide personal feelings and disclose intimate information (Frey et al., 2016; Hall, 2011; Metts, 2006b; Reisman, 1990; Walker, 2004), and they tend to maintain higher expectations for their friends in matters related to trust and intimacy (Felmlee et al., 2012). Consistent with feminine socialization's encouragement of permeable ego boundaries, communication between women friends also tends to be empathic, expressive, and supportive (Campbell, 2002; Kuchment, 2004; Lopez, 2012; Tannen, 2017; Yalom, 2015). While women tend to perceive greater levels of intimacy in face-to-face friendships, online friendships are more likely to be satisfying to women when they include high levels of self-disclosure and person-centered support (Bane et al., 2010; High & Solomon, 2014).

AVA

One of the worst things about being female is not having permission to be selfish or jealous or not to care about a friend. Usually, I'm pretty nice; I feel good for my friends when good things happen to them, and I want to support them when things aren't going well. But sometimes I don't feel that way. Like right now, all my friends and I are interviewing for jobs, and my best friend just got a great offer. I've had 23 interviews and no job offers so far. I felt good for Jessa, but I also felt jealous. I couldn't talk about this with her, because I'm not supposed to feel jealous or to be selfish like this. It's just not allowed, so my friends and I have to hide those feelings.

Because most women are socialized to be attentive, emotionally supportive, and caring, it is difficult for many women to deal with feelings of envy and competitiveness toward friends. It is not that women don't experience these emotions but rather they may think it's wrong to have such feelings (Simmons, 2002, 2004). Many women also find it difficult to override socialization's message that they are supposed to be constantly available and caring. The bottom line is that the supportiveness and caring typical of women's friendships can both enrich and constrain people.

It is not unusual for women friends to talk explicitly about their friendship itself and the dynamics between them. Many women friends are comfortable stating affection explicitly and discussing tensions within a friendship (Lopez, 2012). In online communication as well women are more likely than men to express affection as well as to seek and provide support (Luarn, Kuo, Chiu, & Chang, 2015; Mansson & Myers, 2011).

A final quality typical of women's friendships is breadth. With close friends, women tend not to restrict their communication to specific areas but invite each other into many parts of their lives. Because women talk in detail about varied aspects of their lives, women friends often know each other in complex and layered ways.

In summary, many women's friendships give center stage to communication, which fosters disclosure, verbal expressiveness, depth and breadth of knowledge, and attentiveness to the evolving nature of the relationship.

▬ EXPLORING GENDERED LIVES ▬

When Focusing on Feelings Makes Us Feel Bad

Women who pay attention to their feelings are able to work through feelings. However, there may be a down side.

Researchers have coined the term *co-rumination* to refer to frequent or excessive talk—face-to-face, email, texts, tweets, and posts—between friends about a problem. Co-rumination can lead to heightened anxieties and emotional contagion, in which the person listening to another's problem feels the anxieties and depression as if it is her own (Kershaw, 2008).

Research shows that women generally have a greater tendency than men to brood about bad feelings and to co-ruminate in their friendships (Barstead, Bouchard, & Shih, 2013). Excessive brooding and co-rumination can lead to feeling stuck in unhappy feelings and depression (Nolen-Hoeksema, 2003).

TAKE A STAND: To what extent do you find that talking with friends about problems heightens your anxiety? Have you ever experienced emotional contagion?

Masculine Friendships: Closeness in the Doing

At very young ages, most boys are as emotive and socially oriented as girls (Way, 2013). Even as they engage in vigorous play, they also talk about feelings. However, boys' social and emotional tendencies tend to be tempered by older children, adults, and media models of masculinity. As a result, many boys learn to ground their friendships in shared activities, particularly sports.

Scott Swain's (1989) phrase "closeness in the doing" captures how many men build friendships in ways that reflect masculine socialization (Migliaccio, 2009). More than two-thirds of the men in Swain's study identified activities other than talking as the most meaningful times

Masculine friendships often involve doing things together.

with male friends. Engaging in sports, watching games, and doing other things together cultivate camaraderie and closeness between men. When men do talk, they often talk about activities—reminisce about great games they attended, recall pranks they played or had played on them, and psych themselves up for upcoming activities. Whereas women tend to look for confidantes in friends, men more typically seek companions (Chethik, 2008; Felmlee et al., 2012; Inman, 1996; Swain, 1989; Walker, 2004; Wood & Inman, 1993).

KEITH

My best friend and I almost never sit and just talk. Mainly, we do things together, like go places or shoot hoops or watch games on TV. When we do talk, we talk about what we have done or plan to do or what's happening in our lives, but we don't say much about how we feel. I don't think we need to. You can say a lot without words.

Growing out of the emphasis on activities is a second feature of men's friendships: an instrumental focus. Because many men like doing things for people they care about, their friendships often involve instrumental reciprocity. For example, Brad helps Jake repair his car, and Jake assists Brad with computer problem—an exchange of favors that allows each man to hold his own while helping the other.

A third feature of men's friendship is typically indirect talk about serious feelings. Many men find it uncomfortable to disclose feelings explicitly to other men (Burleson et al., 2005). If they mention serious emotional issues, they often engage in "joke talk" (Fisher, 2009), which couches serious feelings in humor. Rather than verbally expressing sympathy or support for a male friend who is hurting, boys and men are more likely to use joke talk to indicate care indirectly or to suggest diversionary activities that take the friend's mind off his troubles (Rose, Smith, Glick, & Schwartz-Mette, 2016). Recent research in online communication settings suggests that while gendered norms may dissuade men from providing highly person-centered support in face-to-face contexts, computer-mediated communication (CMC) may provide opportunities for men to verbally express greater sympathy and support to friends in need (High & Solomon, 2014; Spottswood, Walther, Holmstrom, & Ellison, 2013).

LEVI

I don't know what girls get out of sitting around talking about problems all the time. What a downer. When something bad happens to me, like I blow a test or break up with a girl, the last thing I want is to talk about it. I already feel bad enough. What I want is something to distract me from how lousy I feel. That's where having buddies really matters. They know you feel bad and help you out by taking you out drinking or starting a pickup game or something that gets your mind off the problems. They give you breathing room and some escape from troubles; girls just wallow in troubles.

Fourth, men's friendships often involve "covert intimacy" (Swain, 1989). Compared to women friends, reports Kory Floyd (1997), men "simply communicate affection in different, more 'covert' ways so as to avoid the possible ridicule that more overt expression might invite" (p. 78). Male friends tend to signal affection by teasing one another, engaging in friendly competition, and exchanging playful punches and backslaps. Most males learn very early in life that physical displays of affection between men are prohibited except in traditionally masculine settings such as sports or the military (Migliaccio, 2009). New research suggests that men are also more likely to offer "invisible support" (High & Solomon, 2014). Invisible support is a form of covert intimacy but emerges in response to a particular stressor or event. It is a form of support that the recipient doesn't have to acknowledge as support, either because it is instrumental (dropping off a meal for a buddy who is stressed over exams) or is otherwise indirect (making extra time to hang out with a friend who is sad). Because it is not obvious help, invisible support allows the recipient to save face. Especially in masculine speech, communities where independence is paramount, invisible support minimizes the chance that the individual in need of support will feel vulnerable or incompetent. Some suggest that this form of support may have especially long-lasting positive effects for the support recipient (High & Solomon, 2014). While covert intimacy is present in most men's friendships regardless of sexual orientation, friendships between gay men tend to be more physically and emotionally expressive than straight men's friendships (Kocet, 2014).

Finally, men's close friendships are often, although not always, more restricted in scope than women's close friendships. Many men have different friends for various spheres of interest (Wright, 1988). Thus, José might play racquetball with Mike, debate politics with Clay, and collaborate with Zach on work projects. Because men tend to focus friendships on particular activities, they may not share as many dimensions of their lives as women friends do. Overall, men's friendships emphasize shared activities, instrumental demonstrations of affection, and covert intimacy within defined spheres of interaction.

In summary, gender-linked communication patterns characterize most same-sex friendships. These gender-linked tendencies, however, are not absolute. Most of us rely on multiple forms of communication in our friendships.

Friendships across Gender

Friendships across gender pose unique challenges and offer special opportunities. Because our culture is heteronormative and heavily emphasizes gender, it can be difficult for women and men not to see each other in sexual terms (Bleske-Rechek et al., 2012; Halatsis & Christakis, 2009; Lemay & Wolf, 2016). In addition, misunderstandings may arise as the result of socialization into distinct gendered speech communities.

Despite these difficulties, friendships across gender are common. For many women, a primary benefit of friendships with men is companionship that is less emotionally intense. For men, an especially valued benefit of closeness with women is access to overt emotional and expressive support. One study of close friendships between gay men and straight women reported a unique benefit shared by both parties—the exchange of dating and relationship advice that was perceived as more trustworthy than that offered by their straight or gay peers (Russell, DelPriore, Butterfield, & Hill, 2013).

LAILA

Last week Jay came by my place to talk. I've known Jay for a year—we're both in band— but we're not close friends or anything. He told me his parents are divorcing and he was really, really upset. He said it just tore him up, and he was crying and everything. Later, I saw Jay's closest friend Rob and asked how Jay was doing with his parents' divorce, but Rob didn't know a thing about it. I thought it was really strange that Jay hadn't told his closest friend but told me.

Both men and women report receiving more emotional support from female than male friends (Burleson et al., 2005). Some researchers suggest that this may be related to the cultural tendency to use a feminine ruler to measure support and thereby overlook the unique forms of support that men tend to provide (High & Solomon, 2014). In friendships across gender, men generally talk more and get more attention, response, and support than they offer. A majority of people, regardless of gender, report that friendships with women are closer and more emotionally rich, that women are their primary confidantes (Barstead et al., 2013), and that they are more comfortable self-disclosing to women than to men (Monsour, 2006).

Gendered Romantic Relationships

Nowhere are gendered roles as salient as in heterosexual romantic relationships. The cultural script for heterosexual romance is well known to most of us (Eaton & Rose, 2011; Metts, 2006a; Mongeau, Serewicz, Henningsen, & Davis, 2006):

- Feminine women and masculine men are desirable.
- Men should initiate, plan, and direct most activities in a relationship.
- Women should facilitate conversation, generally defer to men, but control sexual activity.
- Men should excel in status and earning money, and women should assume primary responsibility for the relationships.

Although many people claim to reject this script, as we will see, it continues to play out in many heterosexual relationships. Compared to their straight peers, gay and lesbian relationships tend to place a greater premium on relationship equality, and there tends to be less role-playing and adherence to the heterosexual script (Hunter, 2012; Patterson, 2000; Rutter & Schwartz, 1996).

Developing Romantic Intimacy

Personal ads and online profiles offer insight into cultural attitudes about what is desirable in romantic partners. Men looking for women often state preferences for stereotypically feminine physical qualities, using words such as *attractive, slender, petite,* and *sexy.* Women's ads for male partners tend to emphasize status and success and include words such as *ambitious, professional,* and *successful.* Whereas LGBT-identified individuals report a larger age range for desirable partners than their heterosexual peers, straight men increasingly prefer younger women as they themselves age; straight women, regardless of their own age, report little interest in men younger than themselves (Conway, Noë, Stulp, & Pollet, 2015).

Gender expectations also shape how individuals present themselves in online communication—heterosexual men are more likely to misrepresent their financial worth and are more likely to be critical of women's physical appearance, and heterosexual women are more likely to enhance their physical attractiveness and misrepresent their weight (Hall, Park, Song, & Cody, 2010; Schmitz, Zillmann, & Blossfeld, 2013; Toma & Hancock, 2010). Gay men's profiles tend to emphasize masculinity, physical fitness, and are more likely than their straight counterparts' profiles to include a shirtless picture or a picture that excludes the individual's face (B. Miller, 2015; Miller & Behm-Morawitz, 2016).

Is one sex more romantic than the other? Contrary to popular belief, research indicates that men tend to fall in love faster and harder than women, profess love earlier, and report greater happiness than women when receiving a declaration of love (Ackerman, Griskevicius, & Li, 2011). Men tend to express love in more impulsive and sexualized ways than women, whose styles of loving tend to be more pragmatic and friendship focused. For instance, men may equate love with travel to romantic places, spontaneous sex, and surprising their partners. Women more typically think of extended conversations and sharing deep feelings and physical contact that isn't necessarily sexual. These gendered preferences for expressing love are also evident in some patterns of relational distress. Consistent across age groups and income levels, heterosexual men are far more likely than heterosexual women, gay men, lesbians, or bisexuals to regard sexual infidelity as more distressing than emotional infidelity (Frederick & Fales, 2016).

Even as premarital and casual sex are more widely accepted, studies conducted on heterosexual, cisgender communities indicate that women who express sexuality openly or have nontraditional relationships and partners are judged more harshly than men who do the same (Bordini & Sperb, 2013). Research also shows that men and women have different primary motives for engaging in sex. Cisgender, heterosexual women more often say intimacy and commitment are their reasons, whereas cisgender, heterosexual men more often say they are motivated by lust and a desire for physical pleasure (Meston & Buss, 2009; Peter & Valkenburg, 2010). This may explain why norms regarding monogamy differ between gay and lesbian relationships—one recent large-scale study across eight European nations demonstrated that while lesbian and gay couples report similar investments in long-term commitment, lesbians place a greater premium on monogamy and gay men report greater comfort with open relationships (Potârcă, Mills, & Neberich, 2015). Regardless of sexual orientation, men are more likely to engage in cuddling and kissing only when those are a prelude to or part of sexual activity (Rosenberger, Herbenick, Novak, & Reece, 2014).

Women of all sexual orientations are more likely than men to focus on relationship dynamics (Metts, 2006a, 2006b; Patterson, 2000). Lesbian partners tend to take mutual responsibility for nurturing and supporting relationships (Goldberg & Perry-Jenkins, 2007). Gay men, conversely, are less likely to focus on nurturing the relationship and providing emotional support (Patterson, 2000).

Committed heterosexual relationships, in general, continue to reflect many traditional gender roles. Men tend to be perceived as the head of the family and are expected to be good breadwinners; women tend to assume primary responsibility for domestic labor and child care; and men tend to have greater power in families. As we've noted in earlier chapters, these perceptions are increasingly at odds with reality: Nearly two-thirds of women in the United States work outside of the home (Peters & Wessel, 2014), and approximately 40% of women are the primary or sole breadwinner (Adams, 2014; Coontz, 2014; Shulevitz, 2015).

Because gender distinctions are less salient, many gays and lesbians are not as bound by roles typical in heterosexual couples. Both gay and lesbian commitments often resemble best-friend relationships with the added dimensions of sexuality and romance. Following the best-friends model, long-term lesbian relationships tend to be monogamous and high in emotionality, disclosure, and support, and partners have the most equality of all types of relationships (Parker-Pope, 2008; Potârcă et al., 2015).

Despite relatively high levels of relationship satisfaction, social stigma and anti-LGBTQ discrimination can negatively impact the health of LGBTQ relationships. Studies demonstrate that contextual factors, such as perceived community support, legal rights, and/or political climate, influence levels of depression and anxiety among lesbian and gay couples (Goldberg & Smith, 2011).

KARIN

In Annie's and my relationship, gender roles are pretty interesting. She's more femme than I am, but she also maintains our cars. I'm the one you would think of as the masculine partner if you saw us and I make more money, but I like cooking and baking and Annie doesn't. We've already agreed that I'll stay home with a child when we have one. We're equal when it comes to making decisions, and we take equal responsibility for keeping the house clean.

Gendered Patterns in Committed Relationships

Gendered orientations influence four dimensions of long-term love relationships: modes of expressing care, needs for autonomy and connection, responsibility for relational maintenance, and power.

PHIL

What does my girlfriend want? That's all I want to know. She says, if I really loved her, I'd want to be together and talk all the time. I tell her all I do for her. I fix her car when it's broken; I give her rides to places; I helped her move last semester. We've talked about marriage, and I plan to take care of her then, too. I will work all day and overtime to give her a good home and to provide for our family. But she says, "Don't tell me what you do for me," like do is a bad word. Now, why would I do all this stuff if I didn't love her? Just tell me that.

Gendered Modes of Expressing Affection As we have seen, the masculine mode of expressing affection is primarily instrumental and activity focused, whereas the feminine mode is more emotionally expressive and talk focused. Women often feel hurt and shut out if men don't want to discuss feelings and the relationship. Conversely, some men feel resentful or intruded on when women push them to be emotionally expressive. Thus, gendered socialization may prevent partners from recognizing one another's ways of communicating care.

As we have seen, for many women, ongoing conversation about feelings and daily activities is a primary way to express and enrich personal relationships (Peretti & Abplanalp, 2004; Yalom, 2015). The masculine speech community however, views solving problems and achieving goals as reasons to talk. Thus, unless there is a problem, men often find it pointless to talk about a relationship, whereas many women feel that ongoing talk keeps problems from developing.

The cultural bias favoring feminine modes of expressing love is illustrated by a classic study (Wills, Weiss, & Patterson, 1974). The researchers wanted to know how husbands' demonstrations of affection affected wives' feelings. To find out, they instructed husbands to engage in different degrees of affectionate behavior toward their wives, and then the wives' responses were measured. When one wife showed no indication of receiving affection, the researchers called the husband to see if he had followed instructions. Somewhat irately, the husband said he certainly had—he had thoroughly washed his wife's car. Not only did his wife not experience this as affection, but the researchers themselves concluded that he had "confused" instrumental with affectionate behaviors. Doing something helpful was entirely disregarded as a valid way to express affection! This exemplifies the cultural bias toward feminine modes of communicating love and affection. It also illustrates a misunderstanding that plagues many heterosexual romantic relationships.

TAMARA

Most of this course has been a review of stuff I already knew, but the unit on how men and women show they love each other was news to me. I'm always fussing at my boyfriend for not showing me he cares. I tell him he takes me for granted, and if he really loved me, he'd want to talk more about personal, deep stuff inside him. But he bought me a book I'd been wanting, and a couple of weeks ago he spent a whole day fixing my car because he was worried about whether it was safe for me—I thought of that when we talked about the guy in the experiment who washed his wife's car. I guess he has been showing he cares for me, but I haven't been seeing it.

Gay and lesbian couples tend to share perspectives about how to communicate affection. Gay men generally engage in more emotional and intimate talk than straight men but less than women of any sexual orientation. Lesbians, on the other hand, generally share responsibility for taking care of a relationship and build the most expressive and nurturing communication climates of any type of couple (Goldberg & Perry-Jenkins, 2007; Patterson, 2000). Lesbian partners' mutual attentiveness to nurturing, emotional openness, and conflict resolution may explain why lesbians report more satisfaction with their romantic relationships than gays or heterosexuals (Goldberg & Perry-Jenkins, 2007; Hunter, 2012).

Gendered Preferences for Autonomy and Connection

Autonomy and connection are two basic needs of all humans. We all need to feel that we have both personal freedom and meaningful interrelatedness with others. Yet, gender affects how much of each of these we find comfortable. Masculine individuals tend to want greater autonomy and less connection than feminine people, whose relative priorities are generally the reverse (Umberson, Thomeer, & Lodge, 2015).

Desires for different degrees of autonomy and connection frequently generate friction in close relationships. Many couples engage in a pattern called *demand–withdraw* (Caughlin & Vangelisti, 2000; Holley, Haase, & Levenson, 2013; Wegner, 2005). In this pattern, one partner encourages the other to communicate, and the other partner resists interaction that stifles his or her need for autonomy. The more one demands talk, the more the other withdraws; the more one withdraws from interaction, the more the other demands talk. Both men and women are likely to withdraw when partners demand or request change; however, the intensity of withdrawal is greater when a woman requests change in a man than when a man requests change in a woman (Sagrestano, Heavey, & Christensen, 1998). Socialized toward independence, masculine individuals tend to be more comfortable when they have some distance from others, whereas feminine people tend to be more comfortable with close connections. Ironically, the very thing that creates closeness for one partner sometimes impedes it for the other.

> **JEFF**
>
> *I get really frustrated talking about relationships with girls I've dated. It seems like they feel a need to discuss the relationship every time we're together. I don't get the point. I mean, why talk about a relationship if everything's going along fine? Why not just be in the relationship and enjoy it?*

> **JANELLE**
>
> *I don't know why straight women put up with partners who don't work on their relationship. Angie and I both invest a lot of time and emotion in taking care of our relationship because it matters to both of us. I talk to straight friends and hear them complaining about how their partners never even notice the relationship. I would never settle for that.*

More hurtful than the demand–withdraw pattern itself, however, are partners' tendencies to interpret each other according to rules that don't apply. For instance, to think that a man who wants time alone doesn't love his partner is to interpret his withdrawal according to a feminine ruler. Similarly, to perceive a woman as intrusive because she wants intimate conversation is to judge her by masculine standards. Illustrating this tension over autonomy and connection, a recent study revealed that teenage girls viewed their male peers' texts as brisk and abbreviated, while teenage boys viewed their female peers' texts as too long, intrusive, and including unnecessary information (Ling, Baron, Lenhart, & Campbell, 2014). By understanding gendered patterns and preferences, we can minimize the poison of misinterpretation and respect different needs for autonomy and connection.

Gendered Responsibility for Relational Health

Because most lesbians, like most heterosexual women, learn feminine ways of thinking and acting; both partners tend to be sensitive to interpersonal dynamics and interested in talking about their relationship and working through problems (Canary & Whaba, 2006; Hunter, 2012; Schwartz & Rutter, 1998; Shulevitz, 2015).

Against the standard set by lesbians, heterosexual couples do not fare as well in distributing responsibility for relational health. In heterosexual relationships, both men and women tend to assume that women have primary responsibility for keeping relationships on track.

The expectation that one person should take care of relationships burdens one partner with the responsibility of keeping a relationship satisfying. In addition, it is difficult for one person to meet this responsibility if the other person doesn't acknowledge and work on matters that jeopardize relational health. The partner who is expected to safeguard the relationship may be perceived as a nag by the one who fails to recognize problems until they become very serious. Not surprisingly, research shows that the highest level of couple satisfaction exists when both partners share responsibility for the relationship (Cubbans & Vannoy, 2004; DeMaris, 2007).

Gendered Power Dynamics

Historically, the person who earns the most money has had the greater power in heterosexual romantic relationships, and that person traditionally has been male. As you might predict, problems fostered by believing that men should be more powerful are not prominent in lesbian relationships, and lesbians tend to be particularly skilled at building harmonious relationships with romantic partners (Hunter, 2012). Gay and lesbian couples report a greater desire for shared power and decision-making than do heterosexual couples (Hunter, 2012).

As we noted in Chapter 7, the belief that men should be the primary breadwinners doesn't match reality for the growing number of heterosexual households in which the woman earns as much as or more than her partner (Patten, 2015). Social attitudes reflect these shifts: In 1977, two-thirds of U.S. citizens thought that the ideal family had a male breadwinner and a stay-at-home wife and mom. Today, not even one-third of U.S. citizens think that (Coontz, 2014).

People who adhere to traditional views of gender in relationships are more likely to experience a decrease in both self-esteem and marital satisfaction if the woman earns more money (Helms, Prouiz, Klute, McHale, & Crouter, 2006; Torabi, 2014; Waismel-Manor & Tolbert, 2010).

ERNEST

As a male who was reared by a single mother, I see women differently from most of the white men I know. I and a lot of blacks see women as our equals more than most white men do. We treat the women in our lives with a lot more respect than middle-class white males. Men who were raised by a single mother understand women and their plight better than most white men. We know we and women are in it together.

In heterosexual relationships, the belief that men have more power than women is often reflected in the distribution of labor in the home. Although the majority of two-parent households today have two wage earners, the housework and the care of children, parents, and other relatives continue to be done primarily by women in heterosexual families (Coontz,

2014; Patten, 2015; Schiebinger & Gilmartin, 2010; Sheehy, 2010). In fact, some men who don't have jobs in the paid labor force and whose female partners work outside the home engage in less child care and home maintenance than do men who have jobs in the paid labor force—as few as three hours a day (Dokoupil, 2009; Shulevitz, 2015). As a point of comparison, unemployed women spend twice as much time on child care and housework as employed women do (Dokoupil, 2009).

Gay and lesbian couples are more likely than heterosexual couples to divide child care and household labor equally between partners (Brewster, 2016; Goldberg, Smith, & Perry-Jenkins, 2012). Lesbians report greater equality in division of labor than do gay men, and, in lieu of relying on gendered norms to divide tasks, incorporate factors such as individual capacity and preference (Brewster, 2016; Goldberg, 2013; Kurdek, 2007).

Despite its mundane quality (or perhaps because of it), the division of household labor is not a small matter—the sharing of domestic responsibilities and chores is ranked by married couples as the third most important factor in a successful relationship, following fidelity and sexual intimacy (Klein, Izquierdo, & Bradbury, 2013). Men who share in child care tend to have relationships that have less conflict and more satisfying sex than men who participate less in child care ("Benefits of," 2015).

There are multiple reasons for women's and men's unequal contributions to domestic labor. One key reason is gender ideology. Men and women with more traditional beliefs about gender are more likely than people with less traditional gender beliefs to perceive it as appropriate for women to do most of the domestic labor. A second reason is women's alternatives to a relationship. Women who don't perceive desirable alternatives to their current relationships have little leverage to persuade their partners to participate more in domestic labor. A third reason is commitment to equity. Most people prefer equitable relationships—ones in which they and their partners invest relatively equally and in which both partners benefit equally. The extent to which partners are committed to equity affects how they divide domestic chores.

A fourth reason is gender socialization. Male socialization typically doesn't emphasize developing skills in domestic chores, whereas girls are often socialized to perform more

---

EXPLORING GENDERED LIVES

Fertile Expectations

Social expectations regarding responsibility for the care and nurturance of children may extend into medical treatments for infertility. According to the American Society for Reproductive Medicine (ASRM), male partners are the sole cause of, or a contributing factor to, approximately half of all infertility cases (2014), yet virtually all medical interventions for infertility are designed to treat women.

Assisted reproduction is emotionally, financially, and medically intensive. Women are subject to the most invasive stages of in vitro fertilization. The risks of these interventions include damage to women's internal organs, miscarriage, infections, ectopic pregnancies, multiple births, and babies born with low birth weight.

TAKE A STAND: Given that both sexes can contribute to couples' infertility, what is the fairest way to treat infertility? What connections do you notice between this and other gendered patterns of relational responsibility and care?

traditionally "feminine" tasks such as laundry, cooking, and cleaning. As a result, girls typically have developed skills in these tasks by the time they set up an adult household. In addition, many women have higher standards for housekeeping than their male partners. This may lead women to criticize how their male partners perform the tasks and to redo or take over tasks that their male partners aren't performing to the women's satisfaction (Coontz, 2014; Wiesmann, Boeije, van Doorne-Huiskes, & den Dulk, 2008). Responses like these understandably discourage men from being active in homemaking.

Millennial men have more egalitarian views related to gender, family, and career within marriage than men of older generations (Miller, 2015b). They are more likely to aspire to being hands-on fathers and to strike a balance between family and career. But research has demonstrated that these aspirations do not necessarily translate into equitable divisions of labor in the home, particularly if children join the family. One reason that aspirations may not be realized is inflexible work policies and cultural norms. Paternity leave is not as common or available as maternity leave (Rehel, 2014), and men who take leave for family reasons may be judged more harshly than women (Miller, 2014b; Parker & Wang, 2013).

Dubbing the extra domestic labor that women typically do the **second shift**, sociologist Arlie Hochschild (2003) reports that the majority of wives employed outside the home have a second-shift job in the home. Child care is a big part of the second shift for many women. Mothers with college educations spend an average of 21.2 hours a week with their children and mothers with less education spend 15.2 hours. Women whose wages are lower sometimes work multiple jobs, which leaves less time to spend with children.

Today's fathers are also spending more time with their children than did their own fathers. College-educated fathers spend an average of 9.6 hours a week with their children, and less educated fathers, who may work more than one job, spend an average of 6.8 hours a week with children. That's more than double the amount of time fathers in 1977 spent with children. Fathers under 29 years of age spend more time with children than older fathers do (Choose Your Parents Wisely, 2014; Council on Contemporary Families, 2010; Parker-Pope, 2010c; Shulevitz, 2015).

As Lynn O'Brien Hallstein (2008) points out, many women think that because becoming a mother is a choice, they are responsible for the consequences of that choice. In other words, many women who continue working in the paid labor force after becoming mothers accept the idea that they have to figure out how to manage motherhood and a career. They are reluctant to ask their workplaces to make accommodations, and they often find their partners are not willing to invest equal time and effort in parenting. Further, they may feel as much pressure to succeed at mothering as at their job (Choose Your Parents Wisely, 2014; Hallstein, 2010b).

GLORIA

I'm a mother and a professional and a part-time student, but I am not the only one who takes care of my home and family. That's a shared responsibility in our home. My daughter and son each cook dinner one night a week, and they switch off on chores like laundry and vacuuming. My husband and I share the other chores 50 - 50. Children don't resist a fair division of labor if their parents model it and show that it's expected of them.

■ EXPLORING GENDERED LIVES ■

Dads at Work

More than in past eras, many men today want to be full parts of their families and communities. Compared to dads a decade ago (Bland, 2012; Shulevitz, 2015):

54% take their kids to school once or twice a month, up from 38%

45% attend class events, up from 34%

41% visit their child's classroom once or twice a month, up from 30%

59% attend school-based parents meetings, up from 47%

28% volunteer at school, up from 20%

75% help kids with extracurricular activities, up from 71%

78% help with homework, up from 74%

77% attend parent–teacher conferences, up from 69%

Why do today's dads work so hard at parenting? In their own words (Bland, 2012):

"I know it sounds a bit clichéd, but they do grow up fast, so I want to spend time with them."

"I just want to be part of her life. I want to be there for her."

"I just feel if you're going to be a parent, you should be there."

TAKE A STAND: In your view, how much parental responsibility should fathers take on?

We should also note that much of the domestic work women do is more taxing and less gratifying than that done by men. For instance, whereas many of the contributions men typically make are sporadic, variable, and flexible in timing (e.g., mowing the lawn), the tasks women typically do are repetitive, routine, and constrained by deadlines (e.g., preparing meals) (Canary & Wahba, 2006; Hochschild with Machung, 2003). Women are also more likely to do multiple tasks simultaneously (e.g., helping a child with homework while preparing dinner). When it comes to child care, mothers tend to be constantly on duty whereas fathers more typically take responsibility of occasional fun child care activities, such as trips to the park or zoo.

AIKAU

My mother works all day at her job. She also cooks all of the meals for the family, does all of the housework, and takes care of my younger brother and sister. When my mother goes out of town on business, she fixes all of the family meals and freezes them before she leaves. She also arranges for day care and cleans very thoroughly before she leaves. My father expects this of her, and she expects it of herself.

The recession that began in 2008 propelled changes in men's involvement in home life. Between 2008 and 2010, millions of Americans lost jobs, and the majority of them were men. Although some of these men have returned to work, others have not. In 2014, one in six men in prime earning years is out of work in the United States (Peters & Wessel, 2014). For many of these men, the jobs they once had no longer exist due to globalization and technological innovation (Peters & Wessel, 2014). According to a recent study by the Pew Research Center, two million fathers are now stay-at-home dads by choice or necessity (Ludden, 2014).

EXPLORING GENDERED LIVES

The Mommy Myth

Motherhood in contemporary U.S. culture is cast as an idyllic experience but also subject to much public scrutiny (Douglas & Michaels, 2004; Fixmer-Oraiz, 2015). The ideal mother loves being with her children, never wants time away from them, and certainly never raises her voice or gets frustrated. Unfortunately, a lot of women find that real, day-to-day mothering is very different from the myth. Intense cultural expectations leave many mothers feeling overwhelmed by what they are expected to do and, simultaneously, feeling guilty that they aren't doing enough, doing it well enough, or enjoying the bliss of motherhood (Hallstein, 2010b; Schulte, 2014; Slaughter, 2012).

Media play a big role in creating and sustaining the mommy myth. Television programs and films often show the mythical woman who "has it all"—being a perfect mother and a successful professional. Working mothers in high-profile careers are featured in magazine and newspaper stories. Compounding media is the relentless quest for perfection that characterizes American culture—whatever we do, we should do it perfectly. One way to address this, say Douglas and Michaels, is to learn what the mommy myth is and to name every instance of it you see.

TAKE A STAND: Where do you see examples of the mommy myth in everyday life? Can you think of ways to promote more realistic views of motherhood and ways to lessen the stressors experienced by moms today?

For men who lose their jobs, the shift from paid employment to child care is difficult. Laid off after 20 years in a Fortune 500 company, Andrew Emery says, "It was a big part of my identity; it's who you are. It took me a long time to fill in the blank when people asked me what I do" (Kershaw, 2009, p. E6). Yet, many men find great satisfaction in being fully engaged fathers (Chesley, 2011; Fournier, 2016; Hickenlooper, 2016; Ludden, 2014). For men looking to rejoin the workforce, many hope to find careers that enable them to spend more time with their children, and the experience of being a primary caretaker can inspire more equitable divisions of domestic labor even after fathers rejoin the workforce (Chesley, 2011; Kershaw, 2009).

Another way in which women's contributions to home life have been greater is in terms of **psychological responsibility**—the responsibility to remember, plan, and make sure things get done (Hochschild, 2003; Shulevitz, 2015). Partners may agree to share responsibility for taking children to doctors, but women tend to remember when inoculations are due, schedule appointments, and keep track of whose turn it is to take the child. Similarly, partners may share responsibility for preparing meals, but women usually take on the responsibilities of planning menus, keeping an inventory of supplies, making shopping lists, and going to the grocery store. All of this planning and organization is a psychological responsibility that is often not counted in couples' agreements for sharing the work of a family.

The consequences of the second shift are substantial. Women who do most of the homemaking and child-care tasks are often extremely stressed, fatigued, and susceptible to illness (Babarskiene & Tweed, 2009; Hochschild, 2003), and they are at a disadvantage in their paid work because they are drained by responsibilities at home (McDonald, Phipps, & Lethbridge, 2005; Patten, 2015). Frustration, resentment, and conflict are also likely when one person in a partnership bears the double responsibilities of jobs inside and outside the home ("Benefits of," 2015; Chethik, 2008; Cubbans & Vannoy, 2004; Erickson, 2005). Similar stress has been found in single fathers who work a second shift.

EXPLORING GENDERED LIVES

Scientists and the Second Shift

Carol Greider got the call every scientist dreams of: The person at the other end of the line was in Stockholm and told her she had won a Nobel Prize. Where was Dr. Greider when she got the call? In her lab? Writing a scientific paper? Nope, she was folding laundry, one of the many home responsibilities she assumes.

Greider isn't alone. According to a study of scientists in the United States, female scientists do twice as much cooking, cleaning, and laundry as male scientists (Schiebinger & Gilmartin, 2010). And then there's child care. At the time she won the award, Dr. Greider had two school-age children, and she took much of the responsibility for going to their sports events, taking them to and from play dates, and so forth.

TAKE A STAND: Can you think of ways to reduce the second shift that many women experience?

Another clue to power dynamics is how couples manage conflict. Masculine individuals (whether female or male) tend to use more unilateral strategies to engage in and to avoid conflicts. They are more likely than feminine people to issue ultimatums, to refuse to listen or discuss an issue, or to assert that the partner is blowing things out of proportion. Feminine individuals more typically defer or compromise to reduce tension, and they employ indirect strategies when they do engage in conflict, which is consistent with feminine speech communities' emphasis on maintaining equality and building relationships (Rusbult, 1987; Stafford, Dutton, & Haas, 2000). Early on in lesbian relationships, partners tend to avoid discussions about interpersonal difficulties, but long-term lesbian couples report improvement in managing relational conflict through productive conversation. For gay partners, avoidant styles of managing conflict are more common, unless the relationship itself is perceived as at risk (Hunter, 2012).

EXPLORING GENDERED LIVES

Fathering in Other Species

Most human fathers may engage less in child care than human mothers, but fathering is a big time pursuit in some species (Angier, 2010). Among birds, males and females usually share the tasks of sitting on eggs to hatch them and fetching insects for the baby birds. In certain species of birds, such as emus and rheas, the males exclusively tend the nest.

And birds aren't the only active fathers. Male pipefish and seahorses become pregnant and give birth. Newborn marmosets and emporer tamarins are carried on their father's backs until they are able to move on their own. Some primates also emphasize the role and status of fathers. Male Barbary macaques, for example, appear with infants to increase their standing in their social groups.

TAKE A STAND: Can you think of reasons why males of different species have distinct tendencies toward fathering?

Finally, gendered power dynamics underlie violence, which is a means of exercising dominance over others. We will cover the topic of violence in detail in Chapter 12, but we need to acknowledge here that intimate partner violence is one manifestation of gendered power dynamics. Not confined to any single group, violence cuts across race, ethnicity, class, and sexual orientation. In the United States, one in four women has been violently attacked by her husband or boyfriend, and one is killed by her partner every six hours (Kristof, 2014b). At least 30% of women worldwide have been victims of intimate partner violence (Prevalence of Domestic Violence, 2013). Intimate partner violence is not confined to adult relationships. Approximately 1 in 10 high school students reports being physically hurt by a girlfriend or boyfriend, and 1 in 3 high school students reports psychological violence from a girlfriend or boyfriend (Hoffman, 2012).

Violence is inflicted primarily by men, most of whom have been socialized into masculine identities (Johnson, 2006; Neighbors, Walker, Mbilinyi, Olson & Rauscher, 2011; O'Rourke, Edleson, Zegree, & Roffman, 2010). In the United States, every 12 to 18 seconds a woman is beaten by a man; 4 women each day are reported beaten to death; and women are 600% more likely to be brutalized by an intimate partner than are men (Wood, 2001). We've seen that personal relationships reflect the expectations and orientations encouraged by feminine and masculine socialization. Gender differences surface in the ways that partners express and experience closeness, preferences for autonomy and connection, the distribution of responsibility for maintaining relationships, and power dynamics.

SUMMARY

Communication between friends and romantic partners is a powerful predictor of relationship strength and satisfaction. For this reason, understanding how gender shapes communicative practices can help us create better friendships and romantic relationships. Today, many people feel that traditional gender roles aren't satisfying or realistic. As people discover the limits and disadvantages of traditional gender roles, they are experimenting with new ways to form and sustain relationships and their own identities within those relationships. For instance, some men choose to be stay-at-home dads because they find greater fulfillment in nurturing a family than in pursuing a career in the paid labor force. Some women discover that they are more effective and more fulfilled by work outside the home than by work inside it. And many people balance home and paid work in ways that transcend traditional roles. Examples such as these remind us that we can edit cultural scripts, using our own lives to craft alternative visions of women, men, and relationships.

KEY TERMS

The following terms are defined in this chapter on the pages indicated, as well as in alphabetical order in the book's glossary, which begins on page 261. The text's companion website also provides interactive flash cards to help you learn these terms and the concepts they represent. You can access the site at www.cengagebrain.com.

alternate paths model 175

feminine ruler 175

male deficit model 174

passionate friendship 177

personal relationships 173

psychological responsibility 190

second shift 188

GENDER ONLINE

1. Look at personal ads on OkCupid or Match.com. To what extent do the characteristics sought reflect or challenge gender stereotypes?

2. Online search terms: *cross-sex friends, psychological responsibility, second shift, dual-worker families, division of household labor.*

3. The U.S. government's Violence Against Women office describes its mission, activities, and resources at **http://www.ovw.usdoj.gov/**

REFLECTION, DISCUSSION, AND ACTION

1. Reread the quotation on the opening page of this chapter. How could you apply this quotation to the idea of building and sustaining personal relationships?

2. Do you find more value in the male deficit model or the alternate paths model of closeness? How does the model you prefer affect your behaviors and your interpretations of others' behaviors?

3. To what extent are gendered patterns of interaction described in this chapter present in your current or past romantic relationships?

4. Expand your communication repertoire. If you have relied primarily on talk to build closeness, see what happens when you do things for or with friends to show that you care. If your friendships have tended to grow out of shared activities, check out what happens if you talk with friends without some activity to structure time.

RECOMMENDED RESOURCES

1. Rebecca Traister (2016). *All the Single Ladies: Unmarried Women and the Rise of an Independent Nation.* New York: Simon & Schuster. This book focuses on the relatively new phenomenon of women in developed countries choosing to marry late or not at all. She notes that women today have a range of options that were not available to their foremothers.

2. John Hickenlooper (2016). *The Opposite of Woe.* New York: Penguin. Former Colorado governor, John Hickenlooper recounts his travels with his son Teddy to meet presidents. Teddy and his father shared a love of history so their trips cultivated a deep bond.

3. Niobe Way (2011). *Deep Secrets: Boys' Friendships and the Crisis of Connection.* Boston, MA: Harvard University Press. In this book, psychologist Niobe Way conducts interviews with hundreds of teenage boys from a range of backgrounds about their friendships. She concludes that boy–boy friendships are very close and vital to boys' navigation of adolescence.

10

Gendered Organizational Communication

Knowledge Challenge:

- How large is the pay gap between women and men who work full time?
- Should women who choose to become mothers accept some tradeoffs in their career success? Should men who choose to become fathers expect similar tradeoffs?
- What is the glass escalator and who rides it?
- To what extent are quotas consistent with affirmative action?

Sheryl Sandberg, COO of Facebook since 2008, earned $16.1 million (plus benefits) in 2013 (Miller, 2014a). That same year, she published *Lean In: Women, Work, and the Will to Lead,* which urges women to "lean in" to their careers by aiming higher and working harder and faster (Kantor, 2012). To lean in, women need to squelch personal insecurities, stoke ambition, demand raises and perks, and balance work and the rest of life. The book was a bestseller and media dubbed Sandberg "the voice of contemporary feminism."

But not everyone agrees that Sandberg embodies contemporary feminism. In fact, some scholars and social critics think Sandberg's message is at odds with feminist values and commitments. Respected theorist and cultural critic bell hooks calls Sandberg's ideas as "faux feminism" (hooks, 2013) because they pertain to privileged white women's careers and are irrelevant to most women's jobs. According to hooks, Sandberg, like other power feminists, seems unaware of the profound ways in which race and economic class shape women's lives. Hooks sees Sandberg as advancing a "trickle-down theory: the assumption that having more women at the top of corporate hierarchies would make the work world better for all women, including women on the bottom" (hooks, 2013).

Additional criticism of Sandberg comes from Ann-Marie Slaughter (2013, 2015), an international lawyer and professor of politics and international affairs at Princeton who served as director of policy planning at the U.S. State Department from 2009 to 2011. Yes, many women are held back by a lack of confidence, says Slaughter, but that's not the only or even the most important barrier to women's professional success. Deeply gendered organizational policies and practices create challenges for women that men seldom face. Further, asserts Slaughter, these institutional barriers are not going to collapse simply because women boost their confidence and ambition.

Sandberg, hooks, and Slaughter are particularly visible spokespeople in the heated debate over whether women can "have it all." Yet they are hardly the only people who have stakes in the issue. Although this debate has been framed around women, it isn't about only women; it is also about workplace culture, the well-being of families, and men's lives and success as workers, partners, and parents.

In this chapter, we will examine this debate by looking beneath the surface arguments to gendered stereotypes, practices, and policies that make it necessary to ask whether it's possible to be successful both in the workforce and personal life. First, we examine gender stereotypes that affect how people are perceived and treated in the workplace. Next, we show gendered dynamics in formal and informal networks can result in inequitable treatment. Finally, we consider different ways to reduce sex and gender discrimination.

Gendered Stereotypes in the Workplace

Social expectations attached to sex and gender influence how workers are perceived and treated. Because people are often not aware of using stereotypes to perceive others, they do not notice, much less question, the stereotypes.

Stereotypes of Women

Women in the workforce are often perceived in terms of one of the four stereotypes, each of which is deeply gendered: sex object, mother, child, and iron maiden (Kanter, 1977; Wood & Conrad, 1983).

Sex Object   This stereotype assumes women's value is defined by their sexual attractiveness. Frequently, it leads to perceiving women workers based on their appearance rather than their qualifications and job performance.

MAGGIE

I worked at Hooters for a while. They had a manual you are given when you are hired at Hooters. It explains to you their discrimination policy and says they can discriminate based on age, weight, and level of attractiveness. They also have makeup and hair policies. Hair must be worn down and it must be done (curled or straightened); jewelry and tattoos are not allowed. Makeup is required.

The experience that Maggie describes is not unusual. The Equal Employment Opportunity Commission (EEOC) sued Abercrombie & Fitch, charging the company discriminated against job applicants based on race. The EEOC attorney claimed that Abercrombie & Fitch hired only women who were "white, young, and physically fit." The company paid 50 million dollars to settle the case (Hiring Hotties, 2012).

But is all discrimination illegal? No. Federal law forbids discrimination based on sex, race, national origin, age, disability, and religion. Some qualities are considered bona fide occupational requirements. For example, churches can require that clergy be members of their denomination and being bilingual or multilingual is necessary to work as a translator. There is no law that prohibits a company from discriminating based on attractiveness, and some companies, like Playboy Clubs and Chippendales, argue that attractiveness of staff is a bona fide job qualification.

Stereotyping women as sex objects contributes to sexual harassment, which is a continuing problem. The sex-object stereotype also underlies harassment of LGBTQ people. Like heterosexual women, gays, lesbians, bisexuals, and trans people are often perceived primarily in terms of their sexuality and their conformity—or lack of conformity—to traditional gender roles. Harassment is a means of policing people who dare to transgress conventional identity categories.

> ### MILISSA
> *Women can use the sex-object stereotype to their advantage. I pay for my education by being an exotic dancer, and I make better money than any other student I know. A lot of people think all exotic dancers are sluts, but that's not true. There's no difference between me using my body to fund my education and an athlete using his or her body to fund his or her education. Same thing.*

We saw examples of treating women as sex objects in the 2016 presidential primary. Hillary Clinton was criticized for not performing femininity—she didn't smile enough, gush enough, and so forth (Roodkowsky, 2016).

Mother   In institutional life, the stereotype of woman as mother has both figurative and literal forms. The figurative version of this stereotype is expressed when others expect women employees to take care of everyone—to smile, exchange pleasantries, prepare coffee and snacks, and listen to and help others. In fact, when women decline to help and support others, their careers suffer, whereas men who decline suffer no negative consequences (Grant & Sandberg, 2015).

Stereotyping women as mothers is one basis of job segregation by gender, a subtle and pervasive form of discrimination. A majority of women in the paid labor force are clerks, secretaries, assistants, and other jobs that, like those of mothers, support and care for others. Although at least half of the paid workforce in the United States is female, women account for only 4.6% CEOs of Fortune 500 companies, 19% of corporate board members, and less than 20% of Congress (Kristof, 2016a; Sandberg & Chávez, 2014; van Ogtrop, 2015). Even when they hold the same titles and positions as men, women consistently are paid less— 79 cents, on average, for every dollar a man earns (AAUW, 2013; Kristof, 2016a; Weber & Adamy, 2016).

The woman-as-mother stereotype also has a literal form. Today 71% of women in the United States who have children younger than 18 years work outside of the home (Bidgood, 2014). In addition, 4.8 million undergraduate students are raising children (Merisotis & Slaughter, 2016). These women, as well as women who are perceived as planning to have children, are often viewed as less serious than men or than women who aren't mothers (Kristof, 2016a; Williams & Dempsey, 2014).

████ **EXPLORING GENDERED LIVES** ████

Personal Choice or Institutional Discrimination?

If women choose to have children, shouldn't they expect to have more limited career opportunities than women who don't have children? That's the question many people ask when working mothers complain that they have fewer career options and are paid less than men or child-free women. At first glance, it seems reasonable to think that women should accept the career consequences of their choice to be mothers.

But the word *choice* is misleading. It obscures multiple ways that what is often cast as a "personal choice" is actually an outcome determined by structural factors that are far beyond the control of individual women.

- Women are the only humans able to carry a fetus so they assume all of the responsibilities during gestation.
- Some workplaces allow maternity leave but not paternity leave so mothers are the default primary parents of new children.
- Many coworkers hold stereotypes of woman as mother and man as bread-winner, making it likely the mother will be encouraged to take a leave, downsize

to part-time, or quit altogether and the father will not.

- Some organizations are more open to allowing female employees, but not male employees, to transition from full-time to part-time work in order to have more family time.
- Some men subscribe to traditional views of masculinity and are unwilling to let family responsibilities affect their careers.
- The United States does not provide universal child care or even reasonable support for families with children.
- Because women but not men are expected to be primary caregivers, many highly educated women pursue lower-paying career paths (pediatrics, rather than surgery; probate law rather than criminal law).

The choice to be a mother is constrained by myriad conditions outside of a woman's personal control. And yet, the perception that becoming a mother is a free choice is used to justify lesser jobs and pay for mothers (Kricheli-Katz, 2012; Slaughter, 2016).

TAKE A STAND: To what extent do you see the tendency of women to downsize careers if they have children as a personal choice? What differences do you notice when you compare this to men's career choices if they become fathers?

Mothers are less likely to be hired or promoted, they are offered lower salaries, and they are judged more harshly than non-mothers (Williams, 2013). In one experiment, two résumés were created for fictitious female job applicants. The résumés were identical except that one résumé noted that the applicant was active in the parent–teacher association (PTA), a tip-off that she was a parent. The applicant whose résumé mentioned the PTA was 44% less likely to be hired (Coontz, 2013). In another experiment, women with children were 79% less likely to be hired than equivalently qualified women who did not have children (Williams & Dempsey, 2014). Men who are fathers are not judged as less committed or competent in their careers; in fact, fatherhood tends to benefit male workers—they are seen as more committed to earning an income and offered higher salaries (Andronici & Katz, 2007; Budig, 2014; Miller, 2014b; Williams & Dempsey, 2014).

Law professor Joan Williams (2010) coined the term *maternal wall* to refer to unexamined assumptions held by coworkers and superiors about mothers. For example, a supervisor may assume that mothers are always available to their children. Based on this assumption, the supervisor may encourage Cynthia Cho to cut back on her hours and quit traveling. Later, when the supervisor is looking for someone with experience in different regions the company serves, the supervisor notes that Ms. Cho has not spent time in different regions and attributes this to her being a mother.

CHARLOTTE

I know the mother role all too well. Before coming back to college, I worked as an adjuster for an insurance company. In my office, there were eleven men and one other woman, Anne. I'll bet there weren't more than 10 days in the 3 years I worked there that one of the guys didn't come in to talk with me or Anne about some personal problem. Sometimes, they wanted a lot of time and sympathy; sometimes, they just wanted a few minutes, but always it was Anne and me they came to—never one of the guys. What really burns is that they went to each other to consult about professional matters, but they never came to Anne and me about those. They treated us like mothers, not colleagues.

Child   A third stereotype sometimes imposed on women is that of child, or pet—cute but not to be taken seriously. Women seen through this stereotype are assumed to need the protection of adults. "Protecting" women from challenging work often excludes them from experiences required for promotion and raises, as well as from the personal development that comes with new challenges. Women were first allowed in law enforcement in 1845 when concerned citizens demanded they be appointed as matrons in jails and insane asylums to protect inmates and patients from male staff. In the early 1900s, a few police departments began assigning female officers to supervise dance halls. Even in 1960, women officers (2.3% of all

---

EXPLORING GENDERED LIVES

He Says/She Says

He takes a balanced perspective.
She is wishy washy.

He collaborates.
She is too reliant on others' opinions.

He is decisive.
She is overly aggressive.

How we see others' behaviors depends as much on assumptions and stereotypes we hold as on what others actually do. Cognitive psychologist Therese Huston

(2016) points out that because women are stereotyped as indecisive, they are viewed as wishy washy when they consider multiple points of view; because men are stereotyped as decisive, they are seen as taking a balanced approach when they consider multiple points of view. Research demonstrates that both women and men engage in deliberative, data-driven decision making, but stereotypes often lead others to perceive the same actions by women and men quite differently.

TAKE A STAND: What do you think might lessen gender stereotyping in the workplace?

police) were assigned "safe" jobs in the office. Only in 1972 when an antidiscrimination law was enacted were policewomen allowed to make arrests, go on patrols, and otherwise fight crime. Female officers in heavy crime cities such as New York now make up approximately 20% of police forces, yet they account for only 5% of police shootings. Studies show female officers are only 25 to 33% as likely to fire guns as their male counterparts (Stewart, 2016).

Iron Maiden If a woman in the workforce is not perceived in terms of one of the three stereotypes we've discussed, she may be perceived as fitting a fourth. Women who are independent, ambitious, directive, competitive, and tough may be seen as "iron maidens." They are regarded as competent because they get the job done but unlikable because they are not sufficiently feminine (O'Neill & O'Reilly, 2011; Roodkowsky, 2016; Williams & Dempsey, 2014). During the 2016 Democratic Primary, polls consistently showed that many people considered Hillary Clinton experienced and competent but emotionally cool, aggressive, and ambitious—qualities that violate expectations for femininity. One political commentator asked, "Why is Hillary hatred so intense?" and answered "It's because Hillary isn't feminine or womanly, at least not in the traditional ways. She doesn't emote much publicly, she's not spontaneous, she's not touchy-feely.... Hillary doesn't fit these stereotypes so she's not a proper woman" (Roodkowsky, 2016, p. 13A).

■ EXPLORING GENDERED LIVES ■

Strategies for Women's Success in the Workplace

Joan Williams, who founded the Center for WorkLife Law at the University of California, and her daughter, Rachel Dempsey, coauthored *What Works for Women at Work* (2014). In this book, they identify five patterns of institutional life that pose obstacles to women's success in the workforce:

1. Prove It Again: Unlike men, women have to demonstrate their competence again and again in order to be perceived as competent.
2. The Tightrope: Women in the workforce experience tension between acting (1) feminine enough to be accepted but not so feminine as to be dismissed, and (2) masculine enough to be taken seriously but not so masculine as to be judged hard or too aggressive. As Williams and Dempsey phrase it, the tightrope is to be perceived as neither a "bitch" nor a "bimbo."
3. The Tug of War: Women who work outside of the home often feel they have

to defend their ways of managing work and life and may feel pushed to criticize strategies used by other women.
4. The Maternal Wall: Women who have children experience pressures to be at home rather than at work. In addition, women are perceived as less committed to their jobs if they have children.
5. Double Jeopardy: Women of color face the double whammy of racism and sexism, both of which can be woven into organizational policies and practices. For example, Asian women report that coworkers and supervisors expect them to be naturally good in STEM fields and to be passive.

To deal with these problems, Williams and Dempsey offer practical advice such as don't do "office housework" (taking notes and serving on social committees) and minimize talking about children in the workplace.

TAKE A STAND: Do you find Williams' and Dempsey's advice useful? Would you follow it if you encountered obstacles such as those they identify?

It is a compliment to call a male worker ambitious; it isn't necessarily perceived as a compliment to call a female worker ambitious. Kristen van Ogtrop, the editor of the highly successful *Real Simple*, points out that she and other women professionals "walk a fine line. We have to demonstrate enough ambition to be taken seriously as 'success material' but not so much that we're perceived as a freight train" (van Ogtrop, 2015, p. 54)

The four stereotypes we have discussed disadvantage women by defining them in terms of sex and gender instead of job qualifications and performance.

Stereotypes of Men

Within institutional settings, men are also stereotyped in ways that reflect cultural views of masculinity and that affect how men are perceived and treated. Three stereotypes of men are particularly prevalent in organizations: sturdy oak, fighter, and breadwinner.

Sturdy Oak   The sturdy oak is a self-sufficient pillar of strength that is never weak or reliant on others. When coworkers communicate that men should work independently, men

---

EXPLORING GENDERED LIVES

Gendered Wages

Mark your calendar to celebrate on April 8. That is Equal Pay Day, which is the day at which the average woman's pay catches up to that of the average man for the previous year. For example, if Jason and Janelle both work the same job in 2017, Janelle has to work until April 8, 2018, in order to make the same amount of money that Jason made in 2017. In short, women have to work significantly more days to earn what men do.

Lilly Ledbetter worked 19 years as a supervisor at a plant in Alabama. As she approached retirement, someone anonymously left her a pay schedule that showed she was making significantly less than men in the position she held. Ledbetter sued, but the Supreme Court ruled against her because the law stated that she had to file her suit within 180 days of the first occurrence of pay discrimination (Abrams, 2009; Collins, 2009a). Ledbetter, of course, had not realized that her pay was less for all those

years. The Lilly Ledbetter Fair Pay Act, which became law in 2009, revises the law to state that wage discrimination occurs whenever an employee receives discriminatory pay.

Despite this law, inequity in pay persists (Miller, 2016b; Rowe-Finkbeiner, 2014; The Truth About the Pay Gap, 2014; Waber, 2014; Weber & Adamy, 2016). Even though women of all races and ethnicities earn a larger share of the undergraduate degrees conferred in the United States (U.S. Department of Education, 2016), men continue to be paid more than women on average. Black and Latina women suffer the worst wage inequities—they are paid less than white women, white men, and men of color (National Women's Law Center, 2015).

The difference in earnings isn't fully accounted for by training, experience, or performance. In other words, sex discrimination continues to affect what people are paid for the work they do.

TAKE A STAND: What additional laws might be passed to reduce inequities in what women and men are paid?

may rule out consulting others for advice or assistance. One result can be decision making that is faulty because of insufficient input.

Fighter   Cultural stereotypes also cast men as fighters—superman-like warriors who go to battle, whether literally in war or metaphorically in professional life (Kunitz, 2016). Childhood training to be aggressive and win at all costs translates into professional expectations to beat the competition and to climb the corporate ladder. There is no room for being less than fully committed to the cause, less than ruthless in defeating the competition, or less than zealous in ambition.

Many employed men would like to spend more time with their families but fear that doing so would reduce their status at work (Miller, 2014; Parker & Wang, 2013; Reid, 2015). Writing in the prestigious *Harvard Business Review*, Erin Reid (2015) reported that men who ask for parental leave often experience hostility and discrimination because coworkers perceive them as not putting career first. But men are increasingly resisting the pressure to conform to the fighter stereotype and demanding the right to be involved with families. One man whose daughter was born five weeks prematurely asked for more than the two weeks of leave his company grants to new fathers. His company refused his request, he sued, and the company settled (Scheiber, 2015). The pressure for employers to provide more paternal leave is likely to increase as more millennial men, who place high value on family responsibilities, enter the workforce (Medved, 2016).

> ### GABE
> *A man at the place where I work part-time asked for family leave when his wife had a baby. Our manager gave him two weeks—he had to by company policy—but he really put the guy down behind his back. I heard him kidding with some of the other managers, saying did the guy think he was a mother or something? Nobody has ever said anything when a woman took family leave.*

Breadwinner   Perhaps no other stereotype so strongly defines and confines men in our society as that of breadwinner. Within organizations, stereotyping men as breadwinners has been used to justify paying them more than women. This stereotype is also why men are expected to put work ahead of family time.

Being the primary or sole breadwinner is central to how our society has historically judged men, as well as how many men judge themselves. Yet, men who tie their identity and worth to earning power are in danger in a culture where gender roles are evolving and the economy is uncertain.

Nonbinary Gender in Organizations

For those who do not conform to gender norms, organizational and professional settings pose unique challenges. As we saw earlier, women who challenge traditional femininity in organizations are often negatively stereotyped as iron maidens, and men who don't put career first are often viewed negatively. Similarly, lesbian, gay, bisexual, and trans workers are often met with hostility for challenging gender in the workplace, and they may have fewer legal protections.

For example, the question of what to wear to work is relatively simple for gender conforming individuals. For others, in the words of self-described genderqueer professional Jacob Tobia, "the question of what to wear to work becomes an exhausting question of identity and of survival. For us, the question changes from '*how* do I present my best self at work?' to '*can* I present my best self at work?'" (Tobia, 2014). As Tobia points out, performing nonbinary gender in organizational settings risks hostility by colleagues, eligibility for promotion, or even the job itself.

While many companies have adopted LGBTQ-inclusive policies, there are no consistent federal protections for sexual orientation and gender identity and expression. Thus, it remains legal in many places to discriminate against LGBTQ people in employment, eligibility for public services, education, credit, and housing (Human Rights Campaign Foundation, 2017).

Gendered organizational stereotypes are out of sync with the real people who make up the contemporary workforce. Most cisgender women and men in the paid labor force cannot be easily pigeonholed into gendered stereotypes. And, in addition to feeling hemmed in by gender norms in organizational settings, LGBTQ people are subject to mistreatment and discrimination without legal recourse. Narrow gender stereotypes limit the potential of all workers and the possibilities for robust and humane professional lives.

Masculine Norms in Professional Life

Because men originally designed the workplace—from stockyards to corporations—and laid the blueprint for its operation, masculine norms infuse the workplace. For the most part, individuals are unaware of these norms. Nonetheless, they powerfully shape expectations for conduct in the workplace. We'll examine two of these norms.

Traditionally Masculine Images of Leaders

The skills required to manage and lead are widely associated with communication skills that are cultivated more in masculine speech communities than in feminine ones—assertiveness, independence, competitiveness, and confidence. To the extent that workers engage in traditionally feminine communication, they may not be recognized as leaders or marked for advancement.

The answer isn't for everyone to adopt masculine communication. As we've seen, women who use assertive and instrumental communication may be branded "iron maidens" (Bennett, Ellison, & Ball, 2010; Williams & Dempsey, 2014). Coworkers who hold gender stereotypes may negatively evaluate women—but not men—who communicate assertively and who demand results.

There are some gender differences in how individuals approach work, including leadership. In general, men tend to find having authority to be intrinsically rewarding, whereas women are more likely to find authority rewarding if it is coupled with having influence (Schieman, Schafer, & McIvor, 2013). Also, men are more likely to be ambitious for positions and titles, whereas women are more likely to be ambitious for being valued, included, and recognized for performing well (van Ogtrop, 2015).

TARA

When I first started working, I tried to act like the men at my level. I was pleasant to people, but I didn't talk with coworkers about my life or their lives. I did my work, led my team with firm, directive communication, and stressed results. When I had my first performance review, I got great marks on achieving tasks, but there was serious criticism of "my attitude." A number of people—both my peers and staff I supervised— complained that I was unfriendly or cold. People criticized me for not caring about them and their lives. I pointed out to my supervisor that nobody made those complaints about men, and she told me that I couldn't act like a man if I wanted to succeed in business.

Let's also realize that all of us can develop new skills as we navigate new circumstances. Standpoint theory claims that we develop new skills when we find ourselves in contexts that demand them. If this is true, then as feminine communicators enter into settings that governed by masculine communication norms, they should become proficient complying with those norms. Similarly, as masculine communicators interact with coworkers who use feminine communication styles, they should develop skills in collaboration and support. A study by Patrice Buzzanell and Kristen Lucas (2006) on cisgender workers shows this dynamic— that both men and women develop new communication skills that are needed for effectiveness on the job. All of us can develop communication skills when we find ourselves in positions that require abilities not emphasized in our early socialization.

Finally, let's realize that organizational leadership is not a contest and does not need to promote the interests of one group over another. Research consistently shows that both women and men lead effectively and that groups that include both women and men make better decisions than those that include only men (Kristof, 2016b).

Traditionally Masculine Norms for Career Paths

The view of a normal career path is out of sync with the needs and identities of many of today's workers. Career paths were conventionally defined as linear progressions through which employees work up the ladder by demonstrating competence at each level. Historically careers have also been thought of as being full time.

The assumption that serious careers are linear and full time reflects social relations of previous eras in which most professionals were men who had stay-at-home wives to care for the home and children. Today, most women and men work outside of the home. Few people can afford full-time maids and nannies, so the responsibilities of taking care of home and family are not easily met when both partners work outside of the home. Organizations with the best chance of thriving in the future will adapt to the realities of contemporary workers and their families (Coontz, 2013; Williams, 2010, 2013). To fit the identities and life rhythms of today's workers, organizations need to ponder key questions about how they operate:

- Do all employees need to be at work by 8 or 9 a.m.?
- Must all work be done on site?
- Can employers provide paid family leave?
- Can employees take breaks of several months or years within a serious career?

- Can employees work part-time when they have young children or other family members who need attention and care?
- Can employees work different schedules on different days?
- Can organizations (at least large ones) provide on-site day care?

Both familial and professional commitments fuel our lives. Research indicates that mothers who work outside of their homes are at least as happy and healthy as stay-at-home mothers. This is especially true of employed mothers who have partners, and among single mothers, maternal employment is correlated with higher levels of emotional well-being (Meier, Musick, Flood, & Dunifon, 2016; Wills & Brauer, 2012). It is also clear that men who share the responsibilities of caring for children tend to become more patient, empathic, and flexible and are more satisfied with their jobs and personal lives (Sandberg & Grant, 2015a). Equally important, the research shows children whose parents work outside of the home are as emotionally balanced, socially adjusted, and academically accomplished as children with a stay-at-home parent.

Although most women who leave paid labor to care for children plan to return to the workforce in a few years, many run into barriers when they are ready to resume their careers. Many mothers encounter employers who prefer to hire women who are not mothers (Warner, 2013). Even those who do find jobs often discover that they don't have access to prestigious career ladders because colleagues and supervisors perceive working mothers as less than fully committed to their careers (Miller, 2015; Warner, 2013).

PERRY

I'll admit I was against having a woman promoted to our executive board, but I'll also admit that I was wrong. I thought Linda wouldn't fit in or have anything to add. I voted for a junior male who I thought would fit in with the rest of us executives. But Linda is just superb. What I like most about having her in our group is that she's a real consensus builder, and nobody else is. Linda's first concern always seems to be finding common ground among us, and she has an absolutely amazing lack of ego invested in decisions. I'm not sure it's flattering to admit this, but the guys in the group, including me, operate from ego. Sometimes, winning a point is more important than crafting the best decision. Linda moves us away from that mindset.

Gendered Patterns in Organizations

Organizations have both formal and informal practices. Formal practices include policies regarding leaves, work schedules, performance reviews, who reports to whom, and so on. Informal practices include normative behaviors and understandings that are not covered by explicit policies: advising, mentoring, socializing, and so forth. As we will see, both formal and informal networks entail gendered dynamics.

Formal Practices

Leave Policies   In 1993, the Family and Medical Leave Act (FMLA) was passed so that U.S. employees could take up to 12 weeks of unpaid leave to care for new babies or sick family members. In 2010, President Obama announced family leave was extended to workers in same-sex relationships who need time to care for a partner's child. Since the act was passed, more than 50 million Americans have taken family leave.

However, FMLA isn't available to all workers. Only companies with 50 or more workers in a 75-mile radius are required to grant family leaves, and small companies can refuse to give leave to some employees. All told, FMLA covers only about 60% of employees in the United States (20 Years in, FMLA Too Weak, 2013). Some individual states, however, have enacted more generous family leave laws.

Also realize that FMLA does not require employers to provide pay to employees who take family leave, although some individual states require paid family leave. Because FMLA does not require companies to provide paid leaves, many workers cannot afford a leave.

The United States has the humiliating distinction of being the only high-income country and one of a very few countries in the world that do not have a guaranteed paid family leave policy. As Figure 10.1 shows, of 188 countries in the United Nations according to a most recent study, 180 offer some level of financial payment to new mothers on maternity leave. Those that that do not are Oman, Papua New Guinea, Tonga, and the United States (Rowe-Finkbeiner, 2014; Zarocostas, 2014). Further, at least 70 countries provide paid leave to fathers (Coontz, 2013; Zarocostas, 2014). U.S. law also mandates fewer weeks of leave (unpaid) than other Western countries (Zarocostas, 2014).

The lack of paid family leave forces many workers to choose between taking care of families and earning income. The lack of institutional support also influences some workers' career choices. Some workers are dropping out of careers that don't provide support for families (Easton, 2015; Lien, 2015; van Ogtrop, 2015).

Work Schedules   Rigid work schedules are another reflection of outdated career models that assumed men were breadwinners and women were at home taking care of families.

■ EXPLORING GENDERED LIVES ■

Work-Life Balance for All

Work-life balance is important for all workers, yet most of the attention has focused on the professional class of workers (Merisotis & Slaughter, 2016; Villano, 2011). That's ironic since professionals already enjoy many benefits that enhance work-life balance. Most professionals know their work hours well in advance; they can come in late or leave early to deal with emergencies; and they can take breaks when they wish.

Low-wage workers often have none of those privileges. They have no flexibility about when they start and stop work; they often don't know their work schedules in advance, so they can't plan day care and other aspects of their lives; they can't take breaks when they please. Rigid schedules, inflexibility, and unpredictability add substantial stress to low-wage earners' lives. As many of these workers put it, "I'm one sick child away from losing my job."

The Institute for Workplace Innovation (IWIN) at the University of Kentucky is devoted to finding solutions to these stresses. Its goal is to boost the bottom line, employee health, and work-life fit. A full report from IWIN is available at **http://www.uky.edu/Centers/iwin/ LWPolicyFinal.pdf**

TAKE A STAND: Can you identify benefits other than those described above that most professionals have but that hourly workers do not?

Obviously, this model doesn't accommodate two-worker or single-parent families with young children. Even if parents can afford day care, children are sometimes too sick to attend; day care centers close on occasion, making it necessary for a parent to take responsibility for child care. Women are more likely than men to take time off to care for children, a pattern that reflects and reinforces gendered assumptions that women put families first and men put careers first. A new longitudinal study from the University of Chicago demonstrated that access to high-quality child care for disadvantaged mothers and children had long-term beneficial effects, including higher earnings and educational attainment not only for mothers but eventually for their children as well. Moreover, the return on state investment was 7:1 (Miller, 2017).

If all other developed countries have laws and policies that allow workers to also be good parents, so can the United States. In fact, providing more leave time and flexible working hours can actually save employers money because doing so boosts worker productivity, increases morale, and reduces turnover, making family friendly policies less expensive than training replacement employees (20 Years in, FMLA too weak, 2013; van Ogtrop, 2015).

Sweden is engaged in an interesting experiment. Concerned about employees' well-being, Svartedalens, a nursing home in Gothenburg, Sweden, cut the work shift from eight to six hours per day with no reduction in pay. After just one year, Svartedalens had greatly reduced absenteeism, improved worker health, and increased productivity—that's right: Workers accomplished more in six hours than in eight because they were motivated to be efficient. Similar results were achieved when a Swedish hospital switched to 30 hour work weeks (Alderman, 2016).

Informal Practices

In addition to formal policies, organizations have informal, unwritten understandings that can make or break careers. Through a range of normative practices, some organizations emphasize gender differences, define one sex or gender as standard, or extend different opportunities to individuals based on sex or gender.

Unwelcoming Environments   In some organizations, language and behavior that emphasize men's experiences and interests are normative. Consider the gendered nature of many terms taken from sports (*hit a home run, huddle on strategy, ballpark figures, second-string player, come up with a game plan, be a team player, line up, score a touchdown, put it in your court*), sexuality or sex organs (*hit on a person, X has balls, X is a real prick, screw the competition, get into a pissing contest, stick it to them*), and the military (*battle plan, mount a campaign, plan of attack, under fire, get the big guns*). Intentional or not, language related to sports, sexuality, and the military binds men into a masculine community in which some women and LGBTQ people feel unwelcome.

The Informal Network   Relationships with colleagues create a sense of belonging and provide access to essential information that may not come through formal channels. Because men originally organized most workplaces, many informal networks were created largely or exclusively by men, giving rise to the term *old boy network*. Hiring and promotion decisions are often made through informal communication within these networks. For example, while golfing, Brad tells Nathan about a job candidate; later that candidate stands out in Nathan's mind when he reviews applications for a job.

Is Paid Leave Available for Mothers of Infants?

● No paid leave   ● Less than 14 weeks   ● 14–25.9 weeks
● 26–51.9 weeks   ● 52 weeks or more

The New York Times

Source: WORLD Policy Analysis Center, Adult Labor Database, 2015

Figure 10.1 Paid Maternal Leave around the World.

EXPLORING GENDERED LIVES

"That's So Gay"

- Upon receiving a failing grade on an exam, Mike says to his friend Alvin, "That's so gay." Alvin has a trans twin sister and is an open ally of the LGBTQ community.
- Charlie's boss, a white woman, asks Charlie where he is "really" from. Charlie is third-generation Asian American.
- A man sees a woman changing a tire on her car and says, "Wow! That's pretty impressive, for a girl."

What are the consequences of the examples listed above? How do we describe their meaning and significance?

Some scholars (Campbell & Manning, 2014; Nadal, 2013; Sue, 2010a, 2010b, 2016) believe that comments such as these reflect and reinforce discrimination. Derald Sue (2010b) uses the term **microaggression** to refer to verbal (demeaning language), behavioral (crossing a street when a person of color approaches), or environmental (Confederate flag bumper stickers) insults that, regardless of intent, reflect and communicate negative bias or hostility toward individuals or groups that are marginalized by race, gender, sexual orientation, religion, or ability. According to Sue, microaggressions are different from overt, deliberate acts of bigotry, such as the use of racist epithets, because people who commit microaggressions often intend no offense or harm. For those who are subject to microaggressions on a regular basis, however, these everyday occurrences can lead to feelings of discomfort and alienation. Moreover, microaggressions can foster hostile environments in schools, workplaces, or public settings (Sue, 2016).

Other scholars do not see acts such as the ones at the start of this box as problematic. They argue that calling them microaggressions encourages a victim psychology in members of marginalized groups and atrophies their ability to handle such minor interpersonal scuffs on their own (Campbell & Manning, 2014; Lukianoff & Haidt, 2014). Further, small transgressions are inherent in the hustle and bustle of everyday social interaction and will never cease to exist entirely. Trying to regulate them has a chilling effect on free speech (Etzioni, 2014; Thomas, 2008).

TAKE A STAND: To what extent do you think microaggressions are discriminatory? What, if anything, should be done about them?

One reason that informal networks are comfortable is that they tend to be composed of people who see themselves as being similar—others in the group are "like me." The easy camaraderie among members of informal networks can also create barriers for coworkers who are not like most of the people in a group. Women, people of color, and gender nonconforming workers may not be invited into networks or not made to feel welcome if they try to participate. When only one or two women are in a group, they stand out as different and unlike most of the employees. Only when women or members of any other minority group reach a critical mass are they unlikely to be marginalized (Newton-Small, 2016). In the face of communication that defines them as outsiders, women and racial and sexual minorities may avoid informal networks and thus lose out on these key sources of information and support.

Mentoring Relationships   A **mentor** is an experienced person who guides the development of a less-experienced person. In the workforce, mentors are usually older employees who help younger employees build careers. A mentor is at least helpful, and sometimes indispensable, to career advancement. Women, people of color, and LGBTQ people are less likely than white men to have mentors.

Several factors account for the low number of women, people of color, and gender nonconforming workers who have the benefit of mentors. First, the numbers game works against them. Lower numbers of women and minorities in senior positions mean that there are few who might counsel new female and/or minority employees. Men are sometimes reluctant to mentor young women for a variety of reasons: They may fear gossip about sexual relations; they may assume that women are less serious than men about careers; or they may feel less comfortable with women than with men. Similarly, straight workers may be reluctant to mentor junior gay, lesbian, bisexual, and trans coworkers because they are less comfortable with them than with straight coworkers. Not mentoring women and minorities perpetuates the status quo, in which straight, cisgender white men get more help with career advancement than women; people of color; and gay, lesbian, bisexual, and transgender people. The reluctance to include women and minorities in informal networks and mentoring is a powerful form of favoritism that reproduces privilege by transferring power to people most like those who currently have power (DiTomaso, 2013).

In an effort to compensate for the lack of networks and mentors available in existing organizations, some professional women have formed their own networks, in which women share ideas, contacts, strategies for advancement, and information. In addition to furnishing information, these networks provide women with support and a sense of belonging with other professionals like themselves. As men and women become accustomed to interacting as colleagues, they may become more comfortable mentoring one another and forming sex-integrated communication networks.

Another challenge in professional settings is **workplace bullying**, which is repeatedly acting toward a person or persons in ways that humiliate, intimidate, or otherwise undermine the target's professional credibility (Einarsen, Hoel, Zapf, & Cooper, 2010; Fox & Lituchy, 2012). Workplace bullying may be overt (ridiculing someone's work in front of others) or covert (spreading rumors) or both. When persistent, it can interfere with the target's ability to be effective in doing his or her job.

Women and gender nonconforming workers are more frequently the targets of workplace bullying by both men and women. Men who bully tend to target men and women in roughly equal numbers. Women who bully, however, disproportionately target women (Fox & Lituchy, 2012). One reason for woman-on-woman bullying may be that, from the early years, girls are taught to evaluate and critique other girls (Workplace Bullying Institute, 2009). Recent reports suggest that approximately 10% of LGBTQ workers have left their jobs due to an unwelcoming environment, and 90% of trans people experience bullying or other mistreatment in the workplace (Baksh, 2016).

TANGIA

Where I used to work, the boss was always dropping in on the men who held positions at my level, but he never dropped in to talk with any of the women at that level. He also had a habit of introducing males in our division to visitors from the main office, but he never introduced women to them. It was like there was a closed loop and we weren't part of it.

▬▬▬▬▬▬▬▬▬▬ **EXPLORING GENDERED LIVES** ▬▬▬▬▬▬▬▬▬▬

The Glass Escalator

When Michael Alquicira couldn't find a job, he went back to school to become a dental assistant. After serving in the army, Daniel Wilden enrolled in a nursing school. Unhappy with his job as a data consultant, John Cook also trained to be a nurse. So did Dexter Rodriguez. These men are part of a growing trend for men to work in occupations historically dominated by women (Dewan & Gebeloff, 2012; Zuk & O'Rourke, 2012).

One advantage for men moving into these careers is that they advance more quickly and get paid more than their female peers. The **glass escalator** is an invisible advantage that accelerates men's success in female-dominated spheres of work. Although the glass escalator seems to help all men in women-dominated fields, it is most helpful to white men (Wingfield, 2009, 2013).

TAKE A STAND: Can you think of a reason other than discrimination why men are paid more and advance more quickly than women in careers predominantly pursued by women?

Glass Ceilings and Walls   Many women hit the **glass ceiling**, an invisible barrier that limits the advancement of women and minorities (Williams & Dempsey, 2014). Women's progress is often impeded by subtle discrimination. It might be the stereotype of women as mothers that leads an executive to assume that a working mother would not be interested in a major new assignment that could advance her career. It might be seeing a woman in sexual terms so that her competence is overlooked. It might be misinterpreting an inclusive, collaborative style of communication as lack of initiative. These stereotypes can create a glass ceiling—an invisible barrier—that keeps women out of the executive suite.

But glass ceilings may be only part of the problem. The term **glass walls** is a metaphor for sex segregation on the job, in which women are placed in "pink collar" positions that require skills traditionally associated with women (assisting, organizing, counseling, and human relations). Typically, such jobs do not include career ladders, on which doing well at one level allows advancement to the next. In essence, many of the positions that women are encouraged to take have no advancement paths (Ashcraft, 2006; Coontz, 2013).

Workplace discrimination—whether subtle or blatant—makes it more difficult for some people to get hired, get paid fairly, and advance. This is why there have been repeated efforts to stop discrimination. Assessing those efforts is the final topic in this chapter.

Efforts to Redress Gendered Inequity in Institutions

Five efforts to reduce discrimination in schools and the workforce are equal opportunity laws, affirmative action policies, quotas, goals, and diversity training. Understanding differences among these methods of redressing inequities will allow you to evaluate arguments for and against them and decide your own position (Moses, 2016). Although this chapter focuses specifically on the workplace, these remedies apply to both professional and educational settings, the two contexts in which efforts to end discrimination have been most pronounced. Significantly, none of these efforts explicitly protect LGBTQ workers and students at the federal level (Human Rights Campaign Foundation, 2017).

Equal Opportunity Laws

Laws prohibiting discrimination began with the landmark legal case *Brown v. Board of Education of Topeka, Kansas,* which was tried in 1954. In that case, the U.S. Supreme Court overturned the "separate but equal" doctrine that had allowed separate educational systems for white and black citizens.

Since the *Brown* decision, the United States has passed other **equal opportunity laws**. The two main ones are Title VII of the Civil Rights Act (1964), which prohibits discrimination in employment, and Title IX (1972), which forbids discrimination in educational programs that receive federal aid (Thomas, 2016). Other antidiscrimination laws are Title IV of the 1964 Civil Rights Act, the Women's Educational Equity Acts of 1974 and 1978, an amendment to the 1976 Vocational Education Act, and the Lilly Ledbetter Fair Pay Act passed in 2009.

Equal opportunity laws focus on discrimination against *individuals*. In other words, complaints must claim that a particular person has suffered discrimination because of sex, race, or other criteria named in laws. Equal opportunity law does not ask whether a group (e.g., women, Latinas, and gays) is underrepresented or is treated inequitably. Instead, it is concerned solely with discrimination against individuals.

Equal opportunity laws focus on *present* practices, so historical patterns of discrimination are irrelevant. For example, a university with a record of denying admission to women is not subject to suit unless a particular individual can prove she personally and currently suffered discrimination on the basis of her sex.

The scope of Title IX has changed since it first became law. Title IX was weakened in 1984 when the Supreme Court narrowed its application from whole institutions to specific programs that receive federal money. Recent EEOC rulings have extended protections against sex discrimination to workers based on gender identity and sexual orientation (McKinley, 2012; West, 2014), but these protections vary from state to state. There is no federal law that explicitly names sexual orientation and gender identity as protected classes (Human Rights Campaign, 2015).

Affirmative Action Policies

President Lyndon B. Johnson used his 1965 commencement address at Howard University to announce a new policy that would address historical prejudice, which equal opportunity laws ignored. He said, "You do not take a person who for years has been hobbled by chains and liberate him, bring him to the starting line of a race, and then say, 'you are free to compete with all the others.'"

Affirmative action is based on three key ideas. First, because discrimination has systematically restricted the opportunities of *groups* of people, remedies must apply to entire groups, not just to individuals. Second, to compensate for the legacy of discrimination, there must be *preferential treatment* of qualified members of groups that have suffered discrimination. Third, the effectiveness of remedies is judged by *results*, not intent. If hiring and admissions policies don't result in a greater presence of women and minorities, then they are ineffective in furthering equality.

Affirmative action has two important limitations. First, affirmative action policies recognize the *limited availability* of qualified people from historically underrepresented groups. Because of long-standing discriminatory practices, fewer women and minorities may have the education and experience to be qualified for certain jobs and academic programs.

Second, affirmative action aims to increase the number of *qualified* members of historically marginalized groups. It does not advocate admitting, hiring, or promoting women and minorities who are not qualified. To understand how affirmative action policies work, it's important to distinguish between *qualified* and *best qualified*. Consider an example: Janelle Evans and Jason Powell are candidates for the last opening in a medical school that requires a 3.2 undergraduate grade point average and a score of 1200 on the medical aptitude exam. Janelle's undergraduate average is 3.4, whereas Jason's is 3.5. On the entrance exam, she scores 1290, and he scores 1300. Although his qualifications are slightly better than hers, both individuals clearly meet the school's requirements, so both are qualified. Under affirmative action guidelines, the school would admit Janelle because she meets the qualifications and does so despite historical patterns that discourage women from studying science and math.

Affirmative action attempts to compensate for the effects of a history of bias by giving preference to members of groups who are qualified despite discrimination. As Thomas Shapiro (2007) points out, one reason that many African Americans are economically less well-off than Caucasians is that "one generation passes advantage and disadvantage to the next" (p. 133). Thus, whites who owned property in the 1700s passed it along to their children who passed it along to their children and so forth. Black people who were slaves owned no land, so they could not pass it on to future generations.

JOHNSON

I've never done anything to discriminate against members of other races, so I don't think I should have to step aside so they can have special advantages now. I don't owe them anything, and I earned everything I've got.

SHERETTA

I get so ripped off when I hear white guys badmouth affirmative action. They don't know what they're talking about. They speak totally from their self-interest and their ignorance. One thing that white guys say a lot is that they didn't hold blacks down in the past, so they shouldn't be penalized today. To that, I'd like to say they sure as hell don't mind taking a heap of advantages they didn't earn, like good schools and clothes and financial support. Do they think they earned those things? How do they think their daddies and granddaddies earned them? I'll tell you how: off the labor of black people that they were holding back, that's how.

Ever since affirmative action policies were enacted, public debate about them has been vigorous. A key issue is whether people hired or admitted under affirmative action guidelines succeed. A controversial study claimed that students admitted under affirmative action policies were less likely to be able to succeed at elite schools (Sander, 2004;

Sander & Taylor, 2012). But many scholars refute these findings (Chambers, Clydesdale, Kidder, & Lempert, 2005; Kennedy, 2015; Moses, 2016; Rothstein & Yoon, 2008). Some note significant evidence that the beneficiaries of affirmative action are not only equally successful in their own careers (Dreier & Freer, 1997; Mangan, 2004; Rothstein & Yoon, 2008) but are more likely to help other minorities achieve success as well (Bowen & Bok, 1998; Eisenberg, quoted in Slater, 2013). Moreover, some argue that the benefits of diverse classrooms are important for everyone—not just the individual beneficiaries of affirmative action (Kennedy, 2015; Liptak, 2016).

The Supreme Court has issued a number of rulings that clarify and refine affirmative action. In 2003, the Court ruled that race cannot be *the deciding factor*, but it may be a factor in admissions decisions because universities have compelling reasons to create diverse student bodies. Ten years later, in 2013, the Supreme Court reaffirmed this ruling with a 7 to 1 decision that racial diversity in college admissions may be a compelling state interest. In a 2013 case involving a Florida school, the Court tweaked earlier rulings by stating that race could be used as an admissions criterion only if no other measure would ensure a diverse student body. In 2014, the Supreme Court ruled that a lower court did not have the authority to overrule a Michigan law that "bars publicly funded colleges from granting preferential treatment to any individual or group on the basis of race, sex, color, ethnicity or national origin" (Mears, 2014). This decision empowers voters to enact laws that ban using race or other factors in admissions decisions (Dunn, 2013).

The most recent affirmative action case is *Fisher v. University of Texas*. When Abigail Fisher, a white woman, was not accepted at the University of Texas, she sued the university, claiming it had denied her admission based on her race. She argued that University of Texas's admissions standards, which include academic achievement and race, create discrimination against white students. In 2016, the Supreme Court ruled against Fisher and once again upheld a university's right to define the characteristics of a student body that are central to its identity and educational mission (Bollinger, 2016; Liptak, 2016).

LAKISHA

I don't know how anyone can say the playing field is even today. It's not. I'm the first in my family to go to college. Actually, I'm the first to finish high school. My school didn't have SAT prep courses. My parents didn't know how to help me with my homework or applications to colleges. I didn't have any of the breaks that most students at this college did. So don't tell me the playing field is even. If it weren't for affirmative action, I wouldn't even be on the playing field!

There is growing interest in revising affirmative action to give preference based on socioeconomic status rather than race and ethnicity (Kahlenberg, 2010a, 2012). Supporters of preference based on socioeconomic factors argue that focusing on socioeconmic status gets at the root of the underlying problem, whereas focusing on race and ethnicity treats only the symptom. People who are economically disadvantaged face numerous barriers to advancement in education and the job market. For instance, a white high school student from a working- or poverty-class family who has a 3.6 grade point average and a 1200 on the SAT has worked against significant disadvantages and, thus, may merit some preferential treatment over more affluent students.

EXPLORING GENDERED LIVES

When Quotas Raise Questions—and When They Don't

Some people think it's unfair to reserve places for women and minorities. They advocate evaluating all applicants on individual merit. It's interesting that questions aren't raised about a long-standing quota system that has benefited wealthy, white, and male students. Legacy policies accord preferential consideration to the children and/or grandchildren of alumni, especially those alumni who donate generously to the schools. Over 90% of elite institutions consider legacy status in admissions, and legacy applicants are 2 to 5 times more likely to be admitted to Ivy Leagues schools than non-legacy applicants (Dewan, 2016).

TAKE A STAND: Do you approve of schools giving preferential treatment to children of alumni?

Quotas

Perhaps the most controversial effort to redress discrimination is quotas. A **quota** specifies a number or percentage of some group that must be admitted, hired, or promoted. For instance, a company might stipulate that 30% of promotions must go to women. If there are not enough qualified women to meet the 30% quota, then women who lack qualifications must be promoted.

A famous case relevant to quotas was brought in 1978, when Alan Bakke sued the University of California at Davis's medical school for rejecting him, a white male, in favor of less-qualified minority applicants. Bakke won his case on the grounds that he had been a victim of "reverse discrimination" because the University of California at Davis violated his Fourteenth Amendment right to equal protection under the law. However, the Court did not outlaw the use of race as one factor that may influence admissions. It ruled only that schools may not set aside specific numbers of spaces for minorities.

NICOLA

The quota system is the only thing that can work. The laws aren't enforced, so they don't help, and affirmative action is just a bunch of talk. I've watched both my parents be discriminated against all of their lives just because of their skin color. All the laws and pledges of affirmative action haven't done a damned thing to change that. Quotas cut through all of the crap of intentions and pledges and say pointblank there will be so many African Americans in this company or this school or whatever. That's the only way change is ever going to happen. And when I hear white guys whining about how quotas are unfair to them, I want to throw up. They know nothing about unfair.

Goals

A goal is different from a quota, although the two are frequently confused. A **goal** is a stated intention to achieve representation of minorities or women. For instance, a company could establish the goal of awarding 30% of its promotions to women by the year 2020. If the company awarded only 10% of its promotions to women by 2020, there would be no penalty; the company could simply announce a new goal: to award 30% of its promotions to women by 2030. There are no penalties for not achieving goals.

Ironically, both quotas and goals can work against women and minorities. The numbers specified by quotas and goals can be interpreted as a maximum number of women and minorities rather than a minimum. In our example, the 30% goal could be used to keep more than 30% of promotions from going to women, even if 40% of qualified applicants were women.

TYRONE

I resent the way so many people at this school assume that any minority student is here only because of affirmative action or quotas. I've heard people say that if it weren't for racial quotas, there wouldn't be anyone here who isn't white. One of my suitemates even said to my face once that, since he hadn't had a quota to get him in here, he had to bust his butt to get into this school. I asked him what his SAT score was. He said 1080. I told him mine was 1164; then I walked out.

Goals and quotas can work against women and minorities in a second way. When goals or quotas are in effect, members of institutions may assume that women and minorities got in only because of their sex or race. When this happens, individual women and people of color are not regarded as capable members of the school, business, or trade. Regardless of their qualifications, women and minorities may be perceived as underqualified.

Diversity Training

A final remedy for persistent discrimination—one that is often combined with one of the other four—is diversity training, which aims to increase awareness of and respect for differences that arise from distinct standpoints shaped by a range of factors including race, economic circumstances, ethnicity, sexual orientation, gender identity, and religion. This strategy assumes that many people are unaware of how their comments and behavior could be offensive or alienating to women, members of minority ethnic communities or races, and people who have nontraditional gender identities.

An important limitation of diversity training is that it requires strong personal commitment from participants. Not everyone cares about inequities, and many people are unwilling to make changes, especially changes that reduce their own privileges. Thus, efforts to deal with discrimination are evolving. As the United States continues to become a truly equal society, we are likely to see new ways of addressing persisting inequities. The next Exploring Gendered Lives box calls attention to a very basic form of workplace discrimination—bias against a particular kind of work.

■ **EXPLORING GENDERED LIVES** ■

Profession or Oppression?

- Prostitution should be illegal because it is dehumanizing and intensifies gender inequality.
- Decriminalizing prostitution would enhance the status and safety of those who do sex work.

The above two points of view are two sides in a robust argument between abolitionists and activists for sex workers' rights.

Abolitionists chose their name to allude to the 1800s battle to end slavery and racial inequality. They believe prostitution should be illegal because it forces women into inequality. Yasmeen Hassan, the executive director of Equality Now, says "If prostitution is legal, and men can buy women's bodies with impunity, it's the extreme sexualization of women. . . . And if women are sex toys you can buy, think about the impact on relationships between women and men, in marriage or otherwise" (Bazelon, 2016, p. 38). For abolitionists, prostitution is a source of oppression and shame (Moran, 2013). Abolitionists tend to favor punishing men who seek paid sex and treating women who provide it as victims. They do not focus on sex workers who are not women.

When an abolitionist group authored a letter calling prostitution "a system of gender apartheid," the letter was signed by 400 people, including high-profile traditional feminists such as Gloria Steinem, Lena Dunham, Kate Winslet, and Meryl Streep (Bazelon, 2016, p. 38).

But big names are on the other side of the debate too. Amnesty International and Human Rights Watch have voiced support for decriminalizing prostitution

as has the World Health Organization and the Global Commission on HIV. These human rights groups argue for decriminalization for two reasons. One is pragmatic: People who do sex work will be safer because they can do it in contexts they choose and expect protection by law officers when that is needed. If their work were legal, they would not risk eviction, loss of custody of children, and deportation. People who hire sex workers would also be safer if regulations such as health checks and condom use were enforced (Bazelon, 2016).

The second reason that human rights group cites is ideological: *Sex work*, the term preferred by activists who favor decriminalization, is not intrinsically bad or dirty. Like any other profession, it is a means of earning income, and sex workers deserve the same respect and rights as other workers (Chateauvert, 2015; Jones, 2016; Kotiswaran, 2012). Most people try to choose work that they enjoy and many sex workers, including middle-class women, state that they like what they do—they enjoy sex and like feeling desired (Bass, 2015). Further, it can be a mode of personal empowerment. Prostitutes can choose when they work; they get paid better than at many jobs; and they learn they have "everything I need to survive" as one sex worker says (Bazelon, 2016, p. 38).

Workers' rights activists draw a sharp distinction between sex work that people choose, which they support and want decriminalized, and sex trafficking or other forced sex, which they oppose and think should remain criminal.

TAKE A STAND: What laws regarding sex work or prostitution, if any, should the United States Have?

SUMMARY

In this chapter, we have considered a variety of ways in which jobs and careers intersect with gender. Cultural views of masculinity and femininity seep into the formal and informal life of organizations and affect everyone who works in them.

Yet, current views of gender and the workplace aren't the only ones that are possible. You and your peers will design the workplaces of the future. One of the challenges for your generation is to remake our institutions so that all of us can live and work in humane and fair ways.

KEYTERMS

The following terms are defined in this chapter on the pages indicated, as well as in alphabetical order in the book's glossary, which begins on page 261. The text's companion website also provides interactive flash cards to help you learn these terms and the concepts they represent. You can access the site at www.cengagebrain.com.

affirmative action 211

equal opportunity laws 211

glass ceiling 210

glass escalator 210

glass walls 210

goal 214

maternal wall 198

mentor 208

microaggressions 208

quota 214

workplace bullying 209

GENDER ONLINE

1. To learn more about efforts to reduce discrimination in the workplace, visit the EEOC's homepage: **www.eeoc.gov**

2. Online search terms: *affirmative action, glass escalator, Lilly Ledbetter*.

3. One innovative organization to support people who have historically experienced job discrimination is the National Center for Faculty Development and Diversity. Learn about its mission, programs, and successes by visiting this site: **http://www. facultydiversity.org/**

4. To learn more about microaggressions and read examples, you can visit the Tumblr page credited with mainstreaming the term: **http://www.microaggressions.com**

REFLECTION, DISCUSSION, AND ACTION

1. Have you observed instances of classifying women or men workers into stereotypes identified in this chapter? How might workers resist being stereotyped?

2. Now that you understand distinctions among equal opportunity laws, affirmative action, goals, quotas, and diversity training, how do you evaluate each?

3. Interview professionals to learn how much they rely on informal networks. To what extent do women and men professionals report that they are equally welcomed into informal networks in their organizations and fields?

4. Talk with staff in the admissions office at your school to learn about admissions policies and enrollment of women and men, students of color, and students who are gender nonconforming. What is your opinion of your school's policies?

RECOMMENDED RESOURCES

1. Peggy McIntosh (2007). White privilege: Unpacking the invisible knapsack. In M. Andersen and P. H. Collins (Eds.), *Race, Class & Gender* (pp. 98–102). Belmont, CA: Thomson Wadsworth. This classic article makes visible white privileges in everyday life that most white people do not perceive.

2. Joan C. Williams and Rachel Dempsey (2014). *What Works for Women at Work: Four Patterns Working Women Need to Know*. New York: New York University Press. This book offers a very accessible description of ways in which discrimination is woven into organizations. It also offers practical suggestions for overcoming obstacles.

3. Jay Newton-Small's book, *Broad Influence*, makes a strong case for the importance of having enough women in powerful positions to promote positive social change.

The media we use and the stories they tell help to make us who we are.
—MARIA MASTRONARDI

11

Gendered Media

Knowledge Challenge:

- How much time does the average U.S. American spend consuming media across devices?
- To what extent do media portrayals of relationships shape expectations for real relationships?
- How effective are social media in organizing for social change?

February 23, 2012: Sandra Fluke, a law student at Georgetown University, appears at a hearing convened by Democrats and testifies that her school's health insurance policies have a harmful impact on women because they do not cover contraception.

February 27, 2012: CNS news proclaims "Sex-crazed co-eds going broke buying birth control."

February 29, 2012: On his radio show, Rush Limbaugh says of Fluke, "It makes her a slut, right. She wants to be paid to have sex."

March 1, 2012: Limbaugh adds fuel to the fire, saying, "If we are going to pay for your contraceptives, we want you to post the videos so we can watch."

March 1–3, 2012: Online outrage condemns Limbaugh's sexist, crude attack on Fluke.

March 3, 2012: Limbaugh posts a statement saying he regrets his "insulting word choices."

March 7, 2012: More than 45 advertisers withdraw from Limbaugh's show.

March 8 and beyond: Fluke is deluged with offers for jobs and speaking engagements. (Cottle, 2012; The Week, 2012)

This episode teaches us a lot about media and gender. One lesson is that media call things to our attention. If CNS and Limbaugh had not attacked Fluke, most people would never have heard of her. A second lesson is that we can discipline media. When blogs, social networking sites, TV broadcasts, and newspapers censured Limbaugh for his attack on Fluke, Limbaugh issued an apology. A third lesson is that social media play an increasingly significant role in negotiating issues related to gender. Finally, it teaches us that social media and traditional media are increasingly intertwined with and responsive to each other.

In this chapter, we explore how mass and social media influence understandings of gender and how social media in particular function as key contemporary sites of education, criticism, and activism.

Media Saturation of Cultural Life

We are the most media-saturated and media-engaged people in history. Mass media are pervasive. Currently 99% of U.S. households have at least one TV and 65% have three or more (Television Watching Statistics, 2016). The average U.S. citizen watches more than five hours of television a day, and children spend more time watching television than attending school (Television Watching Statistics, 2016). While walking, driving, or biking, we stream music or podcasts and take in an endless procession of billboards that advertise various products, services, and companies.

Social media take up more of our time than mass media. Recent surveys show that the average person in the United States spends six hours online every day (S. Bennett, 2015). Much of that time is devoted to social networking. We also use social media to connect with others, organize in our communities, and find out what's happening in the world. In addition, many of us become producers of media as we create blogs, podcasts, and videos to post on sites such as YouTube.

> **CECE**
>
> *Media don't influence what I think or how I dress or act. I can see that a lot of people follow whatever they see online or on TV or films, but I think independently. Sure, I go online and read magazines to see what's in style, but I decide for myself how I like to dress and act and everything else.*

Media Impacts

Like Cece, many people believe others are affected by media but they are immune to media's influences. In fact, that belief is so prevalent that it has a name: **third person effect**, which is the belief that media affect others more than they affect us (Davison, 1983). However, research shows that most of us are not immune to influence from mass and social media (Douglas, 2010a, b). In this section, we'll discuss three ways that media are related to gendered attitudes and behaviors: (1) media set the agenda, (2) media regulate images of gender, and (3) media motivate us to consume.

> **ANDREW**
>
> *Anyone who thinks media don't influence people just needs to spend five minutes on this campus. Everyone dresses alike and everyone changes how they dress when the media hawks new styles. Guys all wear the low slung jeans that nearly fall off their butts. All the girls wear pants so tight they look like they're painted on. Check out shoes. Check out hairstyles. Check out colors. Whatever the fashion gods say is in is what everybody wears. Tattoos? Earrings? If we're told they're cool, we all get them.*

Set the Agenda

A primary impact of media is **agenda setting**, the process by which media tell us what we should attend to. Mass media and some web-based media have the ability to direct public attention to particular issues, events, and people (Vivian, 2011). In setting the agenda, media may not tell us *what* to think, but they tell us what to think *about*—which issues, events, and people merit our attention; and which aspects of people and events are most important. Issues on the front page of the newspaper appear most important; a hashtag or video that goes viral seems more consequential than one that does not. The outrage against Limbaugh was fueled by blogs and print and online newspapers covering and responding to the unfolding drama. It *became* an issue to think about because media put it on our agenda.

The term **gatekeeper** refers to people and groups that control which messages get through to audiences of mass media. Gatekeepers include editors, owners, bloggers, producers, and advertisers. The gatekeepers for newspapers and news programs shape our perceptions by deciding which issues to spotlight, which points of view get a hearing, and how to depict women, men, people of diverse sexual orientations and gender identities.

An example of gatekeeping comes from media coverage of wars. Newspapers routinely feature poignant pictures of teary-eyed children watching mothers go to war, while online polls ask, "Should a woman leave her baby to go to war?" Perhaps this is a reasonable question to ask about any parent, but media tend to ask it only about mothers and not about fathers. By doing this, media encourage us to perceive parenting as central to women and peripheral to men.

Regulate Images of Gender

Acting as gatekeepers, media regulate the images of gender that reach us. In turn, this can affect our views of what women, men, and gender nonconforming people are supposed to be, feel, think, and do. Media underrepresent women as well as people of color and LGBTQ people, and they portray all genders primarily in stereotypical ways that reflect and reproduce conventional views.

Underrepresent Women, Minorities, and LGBTQ People
Although the United States is increasingly demographically diverse and women outnumber men, media overrepresent cisgender heterosexual white men, particularly as substantive characters.

Whether in film, cartoons, or newscasts, males outnumber females. Only 30.2% of characters in top-grossing films who have names or speak are female, and less than 25% of leading characters are female (Dargis, 2015; Dowd, 2015). Despite exceptions such as Meryl Streep, women actors tend to peak when they are 30 while male actors usually peak in their late 40s (Digits, 2015). Fewer than one in five female characters in major films is older than 40 (Dargis, 2015). The majority of women characters on television shows are depicted in interpersonal and secondary roles (Merskin, 2011; Sharp, 2011). Behind the scenes, the underrepresentation of women is even more marked: Only 1.9% of top-grossing movies are directed by women (Dowd, 2015). *A Wrinkle in Time*, released in 2017, made a dent in this glass ceiling: directed by Ava DuVernay of *Selma*, it is the first time a woman of color directed a $100 million movie.

The **Bechdel Test** assesses gender bias in film by asking three simple questions: (1) does the film feature two women (2) who talk to each other (3) about something other than a man? A surprising number of films fail to meet the Bechdel Test. In 2016, half of the Academy Award nominees for best picture failed the Bechdel Test. Interestingly, data suggest that films with strong female characters gross more than those that marginalize women; recent examples include the *Hunger Games* series and Disney's *Frozen* and *Moana* (Dewey, 2014; Hickey, 2014).

News programs rarely present women as authorities. Men make up 66% of quoted material in newspapers and 75% of sources on major news shows (Farhi, 2012). Even on issues

EXPLORING GENDERED LIVES

The Geena Davis Institute

When actress Geena Davis was watching TV with her young daughter, she was stunned by how few female characters there were. Wanting strong role models for her daughter and other young girls, Davis persuaded the Annenberg School for Communication and Journalism to undertake the largest ever study of gender representations in film and TV. The Annenberg study found that there is one female character for every three male characters (the same ratio as in 1946) and females make up a mere 17% of characters in group scenes. These findings led to the establishment of the Geena Davis Institute at the Annenberg School. The Institute's goals are research, education, and advocacy for gender equity in media representations.

TAKE A STAND: What do you think gender equity in media would look like?

where it would be reasonable to think women have more expertise than men—birth control and abortion, for example—men are often the primary sources. Women make up less than one-third of the sources for stories on women's rights (Farhi, 2012). Moreover, while most writers face criticism, female bloggers and journalists are subject to an extraordinary amount of professional intimidation and abuse online, including threats of rape, sexual assault, and even murder (Douthat, 2014; Hess, 2014; Wallace, 2014).

When powerful women make headlines for their professional contributions, journalist Sarah Kendzior notes that the "princess effect" often sets in, making women subject to descriptions of their appearance and clothing and framing them with narratives that open with fashion and close with workout advice (Kendzior, 2014).

These issues are compounded by race for women of color, as media also underrepresent and often negatively portray minorities. In the 500 top-grossing films between 2007 and 2012, 76.3% of speaking characters were white, 10.8% were black, 5% were Asian, 4.2% were Hispanic, and 3.6% were from other or mixed race ethnicities (Smith, Choueiti, & Pieper, 2013). Hispanic women were most likely to be shown with little or no clothing, and black men were those least likely to be portrayed as fathers or in a committed relationship. Media depict Asians and Asian Americans in stereotypical ways as well—for example, women are often portrayed as silent and exotic or as ruthless and evil while men are typically portrayed as asexual and subordinate or villainous (Balaji & Worawongs, 2010; Cortese, 2016; Ono & Pham, 2009). Despite studies demonstrating that viewers are drawn to media with diverse casts and writers, women and minorities are far less likely to be lead actors, writers, and producers (Dowd, 2015; Lee, 2013; Smith, Choueiti, & Pieper, 2013).

Films also give scant representation of people who are not straight and cisgender. Top-grossing films from 2007 until 2014 featured only 19 characters who were gay, lesbian, or bisexual; none were trans (Dargis, 2015). In this sense, the 2016 film, *Moonlight*, broke new ground. Television programs such as *Orange Is the New Black* and *Transparent* have defied the trend by featuring strong roles for LGBTQ characters and actors.

Portray Men Stereotypically   The majority of men on prime-time television are independent, strong, aggressive, and in charge (Katz, 2013). Popular films such as *Captain America: Civil War, Jason Bourne,* and *The Legend of Tarzan* present extreme stereotypes of masculinity: tough, independent, confident, totally in control of all emotions, and—above all—in no way feminine.

Even television news programming is disproportionately male. Men report 65% of political stories in the United States and are on camera 68% of the time on nightly news shows (Women's Media Center, 2015). The five Sunday morning news programs on major channels are all anchored by men, and 74% of guests on those shows are male (Women's Media Center, 2015).

Equally interesting is how men are *not* typically portrayed. The most obvious deficiency is the scarcity of nonwhite men and nonwhite versions of masculinity, a phenomenon that enforces white, cisgender, straight masculinity as the norm. Also, men are seldom shown nurturing others or doing housework. Media have done little to reflect men's increasing involvement in home life and child care.

Yet, traditional representations of men are not the whole story. Media offer some complex portrayals in which male characters combine traditional masculinity and femininity or in which characters do not fit neatly into any of the existing gender-sexuality categories. The men in *Modern Family* and *The Big Bang Theory* deal with emotional issues and friendship across lines of race, class, and sexuality. Tom Hanks embodies versions of masculinity that are unafraid of feelings and relationships in films such as *Philadelphia* and *Saving Mr. Banks*, as does self-proclaimed feminist Matt McGorry in his roles in *Orange Is the New Black* and *How to Get Away with Murder*. Stassa Edwards of *Jezebel* writes, displays of vulnerablity are increasingly available to men: "Chris Pine can weep at the Oscars and still helm a major action franchise; Drake's self-aware sensitivity cuts to the core yet he's still sexually potent... John Boehner can openly weep" (2016). And in 2014, Michael Sam spoke openly with ESPN of his status as one of the few openly gay players in college football, which challenged normative assumptions about masculinity and gay identity. However, displays of vulnerability tend to be viewed more favorably when performed by men otherwise perceived as powerful and traditionally masculine, whether they are professional athletes, star actors in action films, or national political figures.

As important as alternative images of men are, they are exceptions in mass media. Media scholars Deborah Borisoff and Jim Chesebro (2011) report that the version of masculinity that predominates in films and music features "social control and domination by force, a power orientation, and physical strength and determination as the means to achieve social status and prestige" (p. 77).

Portray Women Stereotypically   Media continue to portray girls and women primarily in ways consistent with traditional stereotypes. Media show female characters shopping, grooming, being emotional, talking about and flirting with men, being sexual, and engaging in domestic activities (Cortese, 2016; Smith, Choueiti, & Pieper, 2013; Smith, Choueiti, Scofield, & Pieper, 2013). Even when films or television programs feature strong, competent women characters such as those on *Criminal Minds*, they are usually very attractive, heterosexual, and sensitive to others. The most traditional stereotype of woman is sex object and that continues to dominate media portrayals of women and, increasingly, young girls (Cortese, 2016; Smith, Choueiti, Scofield et al., 2013). Even animated films feature female characters with impossibly small waists, large breasts, and pretty faces.

Like media representations of men, those of women tend to portray whiteness as both the norm and the ideal. According to a recent study, media overwhelmingly stereotype black women as "Gold Diggers, Modern Jezebels, Baby Mamas, Uneducated Sisters, Ratchet

---

EXPLORING GENDERED LIVES

Beyond Sexy Sidekicks and Damsels in Distress

Anita Sarkeesian is a gaming enthusiast who spent much of her free time as a child with her Nintendo. Later, as a college student of gender and women's studies, Sarkeesian was increasingly disturbed by the limited ways in which games depicted women and girls—for example, as rewards, sexy sidekicks, damsels in distress, and decorative or sexual objects that players can use or abuse (Sarkeesian, 2014). In 2009, she launched a video blog titled *Feminist Frequency* to raise awareness about sexism and violence in gaming culture. Her work has been featured on TED Talks, at tech conferences, and is circulated widely through YouTube and social media.

Sarkeesian has not been well received by all, however. Her Wikipedia page was vandalized, she was threatened with rape and assault through Twitter, her Facebook page was bombarded with pornography, and she became the subject of an online game titled *Beat Up Anita Sarkeesian*. Undeterred, Sarkeesian launched a wildly successful online fundraiser to support her work.

In a recent interview, Sarkeesian stated that things were beginning to change: "It's now not uncommon for developers to be challenged directly about the portrayals of women in their games. I've also heard from industry insiders that developers are starting to have conversations about how to improve the representations of women" (Liss-Schultz, 2014). And feminist hackers are beginning to rewrite the stories themselves—refiguring classic games like *Donkey Kong*, *The Legend of Zelda*, and *Mario Brothers* to feature princesses saving the day in games titled *Donkey Kong: Pauline Edition*, *Zelda Starring Zelda*, and *Princess Peach* (Sherr, 2013).

TAKE A STAND: Have you seen evidence of sexism in video games?

Women, Angry Black Women, Mean Black Girls and Black Barbies" (Walton, 2013). Media occasionally offer depictions of black femininity that black women report as more representative of their community: "Young Phenoms, Real Beauties, Individualists, Community Heroines, Girls Next Door, and Modern Matriarchs" (Byng, 2013; Walton, 2013). Perhaps unsurprisingly, depictions of black femininity are far less stereotyped when black women get to tell their own stories, as in Beyoncé's *Lemonade* or Margot Lee Shetterly's *Hidden Figures*.

Media's preference for white norms for female attractiveness explains why many black women in advertising and programming have light skin and straight hair. Asian women and Latinas are often represented as exotic and sexualized (Brooks & Hébert, 2006). Amy Hasinoff's (2008) analysis of *America's Next Top Model* provides further evidence of media's normalization of whiteness. Hasinoff found that judges described women of color as having "an exotic look" or "an urban vibe" but described white women as "classic" and "American" (p. 334). In *Liquorice*, rapper Azealia Banks critiques such fetishized fantasies of black women.

JILL

I hate reading magazines or watching TV anymore. All they tell me is what's wrong with me and what I should do to fix it. I think my butt is too big; my roommate has decided hers is too little. Doesn't anybody have a butt that is right? Same for breasts. I wonder if I should have breast enlargement surgery. It sounds stupid, but I keep thinking that I would look better and be more popular. I pluck my eyebrows and wax my legs and streak my hair. I wonder if it will ever be okay for women to look like they really look!

Pornography, which many consider the ultimate sexualization of women, provides an abundance of free material to an increasingly large audience. One video-sharing site, Pornhub, states that 2.4 million people visit every hour (Luscombe, 2016). A recent study found that the average age for males' first exposure to pornography was 12 years old (Luscombe, 2016).

Makeover reality shows are especially blatant in extolling stereotyped images of attractiveness in women (The Big Reveal, 2009). Judges on *America's Next Top Model* lavish praise on anorexic contestants and call normal-sized contestants "plus sized"; in 2015, *Glamour* magazine featured comedian Amy Schumer in its "plus-size" issue. Makeover shows shine the spotlight on women who are willing to undergo multiple cosmetic surgeries to meet unrealistic and unhealthy ideals for feminine beauty. The message for women is clear: If you aren't gorgeous, your job is to make yourself over until you are (Newsome, 2011).

Media juxtapose images of "good" and "bad" women to dramatize the distinct consequences that befall good and bad women. "Good women" are pretty, deferential, faithful, and focused on home and family. Subordinate to men, they are usually cast as victims, angels, martyrs, and loyal helpmates and they are rewarded with good lives. Cinderella wins the Prince because she is a beautiful, passive, and "good" woman. "Bad" women appear as the witch and evil stepmother in children's stories and programming and as the bitch, slut, or unattractive woman in adult media. Bad women usually come to unhappy ends—they die, are banished into the black forest, or simply disappear.

In recent years, media have featured some women characters that depart from tradition. For instance, Claire Underwood in *House of Cards* and Tris Prior in the *Divergent* series are both strong, capable, and powerful. *Grace and Frankie* revolves around two older women friends, *The Fosters* features a multiracial family headed by a loving lesbian couple, and the groundbreaking web series *Brown Girls* centers queer millennials of color. Disney's wildly successful *Frozen* featured two strong female leads in Princess sisters Elsa and Anna, and Moana's quest was to save her people. These images of women depart from traditional stereotypes in some ways. Yet many images of women, particularly those that appear in mainstream media, continue to center whiteness, thinness, cisgender identity, and youth. What may appear to be radically different images of women remain entwined with familiar, traditional images.

Gendered Images in Advertising   The gendered stereotypes we've discussed appear not only in films, games, and programs but also in advertising. For several reasons, advertising's influence on our views of gender may be even more powerful than that of programmed media content (Berger, 2015; Kilbourne, 2010a, b). First, advertisements on TV, in magazines, on billboards, online, and so forth are repetitive, so we are constantly exposed to them. Second, most ads emphasize visual images, which we tend to analyze less critically than verbal claims. Third, advertising can affect us significantly because we mistakenly think we're immune to it. Research suggests ads do affect what we purchase and what we consider attractive, desirable, feminine, and masculine (Berger, 2015; Kilbourne, 2007, 2010).

Consistent with traditional views of masculinity, advertising generally portrays men as independent, successful, engaged in activities, and strong. The men in ads tend to be tall and muscular, and they are shown as being in control. Men's dominance is also emphasized by positioning them above women, and women are more frequently pictured in varying degrees of undress (Geena Davis Institute, 2010; Katz, 2013). The message is that this is the ideal of masculinity. These unrealistic images can contribute to negative self-images for men with normal bodies and to extreme, sometimes dangerous behaviors aimed at achieving the fabricated ideals.

AF archive/Alamy Stock Photo

Tris Prior is a strong, independent female character.

EXPLORING GENDERED LIVES

Co-opting Feminism

"You've come a long way, baby," was the slogan for Virginia Slims cigarettes, which were aimed to appeal to female smokers. The slogan invoked feminism, supposedly complimenting women on their accomplishments while also linking coming a long way to smoking. T-shirts proclaiming "This Is What a Feminist Looks Like" allow women to wear their politics while also lining the pockets of the shirt manufacturers. Dove's much noted "real woman" campaign explicitly invites women to be their true selves without makeup while also telling them that Dove products are the route to that end.

It's no surprise that capitalist societies, such as the United States, try to sell us products. However, as Andi Zeisler (2016) points out, reducing feminism to personal choices of products to buy is extreme, even in capitalist economies. According to Zeisler, advertising depends on promising to eliminate women's insecurity even as advertisers create that very insecurity.

TAKE A STAND: To what extent do you find Dove's "Real Woman" campaign feminist?

What burns me up is those programs and commercials that show men as absolute idiots. One of the worst is that one where the mother gets sick, and the kids and husband just fall apart without her to fix meals and do laundry. Give me a break. Most guys can do the basic stuff just as well as women, and I'm tired of seeing them made into jokes anytime they enter a nursery or kitchen.

The dominance of males who are shown in ads is paralleled by the authority of men who are not shown but are heard as the voices of authority. For example, women do more house-work than men, so presumably they know more about the products for cleaning. Yet, Mr. Clean tells them how to keep their homes spotless. In many commercials for products, a man's voice is used to explain the superiority of the product that is being sold. Fully 80% of **voice-overs** are by men (Pedelty & Kuecker, 2014), reinforcing the cultural view that men are authorities and women need men to tell them what to do.

The ad that just kills me is the one where a woman is cleaning her carpet with whatever product is being advertised—something you sprinkle on your rug and then vacuum up. This woman is dancing around with her vacuum and seems deliriously happy—like this is what she most loves to do in the world. We may do cleaning, but only a total bimbo would get ecstatic about it. That ad makes women look silly and stupid and trivial.

Central to advertising is sexual objectification of women. Women—usually very young, with minimum clothes, and in highly sexual poses—are used to sell everything from jeans to fishing line (Berger, 2015; Kilbourne a, b, 2010). The relentless emphasis on youth and appearance for women may explain why older women seldom appear in television ads, whereas ads often feature older men in positions of prestige and authority (Baumann & de Laat, 2012).

The influence of ads is more subtle when ads don't stand out because they are blurred with content. One way this happens is when an advertiser pays for an ad in a magazine, and, in return, the magazine gives **complimentary copy**—one or more articles that increase the market appeal of its product (Turner, 1998). A soup company that places an ad might be given a three-page story on how to prepare meals using that brand of soup. A second way in which advertising and content are blurred is **product placement**, showing or mention-ing a particular brand or product in a show, story, film, or other form of media. For exam-ple, glasses with the Coca-Cola logo are in front of the judges on *American Idol*. **Contextual advertising** is embedded in digital content and tailored to specific individuals based on extensive data mining practices by web-based companies. These include tracking patterns in Internet use and online shopping and data culled from personal email and social media accounts (Albergotti, 2014). Have you ever logged on to Facebook and seen advertisements for a product you recently looked at? That's contextual advertising.

If complimentary copy, product placement, and contextual advertising blur the line between advertising and content, **immersive advertising** erases the line. Immersive adver-tising incorporates a product or brand into storylines in books, television programs, and

---

EXPLORING GENDERED LIVES

Is Censorship the Answer?

Should we ban violent, misogynistic media that celebrate violence against women? Even those who are most outraged by the objectification and sexism of media seldom advocate censorship. The U.S. Constitution provides strong protections of freedom of speech and for good reason. The problem with censoring is that somebody decides what all of us can watch, hear, and see.

Who has the right to make this decision for all of us?

A better answer may be to demand that media offer us multiple, diverse images of women and men. Instead of banning what we don't like, perhaps we work to enlarge the range of ways in which people and relationships are portrayed.

TAKE A STAND: Under what conditions, if any, would you support censorship of media?

---

films (Lamb & Brown, 2006). For instance, Naomi Johnson (2010, 2011) critically analyzed romance novels marketed to young girls. She found that storylines in series such as *A List* and *Gossip Girl* revolved around buying products such as La Perla lingerie and Prada bags and relying on services to glamorize the face and body. The characters' identities were defined by particular products and services.

Women appearing as sex objects and men appearing as sexual aggressors are common in many popular music videos and video games. For example, record-breaking singles from Robin Thicke's "Blurred Lines" to Tyler Farr's "Redneck Crazy" depict rape and stalking, respectively, as normal and even desirable; they portray women as possessions and sex objects and portray men as egocentric, violent, and entitled. In some video games, winning requires graphic violence against women (Durham, 2009; Ivory, 2008; Sarkeesian, 2014). In carrying to extremes the stereotyped images of masculinity as aggressive and femininity as passive, these portrayals encourage us to see violence as erotic, normal, and desirable.

Motivate Us to Consume

Media encourage us to consume. In fact, some media analysts say that the primary purpose of media is to convince us we need to buy more products and spend, spend, spend. Media encourage us to think that that buying whatever is advertised will make us happier, more attractive, and more successful (McRobbie, 2009; Zeisler, 2016).

Advertising plays on these insecurities by associating certain products and procedures with happiness and success. It's understandable to wish we weighed a little more or less, had better-developed muscles, and never had pimples. What is not reasonable is to regard healthy bodies as unacceptable or defective. This, however, is precisely the perception that predominant media portrayals of women and men cultivate. Media have convinced millions of American women that what reputable medical sources consider normal body weight is really cause to diet (National Institute of Mental Health, 2016). To achieve constructed and arbitrary ideals, many women continue to endure surgery that sometimes leads to disfigurement and loss of sensation. In 2013, women had over 10.3 million cosmetic procedures, which was 91% of the total number of all cosmetic surgeries for that year (American Society of Plastic Surgeons, 2016). The top five procedures for women were breast augmentation, liposuction, tummy tuck, breast lift, and eyelid surgery. In addition, surgeries to conform to white ideals of beauty are on the rise within and beyond the United States (Hunter, 2011). Skin-lightening or bleaching products are marketed all over the world, but particularly to women and men of the Global South, and are popular in African nations including Ghana, Kenya, Mali, Nigeria, Senegal, South Africa, and Tanzania (Hunter, 2011). One of the most popular—and controversial—cosmetic surgeries for Asians and Asian Americans is eyelid surgery to make the eyes appear more round (American Society of Plastic Surgeons, 2016; Bagalawis-Simes, 2010).

Turning to history helps us to understand how powerful media can be in shaping social attitudes and behaviors about gender. You might be surprised to know that only in the last century have underarm and leg hair been viewed as unfeminine. Beginning in 1915, a sustained marketing campaign persuaded women that underarm hair was unsightly and socially incorrect. (The campaign against leg hair came later.) *Harper's Bazaar*, an upscale magazine, launched the crusade against underarm hair with a photograph of a woman whose raised arms revealed clean-shaven armpits. Underneath the photograph was this caption: "Summer dress and modern dancing combine to make necessary the removal of objectionable hair" (Adams, 1991). By 1922, razors and depilatories were firmly ensconced in middle America. In recent years, the hair removal campaign has targeted men—promoting the clean (usually waxed) chest as the ideal of masculinity. Thus, companies expand the market for products and services to increase their profits.

As demonstrated in this example, the pressure to purchase is not restricted to women. Media also tell men that they are deficient but can fix that by consuming products. The body-building trend has created unrealistic and unhealthy ideals for masculine bodies and has been linked to the increasing abuse of steroids among men. Although media's idealization of extreme musculature and strength is not the only cause of steroid use, we should not dismiss the influence of portrayals of muscle-bound men as ideal (Katz, 2013; Lindgren & Lélièvre, 2009).

Normal changes in men's sexual vigor are also represented as problems to be solved by buying the right products. In recent years, Viagra, Levitra, and Cialis have become blockbuster drugs, making millions for the companies that can solve the "problem." The "problem," of course, was not a problem until drug companies decided they could make money by transforming normal changes in male sexual vitality into problems to be treated by buying drugs. Lured by the promise of greater sexual vitality, men are consuming these drugs, despite warnings of health risks by the American Medical Association and the Food and Drug Administration (Fauber, 2009; Von Drehle, 2014).

Media encourage us to measure up to impossible ideals. When we fail, as inevitably we must, we feel bad about our bodies and ourselves. Accepting these messages, however, is not inevitable: Each of us has the ability to resist those we consider inappropriate or harmful.

CHRISTI

When I used to diet, I remember thinking that I was in control. I believed what all the ads said about taking charge of myself, exerting control. But I was totally not in control. The advertisers and the companies making diet products were in control. So was society with the idea that "you can't be too thin," and that it's more important for girls to look good (read "thin") than to feel good (read "not hungry"). Society and its views of women were in control, not me. I was totally a puppet who was just doing what they told me to do.

Just as we can resist media, so too can we use media, especially social media, for our own reasons and to achieve our own purposes. The next section of this chapter examines how we use social media.

Gender and Social Media

For many of us, social media are seamlessly woven into our lives. We rely on them for everything from checking the weather to shopping to playing games and staying in touch with friends. While there is much debate about how digital culture is shaping the world for younger generations, scholar danah boyd (2014) argues that far from being "passive consumers or pliant sex objects," young people are savvy with their use of social media in constructing and managing their everyday lives and relationships. They are "cultural creators and arbiters who are, at least partially, controlling and scripting their own lives and experiences" (Quart, 2014). Moreover, social and traditional media are increasingly enmeshed in the digital world, as much of the research in this chapter indicates, and thus, social media tends to reflect overall gendered patterns in media.

Still, there are some important and unique intersections between social media and gender. In this section, we'll discuss four distinct functions of social media that are related to gendered attitudes, identities, and activism. We use social media to (1) to network, (2) learn and share information, (3) hold others accountable, and (4) engage in activism (Cox & Pezzullo, 2016). As we discuss these functions of social media, keep in mind that they often overlap as when learning about issues motivates activism.

Social Networking

One of the most popular uses of social media is networking. Girls, women, and LGBTQ individuals are more inclined than heterosexual, cisgender boys and men to regard the online environment as a resource for creating and enriching relationships. In their online communities, girls and women share stories and develop friendships (boyd, 2014; Perrin, 2015), and they engage in video chatting more than boys (Teens & Online Video, 2012). However, recent research also suggests that while girls and women engage these activities more frequently than men and boys, boys and men are more likely to verbally express support in online communication than in face-to-face communication (High & Soloman, 2014).

Girls and women are also more likely than boys to use social media as a venue for self-development. Teen girls use their blogs and pages on social networking sites to talk about issues such as pressures to be skinny, drink (or not), have sex (or not), and dress particular ways (boyd, 2014; Orenstein, 2016a). As girls work out what they think and want to do in their online communities, they count on comments from others to clarify their own thinking and gain confidence in their ability to reject gender norms they find troubling.

Social networking technologies have also been adapted by LGBTQ and gender nonconforming people in ways that reflect their experiences. Research demonstrates that LGBTQ-identified youth use social networking for identity exploration and formation, locating LGBTQ-positive resources, navigating the process of coming out to family and friends, and building friendships and community with other LGBTQ people (Craig & McInroy, 2014; Fox & Ralston, 2016). One study called social media "a key source for informal learning among LGBTQ individuals" (Fox & Ralston, 2016).

Social networks can be—and too often are—used for **cyberbullying**, which includes text messages, comments, rumors, embarrassing pictures, videos, and fake profiles that are meant to hurt another person and are circulated through email or social media. Social networking sites such as Facebook have not done much to develop anti-bullying policies; in fact, they encourage subscribers to give up privacy (Bazelon, 2013). According to a recent report, 25% of young women report being stalked or harassed online, and even more, 43% report being cyberbullied (Women's Media Center, 2015). For LGBTQ teens the percentage is even higher: 53% (Burney, 2012).

Not all boys and girls are equally likely to be victims of cyberbullying (or face-to-face bullying). Girls who are victims tend to be more physically developed than others in their age cohort and are perceived as less attractive than peers or are perceived as more attractive than peers. Girls who are regarded as less attractive are ridiculed for not measuring up to feminine ideals while girls who are very attractive are bullied out of jealousy. One of the more common tactics for bullying girls is to spread rumors that they are sluts.

Boys, especially nonwhite boys, who are perceived as feminine are most likely to be victims of cyberbullying (Anderson, 2011; Burney, 2012). Collapsing distinctions between gender and sexuality, and reflecting both sexist and homophobic attitudes, bulliers belittle them for not being sufficiently masculine. In fact, posting comments that a boy is gay is a common form of cyberbullying.

Online bullying and harassment are not inconsequential. Victims of cyberbullying are more likely to use drugs and alcohol, refuse to attend school, and have lower self-esteem and more health issues (U.S. Department of Health & Human Services, 2014). More serious consequences are also possible.

- 15-year-old Amanda threw herself in front of a bus when she could face no more of the cruel posts on her Facebook wall.
- 13-year-old Rachel hanged herself after an anonymous text saying she was a slut was circulated through her school.
- 14-year-old Jamey killed himself after an anonymous text saying he was gay became a widely spread rumor.
- 15-year-old Phoebe took the advice of a cyberbullier who urged her to hang herself.
- 14-year-old Megan committed suicide when information she confided to a person who posed as a friend was turned against her online.
- 18-year-old Tyler jumped off a bridge after his roommate Ravi urged friends and Twitter followers to watch via his hidden webcam Tyler having sex with a man.

Cyberbullying differs from face-to-face bullying in two key ways. First, it can be and often is perpetrated anonymously. Through fake accounts and other online maneuvers, an individual can post horribly hurtful messages and photos without ever being accountable for her or his actions. Second, cyberbullying has no geographic boundaries. The school-yard bully pretty much stayed on the school yard. Thus, a victim could escape by going home or visiting a friend. Online bullying can follow the victim anywhere and anytime. It is unremitting.

Learning and Sharing Information

The digital world has boundless sources of news and information about gender issues. For instance, strong interest in gender issues led online newspaper *Huffington Post* to create sections devoted to news for women (**http://www.huffingtonpost.com/section/women**)

EXPLORING GENDERED LIVES

Am I Pretty?

The *New York Times* notes a disturbing YouTube trend among young teens. The practice is to upload a video posing the question: "Am I pretty?" and await public response. The vast majority of video uploads are from girls between the ages of 13 and 15. The *Times* reports that a YouTube search for "Am I Pretty" videos results in more than 23,000 hits; some date as far back as 2009 but most are from 2013 or 2014. And the responses to the videos are critical and harsh: "You are really ugly. Now go cry to someone that actually cares" or "Ugly. At first I thought you were a boy" (quoted in Quenqua, 2014).

While some dismiss the trend as yet another example of youth narcissism and superficiality, others have noted that social media amplify gendered pressures facing young women and girls. Certainly, the pressure to conform to femininity encourages adolescent girls to invite others to rate their attractiveness and to hold themselves to unrealistic and damaging beauty standards. The *Huffington Post* refers to the phenomenon as "forcing girls to participate in their own self-abuse and then blaming them for it." Jezebel has asked YouTube to stop allowing the videos on its site.

TAKE A STAND: What, if anything, do you believe can or should be done about "Am I Pretty" videos?

---

and LGBTQ communities (**http://www.huffingtonpost.com/section/queer-voices**). Many people check in with feminist blogs such as Jezebel (**http://jezebel.com/**), Guerrilla Feminism (**http://www.guerrillafeminism.org**), and Black Girl Dangerous (**http://www .blackgirldangerous.com**). College students across the United States have created informal online networks to share information and strategize about sexual assault on campuses (Pérez-Peña, 2013), and activists use microblogging platforms like Tumblr to raise gender awareness, as in popular sites such as Racialicious, Project Unbreakable, and Microaggressions.

The National Organization for Men against Sexism (**http://www.nomas.org/**) provides information on issues in men's lives as well as issues in women's lives that matter to men who care about women. Likewise, the National Organization for Women (**http://www.now.org/**) provides news on political matters relevant to gender equity.

In addition to sites, Twitter feeds and news apps are ways to stay on top of information as it unfolds. You can follow particular individuals—for example, Michael Kaufman (@ GenderEQ) blogs and tweets about issues in men's lives and Rachel Maddow (@maddow) covers a range of public affairs. News apps such as the *New York Times* and National Public Radio will push alerts to your smart phone so that you stay on top of the headlines.

There are also online communities that provide information and support related to specific issues. There are online sites for kids and teens who experience bullying (e.g., **http:// www.stompoutbullying.org/livechat_portal.php**), male victims of sexual abuse (e.g., **http:// www.rainn.org/get-information/types-of-sexual-assault/male-sexual-assault**), surviving rape (e.g., **http://www.aftersilence.org/**), and human rights relevant to gender (e.g., **http:// www.ips.org/institutional/global-themes/human-rights-and-gender-issues/**).

Providing information about gender issues is not restricted to big organizations and high-profile reporters. Social media allow ordinary individuals to document what's happening in their communities and broadcast those reports (Cox & Pezzullo, 2016). For instance,

Hollaback is an online grassroots effort to end street harassment that you'll read more about in Chapter 12. On Hollaback's site (**http://www.ihollaback.org**), women who are harassed can post photos and stories, thereby documenting the harassment and the harasser.

Holding Others Accountable

Mass media have historically been voices against corrupt, immoral, or harmful actions by powerful interests. The long-airing *Sixty Minutes* television show often exposed corporate and political misconduct as have courageous journalists throughout history. Picking up this function of traditional media, social media have emerged as vital forces in holding corporations and other powerful interests accountable for sexism and gendered violence.

Activism

Social communities are fertile ground for cultivating activism. A number of large and small national organizations use social media sites to get their messages to the public by creating their own pages and posting action alerts, and politically engaged young people see social media as a key feature of their activism and organizing (Vromen, Xenos, & Loader, 2015). For example, Black Lives Matter (**http://blacklivesmatter.com**) began as a hashtag and was rapidly transformed into a national grassroots movement. Another example of cultivating activism is Amy Poehler's *Smart Girls at the Party* series (**http://amysmartgirls.com/**), which includes interviews with young feminists (some are under 5 years old) who give a young and contemporary face to girl power and gender equity.

▌ EXPLORING GENDERED LIVES ▐

Watch Out for Sparks

Eighth grader Julia Bluhm was sick of airbrushed, digitally altered photos of underweight women in her *Seventeen* magazine. She sparked change by turning to her online network of activists at SPARK. It didn't take her long to get 84,000 signatures and that led to a meeting with executives at *Seventeen* (Considine, 2012). Following the meeting, Ann Shoket, *Seventeen's* editor, announced that every member of the staff had signed a Body Peace Treaty in which they promise the magazine will "never change girls' body or face shapes" and will include exclusively images of "real girls and models who are healthy" (Haughney, 2012).

SPARK works to end the sexualization of women and girls in media. In the SPARK community, girls 13 and older work together and partner with other organizations to develop and implement strategies to challenge media's hypersexualization of girls and women.

SPARK was started by college professors in 2010 to empower young girls to fight against the unrealistic images of girls and women that media create. Overseeing SPARK are experienced activists, who mentor young girls and connect them with SPARK's network of 60-plus partners including Girls Inc. and NOW. Visit SPARK at **http://www.sparksummit.com/**

TAKE A STAND: What forms of hyper-sexualization of women do you consider most damaging to college-aged women? How might you develop strategies to challenge those?

Social media are ideal platforms for activism, allowing for community organizing that is nimble and almost immediately responsive. An example of this happened in June of 2013, when Texas state senator Wendy Davis filibustered an antiabortion bill on the floor of the Texas state senate for over 11 hours, during which she was not allowed breaks for food, water, the restroom, or sitting. The night prior to her filibuster, she tweeted the following to her roughly 1,200 followers: "The leadership may not want to listen to TX women, but they will have to listen to me. I intend to filibuster this bill" (Recent Legislative Debate, 2013, p. 844). Thanks to social media, people all over the world began to tune into her filibuster, which was broadcast live through YouTube into the wee hours of the morning. At its peak, over 180,000 viewers were watching the event streaming live online. Davis's filibuster provoked significant public awareness and commentary concerning women's health and rights, and significantly for this chapter, it demonstrated the power of social media to initiate an important conversation. In the days that followed, Davis's filibuster gained headlines in major, traditional news outlets (Fernandez, 2013; Tumulty & Smith, 2013).

Thus, social media allow us to communicate in multiple ways that are related to gendered attitudes, identities, and activism. We use social media to network, learn and share information, hold others accountable, and engage in activism.

Consequences of Gendered Media

The images and messages that media advance are not innocent; they have consequences. Throughout our discussion of media's effects on people, we've hinted at harms. Let's now look more closely at two specific ways that media's unrealistic images of gender can affect us adversely.

Normalize Unrealistic Standards

Media's unrealistic images of men, women, and relationships encourage us to see ourselves as inadequate. Regardless of how many products we buy and how many surgeries we have, few of us are going to look like Jennifer Lawrence, Beyoncé, Channing Tatum, or Ryan Gosling. In fact, even those celebrities don't really look like they appear in magazines and on-screen.

Media efforts to pathologize natural bodies can be very dangerous. As we have seen in previous chapters, the emphasis on excessive thinness contributes to severe and potentially lethal dieting and eating disorders. Nonetheless, most of the top female models are skeletal. Seeing anorexic models as the ideal motivates many women and girls to diet excessively in an effort to force their bodies to fit a socially constructed ideal that is unrealistic and unhealthy. Dangers—including heart attack, stroke, and liver disease—also exist for men who use steroids or diet in an effort to meet the ideal masculine form promoted by media.

The selfie culture invites online evaluations of appearance and also encourages people to view themselves as objects for others' evaluation (Orenstein, 2016a). As people post photos of themselves, others respond, sometimes very judgmentally. In her study of how teenage girls use social media, Nancy Jo Sales reported an example of a girl who posted photos of herself in casual clothes and received few likes from others. She then posted photos of herself that were more revealing and sexy and got more likes (Sales, 2016). Our students report that photo apps that feature filters and other editing options (e.g., Instagram) often invite harsh peer criticism of appearance, especially for girls and young women, many of whom respond by carefully editing their photos before posting them.

The abundance and availability of pornography create unrealistic standards for sexual partners and sexual activity. A growing number of men are reporting that they can't have sex or have difficulty having sex with women they find sexy because they have watched so much porn that they can't respond to "normal" women and sex (Wilson, 2014). Some doctors have labeled this problem PIED, porn-induced erectile dysfunction (Luscombe, 2016). Gabe Deem watched a lot of porn as a young boy and adolescent. He reports "I got with a gorgeous girl and we went to have sex and my body had no response at all" (Luscombe, 2016, p. 42). After determining that his problem was what he calls porn addiction, Gabe started Reboot Nation, which is an online video channel that provides support and advice to people experiencing PIED.

For girls and women, mainstream pornography poses a different problem. Many girls watch pornography out of curiosity or interest or to learn how sex occurs. Because a majority of porn includes some aggression toward women who often respond pleasurably, young girls may learn that this is how sex happens. They also see porn actors writhing and moaning and responding very actively to sex. A girl in her senior year of high school explains that "I'll be hooking up with some guy who's really hot, then things get heavier and all of a sudden my mind shifts and I'm not a real person: it's like, This is me performing. It's some fantasy girl" (Orenstein, 2016b, p. 47). In other words, their sense of their own female sexuality is obscured by an effort to perform sexuality in ways that please men (Orenstein, 2016a). Feminists have long debated whether a feminist alternative to mainstream pornography is possible. Although many do not think so, some feminists argue that making sexually explicit material "more politically progressive for those who consume it and making [filming] sets safer for performers are critical issues for feminist intervention" (Potter, 2016).

You might think that we know the difference between fantasy and reality, and we don't use media images as models for our own lives. Research, however, suggests that the unrealistic ideals in popular media do influence how many of us feel about ourselves. For centuries, the people of Fiji were a food-loving society. People enjoyed eating and considered fleshy bodies attractive in both women and men. All that changed when television stations in Fiji began to broadcast American television programs. Within three years, many Fijian women began to diet and developed eating disorders. When asked why they were trying to lose weight, young Fijian women cited very thin characters on American television programs as their model (Becker, Burwell, Gilman, Herzog, & Hamburg, 2002).

Normalize Violence against Women

Gendered violence is so pervasive that all of Chapter 12 is devoted to it. Yet, it would be irresponsible not to mention violence in the context of media. Although it would be naïve to claim that media *cause* violence, there is evidence that violence in media contributes to increasing violence in real life. Some studies have linked exposure to violent media with aggression, violence, and antisocial behavior (Pozios, Kambam, & Bender, 2013). Studies have also shown that men who watch music videos and pro wrestling are more likely to believe that forcing a partner to have sex is sometimes okay (Ensslin & Muse, 2011). When we continually see violence in media, we may come to view it as a normal and increasingly acceptable as part of ordinary life (Katz, 2013; Kilbourne, 2010a, b; Orenstein, 2016b; Yao, Mahood, & Linz, 2010).

> ### RYAN
>
> *Some pretty wild stuff goes down in online worlds. There are virtual rapes like when one avatar asks another to go swimming and then forces sex. I can't decide if virtual rape or assault or whatever is really rape or just part of the game.*

Video games push the envelope of mediated violence because they invite players not just to watch violence (as with films and TV) but to engage virtually in violence, including violence against women (Bugeja, 2010; Ivory, 2008; Sarkeesian, 2014). Male characters outnumber female ones in video games and female characters are frequently sex objects (Wiseman, 2015). In *Grand Theft Auto: San Andreas*, players earn points by having sex with prostitutes and then killing them. Within the game was a hidden scene in which players could use a joystick to control a character that is having sex with a naked woman. When a website published instructions for unlocking the scene, the video's rating went immediately from M (Mature) to AO (Adults Only)—but not before more than six million copies had been sold (Levy, 2005). In addition, gaming culture sometimes promotes psychological violence. At the 2012 Cross Assault video game tournament, competitive gamer and contestant Miranda Pakozdi was asked, on camera, what size bra she wore and told to take off her shirt. Her team's webcam focused directly on her breasts for extended periods and her coach leaned over her neck to smell her. She finally forfeited when she overheard a man at the tournament say that sexual harassment is part of the community of fight gamers (O'Leary, 2012).

Several theories about gender development offer insight into the relationship between mediated violence and real-life violence. Social learning theory claims we engage in behaviors that are rewarded and avoid behaviors that are punished. What happens when boys and men watch music videos that show men being rewarded for exploiting and violating women? Cognitive development theory focuses on our use of role models on which to base our behaviors and identities. If girls and women watch programs and videos in which women allow or invite violence against them, are they more likely to think they should accept violence to be desirable women? Symbolic interactionism highlights the importance of social views in shaping individuals' identities. When disrespect toward women and abusive male–female relationships pervade music videos, is it any wonder some of this content may get inside our own heads?

SUMMARY

Media influence how we perceive people of all genders, in general, and ourselves, in particular. The historical trend of emphasizing gender-stereotyped roles and images continues today and is sometimes challenged by alternative images of women, men, LGBTQ people, and relationships. Below the surface, however, most media continue to reflect traditional gender norms. These representations foster unrealistic gender ideals, encourage us to pathologize normal human bodies and functions, and normalize violence against women.

Understanding the overt and subtle gender messages in media empowers us to be more critical consumers. As individuals and citizens, we have a responsibility to criticize media representations that demean men and women and that contribute to attitudes that harm us and our relationships. Social media have become a primary platform for education about media's unrealistic images of the sexes, encouraging more accurate and healthy representations of women and men, and organizing political activism.

Media need you. If you refuse to buy their messages and products, they will change. In fact, they *have* changed in response to consumers' criticism and demands. Criticism of dangerously thin fashion models led to new standards that require models to have a body mass index that is within the healthy range. Responding to public demand, Nike launched a campaign that celebrated normal-sized bodies. Dove developed a line of ads that positively portrayed women of all ages, races, and sizes. *Seventeen* magazine promised to change how it represents girls when Julia Bluhm presented a petition signed by 84,000 young girls that *Seventeen* wants as subscribers. Changes such as these don't just happen. They happen when we demand them.

KEY TERMS

The following terms are defined in this chapter on the pages indicated, as well as in alphabetical order in the book's glossary, which begins on page 261. The text's companion website also provides interactive flash cards to help you learn these terms and the concepts they represent. You can access the site at www.cengagebrain.com.

agenda setting 220	*gatekeeper 221*
Bechdel Test 221	*immersive advertising 227*
complimentary copy 227	*product placement 227*
contextual advertising 227	*third person effect 220*
cyberbullying 231	*voice-overs 227*

GENDER ONLINE

1. If you want to learn more about gender and media, or if you want to become active in working against media that devalue women, visit the following websites:

   Jezebel: **http://www.jezebel.com**
   Gender Ads Project: **http://www.genderads.com**
   Media Watch: **http://www.mediawatch.com**
   The Geena Davis Institute: **http://www.thegeenadavisinstitute.org/index.php**

2. If you'd like to learn more about cosmetic surgery to reshape eyelids, view this documentary: **http://www.rawstory.com/rawreplay/2011/02/western-eyes-asian-women-contemplate-eyelid-surgery/**

3. Watch Johanna Blakley's TED talk: Social Media and the End of Gender: **http://www.ted.com/talks/johanna_blakley_social_media_and_the_end_of_gender**. Do you agree with her claim that social media are breaking down gender categories?

4. Online search terms: *third person effect, gender and media, agenda setting.*

REFLECTION, DISCUSSION, AND ACTION

1. Bring advertisements to class. Discuss the images of women, men, and relationships in them. Are they realistic? Are they healthy? What are your options as a consumer?

2. Watch prime-time coverage of sports on ESPN or another channel. Make a record of how much time is devoted to women's and men's sports and how often reporters comment

on male and female athletes' dress and appearance. Are the patterns you identify consistent with those discussed in this chapter?

3. You have just read about how social media can be used to challenge social views of gender, sex, and sexual orientation. Think about the ways that you personally use social media. Do you use them to inform your gender, to speak out, or for other reasons? Now imagine how you might engage social media to be part of shaping what gender means.

4. Apply the Bechdel Test to the last few movies you have seen. Do your results surprise you? For more information or to compare your results, visit: **http://bechdeltest.com**

RECOMMENDED RESOURCES

1. **http://www.about-face.org** This is an excellent site for getting information and taking action. **About-face.org** is devoted to media literacy about gender and self-esteem. Among its features is an ever-changing list of "Top Ten Offenders," which shows ads that destructively stereotype women and men and, in some cases, condone violence toward women. About-Face provides the addresses of companies featured in each ad so you can contact the companies directly.

2. *Miss Representation*. This 90-minute documentary on the hypersexualized representations of girls and women in media premiered at the 2011 Sundance Festival. Jennifer Siebel Newsom is the writer, director, and producer.

12

Gendered Power and Violence

Knowledge Challenge:

- How common are false reports of rape?
- Would victims of intimate partner violence be safer leaving abusive partners?
- How can individuals reduce gendered violence?

Two weeks after moving to campus, first-year student Kerri attended a mixer. When she was ready to leave, a senior named Mitch offered to walk her home. When they reached her room where he pushed her inside, locked the door, and raped her. Kerri later learned that he had raped another woman and that a school organization had found him guilty of a sexual offense the prior year. The penalty for his conviction was watching a short video on sexual violence and writing a paper reflecting on the video (Kort, 2014).

Kerri's story is true. She is one of many students who are raped every year on campuses across the United States. One in five women at U.S. colleges and universities will experience rape or attempted rape, and only 12% of victims will report the crime (Kort, 2014; Kristof, 2015).

Rape is even more common and even less subject to punishment in some other countries. In Kenya, Nairobi, Ida suffered internal injuries when she was violently raped by a neighbor. When her family could not pay the bribe the police demanded, investigation of the crime stalled. Ida was four years old (Kristof, 2014a). This chapter focuses on the distressing topic of gendered violence. In the pages that follow, we will discuss the nature and extent of gendered violence and identify social structures, practices, and attitudes that allow it. We will also ask how we can be part of reducing gendered violence in our communities and around the world.

The Many Faces of Gendered Violence

What comes to mind when you see the terms *gendered violence* and *sexual violence*? Most people think of rape, intimate partner violence, and perhaps sexual harassment. That trilogy of abuses, however, doesn't include many forms of gendered violence. **Gendered violence** refers to physical, verbal, emotional, sexual, and visual brutality that is inflicted disproportionately or exclusively on members of one sex or gender. In the following pages, we'll discuss seven forms of gendered violence.

Gender Intimidation

All of us feel unsafe at times. **Gender intimidation**, however, exists when people, because of their sex, gender, or sexual orientation, are treated in ways that lead them to feel vulnerable or unsafe. Gender intimidation, also called street harassment, includes groping, stalking, sexist comments, and publicly masturbating in someone's presence.

A common form of gender intimidation is sexualized remarks made in public spaces. Examples are comments made by strangers to women about their bodies and dress, invitations for sexual activity, and unsolicited advice on how to behave—for instance, to smile. Many women students take longer, less-direct routes around campus to avoid people who assault them with sexual comments and suggestions (Gold, 2014).

> **TIM**
>
> *I think gay bashing is a kind of gender intimidation. I've been a victim of insults and really gross remarks just because I'm gay. I'll be just walking along minding my own business, and someone will shout "fag" at me or even come at me screaming, "We don't want any queers around here." When I go into bathrooms on campus, I usually see gay-bashing graffiti. I have to tolerate these hassles strictly because I'm gay. That makes it gender intimidation.*

Tim's commentary highlights another form of gender intimidation: humiliating, disrespecting, or imposing violence on LGBTQ people or people who do not conform to gender norms.

EXPLORING GENDERED LIVES

Hollaback!

Tired of having strangers comment on your body? Hollaback! Hollaback! is an international grassroots organization that uses social networking and crowd sourcing to tackle the problem of street harassment. Hollaback! encourages victims of street harassment to shoot the harassers—with cameras. The photos are then posted, along with the photographer's comments, on Hollaback!'s site: **http://www.ihollaback.org**

A group of women in India responded similarly to "Eve-teasing," which is what Indians call street harassment. They founded Blank Noise—blank for the silence that had surrounded Eve-teasing and noise for breaking the silence. Blank Noise has developed several responses to Eve-teasing. One is posting "Unwanted" photos of perpetrators or telling stories on their action heroes site: **http://actionheroes .blanknoise.org/**. Another is "Did You Ask for It?," a collection of clothing worn by women who were Eve-teased. The fact that most of the items are very modest testifies that women's dress is not the cause of Eve-teasing (Girish, 2007).

TAKE A STAND: Can you think of ways to resist or challenge street harassment of women on your campus?

Hollaback! holds marches to raise awareness and encourage activism.

Sexual Harassment

Sexual harassment is unwelcome verbal or nonverbal behavior of a sexual nature that links academic or professional standing or success to sexual favors or that interferes with work or learning. Although women are the predominant targets and men the predominant harassers, the Supreme Court has recognized that either sex can be the target or perpetrator and that people can be harassed by members of their own sex or a different sex.

Two broad categories of sexual harassment are quid pro quo harassment and hostile environment harassment.

Quid Pro Quo

Quid pro quo is a Latin phrase that means "this for that." **Quid pro quo harassment** is the actual or threatened use of professional or academic rewards and/or punishments to gain sexual compliance from a subordinate or student. For instance, a professor might promise a student a good grade in exchange for a date, or a manager might offer a subordinate a promotion in exchange for sex. Quid pro quo harassment may also involve punishing someone for not providing sexual favors. For example, a manager might withhold a promotion from an employee who refuses to have sex.

Quid pro quo sexual harassment depends on power differences. The person seeking sexual favors must have some kind of power over the other person—for instance, assigning a grade or controlling wages. The person with less power may be reluctant or unable to say "no."

Hostile Environment

Hostile environment harassment is unwelcome conduct of a sexual nature that interferes with a person's ability to perform a job or to gain an education, and/or conduct that creates a hostile, intimidating, or offensive working environment because of sexualized content or behavior. Whereas quid pro quo harassment pivots on the power differential between perpetrator and victim, hostile environment sexual harassment is often between peers. In fact, the Education Department holds campuses responsible for responding to student-on-student harassment (Lukianoff, 2013).

A hostile environment may be created by lewd remarks, language that demeans one's sex, pinups, and rumors about an individual's real or speculated sexual activities. In addition, a hostile environment may be created when members of one sex (usually women) are disrespected, demeaned, or directly or indirectly excluded from peer groups. LGBTQ individuals also experience hostile environment harassment in workplace settings, and their rights are not explicitly protected under Title VII.

A hostile environment grows out of a pattern of behavior. A single action, even if it is unwelcome and inappropriate, is unlikely to meet the legal standard for sexual harassment. Instead, there must be a clear pattern of unwelcome conduct of a sexual nature, and that pattern must create conditions that a reasonable person would find objectionable. This standard ensures that isolated misconduct, which might be deliberate or inadvertent, doesn't result in excessive penalties.

In 2006, the U.S. Supreme Court ruled that a company cannot suspend or reassign workers who complain about sexual harassment because doing so would constitute retaliation and thus would undercut laws protecting workers against sexual harassment (Andronici & Katz, 2007).

Sexual Assault

Sexual assault is any sexual activity that occurs without the informed consent of at least one of the people involved. Both perpetrators and victims may be of any sex, gender, sexual orientation, and gender identity. One type of sexual assault is **rape**, which is one or more acts of nonconsensual oral, anal, or vaginal penetration by a body part or object. In the United States alone, 10% of women under 20 years are forced into sexual acts (Remmick, 2015). For many years, marital rape was not recognized as a crime in the United States—assuming that a woman, once married, gave up the right to refuse sex with her husband. Some countries still don't recognize marital rape as a crime. Trans people are particularly vulnerable—one in two are sexually abused or assaulted in their lifetimes (Office for Victims of Crime, n.d.).

For many years, the United States defined *rape* as carnal knowledge of a female forcibly and against her will. According to this definition, a man who is forced to have sex with another man has not been raped nor has someone who is forced to engage in oral sex. In 2012, the FBI definition was revised to define *rape* as "penetration, no matter how slight, of the vagina or anus with any body part or object, or oral penetration by a sex organ of another person without the consent of the victim" (Savage, 2012, p. A10). This means that nonconsensual vaginal, anal, and oral penetrations of anyone, regardless of sex, are now recognized as rape.

Sexual assault, including rape, occurs whenever one person doesn't give **informed consent** for sexual activity. Informed consent can be given only by an adult who has normal mental abilities, who is not being coerced, and whose judgment is not impaired by alcohol, other drugs, or circumstances. Informed consent can neither be given by children, nor by inmates who are coerced because they fear violence if they refuse advances from prison staff or, in some cases, other inmates.

> **ABBY**
>
> *When people think of rape, they think about strangers jumping out of bushes at night. But that's not how it usually happens. Most of the women in my victims' support group were raped by friends or dates—guys they knew and trusted. In some ways, that's worse because it makes you afraid to trust anyone.*

EXPLORING GENDERED LIVES

Ending Assault in Prisons

Rape is a weapon of power and domination, as the incidence of sexual assault against prisoners demonstrates. According to the most recent data available from the U.S. Bureau of Justice Statistics:

- Approximately 200,000 people—men and women—were sexually assaulted while in detention in 2012.
- Half of the adult prisoners reporting sexual assault cited prison staff as perpetrators.
- 80% of youth who are sexually assaulted in juvenile facilities are victimized by staff.
- LGBTQ prisoners are 10 times more likely than their straight counterparts to be sexually assaulted.

The U.S. Prison Rape Elimination Act of 2003 was designed to end violence against inmates, but it has proven a difficult endeavor. It took over 10 years to develop standards and protocols for prisoner protections such as staff training, adequate resources for prisoners, and means to identify and protect particularly vulnerable populations. And while states are required to adopt these standards or lose federal funding, some like the state of Texas refuse to comply (Sullivan, 2014).

In a 2015 speech to the National Association for the Advancement of Colored People (NAACP), President Barack Obama stated, "We should not be tolerating rape in prison. And we should not be making jokes about it in our popular culture. That's no joke. These things are unacceptable" (Just Detention International, 2015). The leaders of Just Detention International, a human rights organization working to end sexual abuse of incarcerated peoples all over the world, applauded the president's remarks for demonstrating the leadership necessary to end "the crisis of sexual abuse in U.S. detention facilities" (Stannow, quoted in Just Detention International, 2015, n.p.).

TAKE A STAND: To what extent do you think inmates are entitled to legal protection against sexual assault?

Sexual assault is prevalent on college campuses and fear of rape haunts many women students across the nation (Harris, 2016; Kristof, 2015; Pryor & Hughes, 2013). One reason that rapes are common at colleges and universities is the existence on many campuses, as well as the larger culture, of a **rape culture**, defined as common attitudes, beliefs, and practices that ignore, excuse, encourage, or normalize sexual violence. Examples are rape jokes; media coverage that blames the victim; and popular music, films, and video games that glorify violence against women. Many people, including college students, believe rape myths (such as women say "no" when they mean "yes" and nice girls don't get raped) (Krakauer, 2015).

RAE

I think people blame rape victims because we like to think there was a reason that someone was raped. They were alone, or it was late at night, or they dressed suggestively, or they drank too much. If we can find a reason why someone was raped, then we think we're safe if we don't go out alone or drink too much or whatever. But really we should start teaching people how to not rape as opposed to how to not get raped. We have to educate ourselves and take a stand! Stop yourself the next time you call a girl a slut, or judge a girl for what she's wearing, or assume that a man isn't capable of feeling, or being an ally.

One of the most prevalent rape myths is that rape is usually perpetrated by someone who is a stranger to the victim. Just the opposite is true. An estimated 90% of rape victims know their assailant (Kort, 2014; Kristof, 2015). Kate Harris (2009, 2011a) interviewed women who had engaged in nonconsensual sex with acquaintances or dates. She found that many of these women felt confused because they didn't associate "rape" with friends.

CARRIE

I went to a club with some friends, and we were dancing in a circle. I was wearing this great top that makes me feel really sexy and pretty. This guy I had met once pulled me out of the group and started to dirty dance. Then he groped me, my genitals. I backed off, and he said "What?" like he hadn't done anything wrong. I know he violated me, but I can't help thinking that maybe I was "asking for it" because I was wearing a sexy outfit and all. I know my mother would say I was asking for it because I was dressed in a sexy way.

Saying that rape happens because of the way a woman is dressed or dances or where she goes is **blaming the victim**—holding a person responsible for the harm that another person inflicts. The commentaries by Carrie and Austin offer examples of how both men and women, including women who are victims, can blame the victim.

Fewer studies have focused on perpetrators of sexual assault and rape. In one well-known study on college campuses, 6% of men reported that they had raped or had attempted to rape someone they knew. Of those men, approximately two-thirds were serial offenders—the average rapist had committed six sexual assaults. None of the assaults had been reported (Lisak & Miller, 2002; Starecheski, 2014). These numbers are shocking because they suggest that many perpetrators often repeat their crime. But importantly, they also underscore the fact that most men do not rape women, and subsequent reports suggest that men can use the power of peer influence to reduce rape (Starecheski, 2014).

Sexual assault is not confined to civilian contexts. It is also a serious problem in the military. The three military academies overseen by the Department of Defense are West Point, the Naval Academy, and the Air Force Academy. These academies are not subject to Title IX so cadets who face sexual assault or discrimination have limited means of redress. The Department of Defense's own surveys reveal that 90% of female cadets experience various forms of sexism, including assault (Anderson & Deutsch, 2015).

In 2008, the United Nations officially designated rape a "weapon of war" after the release of a report by the humanitarian group Refugees International, which documented the systematic use of rape as a means of ethnic cleansing in Darfur. In violation of the Geneva Convention, the government-backed Janjaweed military routinely raped women without fear of consequence because Sudanese laws harshly punish women who have sex—even against their wills—outside of marriage (Searcey, 2016). In Zimbabwe, hundreds of women have been raped

AUSTIN

What do girls expect if they go to a club where hookups happen, and they're wearing revealing clothes that are meant to excite and provoke guys, and they are dancing suggestively? It's like sending out an invitation to a guy. So why, when a guy accepts, do they blame him for responding to their invitation?

EXPLORING GENDERED LIVES

The Victim

One of our students adapted this story from one he found on the Web. A variation on the story is posted at **https://feministphilosophers.wordpress.com/2011/09/17/a-useful-rape-analogy/**

Bob Smith was robbed by John Jones. Jones was caught, and Smith pressed charges. Following is the transcript of the defense attorney's cross-examination of Mr. Smith.

"Mr. Smith, were you held up on the corner of 16th and Locust by Mr. Jones?"

"Yes."

"Did you struggle with Mr. Jones?"

"No."

"Why not?"

"He had a gun to my head and told me he'd kill me if I didn't give him my wallet."

"So you decided to comply with his demands instead of resisting. Did you at least scream for help?"

"No. I was afraid."

"Is it true that, earlier on the evening of the alleged robbery, you gave money to some friends who asked for it?"

"Yes."

"Isn't it true that you often give money to others?"

"Yes, I like to help people I care about."

"In fact, don't you have quite a reputation for generosity—for giving money away?

How was Mr. Jones supposed to know you didn't want to give him money? I mean, you give it away to lots of people, so why shouldn't Mr. Jones have assumed you would give him some?"

"What are you getting at?"

"Never mind. When did the robbery take place?"

"About 11 p.m."

"11 p.m.? You were out walking alone at 11 p.m. at night? You know it's dangerous to be out on the streets alone at night. Why were you there at that time of night?"

"I just felt like walking home instead of taking a cab."

"Okay. What were you wearing?"

"A suit. I'd worked late at the office, gone out with friends, and was walking home."

"A suit. An expensive suit, right?"

"Well, yes. It is a very nice suit. What's your point?"

"So, you were walking around a deserted street late at night in an expensive suit that practically advertised you had money. The way you were dressed was really provocative, isn't that so? In fact, we could think that, being dressed that way and out on the streets alone late at night, you were asking to be robbed."

TAKE A STAND: Why do you think some people would not think Mr. Smith asked to be robbed but might think a woman wearing sexy clothes and out late at night asked to be raped?

by opposition soldiers. Some of the rape victims were children who had not even reached puberty; others were pregnant women (Kristof & WuDunn, 2014). Increasingly, males are also victims of rape in wars. Research shows that 40% of women and 25% of men in Liberia, Sierra Leone, Kenya, and Myanmar have been victims of sexual crimes (Drawing a Line, 2014).

A White House report states that the financial costs of rape range from $87,000 to $240,776 (Hilgers, 2016). Costs may include lost wages, lost tuition and fees for students who cannot complete the semester in which a rape occurred, and counseling, including residential treatment centers.

Sexual assault includes forced prostitution, also called sexual slavery. During World War II, the Japanese forced women to be "comfort women" for Japanese soldiers. The repeated and sometimes brutal rapes by as many as 30 Japanese soldiers a day caused some of these women to become sterile. Many committed suicide (Onishi, 2007).

Sexual slavery is not confined to history. Even today, in countries such as India, Pakistan, Bangladesh, and Nepal, girls are sold by their families or kidnapped and forced to be prostitutes (Kristof & WuDunn, 2009). Between 800,000 and 1.8 million women and children, some who have not even gone through puberty, are trafficked each year (Kristof, 2011a). Virgins bring particularly high prices since some men with HIV/AIDS believe that having sex with a virgin will cure them (Norlund & Rubin, 2010).

Sex trafficking is also not limited to developing nations. In the United States, there are an estimated 300,000 child prostitutes who began that work at an average age of 13 to 14. The pimps who manage sex slaves earn $150,000 to $200,000 per slave per year (The Covering House, 2014). Traffickers target youth through social media and chatlines, in shopping malls, on public transportation, and on school campuses through peer recruiters and after-school programs (U.S. Department of Education, 2013).

Intimate Partner Violence

In 2014, the video of Ray Rice punching his then-fiancée Janay Palmer unconscious in an elevator was shown repeatedly on television and the Internet. This incident focused public attention on **intimate partner violence**, which is physical, mental, emotional, verbal, or economic

---

EXPLORING GENDERED LIVES

Myths and Facts about Rape

Myth	Fact
Only men can commit rape.	Rape can be committed by anyone who forces another person to penetrate or be penetrated orally, anally, or vaginally.
Rape is motivated by sexual urges.	Rape is an aggressive act used to dominate another person.
Most rapes occur between strangers.	More than 75% of rapes are committed by a person known to the victim.
Most rapists are African-American men, and most victims are European-American women.	More than three-fourths of all rapes occur within races not between races.
False reports of rapes are frequent.	False reports of rapes constitute only 2% of all reported rapes.
The way a woman dresses affects the likelihood that she will be raped.	Most rapes are planned in advance, without knowledge of how victims will be dressed.
Women who don't drink too much are alert enough to protect themselves from being raped.	Date rape drugs such as Rohypnol, GHB (gamma hydroxybutyric acid), and Ketamine have no color, smell, or taste, so you can't tell if you are being drugged. The drugs make you weak and confused— or even pass out—so that you are unable to refuse sex or defend yourself.

TAKE A STAND: Which of the rape myths identified above do you think are most prevalent on your campus?

■ **EXPLORING GENDERED LIVES** ■

Sexual Assault of Boys and Men

Boys and men are not immune to sexual assault. On June 22, 2012, Penn State's assistant football coach, Jerry Sandusky, was found guilty of 45 counts of sexual abuse of 10 young boys over a 15-year period. Also in 2012, The *New York Times Magazine* published the story of sexual abuse of boys and girls that occurred at the prestigious private Horace Mann School in New York City (Kamil, 2012). According to the Rape, Abuse, and Incest National Network (RAINN), 1 in 9 girls and 1 in 53 boys are sexually assaulted by adults; in addition, 10% of all rape victims are male (2016).

As with most victims of sexual abuse, boys often stay silent for years. There are many reasons for male victims' silence. Like female victims, males don't want the public scrutiny that accompanies reporting. In addition, men have distinct reasons not to speak up. Richard Gartner (2005, 2012), a psychotherapist who works with male victims of childhood abuse, says that male victims put their emotions in a "deep freeze" because they believe that "real men should be resilient and certainly not victims" (2012, p. A23). Male victims may fear others would think they are gay because a man engaged in sexual activity with them. Despite social pressures, some male victims refuse to stay silent.

TAKE A STAND: Can you think of ways to make it more acceptable for men to report sexual assaults against them?

power used by one partner against the other partner in a romantic relationship. Intimate partner violence cuts across many demographics—it is experienced and perpetrated by both sexes, members of all races and economics classes, as well as by gays, lesbians, bisexuals, straights, cisgender, and transgender people (Douglas, 2012; Prevalence of Domestic Violence, 2013).

The prevalence of intimate partner violence is staggering. Over 360,000 incidents are reported per year in the United States. That is almost 1,000 per day. Twenty-five percent of U.S. women have been violently attacked by husbands or boyfriends, and one U.S. woman dies every six hours from a partner's violence (Kristof, 2014b). Bisexual women are far more likely than their lesbian or heterosexual peers to be beaten, stalked, or sexually assaulted by an intimate partner; the vast majority of perpetrators in these cases are male (Walters, Chen, & Breiding, 2013). At least 30% of women worldwide have been victims of intimate partner violence, which is legal in 30 countries (Prevalence of Domestic Violence, 2013; Remmick, 2015). Intimate partner violence is also common in dating relationships, including those of very young people.

Control is a key issue for many abusers. They want to control their partners' appearances, behaviors, relationships, and lives. In some cases, this is done without physical violence. Abusers humiliate, isolate, spy on, and otherwise dominate partners. If there is no physical assault, some victims of control do not realize they are experiencing intimate partner abuse (Ellin, 2016; Fontes, 2015).

Intimate partner violence typically follows a cyclical pattern (Johnson, 2006). In the first stage, the perpetrator experiences mounting tension, which may have little to do with the victim—perhaps the perpetrator has problems at work or feels insecure. The second stage is defined by an explosion, which may involve verbal, emotional, sexual, or physical violence. The third stage is called remorse because the perpetrator typically acts ashamed, apologizes, and promises never to do it again. In the fourth stage, the honeymoon phase, the violent partner acts lovingly and often brings gifts to the victim. The apologies of stage three and the

---

EXPLORING GENDERED LIVES

The Cycle of Intimate Partner Violence

Stage 1, Tension: One partner experiences mounting tension. The source of the tension may be frustration or dissatisfaction with the relationship or issues external to the relationship such as financial problems, difficulties at work, or being unable to get work. The person experiencing tension blames the partner for problems or for not being supportive.

Stage 2, Explosion: Tension erupts, often facilitated by alcohol or other drugs. Initially, the explosion may take the form of psychological battering, using insults, threats, taunts, and intimidation with weapons. If the couple continues through

multiple iterations of the cycle, explosions often involve physical violence, which may be severe and even lethal.

Stage 3, Remorse: The violent partner appears contrite and remorseful. The perpetrator may apologize to the victim and promise it will never happen again. The victim sees the "good person" inside and remembers what led to commitment.

Stage 4, Honeymoon: The violent partner acts devoted to convince the victim that the assault was an aberration that will not recur—even if it has repeatedly. And then the whole cycle begins anew, often with greater intensity.

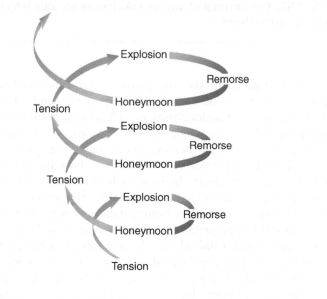

TAKE A STAND: How does what you have learned about typical patterns of gender socialization shed light on why Stages 3 and 4 so often work to keep a woman in a violent relationship?

---

loving acts of stage four often revive the victim's faith in the perpetrator and the possibility of a loving relationship. If the victim stays, the cycle is likely to keep repeating. There may be years between violent explosions or cycles may repeat many times within a year, month, or week. Over time, the level of violence may increase so that each iteration of the cycle is more dangerous.

■ **EXPLORING GENDERED LIVES** ■

Myths and Facts about Violence between Intimates

Myth	*Fact*
Victims of battering can just leave the abusive relationship.	Many victims of battering have nowhere to go and no means of supporting themselves and their children.
Abuse of intimates often stops on its own.	Abuse of intimates seldom stops without intervention or other radical measures.
Abuse is confined primarily to the working and poverty classes.	Abuse occurs in relationships between members of the upper and middle classes as well as members of the working and poverty classes.
Victims of battering would be safer if they left abusive relationships.	Victims of battering are most likely to be murdered by abusive partners if they try to leave.

TAKE A STAND: To what extent do you think your friends believe the myths identified above?

BRICE

Growing up, I saw my father shove Mom around whenever he was having a rough time at work. Sometimes, it was more than shoving—he would actually hit her. Always, the next day he would be Mr. Nice, and things would go along fine for a while until he got upset about something else; then it would start all over again. I hated him because of what he did to her, and I swore I would never be like him. But last year, when I was going through a really rough time, the girl I was dating kept nagging me, and I hauled off and hit her. I never thought I could do that.

Brice's experience, as presented in his commentary, is not unusual. Our families of origin give us our first blueprints for what is normal and allowable in relationships. What we learn in families, however, need not be the blueprint for our lives. We can choose not to repeat destructive patterns that we have observed in our families.

Although people of all genders commit violence, there are general differences in the type of violence committed by women and men. Women who are violent toward partners most often verbally abuse or push, slap, or shove. In contrast, men are more likely to use their bodies, weapons, and even acid to commit assaults (M. Johnson, 2006, 2008). Although both men and women may engage in violence, men more often inflict moderate to severe physical injuries. Men who perpetrate physical violence tend to justify their violence by overestimating how common such behavior is, underestimating the damage their violence does, and claiming it is an appropriate way of controlling women (Derry, 2015; Neighbors, Walker, Mbilinyi, O'Rourke, Edleson, Zegree, & Roffman, 2010; Olson & Rauscher, 2011).

Women and men between 18 and 25 years old are equally likely to engage in relational aggression in friendships. However, in romantic relationships, women exceed men in engaging in this kind of aggression, which is intentionally designed to hurt romantic partners by manipulating social relationships (Goldstein, 2011).

> **PAULA**
>
> *The worst thing I ever went through was being stalked by my ex-boyfriend. We'd dated for about a year when I broke up with him. He was so jealous—wouldn't let me go out with friends or anything, so I just decided to end the relationship. But he didn't want it to end. He followed me around campus, showed up at movies when I was out with other guys, and called at all hours of the night. Sometimes, he would tell me he loved me and beg to get back together; other times, he would threaten me. I finally called the police, and that put an end to his terrorism.*

Stalking is a form of intimate partner violence. **Stalking** is repeated pursuit that is uninvited and unwanted, that seems obsessive, and that makes the target of pursuit concerned for her or his safety (Cupach & Spitzberg, 2015). Updates on social networking sites such as Facebook give stalkers more ways to learn about (potential) victims' habits and current whereabouts.

Genital Surgery

Some people have never heard of genital surgery, which is also called genital mutilation and genital cutting. Of those who have, many think it is an ancient procedure that is no longer practiced. Yet, genital surgery continues to be practiced in some countries, especially some in Africa and the Middle East. More than 200 million women and girls, some as young as 6 years old, have been cut (Belluck & Cochrane, 2016; Blow, 2014b; Dugger, 2013; Eltahawy, 2014).

Male Circumcision   **Male circumcision** is the removal of the sheath, or prepuce, of the penis. In many countries, including the United States, male babies are routinely circumcised because of possible health benefits such as reduction of urinary tract infections and penile cancer. Yet some people view male circumcision as a form of genital mutilation that is unnecessary, dangerous, and painful.

Sunna   The word *sunna* comes from the Arabic word for "religious duty" (Trangsrud, 1994). Sunna, or female circumcision, is practiced primarily in African countries. It is usually performed on girls between the ages of 4 and 14, although it is sometimes performed on infants (Johnson, 2008). Sunna involves removing both the sheath and the tip of the clitoris. Sunna is not equivalent to male circumcision. Removal of the foreskin of a penis doesn't preclude a man's sexual pleasure, but removal of the prepuce and tip of the clitoris significantly lessens women's sexual pleasure. Sunna also has greater potential for medical complications.

Excision or Clitoridectomy   A second type of female genital surgery is excision or **clitoridectomy**, in which the entire clitoris and parts of the labia minora are removed. Because this surgery greatly diminishes women's ability to experience sexual pleasure, it is believed to reduce the likelihood of women being sexually active before marriage or unfaithful after marriage. Of lesser concern to those who endorse the practice is that it often has medical complications and increases pain and danger in childbirth.

■ **EXPLORING GENDERED LIVES** ■

To Circumcise or Not to Circumcise: That Is the Question

In 1999, 63% of Western males were circumcised, whereas only 55% of Western males were circumcised a decade later (Rabin, 2012). Why the change? Questions about the health benefits of removing the foreskin from the penis have stoked opposition to the procedure in the United States and many European countries. In addition, some critics of circumcision consider it cruel and unethical to subject an infant to surgery to remove a healthy body part. In 2012, the influential American Academy of Pediatrics stopped short of recommending circumcision but noted research suggests the procedure may reduce urinary tract infections and penile cancer. These possible health benefits are balanced against complications that occur in 1 in every 500 circumcisions and result in 100 deaths annually (Circumcision, 2012; Rabin, 2012).

And then there's the pain of the surgery. Traditionally, circumcision is performed without anesthesia, and some religions ban even local anesthesia (Circumcision, 2012). Some Austrian provinces have prohibited state hospitals from performing circumcisions, and the Royal Dutch Medical Society discourages the procedure.

TAKE A STAND: Do you think circumcision should be regulated by governments or is it a personal decision parents should make?

You might be surprised to learn that clitoridectomies were performed in the United States and Europe as late as the twentieth century to "cure" masturbation and prevent orgasm, which was considered an "ailment" in women (Dreifus, 2000).

Infibulation   The most radical form of genital surgery is **infibulation**. This operation, which is usually performed on girls between ages five and eight, removes the clitoris and labia minora. Next, the flesh of the labia majora is scraped raw and sewn together to form a hood over the vagina, with a small opening left for urination and menstruation, and the girl is kept immobile until the labia grow together. When an infibulated female marries, an opening is cut to permit intercourse. Sometimes the opening is deliberately made extremely small to increase male sexual pleasure, although this makes intercourse painful for women. Husbands may order their wives resewn when they travel.

Genital surgery is often performed by people with little or no medical training who operate in unsanitary conditions and without anesthesia (Turkewitz, 2015). The immediate consequences may include excruciating pain, hemorrhage, tetanus, gangrene, blood poisoning, and fractured bones from the force needed to hold girls down during the operation. Long-term consequences include sterility, agonizing pain during intercourse, cysts, difficulty delivering babies, permanent incontinence, and stillbirths of babies who cannot emerge through birth canals that have been scarred and deformed (Browne, 2003/2004; Turkewitz, 2015).

Genital surgery is rooted in cultural traditions, which change only when members of the culture resist them. In China, for centuries women's feet were bound. Yet, this practice was eliminated in a mere 17 years (1895–1912) in urban China when progressive Chinese citizens launched an education campaign against foot binding. Also critical to ending the practice were fathers who refused to bind their daughters' feet and prohibited their sons from marrying women whose feet had been bound (Lorber, 1997). When enough fathers made these commitments, women with unbound feet became desirable as marriage partners.

■ EXPLORING GENDERED LIVES ■

Vacation Cutting

African immigrants to the United States have quadrupled in the past 20 years. Like most immigrants, Africans bring the traditions of their culture with them to their new home. One tradition is female genital surgery or cutting, which is still practiced in many African countries, but this practice has been illegal in the United States since 1996.

For some immigrant parents, the solution is "vacation cutting" in which a daughter is sent to the parents' home country for a vacation with relatives who arrange for the child to be cut (Turkewitz, 2014). It's natural for parents to want to bring their children up in the customs of their culture of origin. However, argue opponents of vacation cutting, this practice is not endorsed in the United States where the parents have chosen to live. Further, beginning in 2013, U.S. law made it illegal to transport girls for the purpose of genital surgery (Turkewitz, 2014).

TAKE A STAND: What should be the balance between parental and government authority in matters concerning genital surgery on children?

Gender-Based Murder

Consider two facts: (1) When both sexes are given adequate care, females outnumber males; and (2) in many countries today, men substantially outnumber women. How can both of these facts be true? Because millions of females are killed before or after birth.

One way to reduce the number of women is reproductive technologies to either selectively abort female fetuses or select for sex prior to in vitro fertilization (Bring Back the Girls, 2014). A second way to reduce the number of women is female infanticide, which is the active or passive killing of female children. Active female infanticide may take the form of smothering a newborn female or drowning her in a bucket of water kept by the birthing bed. Passive methods of female infanticide include feeding girl babies little or nothing and denying them essential medical care (Patel, 2006).

Women who survive to adulthood aren't necessarily safe. **Femicide** is the killing of women. In many places, including India, Pakistan, Albania, Mexico, and United Arab Emirates, adult women are killed and official efforts to find and prosecute the perpetrators are often weak or nonexistent. Femicide includes dowry deaths or bride burnings (Lahiri & Sharma, 2013). Some groups in India still follow the custom in which a woman's parents give money or other goods to the man who marries their daughter. After the marriage, the new husband may demand additional payments from the bride's parents. If the demands aren't met, the husband's family may hold the bride near the cooking stove until her sari catches fire and she burns to death. The husband is then free to get another wife and another dowry.

Femicide is not confined to developing nations. It happens in highly developed countries, including the United States. The statistics on intimate partner violence noted earlier are chilling—each year in the United States, 1,460 women are murdered or suffer fatal injuries at the hands of an intimate partner. In May of 2014, Elliot Rodger slaughtered 6 women students and injured 13 others at the University of California, Santa Barbara. Prior to perpetrating mass murder of women, Rodger spent substantial time on websites that are part of the manosphere, a digital subculture "run by men's rights activists that is typified by its loathing for women in general and feminism in particular" (Bellafante, 2016; Potok, 2014). Rodger's carnage is not an isolated case. In 2009, George Sodini carried several handguns into a Pennsylvania fitness club, killed three women, and wounded nine others. In 2011, Scott Dekraai entered the business where his ex-wife worked and shot her and six other women as well as two men who were in the line of fire.

Reproductive Violence   **Reproductive violence** is coerced or discriminatory infringement on reproductive rights. It includes force or exploitation that inhibits an individual's free choice of whether, when, and with whom to reproduce, to become a parent, and to parent existing children (Ross, 2009). In America's early history, these basic rights were denied to slaves. Any children of slaves were legally the "property" of the slave owner; so enslaved mothers, many of whom were raped by owners, had no legal claim to parentage (Fixmer-Oraiz, 2015; Roberts, 1997).

In the twentieth century, the United States saw the emergence of eugenics, a set of reproductive procedures to reduce the births of "undesirable" people and increase the births of "desirable" people. Those designated undesirable were almost always low-income, socially marginalized minorities (Solinger, 2005). State-funded programs in the United States forcibly sterilized numerous women involuntarily who were immigrants, minorities, lesbians, poor, disabled, and/or incarcerated (Roberts, 2009; Solinger, 2005).

Other forms of reproductive injustice do not involve the clear-cut violence of eugenics, forced abortion, and slavery but do severely constrain decisions about reproduction. Consider three instances of highly constrained reproductive choices. First, the link between racism and regulation of reproductive rights is clear in U.S. programs during the twentieth century that promoted free birth control to minority women and women with low incomes while denying other health care services (Gordon, 2007; Roberts, 1997). Second, while low-income women in our era are more likely to suffer from infertility, assisted reproduction is used almost exclusively by privileged women and couples due to its expense and lack of insurance coverage.

EXPLORING GENDERED LIVES

Whose Rights? Whose Protection?

When Alicia Beltran discovered she was pregnant, she was happy to have recently weaned herself off pills to which she had been addicted. At a prenatal checkup, she mentioned her prior addiction when she provided her medical history. The health care provider then demanded that Ms. Beltran take an anti-addiction drug. Ms. Beltran resisted because she had beaten the addiction on her own, which a urine test later verified. Unconvinced that the expectant mother's word could be trusted, state authorities shackled Ms. Beltran and took her to court where she was sentenced to a 90-day stay at a drug treatment center for an addiction she didn't have (Fixmer-Oraiz, 2015). She served 78 days.

Ms. Beltran lives in Wisconsin, which is one of four states that have passed laws that empower authorities to confine pregnant women for substance abuse. A number of other states use assorted criminal laws to force women into treatment programs or punish them for taking drugs.

Alicia Beltran is not an isolated case. Hundreds of pregnant U.S. women, mostly low income and minority, have been detained, arrested or forced to accept medical procedures. Ironically, laws that claim to protect fetuses may actually increase risk to fetuses because some pregnant women will not seek prenatal care for fear of being confined or forced to endure medical treatment (Eckholm, 2013).

TAKE A STAND: How do you balance rights of pregnant women and those of fetuses?

For example, 80% of the women who freeze eggs for possible later gestation are white, and the starting cost of this procedure is $10,000 (Allen, 2016). Third, in Africa and parts of Asia arranged marriages are common, and the brides may be children younger than 15. UNICEF reports that more than 700 million women living now were married before they were 18, and 250 million were married before they were 15 (Progress but Too Slow, 2014).

One infamous infringement on reproductive rights in the United States involved Norplant, a long-term, implanted contraceptive that came on market in the early 1990s. Within days of Norplant's entry into the market, prominent publications such as the *Philadelphia Inquirer* (Kimelman, 1990), *The Richmond-Times Dispatch* (Journalistic Thought Police, 1990), and *Newsweek* (Alter, 1990) published editorials noting that the new contraceptive might "curb the expansion of an underclass" (Journalistic Thought Police, 1990, p. A12). Every state and the District of Columbia made Norplant available to poor women (Roberts, 1997). In some instances, judges offered women the "choice" between having Norplant implanted and serving jail terms (Bigham, 1991). However, states refused to pay to remove Norplant when women wanted to conceive and even when they experienced serious medical complications including nerve injury, ovarian cysts, phlebitis, significant weight gain, and gallbladder disease (Norplant, 2012; Roberts, 1997).

Both the American Medical Association and the American Bar Association oppose state or judicial efforts to coerce a woman to use any method of contraception or sterilization. Even Dr. Sheldon Segal, the originator of Norplant, stated, "I am totally and unalterably opposed to the use of Norplant for any coercive or involuntary purpose. It was developed to improve reproductive freedom, not to restrict it" (Norplant, 1994).

Another infringement on reproductive rights that involves risks for poor women is commercial surrogacy. Women or couples with sufficient wealth can hire other women to carry pregnancies to term. In one sense, this is potentially a win-win situation: Women who cannot give birth are able to become mothers, and women who are poor or otherwise unable to earn a living are able to earn income by carrying a child. Without denying this potential for mutual benefit, we should also recognize the power dynamics involved (Fixmer-Oraiz, 2013). The surrogate mothers often have no other means of earning income so their "choice" to be surrogates is constrained. Some surrogate mothers are required to live in supervised gestational dormitories, leaving their own children for nine months. Some must agree to caesarian births so that the birth date is convenient for the hiring woman or couple. If the surrogates later have other children by vaginal delivery, the prior caesarian delivery may cause complications, including ones that are life-threatening. Thus, surrogates may compromise their ability to carry and give birth to their own children (Jaiswal, 2012).

The gendered violence we've discussed is not inevitable. Throughout this book, we have seen that what is considered acceptable or normal is socially constructed. In the next section of this chapter, we discuss social processes that allow or encourage gendered violence.

Cultural Foundations of Gendered Violence

Although particular individuals commit violent acts and should be held responsible for them, individual pathologies alone cannot explain the pervasiveness of gendered violence. To unravel cultural forces that cultivate tolerance for gendered violence, we will consider how media, institutions, and language normalize gendered violence.

The Normalization of Violence in Media

As we noted in Chapter 11, violence is customary—not unusual—in films, on MTV and television programs, in music and video games. Popular music includes lyrics that refer to women as "hos" (whores) and "bitches" and glorify killing for sport, which reflects a widespread and deeply ensconced cultural ideology that esteems violence, including rape.

Pornography is sexually explicit material that favorably depicts subordination, degradation, and nonconsensual sexual behavior. Pornography is distinct from **erotica**, which depicts consensual activities that are desired by and pleasurable to all parties. Unlike erotica, mainstream pornography portrays violence as normal and acceptable. A recent survey found that 83% of men in U.S. colleges who viewed mainstream pornography were more likely to say they would commit rape than men who did not view pornography (The Week, 2016).

The Normalization of Violence by Institutions

Many of the basic structures and institutional practices of Western culture uphold violence, including violence toward women. They do this by refusing to interfere in domestic disputes, praising men for aggression, advising victims not to prosecute rapists, and encouraging victims to fulfill social prescriptions for femininity by standing by their men.

Schools   In 2014, the Education Department named 55 colleges and universities that are subject to investigation because they have or may have mishandled investigations of sexual assault on their campus (Crampton, 2014; Kristof, 2015). Many students, primarily women, state that when they report a rape or other sexual assault, they are not taken seriously and are discouraged from pursuing their cases. Many colleges and universities have failed to train officials who adjudicate cases of campus sexual assault (Bogdanich, 2014). Former president Jimmy Carter notes that 95% of victims of campus rape do not report the crimes because their schools don't support victims. As a result, "most on-campus rapes are perpetrated by serial rapists, who can safely assume that their crimes will not be revealed" (2014, p. 43).

Colleges and universities want to preserve their reputations, which is an incentive to keep victims of sexual assault from going public. Students have reported a number of techniques used by school officials to discourage them from pursuing their cases. In some cases, the very officials who are supposed to support victims of sexual assault engage in blaming the victim by asking about the victim's dress and behaviors (Kort, 2014). Officials may also encourage the victim to doubt what happened, asking: "Are you *sure* it was rape?" (Kort, 2014). And officials may blame the victim as was the case with one campus police officer who told a woman who had been raped, "Women have to just stop spreading their legs like peanut butter [or rape] will keep on happening till the cows come home" (Schlossberg, 2014).

Widespread neglect and mismanagement of campus sexual assaults led the White House to establish a special Task Force to Protect Students from Sexual Assault in 2014. Named *Not Alone*, the task force provides information and resources on preventing and responding to sexual assaults on campus. **Notalone.gov**, the website created by the task force, provides information on victims' rights and reporting procedures and also allows students to see incidence reports for their campus.

Family   One of the most important institutions shaping cultural consciousness, including perspectives on violence, is the family. In families where violence exists, children may grow up assuming that violence is part of marriage. Families may also encourage women to stay with violent men for economic security, because that is a woman's duty, or "for the sake of the children" (Shoener, 2014). Immigrant women or women of color may be especially vulnerable to pressures not to report intimate partner violence for fear that reporting would further stigmatize or enable state violence against their communities.

Law Enforcement   The current legal system does not offer sufficient safeguards for victims, and some law enforcement officials and judges give greater priority to maintaining a two-parent family than to the safety of victims of intimate partner violence (Shoener, 2014). The laws governing restraining orders need to be strengthened so that people can get protection before tragedy happens. For instance, Massachusetts now requires perpetrators of intimate partner violence who are deemed highly dangerous to wear GPS locators, which have proven remarkably effective in preventing further attacks (Carter, 2014).

Language   Another cultural practice that reflects and sustains tolerance of violence is the use of language that obscures the seriousness of the issue. Too often, the language used to describe violence between intimates conceals the brutality of what happens. Why do newspapers and news programs use inappropriately gentle terms, such as *domestic dispute* or *spousal conflict*, to camouflage acts such as smashing women's faces with hammers, slashing women with knives, and stomping on women (Lamb, 1991, 1999)? Why did reporters use the term *sex scandal* to describe former mayor of San Francisco Bob Filner's years' long habit of groping women (Bruni, 2013)? This is an incidence of violence, not a sex scandal.

Responsibility for violence is also diminished by passive language that fails to name aggressors—for example, "The battery occurred on Sunday," "Women are abused frequently," or "Many women are beaten." The horror of intimate partner violence is also diminished when the language of love is used to describe physical abuse. Media accounts of battering of women often include phrases such as "He loved her too much," "She was the victim of love," and "It was love that went too far" (Meyers, 2004).

Resisting Gendered Violence: Where Do We Go from Here?

We suspect that this chapter has been as distressing for you to read as it was for us to research and write. But being distressed doesn't lessen gendered violence. We must ask how we can be agents of change to make our world safer for all.

Personal Efforts to Reduce Gendered Violence

Each of us can do something to lessen gendered violence. The most basic personal choice is to decide that you will not engage in or tolerate violence in your relationships. You can also make conscious choices about the language you use. You can heighten others' awareness by using language that accurately represents the brutality and inhumanity of gendered violence.

Another choice, one emphasized by Mentors in Violence Prevention, is to refuse to be a silent bystander. In 2009, a homecoming dance in Richmond, California, turned into a horrific tragedy when a 15-year-old girl was beaten and gang-raped for hours. More than a dozen people watched during this extended attack, yet none of them chose to intervene to stop the brutal assault (California, 2009). If you are a bystander, you can choose to speak or act to prevent violence (Katz & Moore, 2013).

There are other ways you personally can take a stand against gendered violence. Most campuses and communities have a number of groups that provide support to victims and offer outreach programs to educate citizens about gendered violence. Men on many campuses work to get other men involved in combating violence toward women. You can also make a personal statement by writing or calling in to object to magazine stories, radio programs, and television shows that present violence as normal or acceptable. You can use your social media networks to raise awareness about violence and local efforts to end it. If you are a parent or plan to be one, you can teach your children that nobody has a right to touch them in a sexual way without their permission. And all children should learn that it is wrong to coerce others into sexual activities.

For too many years, people have looked away from gendered violence. We've pretended not to see bruises, looked the other way when there was on-the-job harassment. If you suspect that a friend or colleague is experiencing violence, don't tell yourself, "It's none of my business." It *is* your business. Speaking up to support someone who is being harmed is a concrete way to use your voice to resist violence.

Social Efforts to Reduce Gendered Violence

We must also change cultural practices and structures. Here, too, there are many ways to be an agent of change. You can vote for tax increases to underwrite education and social services. If you become an educator or administrator, you can implement educational programs.

You may support international programs whose mission is reducing gendered violence. For example, South Asian women formed *Saheli*, which protests dowry deaths. *Saheli* was successful in getting a law passed that requires thorough investigation of any "accidental death" of a woman during the first seven years of marriage. In India, a group of women

---

■ EXPLORING GENDERED LIVES ■

Refusing to Be Defeated

In 2002, when Pakistani Mukhtar Mai was 32, her 12-year-old brother was accused of having sexual relations with the daughter in a higher-caste family. The village council found him guilty and decided to punish his family by sentencing Mukhtar to be gang-raped. A group of men stripped her, carried out the sentence, and then forced her to walk home naked while 300 villagers watched. A woman who has been raped in Pakistan is dishonored (Minhas, 2009), so Mukhtar was expected to commit suicide.

She didn't. Instead, she fought back— and not just for herself. She prosecuted her rapists and was awarded $8,300, which she used to start two schools in her village, one for boys and one for girls (Kristof, 2005a, b, c, d). On March 3, 2005, a Pakistani appeals court overturned the death sentences of six of the men convicted of attacking her and set five of them free to live in her neighborhood. The Pakistani authorities placed Mukhtar under house arrest and refused to let her leave the country.

In June 2005, the Pakistani Supreme Court yielded to international pressure and freed Mukhtar from house arrest. In 2011, Pakistan's Supreme Court freed five of the six men who were imprisoned for gang-raping Mukhtar (Shah, 2011).

TAKE A STAND: Rather than asking you to reflect on the material in this box, we encourage you to read Mukhtar's autobiography, *In the Name of Honor*, or view "Shame," a documentary produced by Showtime in 2007.

formed *Vimochana*, an organization that helps battered women get legal assistance and orga-nizes consciousness-raising groups that help women work together to redefine battering and dowry murders as unacceptable. Asian men have formed "Men Oppose Wife Abuse" to end intimate partner violence (Cuklanz & Moorti, 2009). Chilean women are risking imprison-ment and death to demand that *desaparecidas*, "disappeared women," be returned. Playwright Eve Ensler (2000, 2001, 2004) founded V-day, an organization that works to stop all kinds of violence against women, including rape, incest, female genital mutilation, and sexual slavery.

Athletes who commit violence against women have seldom been punished seriously. For example, when Baltimore Raven Ray Rice knocked his fiancée unconscious in an elevator and dragged her out, the National Football League (NFL) gave him a tap on the wrist by suspending him from a mere two games. In response, multiple groups pressured the NFL to take violence more seriously. In August of 2014, NFL commissioner Roger Goodell announced he agreed that violence is a serious issue and should be treated that way. He promised that the NFL would take strong measures against players who perpetrate assault, battery, intimate partner violence, or sexual assault. A first-time offender receives a six-game ban. A second offense results in life-time banishment from NFL. However, after one year, offenders may appeal the lifetime ban and request reinstatement. Commissioner Goodell also announced the NFL's youth league will now teach men to respect women and not be violent toward them (Macur, 2014).

Taking a Voice

You cannot escape involvement with gendered violence. Just as speaking out is a choice, so, too, is silence. You can't avoid having influence. Instead, your only options are to decide what influence you will exert and how and where you will do it. In his study of how people respond to toxic chemical disasters, Michael Reich (1991) identified three ways in which citizens affect public awareness, public policy, and redress for victims of chemical disasters. Translat-ing his ideas to our concern with gendered violence, we can identify three forms of influence: direct power, agenda setting, and voice.

Direct power is the ability to make others do what they would not do on their own. If you have children, you will exercise direct power when you encourage or discourage playing with particular toys and engaging in various kinds of activities. If you become a medical pro-fessional, you will decide how to treat transgender patients and how to help your colleagues develop competence with transgender patients. As a citizen, you exercise direct power by voting, supporting candidates, and entering politics yourself.

A second form of power is agenda setting. If you pursue a career in advertising, pub-lic relations, popular music, or journalism, you will have opportunities to shape the public agenda. You can also participate in agenda setting by blogging and calling in to talk shows to state your opinions and to get issues on the public agenda. Likewise, you can engage in agenda setting in your professional and social relationships by calling out practices that oper-ate covertly to normalize gendered violence or, more broadly, gender discrimination.

A third way to exercise power is through voice—communicating with others and engaging in everyday acts of principled resistance. One means of enacting voice is adopting a traitorous identity, which we discussed in Chapter 4. Other examples of voice come from third-wave feminists who challenge sexist attitudes and practices in everyday life. They challenge peers who make racist, sexist, and homophobic comments, which lay a foundation for violence. When you witness violence, you can choose to be an engaged bystander, rather than a passive one. It's important to realize that voice and resistance are processes. We notice outcomes such as a protest or passage of a law. But those visible results grow out of prolonged processes of listening, reading, reflecting, and talking with others. We are often cultivating our voices in quiet moments. Making time to think about issues is part of developing a strong voice.

In speaking about the financial crisis that began in 2008, President Obama observed that some of us are to blame for the crisis, but all of us are responsible for it. Those words apply equally to other facets of our lives, including gendered violence. We are all responsible. We owe it to ourselves and each other to take responsibility for our shared future.

SUMMARY

We can do much to reduce gendered violence in our personal lives and to contribute to broader changes in the social structures and practices that sustain acceptance of it. We need to provide safe refuges for victims of violence and counseling to both victims and perpetrators. In addition, we need to develop educational programs that teach very young children that violence toward others is unacceptable and that sexual activity should always be consensual. These and other changes in social structures and practices can reform cultural attitudes toward gendered violence. The changes will not be easy, but they are possible. Continuing to live with pervasive and relentless violence is not acceptable.

In the time it has taken you to read this chapter, at least one woman has been raped and at least two have been beaten by a friend, lover, or family member. We need to be part of changing this.

KEY TERMS

The following terms are defined in this chapter on the pages indicated, as well as in alphabetical order in the book's glossary, which begins on page 261. The text's companion website also provides interactive flash cards to help you learn these terms and the concepts they represent. You can access the site at www.cengagebrain.com.

blaming the victim 244	*male circumcision 250*
clitoridectomy 250	*pornography 255*
erotica 255	*quid pro quo harassment 241*
femicide 252	*rape 242*
gendered violence 239	*rape culture 243*
gender intimidation 240	*reproductive violence 253*
hostile environment harassment 241	*sexual assault 242*
infibulation 251	*sexual harassment 241*
informed consent 242	*stalking 250*
intimate partner violence 247	*sunna 250*

GENDER ONLINE

1. Many organizations provide up-to-date information on ways you can help stop gendered violence around the world. Visit these websites: Office of Violence Against Women: **http://www.usdoj.gov/ovw**; National Domestic Violence Hotline: **http://www.ndvh.org**

2. To learn more about men who are committed to stopping men's violence, visit this website **http://menstoppingviolence.org**

3. The Department of Justice has a special office that focuses exclusively on violence against women. Its website is **http://www.ovw.usdoj.gov**. You might want to pay particular attention to the "Campus Grants" link, which is a relatively new feature that emphasizes dealing with and reducing violence against women on campuses.

4. **Notalone.gov** is the website set up by the Task Force to Protect Students from Sexual Assault. *The Invisible War* is a 2012 feature-length documentary about sexual assault in the military in which 35 former soldiers and sailors recount being raped and otherwise sexually assaulted while in the military. **Warning:** This film is disturbing.

5. Online search terms: *bride burning, informed consent, sexual harassment.*

REFLECTION, DISCUSSION, AND ACTION

1. Conduct a survey to see if students on your campus believe the rape myths discussed in this chapter.

    -   On the left-hand side of a sheet of paper, type the five myths about rape that are listed in the "Exploring Gendered Lives: Myths and Facts about Rape" box. To the right of the statements, type five categories of answer: strongly agree; somewhat agree; not sure; somewhat disagree; strongly disagree.

    -   Print 15 copies of the sheet. Use two different colors of paper; give one color to women students and the other color to men students. Ask the students to respond anonymously. Ideally, members of the class should poll students at different places, such as the library, the student center or union, a fraternity house, and so forth.

    -   Compile and analyze the data gathered by all the students in your class.

2. Is bombing abortion clinics or killing doctors who provide abortion reproductive violence? If bombings and threats of them discourage medical professionals from performing abortions or if fear of harm discourages women from going to clinics, is that interference with their right to choose whether, when, and with whom to reproduce?

RECOMMENDED RESOURCES

1. Mukhtar Mai (2006). *In the Name of Honor.* New York: Simon Schuster/Atria. This is Mukhtar Mai's autobiography.

2. Jimmy Carter (2014). *A Call to Action: Women, Religion, Violence, and Power.* New York: Simon and Schuster. Carter documents widespread violence against women both in the United States and internationally.

3. Nicholas Kristof and Sherryl WuDunn (2014). *A Path Opens: Transforming Lives, Creating Opportunity.* New York: Knopf. This book provides inspirational accounts of people and groups that have made a difference in the effort to end gendered violence.

4. Jeremy Schaap's documentary video on "corrective rape" in South Africa details the rape of lesbians to punish them for being lesbian and "correct" their sexual orientation. These assaults, some of which end in murder, are perpetrated by men in South African communities and rarely result in criminal charges or conviction. We are providing a link to a site that features Schaap's documentary, but please be aware that it is very disturbing. **http://www.opposingviews.com/i/%e2%80%9ccorrective-rape%e2%80%9d-and-black-lesbian-athletes-in-south-africa**

Glossary

ACT UP A grassroots movement that used street-based, direct action civil disobedience to advocate for people living with HIV and AIDS.

affirmative action Collective term for policies that go beyond equal opportunity laws to redress discrimination. Assumes that historical patterns of discrimination against groups of people justify the preferential treatment of members of those groups; focuses on results, not on the intent of efforts to redress inequities; and attempts to increase the number of qualified members of minorities in education and the workplace, commensurate with their availability.

agenda setting Process by which media tell us to what we should attend.

alternate paths model A relationship theory according to which masculine and feminine ways of creating and expressing closeness are viewed as different from each other and equally valid.

androgyny Combination of qualities that society considers both masculine and feminine. Androgynous people tend to identify with and enact qualities socially ascribed both to women and men.

antifeminism A movement opposing any measures that advance women's equality, status, rights, or opportunities; also called the *backlash against feminism*.

antisuffrage movement A movement that aimed to prevent women from gaining the right to vote in the United States. Opposition to women's suffrage was evident as early as 1848 and was formalized in organizations by 1911.

artifact A personal object that influences how we see ourselves and how we express our identities.

backlash A countermovement that seeks to repudiate and contain feminism by arguing two contradictory claims: that women have never had it so good, so there is no longer any need for feminism; and that feminism has caused serious problems in women's lives and family relationships. Also called *antifeminism*.

Bechdel Test An assessment of gender bias in media that asks three simple questions of a film: Does it feature two women, who talk to each other, about something other than a man?

benevolent sexism Paternalistic attitude that describes women affectionately but assumes they aren't competent to do particular tasks.

biological theory The theory that biological characteristics of the sexes are the basis of differences in women's and men's thinking, communicating, feeling, and other functions.

Black Lives Matter Grassroots movement of people of all genders that challenges racist violence, police brutality, and mass incarceration of black people.

blaming the victim Holding a harmed person responsible for the harm inflicted on him or her by another person.

bullying Behavior intended to hurt, embarrass, shame, or intimidate another person. Also see *cyberbullying*.

cis Prefix that designates someone whose gender identity is consistent with what society considers appropriate for the sex assigned at birth.

clitoridectomy Removal of the entire clitoris. Part or all of the labia minora may also be removed. Also called *excision*.

cognitive development theory A developmental theory according to which children participate in defining their genders by acting on internal motivations to be competent, which in turn lead them to seek out gender models that help them to sculpt their own femininity or masculinity.

communication A dynamic, systemic process in which meanings are created and reflected in and through humans' interactions with symbols.

complimentary copy An article or section of writing about an advertiser's product or service that is placed in a magazine by the publisher at no cost to the advertiser to increase the market appeal of the product or service.

content level of meaning The literal meaning of communication. Content-level meanings are the formal, or denotative, meanings of messages.

contextual advertising Ads embedded in digital content and tailored to specific individuals based on extensive data mining practices by web-based companies.

critical research methods Modes of study that are informed by political commitments to interrogating power dynamics.

cult of domesticity Cultural ideology during the first wave of U.S. feminism that claimed women are suited for and should remain in the domestic sphere.

cultural feminism The viewpoint that women and men differ in fundamental ways, including biology, having different abilities and skills, and being entitled to different rights.

culture The structures and practices, especially those relating to communication, through which a particular social order is produced and reproduced by legitimizing certain values, expectations, meanings, and patterns of behavior.

culture of romance Created when forces in higher education encourage female students to regard being attractive to men as more important than academics and career preparation.

cyberbullying It includes text messages, comments, rumors, embarrassing pictures, videos, and fake profiles that are meant to hurt another person and are sent by email or posted on social networking sites.

ecofeminism A movement that integrates the intellectual and political bases of feminist theorizing with ecological philosophy. The specific oppression of women is seen as a particular instance of a larger ideology that esteems

violence and domination of women, children, animals, and the Earth.

effortless perfection The pressure felt by many female students at colleges to be beautiful, fit, popular, smart, and accomplished, all without visible effort.

ego boundary Psychologically the point at which an individual stops and the rest of the world begins; an individual's sense of the line between herself or himself and others. Ego boundaries range from permeable (a sense of self that includes others and their issues, problems, and so on) to rigid (a sense of self as completely distinct from others).

equal opportunity laws Laws that prohibit discrimination on the basis of race, color, religion, sex, or national origin. Equal opportunity laws seek to protect *individual* members of groups that have been targets of discrimination; they redress only current discrimination, not historical bias.

erotica Depictions of sexual activities that are agreed to and enjoyed by the parties participating in the activities.

essentializing The reduction of a phenomenon to its essential characteristics, which are generally presumed to be innate or unchangeable. To essentialize the sexes is to imply that all women are alike in basic respects, that all men are alike in basic respects, and that the two sexes are distinct from each other because of fundamental, essential qualities.

father hunger From the mythopoetic men's movement, men's yearning to be close to other men and to build deep, enduring bonds with them; based on the mythopoetic belief that most young boys have distant relationships with the primary man in their lives—the father—and that the hunger for meaningful contact with men, of which they were deprived in youth, continues throughout life.

Fathers 4 Justice A British fathers' rights group that relies on the two rhetorical strategies of humor and dramatic stunts to raise public awareness about the custody rights of separated and divorced fathers.

femicide The killing of girls and women.

feminine ruler Measuring closeness or intimacy in a way that gives priority to behaviors more typical of women than of men.

Free Men A branch of the men's movement that seeks to restore the traditional image of men by celebrating and encouraging the qualities of competitiveness, independence, and ruggedness in men.

gatekeeper Person or group that controls which messages get through to audiences of mass media.

gender A social, symbolic construction that includes an internal sense of identity, the external communication of that identity, as well as the cultural expectations assigned to biological sex. Gender varies across cultures, over time within any given society, and in relation to other genders.

gender binary The division of humans into two sexes and two corresponding genders that are presumed to be opposite, distinct, natural, and enduring. The gender binary assumes that a person's sex, gender, and sexuality align in socially prescribed ways.

gender constancy A person's understanding that his/her/their assigned sex is stable or permanent and that it is accompanied by gendered expectations.

gender expression The external communication of one's gender identity through clothing, hairstyles, behavior, and voice.

gender identity A person's private sense of, and subjective experience of, his/her/their own gender.

gender intimidation Groping, stalking, sexist comments, publicly masturbating in someone's presence, or other behaviors that lead people, because of their sex, gender, or sexual orientation, to feel humiliated, vulnerable, or unsafe.

gender-linked language effect Asserts that differences between women's and men's communication are influenced by a variety of factors including topics, speaker status, salience of gender in a communication situation, and other people present.

gender role The cultural expectations assigned to one's sex.

gender schema An internal mental framework that organizes perceptions and directs behavior related to gender.

gender schema theory Claims that cognitive processes are central to our learning what gender means in our culture and to learning how to perform our gender competently. Related to cognitive development theory.

gendered violence Physical, verbal, emotional, sexual, or visual brutality inflicted disproportionately or exclusively on members of one sex or gender. Includes gender intimidation, sexual assault, violence between intimates, sexual harassment, genital mutilation, and gender-based murder.

generic language Words and phrases that are claimed to refer to both women and men yet are denotatively masculine; for example, the word *man* used to refer to all human beings.

glass ceiling An invisible barrier made up of subtle, often unconscious prejudices and stereotypes that limits the opportunities and advancement of women and minorities.

glass escalator An invisible advantage that accelerates men's success in female-dominated spheres of work.

glass walls A metaphor for sex segregation on the job. Glass walls exist when members of a group, such as women, are placed in positions based on stereotypes of that group. Typically, such positions do not entail advancement ladders.

goal A stated intention to achieve a defined representation of minorities or women.

Good Men Project A multifaceted effort to stimulate a national conversation about what it means to be a good man today.

haptics Touch as a form of nonverbal communication.

heteronormativity A view that promotes heterosexuality as natural and preferred and assumes all other sexual identities are abnormal.

hip-hop feminism A contemporary feminist movement rooted in black feminism but responsive to the concerns of the post-civil rights or hip-hop generation.

hostile environment harassment Conduct that has sexual overtones and that interferes with a person's ability to perform a job or gain an education or that creates a hostile, intimidating, or offensive working environment.

immersive advertising Incorporating a particular brand or product into entertainment.

infibulation Removal of the clitoris and labia minora and subsequent joining of the lips of the labia majora so that they fuse together.

informed consent Consent given by a legal adult with normal mental abilities whose judgment is not impaired by circumstances, including alcohol or other drugs.

intersex people Used to describe various circumstances in which individuals are born with anatomical features that do not neatly conform to typical male or female sex classification.

intimate partner violence The use of physical, mental, emotional, verbal, or economic power by one partner against the other partner in a current or past romantic relationship.

invisible hand discrimination The inadvertent application, in discriminatory fashion, of policies that are not inherently biased.

kinesics Facial and body movements; one type of nonverbal communication.

liberal feminism A form of feminism that maintains that women and men are alike in important respects and advocates women's social, economic, educational, and political equality. The National Organization for Women (NOW) is the best-known organization representing liberal feminism.

liking The dimension of relationship-level meaning that expresses affection for another.

mainstream second-wave feminism Branch of feminism that arose in the early 1960s and advocates women's social, economic, educational, and political equality.

mainstream third-wave feminism (1) Aims to be inclusive of diverse peoples; (2) to use personal life and personal action for political impact; and (3) to work to build coalitions with other groups that struggle against oppression.

male circumcision Removal of the sheath, or prepuce, of the penis.

male deficit model A relationship theory according to which men are deficient in forming and participating in close relationships and holds that most men's ways of experiencing and expressing closeness are not simply different from, but inferior to, those of women.

male feminists Men who believe that women and men are alike in important respects and that the sexes should enjoy the same privileges, rights, opportunities, and status in society. Male feminists join liberal women feminists in fighting for equitable treatment of women. In addition, many male feminists seek to rid themselves of what they regard as toxic masculinity promoted in men by socialization and to develop sensitivities more typically inculcated in women. Also called *profeminist men*.

masculinist A category of men's movement that sees men as oppressed and seeks to preserve men's freedom from women and feminization.

maternal wall Unexamined assumptions held by coworkers and superiors about how women will behave once they become mothers.

matriarchal Of or pertaining to matriarchy, "rule by the mothers." The term *matriarchy* is generally used to refer to systems of ideology, social structures, and practices that are created by women and reflect the values, priorities, and views of women as a group.

men's rights activists Members of a men's movement whose goal is to restore traditional roles for men and women and, with that, the privileges men have historically enjoyed.

mentor A more experienced person who helps a less experienced person develop.

Mentors in Violence Prevention (MVP) A male antiviolence program that educates men about socialization that links masculinity to violence and aggression; motivates men to reject violence in themselves and in other men; and emphasizes the role of a bystander.

microaggression Verbal, behavioral, or environmental insults that, regardless of intent, reflect and communicate negative bias or hostility toward individuals or groups that are marginalized by race, gender, sexual orientation, religion, or ability.

Million Man March A branch of the men's movement that began with a march in Washington, DC, in 1995, in which black men atoned for sins and committed themselves to spiritual transformation and political action. Annual marches were also held in subsequent years.

Million Woman March A grassroots gathering of African-American women launched in Philadelphia in 1997 to celebrate and foster solidarity among black women.

minimal response cues Nominal indicators of listening or attending. "Um" and "yeah" are minimal response cues.

misogyny Hatred of women.

mixed research methods Scholarship that combines quantitative, qualitative, and critical methods of doing research.

multiracial feminism A branch of the women's movement that is characterized by global perspective, coalition-building, and emphasis on multiple systems of domination that shape women's lives.

mythopoetic movement A branch of the men's movement headed by poet Robert Bly and active in the 1990s. Mythopoetics believe that men need to rediscover their distinctively masculine modes of feeling, which they regard as rooted largely in myth.

NOMAS An activist men's organization that promotes personal, political, and social changes that foster equality of men and women and gay and straight people through workshops and informal group discussions, public speaking, educational outreach programs, and enactment of traitorous identities.

nonverbal communication All elements of communication other than words themselves. Estimated to carry 65 to 93% of the total meaning of communication and includes visual, vocal, environmental, and physical aspects of interaction.

paralanguage Vocal cues that accompany verbal communication, such as accent, volume, and inflection.

passionate friendship A unique interpersonal relationship, typically occurring between women, that blends aspects of romance and friendship

patriarchal Of or pertaining to patriarchy, "rule by the fathers." The term *patriarchy* generally refers to systems of ideology, social structures, and practices created by men, which reflect the values, priorities, and views of men as a group.

performative theory Claims that identity, including gender, is not something individuals have, but rather something they do through performance or expression.

personal relationships Connections in which partners are interdependent, consider each other irreplaceable, and are strongly and specifically connected to each other as unique individuals.

polarized thinking Conceiving things in terms of opposites (e.g., good or bad, right or wrong).

pornography Written, oral, or visual material that favorably shows subordination and degradation of individuals by presenting sadistic behaviors as pleasurable, pain as enjoyable, and forced sex as positive. Distinct from erotica, which depicts consensual activities desired by and pleasurable to all parties.

postfeminist era Cultural assumption that sexism is fully eradicated. Uses the language of feminism to undermine feminist commitments to collective justice and change.

power Dimension of relationship-level meaning that expresses the degree to which a person is equal to, dominant over, or deferential to others.

power feminism A movement that emerged in the 1990s as a reaction to feminist emphasis on women's oppression. Urges women to take the power that is theirs and to reject seeing themselves as victims of men or society.

product placement Showing or mentioning a particular brand or product in a show, story, film, or other form of media.

profeminists See *male feminists*.

Promise Keepers Begun in 1990, a Christian branch of the men's movement that calls men together to pray and commit to Christ-centered living.

proxemics Space and the human use of space, including personal territories.

psychodynamic theory The theory that family relationships, especially between mother and child during the formative years of life, have a pivotal and continuing impact on the development of self, particularly gender identity.

psychological responsibility The responsibility to remember, plan, think ahead, organize, and so forth. In most heterosexual relationships, even when physical labor is divided between partners, women assume greater psychological responsibility for the home and children.

qualitative research methods Aim to understand the nature or meaning of experiences, which cannot be quantified into numbers.

quantitative research methods Way of gathering data that can be quantified and analyzing the data to draw conclusions.

queer performative theory Integration of queer and performative theories into a perspective on performances as means of challenging and destabilizing conventional cultural categories and the values attached to them.

queer theory Critique of conventional categories of identity and cultural views of "normal" and "abnormal," particularly in relation to sexuality. Queer theory argues identities are not fixed but fluid.

quid pro quo harassment Actual or threatened use of professional or academic rewards or punishments to gain sexual compliance from a subordinate or student.

quota A particular number or percentage of women or minorities who must be admitted to schools, hired in certain positions, or promoted to certain levels in institutions.

radical feminism A branch of feminism that grew out of New Left politics and demanded the same attention to women's oppression that New Left organizations gave to racial oppression and other ideological issues. Radical feminists pioneered revolutionary communication techniques such as consciousness raising, leaderless group discussion, and guerrilla theater.

rape One or more acts of nonconsensual oral, anal, or vaginal penetration by a body part or object.

rape culture Common attitudes, beliefs, and practices that ignore, excuse, encourage, or normalize sexual violence.

relationship level of meaning The nonliteral meaning of communication. Expresses how a speaker sees the relationship between self and other. May provide cues about how to interpret the literal meaning of a message, for instance, as a joke.

reproductive violence Coerced or discriminatory infringement on reproductive rights. It includes force or exploitation that inhibits an individual's free choice of whether, when, and with whom to reproduce, become a parent, and parent existing children.

responsiveness The dimension of relationship-level meaning that expresses attentiveness to others and interest in what they say and do.

revalorism Feminist group that focuses on valuing traditionally feminine skills, activities, and perspectives and their contributions to personal, interpersonal, and cultural life.

Riot Grrrl An underground feminist movement that began in the late 1980s and aligned with punk music, radical politics, and DIY ethics. Riot Grrrls created their own music, art, and zines to tackle a range of feminist issues.

role social definitions of expected behaviors and the values associated with them; typically internalized by individuals in the process of socialization.

second shift The work of homemaking and child care performed by a member of a dual-worker family after and in addition to that person's job in the paid labor force.

separatism Feminist group that believes that, because patriarchal culture cannot be changed or reformed, women who find it oppressive must create and live in their own women-centered communities separate from the larger culture.

sex A personal quality determined by biological and genetic characteristics. *Male, female, man,* and *woman* indicate sex.

sexual assault Sexual activity to which at least one participant has not given informed consent.

sexual harassment Unwelcome sexualized conduct that is linked to the target's academic or professional standing.

sexual orientation A person's preferences for romantic and sexual partners.

social learning theory Theory that individuals learn to be masculine and feminine (among other things) by observing and imitating others and by reacting to the rewards and punishments others give in response to imitative behaviors.

speech community A group of people who share assumptions regarding how, when, and why to communicate and how to interpret others' communication.

stalking Repeated pursuit that is uninvited and unwanted, that seems obsessive, and that makes the target of pursuit concerned for her/his/their safety.

standpoint theory A theory that focuses on the influence of gender, race, class, and other social categories on circumstances of people's lives, especially their social positions and the kinds of experiences fostered within those positions. According to standpoint theory, political consciousness about social location can generate a standpoint that affects perspective and action.

stereotype A broad generalization about an entire class of phenomena based on some knowledge of limited aspects of certain members of the class.

sunna Genital mutilation involving removal of the sheath and tip of the clitoris. Also called *female circumcision.*

symbolic interactionism The theory that individuals develop self-identity and an understanding of social life, values, and codes of conduct through communicative interactions with others in a society.

territoriality An aspect of proxemics; the sense of personal space that one does not want others to invade.

theory A way to describe, explain, and predict relationships among phenomena.

third person effect The belief that media affect others more than they affect us.

Title IX The section of the Educational Amendment of 1972 that makes it illegal for schools that accept federal funds to discriminate on the basis of sex.

traitorous identity A group member's criticism of particular attitudes and actions—for example, sexist jokes—that are accepted and normative within the group.

transfeminism A movement by and for trans and gender-nonconforming people that advances an intersectional view of liberation.

transgender Someone whose biologically assigned sex and its accompanying gendered expectations do not match their gender identity.

voice-over A technique used in audiovisual media, particularly television commercials; over the action on the screen, viewers hear a voice that makes claims about the product, gives advice, or explains the action.

Walk a Mile in Her Shoes An organization that works to end men's violence against women through community awareness and fundraising.

White Ribbon Campaign (WRC) An international group of men who work to end men's violence against women.

womanism Activism started by black women to define *oppression* as resulting from both race and sex. The womanist movement arose out of dissatisfaction with mainstream feminism's predominant focus on white, middle-class women and their interests.

women's liberation movement See *radical feminism.*

women's rights movement From the mid-1800s to the 1920s, a movement that focused on gaining basic rights for women, such as the rights to vote, to pursue higher education, and to enter professions.

workplace bullying Repeatedly acting toward a person or persons in ways that humiliate, intimidate, or otherwise undermine the target's professional credibility.

References

AAUW (American Association of University Women). (2013). *The simple truth about the gender pay gap.* Retrieved June 30, 2013, from http://www.aauw .org/files/2013/03/The-Simple-Truth-Fall-2013.pdf

Abadi, P. (2013, June 5). Kids' toys: More gendered than ever. *Ms. Blog.* Retrieved June 18, 2014, from http://msmagazine.com/blog/2013/06/05/kids-toys-more-gendered-than-ever

Abrams, J. (2009, January 23). Bill lifting limits on equal-pay lawsuits clears Senate. *Raleigh News & Observer*, p. 6A.

Acitelli, L. (1988). When spouses talk to each other about their relationship. *Journal of Social and Personal Relationships, 5*, 185–199.

Ackerman, J. M., Griskevicius, V., & Li, N. P. (2011). Let's get serious: Communicating commitment in romantic relationships. *Journal of Personality and Social Psychology, 100*, 1079–1094.

Adams, C. (1991, April). The straight dope. *Triangle Comic Review*, p. 26.

Adams, S. (2014, April 21). How women breadwinners can save their relationships. *Forbes.* Retrieved August 3, 2014, from http://www.forbes.com/sites/susanadams/2014/04/21/how-women-breadwinners-can-save-theirrelationships/

Adichie, C. (2015). *We should all be feminists.* New York: Anchor.

Adler, J. (2007, March 12). The great sorority purge. *Newsweek*, p. 47.

Afful, A. A., & Ricciardelli, R. (2015). Shaping the online fat acceptance movement: Talking about body image and beauty standards. *Journal of Gender Studies, 24*(4), 453–472. Retrieved from https://doi.org/10.1080/09589236.2015.1028523

Albergotti, R. (2014, June 12). Facebook to target ads based on web browsing. *Wall Street Journal.* Retrieved from http://online.wsj.com/articles/facebook-to-give-advertisers-data-about-users-web-browsing-1402561120

Alcantara-Tan, S. M. (2000). The herstory of "Bamboo Girl" zine. *Frontiers: A Journal of Women's Studies, 21*(1/2), 159–170.

Alderman, L. (2016, May 21). The 6-hour workday. *New York Times*, pp. B1, B5.

Allen, R. (2016, May 22). Is egg freezing only for white women? *New York Times*, pp. SR 4, 5.

Allis, S. (1990, Fall). What do men really want? *Time*, pp. 80–82.

Alter, J. (1990, December 31). One well-read editorial. *Newsweek*, pp. 85, 86.

American Association of University Women. (2016). The simple truth about the gender pay gap. Retrieved from http://www.aauw.org/research/the-simple-truth-about-the-gender-pay-gap/

American Society for Reproductive Medicine (ASRM). (2014a). *Quick facts about infertility.*

American Society for Reproductive Medicine. (2014b). *In vitro fertilization: What are the risks?* Retrieved from http://www.reproductivefacts.org/globalassets/rf/news-and-publications/bookletsfact-sheets/english-fact-sheets-and-info-booklets/in_vitro_fertilization_ivf_what_are_the_risks_factsheet.pdf

American Society of Plastic Surgeons. (2016). *2015 plastic surgery statistics report.* Retrieved from http://www.plasticsurgery.org

Anchalee, I. (2015, August 1). You may have seen my face on BART. Retrieved August 30, 2016, from https://medium.com/the-coffeelicious/you-may-have-seen-my-face-on-bart-8b9561003e0f#.mh8kzlnak

Andelin, H. (1975). *Fascinating womanhood.* New York: Bantam.

Andersen, P. (2006). The evolution of biological sex differences in communication. In K. Dindia & D. Canary (Eds.), *Sex differences and similarities in communication* (pp. 117–135). Mahwah, NJ: Erlbaum.

Anderson, A., & Deutsch, E. (2015, May 12). Stop assaults on military campuses. *New York Times*, p. A23.

Andronici, J. F., & Katz, D. S. (2007, Winter). Scaling the maternal wall. *Ms.*, pp. 63–64.

Angier, N. (2007a, May 1). For motherly X chromosome, gender is only the beginning. *New York Times*, pp. D1, D6.

Angier, N. (2007b, June 12). Sleek, fast and focused: The cells that make dad dad. *New York Times*, pp. D1, D6.

Angier, N. (2010, June 15). Paternal bonds, special and strange. *New York Times*, pp. D1, D2.

Anzaldúa, G. (2002, October 11). Beyond traditional notions of identity. *Chronicle of Higher Education*, pp. B11–B13.

Anzaldúa, G., & Keating, A. (Eds.). (2002). *This bridge called home*. New York: Routledge.

Arneson, P. (2014). *Communicative engagement and social liberation: Justice will be made*. Madison, WI: Farleigh Dickinson University Press.

Arroyo, A., & Harwood, J. (2012). Exploring the causes and consequences of engaging in fat talk. *Journal of Applied Communication Research, 40,* 167–187.

Aschwanden, C. (2014, August 12). Harassment in science, replicated. *New York Times*, pp. D1, D2.

Ashcraft, K. (2006). Back to work: Sights/sites of difference in gender and organizational communication studies. In B. Dow & J. T. Wood (Eds.), *Handbook of gender and communication* (pp. 97–122). Thousand Oaks, CA: Sage.

The Associated Press. (2016, August 31). Texas, other states file to support North Carolina's HB2 bathroom law. *NBC News*. Retrieved September 1, 2016, from http://www.nbcnews.com/feature/nbc-out/texas-other-states-file-support-north-carolinas-hb2-bathroom-n640846

Babarskiene, J., & Tweed, R. (2009). Marital adjustment in post-Soviet Eastern Europe: A focus on Lithuania. *Personal Relationships, 16,* 647–658.

Babel, C., & Kwan, S. (Eds.). (2011). *Embodied resistance: Challenging the norms, breaking the rules*. Nashville, TN: Vanderbilt University Press.

Bagalawis-Simes, J. (2010). Saving face: More Asian Americans opting for plastic surgery. *Hyphen*. Retrieved from http://hyphenmagazine.com/magazine/issue-22-throwback-winter-2010/saving-face-more-asian-americans-opting-plastic-surgery

Baird, J. (2014, April 7). Neither female nor male. *New York Times*, p. A21.

Bakalar, N. (2006, June 13). Men are better than women at ferreting out that angry face in a crowd. *New York Times*, p. D5.

Baker, J. (2006). *Sisters: The lives of America's suffragists*. New York: Hill and Wang.

Baksh, K. (2016, June 22). Workplace discrimination: The LGBT workforce. *The Huffington Post*. Retrieved April 26, 2017, from http://www.huffingtonpost.com/kurina-baksh/workplace-discrimination-_b_10606030.html

Balaji, M., & Worawongs, T. (2010, June). The new Suzie Wong: Normative assumptions of white male and Asian female relationships. *Communication, Culture & Critique, 3,* 224–241.

Banchefsky, S., Westfall, J., Park, B., & Judd, C. M. (2016). But you don't look like a scientist!: Women scientists with feminine appearance are deemed less likely to be scientists. *Sex Roles, 75*(3–4), 95–109. Retrieved from http://doi.org/10.1007/s11199-016-0586-1

Bandura, A. (2002). Social cognitive theory of mass communication. In J. Bryant & D. Zillmann (Eds.), *Media effects: Advances in theory and research* (2nd ed., pp. 121–153). Mahwah, NJ: Erlbaum.

Bandura, A., & Walters, R. H. (1963). *Social learning and personality development*. New York: Holt, Rinehart & Winston.

Bane, C., Cornish, M., Erspamer, N., & Kampman, L. (2010). Self-disclosure through weblogs and perceptions of online and "real-life" friendships among female bloggers. *Cyberpsychology, Behavior, and Social Networking, 32,* 131–139.

Banyard, V. L. (2015). *Toward the next generation of bystander prevention of sexual and relationship violence*. London: Springer.

Barash, D. (2002, May 24). Evolution, males, and violence. *Chronicle of Higher Education*, pp. B7–B9.

Barash, D., & Lipton, J. (2002). *Gender gap: The biology of male-female differences*. New Brunswick, NJ: Transaction Publishers.

Barbu, S., Cabanes, G., & Le Maner-Idrissi, G. (2011). Boys and girls on the playground: Sex differences in social development are not stable across early childhood. *PLOS ONE, 6.* Retrieved May 6, 2016 from www.ncbi.nlm.nih.gov/pmc/articles/PMC3030561

Barnett, R., & Rivers, C. (1996). *She works, he works: How two-income families are happier, healthier, and better off*. San Francisco, CA: HarperCollins.

Barry, K. (1998). Radical feminism. In W. Mankiller, G. Mink, M. Navarro, B. Smith, & G. Steinem (Eds.), *The reader's companion to U.S. women's history* (pp. 217–218). New York: Houghton Mifflin.

Barstead, M. G., Bouchard, L. C., & Shih, J. H. (2013). Understanding gender differences in co-rumination and confidant choice in young adults. *Journal of Social and Clinical Psychology, 32,* 791–808.

Bartlett, N. B., & Vasey, P. L. (2006). A retrospective study of childhood gender-atypical behavior in Samoan fa'afafine. *Archives of Sexual Behavior, 35,* 559–566.

Baruh, L., Chisik, Y., Bisson, C., & Şenova, B. (2014). When sharing less means more: How gender moderates the impact of quantity of information shared in a social network profile on profile viewers' intentions about socialization. *Communication Research Reports, 31*(3), 244–251. Retrieved from https://doi.org/10.1080/08824096.2014.924302

Basow, S. A., & Rubenfeld, K. (2003). "Troubles talk": Effects of gender and gender-typing. *Sex Roles, 48,* 183–187.

Bass, A. (2015). *Getting screwed: Sex workers and the law*. Lebanon, NH: University Press of New England/ForEdge.

Bates, L. (2016). *Everyday sexism*. New York: Thomas Dunn-St. Martin's.

Baumann, S., & de Laat, K. (2012). Socially defunct: A comparative analysis of the underrepresentation of older women in advertising. *Poetics, 40,* 514–541.

Baumgardner, J., & Richards, A. (2000). *Manifesto: Young women, feminism, and the future*. New York: Farrar, Straus & Giroux.

Baxter, L. A. (2014). Introduction. In L. A. Baxter (Ed.), *Remaking "family" communicatively*. New York: Peter Lang.

Bazelon, E. (2013). *Sticks and stones: Defeating the culture of bullying and rediscovering the power of character and empathy*. New York: Random House.

Bazelon, E. (2015, September 13). Reframing the victim. *New York Times Magazine*, pp. 56–59, 72–73.

Bazelon, E. (2016, May 8). Oppression or profession? *New York Times Magazine*, pp. 34–43, 55–57.

Beatie, T. (2008). *Labor of love: The story of one man's extraordinary pregnancy*. Boston, MA: Seal.

Beck, R. (2008, January 23). When they couldn't even vote. *Raleigh News & Observer*, p. A14.

Becker, C. S. (1987). Friendship between women: A phenomenological study of best friends. *Journal of Phenomenological Psychology, 18*, 59–72.

Becker, A., Burwell, R., Gilman, S., Herzog, D., & Hamburg, P. (2002). Eating behaviours and attitudes following prolonged exposure to television among ethnic Fijian adolescent girls. *British Journal of Psychiatry, 180*, 509–514.

Begley, S. (2009, June 29). Don't blame the cavemen. *Newsweek*, pp. 50–62.

Bellafante, G. (2016, October 16). This election, misogyny is back. Did it ever go away? *New York Times*, p. 28Y.

Belluck, P. (2011, September 13). Fatherhood cuts testosterone, study finds, for good of the family. *New York Times*, pp. A1, A3.

Belluck, P. (2015, August 4). Chilly at work? Icy office temperature was devised with men in mind. *New York Times*, pp. A1, A3.

Belluck, P., & Cochrane, J. (2016, February 5). Female genital cutting: Not just "an African problem." *New York Times*, p. A6.

Bendavid, N. (2013, October 31). Countries expand recognition for alternative "intersex" gender. *Wall Street Journal*, p. A9.

Benefits of shared child sare. (2015, September 1). *New York Times*, p. D4.

Benenson, J., Del Bianco, R., Philippoussis, M., & Apostoleris, N. (1997). Girls' expression of their own perspectives in the presence of varying numbers of boys. *International Journal of Behavioral Development, 21*, 389–405.

Bennett, J. (2015, August 9). Man deconstructed. *New York Times*, pp. ST 1, 7.

Bennett, J., Ellison, J., & Ball, S. (2010, March 29). Are we there yet? *Newsweek*, pp. 42–46.

Bennett, S. (2015, January 27). 28% of time spent online is social networking. *Social Times*. Retrieved May 18, 2016, from http://www.adweek.com/socialtimes/time-spent-online/12374

Berger, A. (2015). *Ads, fads, and consumer culture* (5th ed.). Lanham, MD: Rowman & Littlefield.

Bergeron, C. (2009, November 2). A few "Good Men": Authors spread wisdom of manhood. *Metrowest Daily News*. Retrieved from http://www.metrowestdailynews.com/news/x1659494253/A-few-Good-Men-Authors-spread-wisdom-of-manhood?zc_p=0

Berkowitz, D. (2011). Maternal instincts, biological clocks, and soccer moms: Gay men's parenting and family narratives. *Symbolic Interaction, 34*(4), 514–535. Retrieved from http://doi.org/10.1525/si.2011.34.4.514

Berry, L. (2014, May 21). "Ideal" body image differs by race. *Medscape Medical News*. Retrieved from www/medscape.com/viewarticle/825489

Bianchi, S. M., Robinson, J., & Milkie, M. (2006). *Changing rhythms of American family life*. New York: Russell Sage Foundation.

Bidgood, J. (2014, April 9). Number of mothers in U.S. who stay at home rises. *New York Times*, p. A15.

Bigham, J. (1991, January 11). Birth control order stands until appeal. *Oregonian* [Portland, Oregon], p. A16.

The big reveal. (2009, October 29). *Chronicle of Higher Education*, p. B18.

Binker, M. (2016, May 4). Obama administration says HB2 violates federal civil rights laws. *WRAL News*. Retrieved September 1, 2016, from http://www.wral.com/obama-administration-says-hb2-violates-federal-civil-rights-laws/15682472/

Birdwhistell, R. (1970). *Kinesics and context*. Philadelphia, PA: University of Pennsylvania Press.

Blackwell, A. G. (2014, July 25). The missing piece for young men of color: Jobs. Retrieved September 25, 2016, from http://www.huffingtonpost.com/angela-glover-blackwell/the-missing-piece-for-unemployment_b_5618585.html

Bland, K. (2012, June 29). *Dad on duty*. Retrieved from http://www.azcentral.com/arizonarepublic/news/articles/2009/06/21/20090621dadtoday06210.html

Bleske-Rechek, A., Somers, E., Micke, C., Erickson, L., Matteson, L., Stocco, C., & Ritchie, L. (2012). Benefit or burden? Attraction in cross-sex friendship. *Journal of Social and Personal Relationships, 29*(5), 569–596. Retrieved from https://doi.org/10.1177/0265407512443611

Blow, C. (2012, June 23). Bullies on the bus. *New York Times*, p. A19.

Blow, C. (2014a, March 1). Fathers' sons and brothers' keepers. *New York Times*, p. A19.

Blow, C. (2014b, June 2). Yes, all men. *New York Times*, p. A17.

Blow, C. (2015, September 7). Sexual attraction and fluidity. *New York Times*, p. A17.

Blum, D. (1998). The gender blur: Where does biology end and society take over? *Utne Reader*, pp. 45–48.

Boboltz, S. (2014, April 16). 9 facts that prove traditional definitions of gender roles are bulls*it. *Huffington Post*. Retrieved April 17, 2014, from http://www.huffingtonpost.com/2014/04/16/gender-facts-traditionalroles_n_5115265.html?utm_hp_ref=women&ir=Women

Bogdanich, W. (2014, July 13). Reporting rape, and wishing she hadn't. *New York Times*, pp. A1, 14–15.

Bollinger, L. (2016, June 25). Affirming affirmative action. *New York Times*, p. A19.

Bologna, C. (2016, February 1). Mom combats gender stereotypes with #StillABoy campaign. Retrieved September 29, 2016, from http://www.huffingtonpost.com/entry/mom-combats-gender-stereotypes-with-stillaboy-campaign_us_56ab-be47e4b00b033aaf0587

Bonnett, A. (1996). The new primitives: Identity, landscape and cultural appropriation in the mythopoetic men's movement. *Antipode*, *28*, 273–291.

Bordini, G. S., & Sperb, T. M. (2013). Sexual double standard: A review of the literature between 2001 and 2010. *Sexuality & Culture*, *17*(4), 686–704. Retrieved from https://doi.org/10.1007/s12119-012-9163-0

Borenstein, K. (1994). *Gender outlaws: On men, women, and the rest of us*. New York: Psychology Press.

Borenstein, S. (2010, January 14). Ladies first? Chromosomes say no. *Raleigh News & Observer*, p. 4A.

Borisoff, D., & Chesebro, J. (2011). *Communicating power & gender*. Long Grove, IL: Waveland.

Boston proclaims April 9 Riot Grrrl Day in honor of Kathleen Hanna. (2015, April 9). Retrieved April 10, 2016, from http://www.factmag.com/2015/04/08/boston-proclaims-april-9-riot-grrrl-day-in-honor-of-kathleen-hanna/?utm_source=social&utm_medium=facebook&utm_context=v1buttons

Bowen, W., & Bok, D. (1998). *The shape of the river*. Princeton, NJ: Princeton University Press.

boyd, danah. (2014). *It's complicated: The social lives of networked teens*. New Haven, CT: Yale University Press.

Boylan, J. (2013a). *She's not there*. New York: Roadway.

Boylan, J. (2013b). *Stuck*. New York: Crown.

Boylan, J. (2016, July 23). Bring moral imagination back in style. *New York Times*, p. A17.

Breines, W. (2006). *The trouble between us: An uneasy history of white and black women in the feminist movement*. New York: Oxford University Press.

Brescoll, V. (2012). Who takes the floor and why: Gender, power, and volubility in organizations. *Administrative Science Quarterly*, *56*, 621–640.

Brettell, C., & Sargent, C. (2012). *Gender in cross-cultural perspective* (6th ed.). Upper Saddle, NJ: Pearson.

Brewster, M. E. (2016). Lesbian women and household labor division: A systematic review of scholarly research from 2000 to 2015. *Journal of Lesbian Studies*, *3*, 1–23. Retrieved from https://doi.org/10.1080/10894160.2016.1142350

Bridges, V. (2017, January 15). Pauli Murray's childhood home in Durham recognized as National Historic Monument. *Chapel Hill News*, p. 5A.

Bring back the girls. (2014, July 19). *Economist*, p. 44.

Brizendine, L. (2007). *The female brain*. New York: Doubleday/Broadway.

Brooks, D. (2012, July 10). The opportunity gap. *New York Times*, p. A19.

Brooks, D. E., & Hébert, L. P. (2006). Gender, race and media representation. In B. Dow & J. T. Wood (Eds.), *Handbook of gender and communication* (pp. 297–317). Thousand Oaks, CA: Sage.

Brown, L. M., Lamb, S., & Tappan, M. (2009). *Packaging boyhood*. New York: St. Martin's Press.

Browne, K. (2003/2004, Winter). Fighting fistula. *Ms.*, p. 20.

Bruni, F. (2013, August 13). Tackling the roots of rape. *New York Times*, p. A19.

Bruni, F. (2016, April 10). Building a better father. *New York Times*, p. SR 3.

Bruns, G. L., & Carter, M. M. (2015). Ethnic differences in the effects of media on body image: The effects of priming with ethnically different or similar models. *Eating Behaviors*, *17*, 33–36. Retrieved from http://doi.org/10.1016/j.eatbeh.2014.12.006

Budig, M. (2014). The fatherhood bonus & the motherhood penalty: Parenthood and the gender gap in pay. Washington, DC: Third Way.

Bugeja, M. (2010, February 25). Avatar rape. *Inside Higher Ed*. Retrieved from http://www.insidehighered.com/views/2010/02/25/bugeja

Bulik, C. (2011). *The woman in the mirror: How to stop confusing what you look like with who you are*. New York: Walker & Co.

Burleson, B. R., Hanasono, L. K., Bodie, G. D., Holmstrom, A. J., McCullough, J. D., Rack, J. J., & Rosier, J. G. (2011). Are gender differences in responses to supportive communication a matter of ability, motivation, or both? Reading patterns of situation effects through the lens of a dual-process theory. *Communication Quarterly*, *59*(1), 37–60. Retrieved from https://doi.org/10.1080/01463373.2011.541324

Burleson, B. R., Holmstrom, A. J., & Gilstrap, C. M. (2005). Guys can't say that to guys: Four experiments assessing the normative motivation account for deficiencies in the emotional support provided by men. *Communication Monographs*, *72*, 468–501.

Burn, J. (1996). *The social psychology of gender*. New York: McGraw-Hill.

Burney, M. (2012, March 15). Standing up to bullies. *Chronicle of Higher Education*, pp. 50–53.

Buss, D. (1995). Evolutionary psychology: A new paradigm for psychological science. *Psychological Inquiry, 6*, 1–30.

Buss, D. (1996). The evolutionary psychology of human social strategies. In E. Higgins & A. Druglanski (Eds.), *Social psychology: Handbook of basic principles* (pp. 3–38). New York: Guilford.

Buss, D. (1999). *Evolutionary psychology: The new science of the mind*. Boston, MA: Allyn & Bacon.

Buss, D., & Kenrick, D. (1998). Evolutionary social psychology. In D. Gilbert, S. Fiske, & G. Lindzey (Eds.), *The handbook of social psychology* (4th ed., Vol. 2, pp. 982–1026). Boston, MA: McGraw-Hill.

Butler, J. (1990). Performative acts and gender constitution: An essay in phenomenology and feminist theory. In S. Case (Ed.), *Performing feminisms: Feminist critical theory and theater* (pp. 270–282). Baltimore, MD: Johns Hopkins University Press.

Butler, J. (1993a). *Bodies that matter: On the discursive limits of "sex."* New York: Routledge.

Butler, J. (1993b). *Gender trouble: Feminism and the subversion of identity*. New York: Routledge.

Butler, J. (2004). *Undoing gender*. London: Routledge.

Buzzanell, P. M., & Lucas, K. (2006). Gendered stories of career: Unfolding discourses of time, space, and identity. In B. Dow & J. T. Wood (Eds.), *Handbook of gender and communication* (pp. 161–178). Thousand Oaks, CA: Sage.

Byng, R. (2013, October 15). The images of black women in media still "only scratch the surface," Essence study finds. *Huffington Post*. Retrieved from http://www.huffingtonpost.com/2013/10/15/the-images-of-black-womenin-media_n_4102322.html

Caldwell, M., & Peplau, L. (1982). Sex differences in same-sex friendship. *Sex Roles, 8*, 721–732.

California: Gang rape is investigated. (2009, October 27). *New York Times*, p. A21.

Callimachi, R. (2007, February 5). Here, women woo, men wait. *Raleigh News & Observer*, p. 10A.

Campbell, A. (2002). *A mind of her own*. Oxford: Oxford University Press.

Campbell, K. (2005). Agency: Promiscuous and protean. *Communication and Critical/Cultural Studies, 2*, 1–19.

Campbell, K. K. (1989a). *Man cannot speak for her: I. A critical study of early feminist rhetoric*. New York: Praeger.

Campbell, K. K. (1989b). *Man cannot speak for her: II. Key texts of the early feminists*. New York: Greenwood.

Campbell, B., & Manning, J. (2014). Microaggressions and moral culture. *Comparative Sociology, 13*, 692–726.

Canary, D., & Wahba, J. (2006). Do women work harder than men at maintaining relationships? In K. Dindia & D. Canary (Eds.), *Sex differences and similarities in communication* (2nd ed., pp. 359–377). Mahwah, NJ: Erlbaum.

Cancian, F. (1987). *Love in America*. Cambridge, MA: Cambridge University Press.

Cancian, F. (1989). Love and the rise of capitalism. In B. Risman & P. Schwartz (Eds.), *Gender and intimate relationships* (pp. 12–25). Belmont, CA: Wadsworth.

Carey, B., & Hoffman, J. (2016, October 13). Stopping offensive speech in its tracks. *New York Times*, p. A18.

Carothers, B., & Reis, H. (2013, April 21). The tangle of the sexes. *New York Times*, p. SR9.

Carter, J. (2014). *A call to action: Women, religion, violence, and power*. New York: Simon and Schuster.

Casey, E., & Smith, T. (2010). "How can I not?": Men's pathways to involvement in anti-violence against women work. *Violence against Women, 16*, 953–973.

Caughlin, J., & Vangelisti, A. (2000). An individual differences explanation of why married couples engage in the demand/withdraw pattern of conflict. *Journal of Social and Personal Relationships, 17*, 523–551.

Caughlin, P., & Caughlin, P. (2005). *No more Christian nice guy*. Minneapolis, MN: Bethany House.

Centers for Disease Control and Prevention. (2015). *Suicide: Facts at a glance*. National Center for Injury Prevention and Control, CDC (producer). Retrieved from http://www.cdc.gov/violenceprevention/pdf/suicide-datasheet-a.PDF

Chambers, D. L., Clydesdale, T. T., Kidder, W. C., & Lempert, R. O. (2005). The real impact of eliminating affirmative action in American law schools: An empirical critique of Richard Sander's study. *Stanford Law Review, 57*(6), 1855–1898.

Chang, A., Sandhofer, C., & Brown, C. (2012). Gender biases in early number exposure to preschool-aged children. *Journal of Language and Social Psychology, 30*, 440–450.

Chapman, M., & Hendler, G. (Eds.). (1999). *Sentimental men: Masculinity and the politics of affect in American culture*. Berkeley, CA: University of California Press.

Chateauvert, M. (2015). *Sex workers unite: A history of the movement from Stonewall to slutwalks*. Boston, MA: Beacon.

Chaudhry, L. (2005, November 21). Babes in Bushworld. *In These Times*, pp. 38–39.

Chemaly, S. (2012, January 6). Definition of rape: 7 ways to rethink how we approach sexual assault. Retrieved from http://www.huffingtonpost.com/soraya-chemaly/definition-ofrape_b_1190255.html

Chemaly, S. (2013, Fall). Mapping a feminist world: Violence against women activates new global network. *Ms. Magazine*, pp. 20–21.

Chernik, A. F. (1995). The body politic. In B. Findlen (Ed.), *Listen up: Voices from the next generation of feminists* (pp. 75–84). Seattle, WA: Seal Press.

Chesler, E. (1992). *Woman of valor: Margaret Sanger and the birth control movement in America*. New York: Simon & Schuster.

Chesley, N. (2011). Stay-at-home fathers and breadwinning mothers: Gender, couple dynamics, and social change. *Gender & Society, 25*(5), 642–664.

Chethik, N. (2001). *Father loss: How sons of all ages come to terms with the deaths of their dads*. New York: Hyperion.

Chethik, N. (2008). *Voice male: What husbands really think about their marriages, their wives, sex, housework and commitment*. New York: Simon & Schuster.

Chodorow, N. J. (1978). *The reproduction of mothering: Psychoanalysis and the sociology of gender*. Berkeley, CA: University of California Press.

Chodorow, N. J. (1989). *Feminism and psychoanalytic theory*. New Haven, CT: Yale University Press.

Chodorow, N. J. (1999). *The power of feelings: Personal meaning in psychoanalysis, gender, and culture*. New Haven, CT: Yale University Press.

Choose your parents wisely. (2014, July 26). *Economist*, pp. 21–25.

Chow, E. N. L. (1989). The feminist movement: Where are all the Asian American women? In Asian Women United of California (Ed.), *Making waves: An anthology of writings by and about Asian American women* (pp. 362–377). Boston, MA: Beacon Press.

Chrisafis, A. (2016, August 28). French mayors refuse to lift burkini ban despite court ruling. *The Guardian*. Retrieved from https://www.theguardian.com/world/2016/aug/28/french-mayors-burkini-ban-court-ruling

Circumcision. (2012, September 15). *Economist*, pp. 57–58.

Citadel. (2001, May). The Citadel leads S.C. public colleges in four-year graduation rates. Retrieved April 22, 2017, from http://www.citadel.edu/root/news-archives-sy00-01-grad_rates

Clark, R. A. (1998). A comparison of topics and objectives in a cross section of young men's and women's everyday conversations. In D. J. Canary & K. Dindia (Eds.), *Sex differences and similarities in communication: Critical essays and empirical investigations of sex and gender in interaction* (pp. 303–319). Mahway, NJ: Erlbaum.

Clinton, K. (2001, May). Unplugged: Surrendered wives. *Nation*, p. 17.

Cobble, D., Gordon, L., & Henry, A. (2015). *Feminism unfinished*. London: Liveright.

Colapinto, J. (2006). *As nature made him*. New York: HarperPerennial.

Coles, R. L. (2015). Single-Father Families: A Review of the Literature: Single-Father Families. *Journal of Family Theory & Review, 7*(2), 144–166. Retrieved from http://doi.org/10.1111/jftr.12069

Collins, G. (2009a, January 29). Lilly's big day. *New York Times*, p. A21.

Collins, G. (2009b). *When everything changed: The amazing journey of American women from 1960 to the present*. New York: Little, Brown, & Co.

Collins, G. (2015, November 8). Hillary in history. *New York Times*, pp. SR 1, 6.

Collins, P. H. (1986). Learning from the outsider within. *Social Problems, 33*, 514–532.

Collins, P. H. (1998). *Fighting words: Black women and the search for justice*. Minneapolis, MN: University of Minnesota Press.

Considine, A. (2012, May 16). Saying "no" to picture perfect. *New York Times*. Retrieved from http://www.nytimes.com/2012/05/17/fashion/saying-no-to-picture-perfect.html

Conway, J. R., Noë, N., Stulp, G., & Pollet, T. V. (2015). Finding your Soulmate: Homosexual and heterosexual age preferences in online dating: Age preferences in online dating. *Personal Relationships, 22*(4), 666–678. Retrieved from https://doi.org/10.1111/pere.12102

Coontz, S. (2013). Why gender equality stalled. *New York Times*, pp. 1, 6, 7.

Coontz, S. (2014, July 27). The new instability. *New York Times*, pp. SR1, 7.

Cooper, A. (2006, November–December). One of the guys: Transgender performance artist Scott Turner Schofield explores gender issues for the average Joe. *Utne Reader*, pp. 34–35.

Cornwell, C., Mustard, D., & Van Parys, J. (2013). Noncognitive skills and the gender disparities in test scores and teacher assessments: Evidence from primary school. *Journal of Human Resources, 48*, 236–264.

Cortese, A. (2016). *Provocateur: Images of women and minorities in advertising* (4th ed.). Lanham, MD: Rowman & Littlefield.

Cose, E. (1997, October 13). Promises. *Newsweek*, pp. 30–31.

Cottle, M. (2012, May 28). Thank you, Rush Limbaugh! *Newsweek*, pp. 18–19.

Council on Contemporary Families. (2010). *Unconventional wisdom*. Retrieved April 14, 2010, from https://contemporaryfamilies.org/unconventional-wisdom-3/

The Covering House. (2014). Retrieved July 4, 2014, from http://thecoveringhouse.org

Cox, J. R. (2013). *Environmental communication and the public sphere* (3rd ed.). Thousand Oaks, CA: Sage.

Cox, J. R., & Pezzullo, P. (2016). *Environmental communication and the public sphere* (4th ed.). Thousand Oaks, CA: Sage.

Craig, S. L., & McInroy, L. (2014). You can form a part of yourself online: The influence of new media on identity development and coming out for LGBTQ youth. *Journal of Gay & Lesbian Mental Health*, *18*(1), 95–109. Retrieved from http://doi.org/10.10 80/19359705.2013.777007

Crampton, L. (2014, June 10). Sexual assaults on the response students deserve. *Raleigh News & Observer*, p. 9A.

Crary, D. (2014, June 20). As NOW turns 50, feminists hail gains but 'battle goes on.' *Raleigh News & Observer*, p. 13A.

Cubbans, L. A., & Vannoy, D. (2004). Division of household labor as a source of contention for married and cohabiting couples in Metropolitan Moscow. *Journal of Family Issues*, *25*, 182–185.

Cuklanz, L. M., & Moorti, S. (Eds.). (2009). *Local violence, global media*. New York: Peter Lang.

Cupach, W., & Spitzberg, B. (2015). Unilateral union: Obsessive relational intrusion and stalking in a romantic context. In D. O. Braithwaite & J. T. Wood (Eds.), *Casing interpersonal communication* (pp. 131–136). Dubuque, IA: Kendall-Hunt.

Curtis, J. W. (2010, Spring). "Faculty salary equity: Still a gender gap?" *On campus with women* (Association of American College and Universities), p. 1. Pay Equity (event). Retrieved from http://www .aacu.org/ocww/volume39_1/feature .cfm?section=2

Curtis, J. W. (2011, April 11). *Persistent inequity: Gender and academic employment*. Paper presented at the New Voices in Pay Equity: An Event for Equal Pay Day. Retrieved from https://www.aaup.org/ NR/rdonlyres/08E023AB-E6D8-4DBD-99A0- 24E5EB73A760/0/persistent_inequity.pdf

Damaske, S. (2011). A "major career woman"? How women develop early expectations about work. *Gender & Society*, *25*, 409–430.

Dana, R. (2011, December 19). All I want for Christmas is a brand-new face. *Newsweek*, pp. 13–15.

Dargis, M. (2015, August 6). Young, white and male? The role is yours. *Raleigh News & Observer*, p. C1.

Davies-Popelka, W. (2015). Mirror, mirror on the wall. In D. O. Braithwaite & J. T. Wood (Eds.), *Casing interpersonal communication* (2nd ed., e-book). Dubuque, IA: Kendall Hunt.

Davison, W. P. (1983). The third-person effect in communication. *Public Opinion Quarterly*, *47*, 1–15.

Dawson, I. (2005, Summer). Good rap, bad rap. *Ms.*, p. 18.

DeMaris, A. (2007). The role of relationship inequity in marital disruption. *Journal of Social and Personal Relationships*, *24*, 177–195.

Denizet-Lewis, B. (2014, March 20). The scientific quest to prove—once and for all-that someone (even a man) can be truly attracted to both a man . . . and a woman. *New York Times Magazine*, pp. 20–29, 44.

Dennis, A., & Wood, J. T. (2012). "We're not going to have this conversation, but you get it.": Black mother–daughter communication about sexual relations. *Women's Studies in Communication*, *35*(2), 204–223. doi: 10.1080/07491409.2012.724525

Derry, C. (2015, Fall). Abusive men describe the benefits of violence. *Male Voice*, *19*, 12–13.

De Ruijter, E., Treas, J. K., & Cohen, P. N. (2005). Outsourcing the gender factory: Living arrangements and service expenditures on female and male tasks. *Social Forces*, *84*(1), 305–322.

DeSantis, N. (2013, February 13). Brown U. will cover transgender surgery under student insurance plan. *Chronicle of Higher Education*. Retrieved July 9, 2014, from http://chronicle.com/blogs/ticker/ jp/brown-u-will-cover-transgender-surgery-under-student-insurance-plan

Dewan, B. (2016, May 2). Why do colleges still give preference to kids whose parents went there? Retrieved September 21, 2016, from https:// thinkprogress.org/why-do-colleges-still-give-preference-to-kids-whose-parents-went-there-ef3abe20407b#.keogie6un

Dewan, S., & Gebeloff, R. (2012, May 21). More men enter fields dominated by women. *New York Times*, pp. A1, A3.

Dewey, C. (2014, January 17). How many of this year's Oscar nominees pass the Bechdel test? Not many. *Washington Post Style Blog*. Retrieved from http:// www.washingtonpost.com/blogs/style-blog/ wp/2014/01/17/how-many-of-this-years-oscar-nominees-pass-the-bechdel-test-not-many/

Diamond, L. M. (2000). Passionate friendships among adolescent sexual-minority women. *Journal of Research on Adolescence*, *10*(2), 191–209.

Differences between male and female full-time professors. (2014, August 18). *Chronicle of Higher Education*. Retrieved from http://chronicle.com/article/ Differences-Between-Male-and/147307/

Digits. (2015, October 26). *Time*, p. 16.

DiTomaso, N. (2013, May 12). Not discrimination but favoritism. *Raleigh News & Observer*, p. 17A.

Dokoupil, T. (2009, March 2). Men will be men. *Newsweek*, p. 50.

Douglas, S. (2010a). *Enlightened sexism: The seductive message that feminism's work is done*. New York: Times Books.

Douglas, S. (2010b). *The rise of enlightened sexism: How pop culture took us from girl power to girls gone wild*. New York: St. Martin's.

Douglas, S., & Michaels, M. (2004). *The mommy myth: The idealization of motherhood and how it has undermined women*. New York: The Free Press.

Douglas, W. (2012, May 17). House Oks anti-domestic violence bill. *Raleigh News & Observer*, p. 3A.

Douthat, R. (2014, January 14). The war on women. *New York Times*, p. SR11.

Dow, B. J. (1991). The "womanhood" rationale in the woman suffrage rhetoric of Frances E. Willard. *Southern Communication Journal, 56*, 298–307.

Dow, B. J. (2014). *Watching women's liberation 1970: Feminism's pivotal year on the network news*. Urbana, IL: University of Illinois Press.

Dow, B. J., & Wood, J. T. (Eds.). (2006). *The handbook of gender and communication*. Thousand Oaks, CA: Sage.

Dow, B. J., & Wood, J. T. (2014). Repeating history and learning from it: What can SlutWalks teach us about feminism? *Women's Studies in Communication, 37*(1), 22–43.

Dowd, M. (2015, November 22). Waiting for the green light. *New York Times Magazine*, pp. 40–47, 60–61.

Doyle, J. (1997). *The male experience* (3rd ed.). Dubuque, IA: Brown & Benchmark.

Doyle, L. (2001). *The surrendered wife: A practical guide for finding intimacy, passion and peace with a man*. New York: Fireside.

Drawing a line. (2014, June 14). *Economist*, pp. 55–56.

Dreger, A. (n.d.). *Shifting the paradigm of intersex treatment*. Retrieved August 23, 2016, from http://www.isna.org/compare

Dreier, P., & Freer, R. (1997, October 24). Saints, sinners, and affirmative action. *Chronicle of Higher Education*, pp. B6, B7.

Dreifus, C. (2000, July 11). A conversation with Nawal Nour. *New York Times*, p. D7.

Dube, K. (2004, June 18). What feminism means to today's undergraduates. *Chronicle of Higher Education*, p. B5.

Dubriwny, T. N. (2013). *The vulnerable empowered woman: Feminism, postfeminism, and women's health*. New Brunswick, NJ: Rutgers University Press.

Duenwald, M. (2005, March 8). Aspirin is found to protect women from strokes, not heart attacks. *New York Times*, p. D5.

Dugger, C. (2013, July 23). Genital cutting found in decline in many nations. *New York Times*, pp. A1, A6.

Duncan, G., & Murane, R. (2011). *Whither opportunity?* New York: Russell Sage Foundation.

Dunn, S. (2013, February 15). U.S. high court is urged to rule on Mich. affirmative-action case. *Chronicle of Higher Education*, p. A17.

Durham, M. G. (2009). *The Lolita effect: The media sexualization of young girls and five keys to fixing it.* New York: The Overlook Press.

Durham, A., Cooper, B. C., & Morris, S. M. (2013). The stage hip-hop feminism built: A new directions essay. *Signs, 38*, 721–737.

Easton, N. (2015, March 15). The jobless gender. *Fortune*, pp. 22–24.

Eaton, A. A., & Rose, S. (2011). Has dating become more egalitarian? A 35 year review using *Sex Roles*. *Sex Roles, 64*, 843–862.

Eckholm, E. (2013, October 23). Case explores rights of fetus versus mother. *New York Times*. Retrieved July 1, 2014, from http://www.nytimes.com/2013/10/24/us/case-explores-rights-of-fetus-versus-mother.html?_r=0

Edwards, S. (2016, May 6). Cheer up! The vulnerable, weeping man is back in style. Retrieved August 4, 2016, from http://jezebel.com/cheer-up-the-vulnerable-weeping-man-is-back-in-style-1767495371

Ehrensaft, D. (2016). *The gender creative child*. New York: The Experiment.

Ehrmann, J. (2013, January 25). *Joe Ehrmann TED Talk: Be a man* [video file]. Retrieved from http://www.coachforamerica.com/meet-joe

Einarsen, S., Hoel, H., Zapf, D., & Cooper, C. (Eds.). (2010). *Bullying and harassment in the workplace: Developments in theory, research, and practice* (2nd ed.). Boca Raton, FL: Taylor & Francis/CRC.

Eisenberg, N. (2002). Empathy-related emotional responses, altruism, and their socialization. In R. Davidson & A. Harrington (Eds.), *Visions of compassion: Western scientists and Tibetan Buddhists examine human nature* (pp. 131–164). London: Oxford University Press.

Elam, P. (2010, November 14). Challenging the etiology of rape. *A Voice for Men*. Retrieved September 7, 2014, from https://archive.today/eIlgf

Elam, P. (2014, October 14). If you see Jezebel in the road, run the bitch down. *A Voice for Men*. Retrieved September 7, 2014, from http://www.wehuntedthemammoth.com/2010/11/28/paul-elam-youre-no-jonathan-swift/

Ellen, A. (2012, August 14). Binge eating among men steps out of the shadows. *New York Times*, pp. D1, D6.

Ellin, A. (2016, July 12). When abuse is psychological. *New York Times*, p. D4.

Elliott, L. (2009). *Pink brain, blue brain: How small differences grow into troublesome gaps—and what we can do about it*. Boston, MA: Houghton Mifflin-Harcourt.

Eltahawy, M. (2014, November 17). Fighting female genital mutilation. *New York Times*, p. A23.

Emens, E. F. (2007). Changing name changing: Framing rules and the future of marital names. *University of Chicago Law Review, 74*, 761–863.

Ensler, E. (2000). *The vagina monologues: The V-Day edition.* New York: Random House, Villard.

Ensler, E. (2001). *Necessary targets: A story of women and war.* New York: Random House, Villard.

Ensler, E. (2004). *The good body.* New York: Random House, Villard.

Ensler, E. (2011). *I am an emotional creature.* New York: Random House, Villard.

Ensslin, A., & Muse, E. (Eds.). (2011). *Creating second lives: Community, identity, and spatiality as constructions of the virtual.* New York: Routledge.

Erickson, R. J. (2005). Why emotion work matters: Sex, gender and the division of household labor. *Journal of Marriage and the Family, 67*, 337–351.

Estioko-Griffin, A., & Griffin, P. (1997). Woman the hunter: The Agta. In C. Brettell & C. Sargent (Eds.), *Gender in crosscultural perspectives* (pp. 123–149). Englewood Cliffs, NJ: Prentice Hall.

Etzioni, A. (2014, April). Don't sweat the microaggressions. *The Atlantic.* Retrieved September 17, 2016, from http://www .theatlantic.com/politics/archive/2014/04/ dont-sweat-the-microaggressions/360278/

Faderman, L. (1999). *To believe in women: What lesbians have done for America—a history.* Boston, MA: Houghton Mifflin Company.

Fagan, K., & Cyphers, L. (2012, April 29). Five myths about Title IX. Retrieved April 21, 2017, from http://www.espn.com/espnw/title-ix/ article/7729603/five-myths-title-ix

Fairfield, H. (2013). Girls vs. boys. *New York Times,* p. D3.

Farhi, P. (2012, June 28). Media often consult men for views on women's issues. *Raleigh News & Observer,* p. 3D.

Farley, S. D., Ashcraft, A. M., Stasson, M. F., & Nusbaum, R. L. (2010). Nonverbal reactions to conversational interruption: A test of complementarity theory and the status/gender parallel. *Journal of Nonverbal Behavior, 34*, 193–206.

Fauber, J. (2009, August 8). UW tied to male hormone marketing: Testosterone prescriptions soar despite weak research, risks. *Milwaukee-Wisconsin Journal Sentinel.* Retrieved from http://archive.jsonline. com/watchdog/watchdogreports/testosterone- courses-downplay-risks-lead-to-overuse-in-older- men-b99595151z1-333591801.html

Fausto-Sterling, A. (1982). Course close up: The biology of gender. *Women's Studies Quarterly, 13*, 30–32.

Fausto-Sterling, A. (1989). Life in the XY corral. *Women's Studies International Forum, 12*, 3.

Fausto-Sterling, A. (1992). Myths of gender: Biological theories about men and women. New York: Basic.

Fausto-Sterling, A. (1993, March/April). The five sexes: Why male and female are not enough. *The Sciences, 33*, 20–24.

Fausto-Sterling, A. (2000). *Sexing the body: Gender politics and the construction of sexuality.* New York: Basic Books.

Federman, D. D., & Walford, G. A. (2007, January 15). Is male menopause real? *Newsweek,* pp. 58–60.

Feeney, N. (2014). A brief history of sexism in TV coverage of the Olympics. *Atlantic.* Retrieved July 7, 2014, from http://www.theatlantic.com/entertain- ment/archive/2014/02/a-briefhistory-of-sexism- in-tv-coverage-of-theolympics/284003/

Feinberg, L. (1997). Transgender warriors : Making history from Joan of Arc to Dennis Rodman. Boston, MA: Beacon Press.

Feinberg, L. (2006). Street transvestite action revolutionaries: *Workers World Party.* Retrieved June 3, 2016, from http://www.workers.org/2006/us/ lavender-red/73/

Felmlee, D., Sweet, E., & Sinclair, H. C. (2012). Gender rules: Same- and cross-gender friendships norms. *Sex Roles, 66*(7–8), 518–529. Retrieved from https://doi.org/10.1007/s11199-011-0109-z

Ferguson, M. L. (2010, March). Choice feminism and the fear of politics. *Perspectives on Politics, 8*(1), 247–253.

Fernandez, M. (2013, June 25). Filibuster in Texas Senate tries to halt abortion bill. *New York Times.* Retrieved from http://www.nytimes.com/2013/06/26/us/pol- itics/senate-democrats-in-texas-try-blocking-abor- tion-bill-with-filibuster.html

Ferraro, S. (2001). Gender affects the course of disease, researchers say. *Raleigh News & Observer,* p. 2E.

Fiebert, M. (1987). Some perspectives on the men's movement. *Men's Studies Review, 4*, 8–10.

Fields, A. (2003). *Katharine Dexter McCormick: Pioneer for women's rights.* Westport, CT: Praeger.

Fincher, L. H. (2014). *Leftover women: The Resurgence of gender inequality in China.* London: Zed Books, Ltd.

Fine, C. (2011). *Delusions of gender.* New York: W. W. Norton.

Fisher, H. (2000). *The first sex.* New York: Bantam.

Fisher, H. (2009, October). Intimacy: His & hers. *O: The Oprah Winfrey Magazine,* p. 138.

Fishman, P. M. (1978). Interaction: The work women do. *Social Problems, 25*, 397–406.

Fishwick, C. (2016, August 31). Why we wear the burkini: Five women on dressing modestly at the beach. *The Guardian.* Retrieved from https://www .theguardian.com/world/2016/aug/31/why-we- wear-the-burkini-five-women-on-dressing-mod- estly-at-the-beach

Fixmer, N. (2003). *Revisioning the political: Feminism, difference, and solidarity in a new generation.* Unpublished master's thesis, University of North Carolina, Chapel Hill.

Fixmer, N., & Wood, J. T. (2005). The political is personal: Difference, solidarity, and embodied politics in a new generation of feminists. *Women's Studies in Communication, 28,* 235–257.

Fixmer-Oraiz, N. (2013). Speaking of solidarity: Surrogacy and the rhetorics of reproductive (in)justice. *Frontiers: A Journal of Women's Studies, 34*(3), 126–164.

Fixmer-Oraiz, N. (2015). Contemplating homeland maternity. *Women's Studies in Communication, 38,* 129–134.

Floyd, K. (1997). Communicating affection in dyadic relationships: An assessment of behavior and expectancies. *Communication Quarterly, 45,* 68–80.

Fontes, L. (2015). *Invisible chains: Overcoming coercive control in your intimate relationships.* New York: Guilford.

Foss, K., Edson, B., & Linde, J. (2015). What's in a name? Negotiating decisions about marital names. In D. O. Braithwaite & J. T. Wood (Eds.), *Case studies in interpersonal communication* (2nd ed.). Dubuque, IA: Kendall-Hunt. (Ebook).

Foucault, M. (1978). *The history of sexuality, volume 1: An introduction* (R. Hurley, Trans.). New York: Pantheon.

Fournier, R. (2016). *Love that boy.* San Jose, CA: Penguin-Harmony.

Fouts, H., Hallam, R., & Purandare, S. (2013). Gender segregation in early childhood social play among the Bofi foragers and Bofi farmers in Central Africa. *American Journal of Play, 5,* 333–356.

Fox, J., & Ralston, R. (2016). Queer identity online: Informal learning and teaching experiences of LGBTQ individuals on social media. *Computers in Human Behavior.* Retrieved from http://doi.org/10.1016/j.chb.2016.06.009

Fox, S., & Lituchy, T. (Eds.). (2012). *Gender and the dysfunctional workplace.* Northampton, MA: Edward Elgar Publishing Limited.

France, D. (2012). *How to survive a plague* [Motion picture]. United States: Sundance Selects.

Frawley, T. J. (2008). Gender schema and prejudicial recall: How children misremember, fabricate, and distort gendered picture book information. *Journal of Research in Childhood Education, 22,* 291–303.

Frederick, D. A., & Fales, M. R. (2016). Upset over sexual versus emotional infidelity among gay, lesbian, bisexual, and heterosexual adults. *Archives of Sexual Behavior, 45*(1), 175–191. Retrieved from https://doi.org/10.1007/s10508-014-0409-9

Freed, B., & Freed, D. (2012, July/August). Why won't men get help? *Pacific Standard,* pp. 34–41.

Freeman, E. (2002). *No turning back.* New York: Ballantine.

Frey, L. L., Beesley, D., Hurst, R., Saldana, S., & Licuanan, B. (2016). Instrumentality, expressivity, and relational qualities in the same-sex friendships of college women and men. *Journal of College Counseling, 19*(1), 17–30. Retrieved from https://doi.org/10.1002/jocc.12028

Friedan, B. (1963). *The feminine mystique.* New York: Dell.

Gallagher, J. (2012). *Black women and politics in New York City.* Urbana, IL: University of Illinois Press.

Galupo, M. P., Bauerband, L. A., Gonzalez, K. A., Hagen, D. B., Hether, S. D., & Krum, T. E. (2014). Transgender friendship experiences: Benefits and barriers of friendships across gender identity and sexual orientation. *Feminism & Psychology, 24,* 193–215.

Galupo, M. P., & Gonzalez, K. A. (2013). Friendship values and cross-category friendships: Understanding adult friendship patterns across gender, sexual orientation, and race. *Sex Roles, 68,* 779–790.

Galvin, K. (2006). Gendered communication in families. In B. Dow & J. T. Wood (Eds.), *Handbook of gender and communication* (pp. 41–55). Thousand Oaks, CA: Sage.

Gannon, M. (2009). (Director & Producer). *The Good Men: One-hour documentary.* Boston, MA: Good Men Foundation.

Garloch, K. (2009, September 29). Saving our sons. *Raleigh News & Observer,* p. D1.

Gartner, R. (2005). *Beyond betrayal: Taking charge of your life after boyhood sexual abuse.* New York: Wiley.

Gartner, R. B. (2012, June 8). A troubled silence. *New York Times,* p. A23.

Garza, A. (n.d.). A herstory of the BlackLivesMatter movement. Retrieved May 26, 2026, from http://blacklivesmatter.com/herstory/

Gastil, J. (1990). Generic pronouns and sexist language: The oxymoronic character of masculine generics. *Sex Roles, 23,* 629–643.

Geena Davis Institute. (2010). *Improving gender portrayals in children's media.* Retrieved from http://www.thegeenadavisinstitute.org/research

Gilenstam, K., Karp, S., & Henriksson-Larsen, K. (2008). Gender in ice hockey: Women in a male territory. *Scandinavian Journal of Medicine & Science in Sports, 18,* 235–249.

Gill, T. (2010). Beauty shop politics: African American women's activism in the beauty industry. Urbana, IL: University of Illinois Press.

Gilligan, C., & Pollack, S. (1988). The vulnerable and invulnerable physician. In C. Gilligan, J. V. Ward, & J. M. Taylor (with B. Bardige) (Eds.), *Mapping the moral domain* (pp. 245–262). Cambridge, MA: Harvard University Press.

Giraldi, W. (2016). *The hero's body*. New York: Liveright Publishing.

Girish, U. (2007, Spring). Don't "tease" these Eves. *Ms.*, p. 27.

Girls Incorporated. (2006). The supergirl dilemma: Girls grapple with the mounting pressure of expectations, summary findings. New York: Girls Incorporated.

Global short takes. (2013, Summer). *Ms. Magazine*, p. 24.

Glover, J. A., Galliher, R. V., & Crowell, K. A. (2015). Young women's passionate friendships: A qualitative analysis. *Journal of Gender Studies, 24*(1), 70–84. Retrieved from https://doi.org/10.1080/09589236.2013.820131

Gold, H. (2014, April 15). Society is starting to wake up to rampant street harassment of women. *Alternet*. Retrieved July 3, 2014, from http://www.alternet.org/gender/international-anti-street-harassment-week

Goldberg, A. E. (2013). "Doing" and "undoing" gender: The meaning and division of housework in same-sex couples: Housework in same-sex couples. *Journal of Family Theory & Review, 5*(2), 85–104. Retrieved from https://doi.org/10.1111/jftr.12009

Goldberg, A., & Perry-Jenkins, M. (2007). The division of labor and perceptions of parental roles: Lesbian couples across the transition to parenthood. *Journal of Social and Personal Relationships, 24*, 297–318.

Goldberg, A. E., & Smith, J. Z. (2011). Stigma, social context, and mental health: Lesbian and gay couples across the transition to adoptive parenthood. *Journal of Counseling Psychology, 58*(1), 139–150. Retrieved from https://doi.org/10.1037/a0021684

Goldberg, A. E., Smith, J. Z., & Perry-Jenkins, M. (2012). The division of labor in lesbian, gay, and heterosexual new adoptive parents. *Journal of Marriage and Family, 74*(4), 812–828. Retrieved from https://doi.org/10.1111/j.1741-3737.2012.00992.x

Goldblum, P., Espelage, D., Chu, J., & Bongar, B. (Eds.). (2014). *Youth suicide and bullying*. New York: Oxford University Press.

Goldstein, S. (2011). Relational aggression in young adults' friendships and romantic relationships. *Journal of Personal Relationships, 18*, 645–656.

Gonzalez, A., Houston, M., & Chen, V. (2012). *Our voices: Essays in culture, ethnicity, and communication* (5th ed.). Los Angeles, CA: Roxbury.

The Good Men Foundation. Retrieved from http://goodmenproject.com/foundation/

Goodwin, M. H. (1990). *He said, she said: Talk as social organization among black children*. Bloomington, IN: Indiana University Press.

Goodwin, M. H. (2006). *The hidden life of girls*. Maiden, MA: Blackwell Publishing.

Gordon, L. (1976). *Woman's body, woman's right: A social history of birth control in America*. New York: Grossman.

Gordon, L. (2007). *The moral property of women: A history of birth control politics in America*. Chicago, IL: University of Illinois Press.

Gorski, E. (2003, October 6). Promise Keepers to shift direction under new chief. *Denver Post*, pp. IB, 3B.

Grant, A., & Sandberg, S. (2015, February 8). Madam C.E.O., get me a coffee. *New York Times*, p. SR2.

Gray, P. (2010). *Fatherhood: Evolution and human paternal behavior*. Cambridge, MA: Harvard University Press.

Gray, R., II. (Ed.). (2012). *The performance identities of Lady Gaga*. Jefferson, NC: McFarland.

Grayling, A. (2013). *Friendship (vices and virtues)*. New Haven, CT: Yale University Press.

Griffith, R. (1997, October 17). The affinities between feminists and evangelical women. *Chronicle of Higher Education*, pp. B6, B7.

Griffiths, S., Murray, S. B., & Touyz, S. (2015). Extending the masculinity hypothesis: An investigation of gender role conformity, body dissatisfaction, and disordered eating in young heterosexual men. *Psychology of Men & Masculinity, 16*(1), 108–114. Retrieved from http://doi.org/10.1037/a0035958

Gross, D. (1990, April 16). The gender rap. *New Republic*, pp. 11–14.

Guarino, C. M., & Borden, V. M. H. (2017). Faculty service loads and gender: Are women taking care of the academic family? *Research in Higher Education*. Retrieved from https://doi.org/10.1007/s11162-017-9454-2

Guerrero, L., Jones, S., & Boburka, R. (2006). Sex differences in emotional communication. In K. Dindia & D. Canary (Eds.), *Sex differences and similarities in communication* (pp. 242–261). Mahwah, MJ: Erlbaum.

Gurian, M., & Stevens, K. (2007). *The minds of boys*. San Francisco, CA: Jossey-Bass.

Haag, P. (2005, February 11). Navigating the new subtleties of sex-discrimination cases in academe. *Chronicle of Higher Education*, p. B20.

Halatsis, P., & Christakis, N. (2009). The challenge of sexual attraction with heterosexuals? Cross-sex friendship. *Journal of Social and Personal Relationships, 26*, 919–937.

Halberstam, J. J. (1998). *Female masculinity*. Durham, NC: Duke University Press.

Halberstam, J. J. (2011). *The queer art of failure.* Durham, NC: Duke University Press.

Halberstam, J. J. (2012). *Gaga feminism: Sex, gender and the end of normal.* Boston, MA: Beacon.

Hall, J. (2006). How big are nonverbal sex differences? The case of smiling and nonverbal sensitivity. In K. Dindia & D. Canary (Eds.), *Sex differences and similarities in communication* (2nd ed., pp. 59–81). Mahwah, NJ: Lawrence Erlbaum.

Hall, J., Park, N., Song, H., & Cody, J. (2010). Strategic misrepresentation in online dating: The effects of gender, self-monitoring, and personality traits. *Journal of Social and Personal Relationships, 27*, 117–135.

Hall, J. A. (2011). Sex differences in friendship expectations: A meta-analysis. *Journal of Social and Personal Relationships, 28*, 723–747.

Hallstein, D. L. O. (2008). Silences and choice: The legacies of white second wave feminism in the new professoriate. *Women's Studies in Communication, 31*, 143–150.

Hallstein, D. L. O. (2015). *Bikini-ready moms: Celebrity profiles, motherhood, and the body.* Albany, NY: SUNY Press.

Hallstein, D. L. O., & O'Reilly, A. (2012). *Academic motherhood in a post second wave context challenges strategies and possibilities.* Toronto, ON: Demeter Press.

Hallstein, L. (2010). *White feminists and contemporary maternity.* New York: Palgrave Macmillan.

Halperin, D. (2007). *What do gay men want? An essay on sex, risk, and subjectivity.* Ann Arbor, MI: University of Michigan Press.

Hamilton, M. C. (1991). Masculine bias in the attribution of personhood: People-male, male-people. *Psychology of Women Quarterly, 15*, 393–402.

Hammer, J. (2001). *What it means to be a daddy: Fatherhood for black men living away from their children.* New York: Columbia University Press.

Hammonds, E. (1998). Science and gender. In W. Mankiller, G. Mink, M. Navarro, B. Smith, & G. Steinem (Eds.), *The reader's companion to U.S. women's history* (pp. 521–522). New York: Houghton Mifflin.

Hanisch, C. (1970). What can be learned? A critique of the Miss America protest. In L. Tanner (Ed.), *Voices from women's liberation* (pp. 132–136). New York: Signet Classics.

Hanish, L., & Fabes, R. (2014). Peer socialization of gender in young boys and girls. *Encyclopedia on early childhood development.* Retrieved April 30, 2016, from www.child-encyclopedia.com/gender-early-socialization/according-experts/peer-socialization-gender-young-boys-and-girls

Hanna, K. (1991). Rebel Girl (Recorded by Bikini Kill). On *Yeah Yeah Yeah Yeah.* Olympia, WA: Kill Rock Stars (1993).

Harding, S. (1991). *Whose science? Whose knowledge? Thinking from women's lives.* Ithaca, NY: Cornell University Press.

Harding, S. (1998). *Is science multicultural?* Ithaca, NY: Cornell University Press.

Harper, A. B. (Ed.). (2010). *Sistah vegan: Black female vegans speak on food, identity, health, and society.* Brooklyn, NY: Lantern Books.

Harper, C. (2007). *Intersex.* New York: Berg.

Harris, K. (2009). *The next problem that has no name: The discourse and politics of "rape."* M. A. Thesis, Department of Communication Studies, The University of North Carolina, Chapel Hill.

Harris, K. (2011a). The next problem with no name: The politics and pragmatics of the word rape. *Women's Studies in Communication, 34*, 42–63.

Harris, K. (2011b). Peanut butter sandwiches: Making sense of acquaintance rape in ongoing relationships. In D. O. Braithwaite & J. T. Wood (Eds.), *Casing interpersonal communication* (pp. 181–285). Dubuque, IA: Kendall-Hunt.

Harris, K. (2016). Re-situating organizational knowledge: Violence, intersectionality, and the privilege of partial perspective. *Human Relations, 69*, 1–23.

Harrison, C. E. (1988). *On account of sex: The politics of women's issues, 1945–1968.* Berkeley, CA: University of California Press.

Harrison, K. (2008). Adolescent body image and eating in media: Trends and implications for adolescent health. In P. E. Jamieson & D. Romer (Eds.), *The changing portrayal of adolescents in the media since 1950* (pp. 165–197). New York: Oxford University Press.

Hasinoff, A. (2008). Fashioning race for the free market on America's next top model. *Critical Studies in Media Communication, 25*, 324–343.

Haskell, M. (2013). *My brother my sister.* New York: Viking.

Haughney, C. (2012, July 4). A magazine vows to ease retouching. *New York Times*, pp. B1, B2.

Hayden, S. (2009). Revitalizing the debate between life and choice: The 2004 march for women's lives. *Communication and Critical/Cultural Studies, 6*(2), 111–131.

Hayden, S. & O'Brien Hallstein, L. (Eds.). (2010). *Contemplating maternity in an era of choice: Exploring discourses of reproduction.* New York: Lexington.

Haynes, J. (2009). Exposing domestic violence in country music videos. In L. Cuklanz & S. Moorti (Eds.), *Local violence, global media* (pp. 201–221). New York: Peter Lang.

Heath, M. (2003). Soft-boiled masculinity: Renegotiating gender and racial ideologies in the Promise Keepers movement. *Gender & Society, 17*, 423–444.

Hegel, G. W. F. (1807). *Phenomenology of mind* (J. B. Baillie, Trans.). Germany: Wurzburg & Bamberg.

Helgeson, V. (2016). *The psychology of gender* (5th ed.). New York: Routledge.

Helms, H., Prouix, C., Klute, M., McHale, S., & Crouter, A. (2006). Spouses' gender-typed attributes and their links with marital quality: A pattern analytic approach. *Journal of Social and Personal Relationships, 23,* 343–364.

Henig, R. M. (2017, January). Rethinking gender. *National Geographic,* 48–73.

Henry, A. (2004). *Not my mother's sister.* Bloomington, IN: Indiana University Press.

Herdt, G. (1997). *Same sex, different cultures.* Boulder, CO: Westview.

Herrup, M. J. (1995). Virtual identity. In R. Walker (Ed.), *To be real* (pp. 239–252). New York: Anchor.

Herthel, J., Jennings, J., & McNicholas, S. (2014). *I am Jazz.* New York: Dial/Penguin.

Hess, A. (2014, January 6). Why women aren't welcome on the Internet. *Pacific Standard.* Retrieved from http://www.psmag.com/navigation/health-and-behavior/women-arent-welcome-internet-72170/

Hess, A. (2016, April 3). Multiple choice. *New York Times Magazine,* pp. 13–15.

Hewitt, N. A. (Ed.). (2010). *No permanent waves: Recasting histories of U. S. feminism.* Piscataway, NJ: Rutgers University Press.

Hickenlooper, J. (2016). *The opposite of woe.* New York: Penguin.

Hickey, W. (2014, April 1). The dollar-and-cents case against Hollywood's exclusion of women. *FiveThirtyEight Life.* Retrieved from http://fivethirtyeight.com/features/the-dollar-and-cents-case-against-hollywoods-exclusion-of-women/

High, A. C., & Solomon, D. H. (2014). Communication channel, sex, and the immediate and longitudinal outcomes of verbal person-centered support. *Communication Monographs, 81*(4), 439–468.

Hilgers, L. (2016, June 24). What one rape cost our family. *New York Times,* p. A25.

Hill, C. (2016, Spring). The simple truth about the gender pay gap. *AAUW: Empowering Women Since 1881.* Retrived from http://www.aauw.org/research/the-simple-truth-about-the-gender-pay-gap/

Hinshaw, S. (with Kranz, R.). (2009). *The triple bind: Saving our teenage girls from today's pressures.* New York: Ballentine.

Hiphop Literacies Conference. (n.d.). 2016 Hiphop Literacies Conference: Black women and girls' lives matter. Retrieved from http://www.hiphop-literacies.com/2016-black-women-and-girls-lives-matter.html

Hiring hotties. (2012, July 21). *The Economist.* Retrieved April 25, 2017, from http://www.economist.com/node/21559357

Hise, R. (2004). *The war against men.* Oakland, OR: Elderberry Press LLC.

Hochschild, A. (with Machung, A.). (2003). *The second shift: Working parents and the revolution at home* (Rev. ed.). New York: Viking/Penguin Press.

Hochschild, A., & Ehrenreich, B. (Eds.). (2003). *Global women: Nannies, maids and sex workers in the new economy.* New York: Metropolitan.

Hoffman, J. (2012, June 4). A warning to teenagers before they start dating. *New York Times,* pp. A12, A13.

Holland, D., & Eisenhart, M. (1992). *Educated in romance: Women, achievement, and college culture.* Chicago, IL: University of Chicago Press.

Holley, S. R., Haase, C. M., & Levenson, R. W. (2013). Age-related changes in demand-withdraw communication behaviors. *Journal of Marriage and Family, 75,* 822–836.

hooks, b. (1990). *Yearning: Race, gender, and cultural politics.* Boston, MA: South End Press.

hooks, b. (2013, October 28). Dig deep: Beyond lean in. *Feminist Wire.* Retrieved from http://thefeministwire.com/2013/10/17973

Hotz, R. (2013, December 10). Brain wiring in men versus women. *Wall Street Journal,* pp. D1–D2.

Houghton, J., Bean, L., & Matlack, T. (2009). *The Good Men Project: Real stories from the front lines of modern manhood.* Boston, MA: Good Men Foundation.

Housel, T. (2012, November 2). First-generation students need help in straddling their 2 cultures. *Chronicle of Higher Education,* pp. B32–B33.

Human Rights Campaign. (2015, July 16). HRC hails historic EEOC ruling on employment discrimination. Retrieved September 13, 2016, from http://www.hrc.org/press/hrc-hails-historic-eeoc-ruling-on-employment-discrimination/

Human Rights Campaign Foundation. (2017). Corporate equality index 2017: Rating workplaces on lesbian, gay, bisexual and transgender equality (pp. 1–112). Washington, DC: Human Rights Foundation. Retrieved from http://assets.hrc.org/files/assets/resources/CEI-2017-FinalReport.pdf?_ga=1.211807189.1782391019.1473783193

Human Rights Watch. (2016, December 23). "I want to live with my head held high": Abuses in Bangladesh's legal recognition of hijras. Retrieved April 28, 2017, from https://www.hrw.org/report/2016/12/23/i-want-live-my-head-held-high/abuses-bangladeshs-legal-recognition-hijras

Hunter, M. (2011). Buying racial capital: Skin-bleaching and cosmetic surgery in a globalized world. *Journal of Pan African Studies, 4,* 142–164.

Hunter, S. (2012). *Lesbian and gay couples: Lives, issues, and practice.* Chicago, IL: Lyceum Books, Inc.

Hurlemann, R., Patin, A., Onur, O. A., Cohen, M. X., Baumgartner, T., Metzler, S., … Kendrick, K. M. (2010). Oxytocin enhances amygdala-dependent, socially reinforced learning and emotional empathy in humans. *Journal of Neuroscience, 30*(14), 4999–5007. Retrieved from https://doi.org/10.1523/JNEUROSCI.5538-09.2010

Huston, T. (2016). *How women decide: What's true, what's not, and what strategies spark the best choices.* New York: Houghton-Mifflin Harcourt.

Hyde, J. S. (1984). Children's understanding of sexist language. *Developmental Psychology, 20,* 697–706.

Ingber, H. (2016, December 25). Readers reflect on changing their surnames for marriage. *New York Times,* p. Y13.

Ingraham, L. (1997, July 15). Feminists welcome the Promise Keepers. *Raleigh News & Observer,* p. 11A.

Inman, C. (1996). Friendships between men: Closeness in the doing. In J. T. Wood (Ed.), *Gendered relationships: A reader* (pp. 95–110). Mountain View, CA: Mayfield.

Iszler, M. (2016, October 1). Family in spotlight after post on gender-creative son. *Raleigh News & Observer,* p. 3A.

Italie, L. (2014, July 31). Fashion industry, retailers face gender divide. *Raleigh News & Observer,* p. 8D.

Ivory, J. D. (2008). The games, they are a changin'. In P. E. Jamieson & D. Romer (Eds.), *The changing portrayal of adolescents in the media since 1950* (pp. 347–376). New York: Oxford.

Jackson, R., & Murali, B. (Eds.). (2011). *Global masculinities and manhood.* Urbana, IL: University of Illinois Press.

Jacobson, J. (2001, March 9). Why do so many female athletes enter ACL hell? *Chronicle of Higher Education,* p. A45.

Jaiswal, S. (2012). Commercial surrogacy in India: An ethical assessment of existing legal scenario from the perspective of women's autonomy and reproductive rights. *Gender Technology and Development, 1,* 1–28.

Janeway, E. (1971). *Man's world, woman's place: A study in social mythology.* New York: Dell.

Jaret, P. (2014, July–August). Low T: Real problem or ad-driven fad? *AARP Bulletin,* p. 18.

Johnson, A. (2008, August 4). One by one, women in Egypt fight female circumcision. *Raleigh News & Observer,* p. 7A.

Johnson, A. (2017). *Power, privilege, and difference* (3rd ed.). New York: McGraw-Hill.

Johnson, J. W. (1912/1989). *Autobiography of an ex-coloured man.* New York: Vintage-Random.

Johnson, M. (2006). Gendered communication and intimate partner violence. In B. Dow & J. T. Wood (Eds.), *Handbook of gender and communication* (pp. 71–87). Thousand Oaks, CA: Sage.

Johnson, M. (2008). *A typology of domestic violence.* Boston, MA: Northeastern University Press.

Johnson, N. (2011). The whole package: Commodifying the self. In D. O. Braithwaite & J. T. Wood (Eds.), *Casing interpersonal communication* (pp. 9–15). Dubuque, IA: Kendall-Hunt.

Johnson, N. R. (2010). Consuming desires: Consumption, romance, and sexuality in bestselling teen romance novels. *Women's Studies in Communication, 33,* 54–73.

Jones, S. H. (2016). *Sex work and female self-empowerment.* New York: Routledge.

Journalistic thought police. (1990, December 27). *Richmond Times-Dispatch,* p. A12.

Juhasz, A. (2012). Forgetting ACT UP. *Quarterly Journal of Speech, 98,* 69–74.

Jung, K., Shavitt, S., Viswanathan, M., & Hilbe, J. M. (2014). Female hurricanes are deadlier than male hurricanes. *Proceedings of the National Academy of Sciences of the United States of America.* Retrieved from http://www.pnas.org/content/early/2014/05/29/1402786111.full.pdf+html

Just Detention International. (July 15, 2015). Barack Obama says prison rape jokes are never okay [Press release]. Retrieved from http://justdetention.org/barack-obama-says-prison-rape-jokes-are-never-okay/

Kahlenberg, R. (2010). *Affirmative action for the rich: Legacy preferences in college admissions.* New York: Century/Foundation.

Kahlenberg, R. (2012). A new kind of affirmative action can ensure diversity. *Chronicle of Higher Education,* pp. A29–A30.

Kamil, A. (2012, June 6). Prep-school predators. *New York Times.* Retrieved from http://www.nytimes.com/2012/06/10/magazine/thehorace-mann-schools-secret-history-of-sexual-abuse.html?pagewanted=all

Kanter, R. M. (1977). *Men and women of the corporation.* New York: Basic Books.

Kantor, J. (2012, June 22). Elite women put new spin on an old debate. *New York Times,* pp. A1, A14.

Karkazis, K., & Jordan-Young, R. (2014, April 12). The trouble with too much T. *New York Times,* p. A19.

Kaschak, E. (1992). *Engendered lives.* New York: Basic Books.

Katz, J. (2013). *Tough guise, 2.* Northampton, MA: Media Education Foundation.

Katz, J. (n.d.). *Mentors in violence prevention: History and overview.* Retrieved June 30, 2014, from http://www.jacksonkatz.com

Katz, J., & Jhally, S. (2000, June 25). Put the blame where it belongs: On men. *Los Angeles Times,* p. M5.

Katz, J., & Moore, J. (2013). Bystander education training for campus sexual assault prevention: An initial meta-analysis. *Violence and Victims, 28,* 1054–1067.

Kaufman, M., & Kimmel, M. (2011). *The guy's guide to feminism.* Berkeley, CA: Seal.

Kearney, M. C. (2006). *Girls make media.* London: Routledge.

Kellerman, C. J. (2012, May 22). *17-year-old to Face-book: I exist, and gender identity is also a civil rights issue.* Retrieved from http://www.huffing-tonpost.com/cj-kellman/facebook-gender-identi-ty_b_1534832.html

Kendzior, S. (2014, July 2). The princess effect: How women's magazines demean powerful women—even when they're trying to celebrate them. *Politico Magazine.* Retrieved from http://www.politico .com/magazine/story/2014/07/glass-ceilings-glass-mirrors-108516.html#. U-p6Yla3dyH

Kennedy, R. (2015). *For discrimination: Race, affirmative action, and the law.* New York: Vintage.

Kershaw, S. (2008, September 11). Girl talk has its limits. *New York Times,* pp. E1, E6.

Kershaw, S. (2009, April 23). Mr. Moms (by way of Fortune 500). *New York Times,* pp. E1, E6.

Kiernan, D. (2013). *The girls of atomic city: The untold story of girls and women who helped win World War II.* New York: Simon & Schuster: Touchstone.

Kilbourne, J. (2007). "You talkin' to me?" In M. Andersen & P. H. Collins (Eds.), *Race, class, and gender: An anthology* (6th ed., pp. 228–233). Belmont, CA: Thomson.

Kilbourne, J. (2010a, summer). Sexist advertising, then & now. *Ms,* pp. 34–35.

Kilbourne, J. (Writer). (2010b). *Still killing us softly/4.* Northampton, MA: Media Education Foundation.

Kimbrough, A. M., Guadagno, R. E., Muscanell, N. L., & Dill, J. (2013). Gender differences in mediated communication: Women connect more than do men. *Computers in Human Behavior, 29,* 896–900.

Kimelman, D. (1990, December 12). Poverty and Norplant: Can contraception reduce the underclass? *Philadelphia Enquirer,* p. A18.

Kimmel, M. (2008). *Guyland: The perilous world where boys become men.* New York: Macmillan.

Kimmel, M. (2013). *Angry white men.* New York: Nation Books.

Kimmel, M., & Messner, M. (2012). *Men's lives* (9th ed). Upper Saddle Ridge, NJ: Pearson.

Klein, W., Izquierdo, C., & Bradbury, T. N. (2013, March 1). The difference between a happy marriage and miserable one: Chores. *The Atlantic.* Retrieved from https://www.theatlantic.com/sexes/archive/2013/03/the-difference-between-a-happy-marriage-and-miserable-one-chores/273615/

Knapp, M., Hall, J., & Horgan, T. (2013). *Nonverbal communication in human interaction.* Stamford, CT: Cengage.

Kocet, M. M. (2014). The role of friendships in the lives of gay men, adolescents, and boys. In M. M. Kocet (Ed.), *Counseling gay men, adolescents, and boys* (pp. 24–54). New York: Routledge.

Kohlberg, L. (1958). *The development of modes of thinking and moral choice in the years 10 to 16.* Unpublished doctoral dissertation, University of Chicago, Chicago.

Kolata, G. (2012, February 9). Male genes may explain higher heart disease risk. *New York Times,* p. A13.

Kort, M. (2014, February 18). Blowing the whistle on campus rape. *Ms. Magazine.* Retrieved from http://msmagazine.com/blog/2014/02/18/blowing-the-whistle-on-campus-rape/

Kotiswaran, P. (2012). *Dangerous sex, invisible labor.* Princeton, NJ: Princeton University Press.

Koyama, E. (2003). The transfeminist manifesto. In R. Dicker & A. Piepmeier (Eds.). *Catching a wave: Reclaiming feminism for the 21st century* (pp. 244–261). Boston, MA: Northeastern University Press.

Krakauer, J. (2015). *Missoula.* New York: Anchor.

Kreighbaum, A. (2017, February 23). Transgender protections withdrawn. *Inside Higher Ed.* Retrieved from https://www.insidehighered.com/news/2017/02/23/trump-administration-reverses-title-ix-guidance-transgender-protections

Kricheli-Katz, T. (2012, July 6). Choice-based discrimination: Labor force type discrimination against gay men, the obese and mothers. In *7th Annual Conference on Empirical Legal Studies Paper.* Retrieved June 22, 2014, from http://ssrn.com/abstract=2101596 or http://dx.doi.org/10.2139/ssrn.2101596

Kristof, N. (2005a, March 5). When rapists walk free. *New York Times,* p. A27.

Kristof, N. (2005b, June 14). Raped, kidnapped and silenced. *New York Times,* p. A19.

Kristof, N. (2005c, June 19). A free woman. *New York Times,* Section 4, p. 13.

Kristof, N. (2005d, June 21). The 11-year-old wife. *New York Times,* p. A23.

Kristof, N. (2011a, May 26). Raiding a brothel in India. *New York Times,* p. A27.

Kristof, N. (2014a, January 14). In this rape case, the victim was 4. *New York Times,* pp. SR1, 11.

Kristof, N. (2014b, March 9). To end the abuse, she grabbed a knife. *New York Times,* pp. SR1, 11.

Kristof, N. (2015, May 24). When the rapist doesn't see it as rape. *New York Times,* p. SR9.

Kristof, N. (2016a, May 3). Less than worthless 'woman card.' *New York Times,* p. 15A.

Kristof, N. (2016b, July 31). When women win, men win, too. *New York Times,* p. SR9.

Kristof, N., & WuDunn, S. (2009). *Half the sky*. New York: Knopf.

Kristof, N., & WuDunn, S. (2014). *A path appears: Transforming lives, creating opportunity*. New York: Knopf.

Kuchment, A. (2004, May 10). The more social sex. *Newsweek*, pp. 88–89.

Kunitz, D. (2016). *Fitness culture, from naked Greeks and acrobats to Jazzercise and Ninja Warriors*. New York: HarperCollins.

Kunkel, A., Hummert, M., & Dennis, M. (2006). Social learning theory: Modeling and communication in the family context. In D. Braithwaite & L. Baxter (Eds.), *Engaging theories in family communication* (pp. 260–275). Thousand Oaks, CA: Sage.

Kurdek, L. A. (2007). The allocation of household labor by partners in gay and lesbian couples. *Journal of Family Issues, 28*(1), 132–148. Retrieved from https://doi.org/10.1177/0192513X06292019

Labov, W. (1972). *Sociolinguistic patterns*. Philadelphia, PA: University of Pennsylvania Press. Lacey, M. (2008, December 7). A lifestyle distinct: The Muxe of Mexico. *New York Times*, p. WK4.

LaFraniere, S. (2007, July 4). In Mauritania, seeking to end an overfed ideal. *New York Times*, p. 1A.

Lahiri, T., & Sharma, A. (2013, May 18–19). To wed your rapist, or not: Indian women on trial. *Wall Street Journal*, pp. A1, A11.

Lakoff, R. (1975). *Language and woman's place*. New York: Harper & Row.

Lamb, S. (1991). Acts without agents: An analysis of linguistic avoidance in journal articles on men who batter women. *American Journal of Orthopsychiatry, 61*, 87–102.

Lamb, S. (Ed.). (1999). *New versions of victims*. New York: New York University Press.

Lamb, S., & Brown, L. (2006). *Packaging girlhood: Rescuing our daughters from marketers' schemes*. New York: St. Martin's Press.

Lamb, S., Brown, L., & Tappan, M. (2009). *Packaging boyhood: Saving our sons from superheroes, slackers, and other media stereotypes*. New York: St. Martin's.

Lang, S. S. (1991, January 20). When women drink. *Parade*, pp. 18–20.

Langer, S. K. (1953). *Feeling and form: A theory of art*. New York: Scribner's.

Langer, S. K. (1979). *Philosophy in a new key: A study in the symbolism of reason, rite and art (3rd ed.)*. Cambridge, MA: Harvard University Press.

Langfield, A. (2013, May 29). Pew study shows women leading breadwinners in 40 percent of households. CNBC. Retrieved June 20, 2014, from http://www.thedailybeast.com/articles/2013/05/29/pew-study-shows-women-leading-breadwinners-in-40-percent-of-households.html

Langston, D. H. (2003). American Indian women's activism in the 1960s and 1970s. *Hypatia, 18*, pp. 114–132.

Lanzieri, N., & Hildebrandt, T. (2011). Using hegemonic masculinity to explain gay male attraction to muscular and athletic men. *Journal of Homosexuality, 58*, 275–293.

LaPuma, J. (2014, February 4). Don't ask your doctor about 'low t.' *New York Times*, p. A19.

Lazebnik, R. (2013, April 27–28). Hollywood's new arms race. *Wall Street Journal*, p. C3.

Lazo, A. (2014, January 28). California law gives new options to transgender students. *Wall Street Journal*, p. A4.

Leaper, C. (2014). Gender: Early socialization. In M. Boivin, R. D. Peters, & Tremblay (Eds.), *Encyclopedia on Early Childhood Development*. Quebec, Canada: Centre of Excellence for Early Childhood Development and the Strategic Knowledge Cluster on Early Child Development. Retrieved from www.child-encyclopedia.com

Leaper, C., & Ayres, M. (2007). A meta-analytic review of gender variations in adults' language use: Talkativeness, affiliative speech, and assertive speech. *Personality & Social Psychology Review, 11*, 328–363.

Lee, C. (2013, October 8). Study finds TV shows with ethnically diverse casts, writers have higher ratings. *UCLA newsroom*. Retrieved from http://newsroom.ucla.edu/releases/study-finds-that-tv-shows-with-248757

Lee, S. (1997). *Get on the bus* [Motion picture]. United States: Columbia/Tristar.

Lelchuk, I. (2007, May 20). Being Mr. Dad. *San Francisco Chronicle Magazine*, pp. 8, 9, 19.

Lindgren, S., & Lélièvre, M. (2009). In the laboratory of masculinity: Renegotiating gender subjectivities in MTV's Jackass. *Critical Studies in Media Communication, 26*, 393–410.

Lemay, E. P., & Wolf, N. R. (2016). Projection of romantic and sexual desire in opposite-sex friendships: How wishful thinking creates a self-fulfilling prophecy. *Personality and Social Psychology Bulletin, 42*(7), 864–878. Retrieved from https://doi.org/10.1177/0146167216646077

LePoire, B. A., Burgoon, J. K., & Parrott, R. (1992). Status and privacy restoring communication in the workplace. *Journal of Applied Communication Research, 4*, 419–136.

Levy, S. (2005, August 1). Sex, secret codes, and videogames. *Newsweek*, p. 14.

Lien, T. (2015, March 8). Why women are leaving the tech industry in droves. *Raleigh News & Observer*, pp. 1E, 2E.

Lindsey, T. B. (2015). Let me blow your mind: Hip hop feminist futures in theory and praxis. *Urban*

Education, 50(1), 52–77. Retrieved from http://doi.org/10.1177/0042085914563184

Ling, R., Baron, N. S., Lenhart, A., & Campbell, S. W. (2014). "Girls text really weird": Gender, texting and identity among teens. *Journal of Children and Media, 8*(4), 423–439. Retrieved from https://doi.org/10.1080/17482798.2014.931290

Liptak, A. (2016, June 24). Justices uphold race-aware admissions. *New York Times*, pp. A1, A16.

Lisak, D., & Miller, P. M. (2002). Repeat rape and multiple offending among undetected rapists. *Violence and Victims, 17*(1), 73–84.

Liss-Schultz, N. (2014, May 30). This woman was threatened with rape after calling out sexist video games—and then something inspiring happened. *Mother Jones*. Retrieved from http://www.motherjones.com/media/2014/05/pop-culture-anita-sarkeesian-video-games-sexismtropes-online-harassement-feminist

Livingston, G. (2014, June 5). Growing number of dads home with kids. PA: Pew Research Foundation.

Loflin, D. C., & Barry, C. T. (2016). "You can't sit with us": Gender and the differential roles of social intelligence and peer status in adolescent relational aggression. *Personality and Individual Differences, 91*, 22–26. Retrieved from https://doi.org/10.1016/j.paid.2015.11.048

Lopez, A. (Ed.). (2012). *Count on me: Tales of sisterhood and fierce friendships*. New York: Simon & Schuster/Atria.

Lorber, J. (1997). A woman's rights/cultural conflict. *Democratic Left, 2*, 3–5.

Lorber, J. (Ed.). (2012). *Gender inequality* (5th ed.). New York: Oxford University Press.

Louis, C. S. (2010a, April 29). Cosmetic surgery gets a nip and tuck. *New York Times*, p. E3.

Louis, C. S. (2010b, August 12). This teenage girl uses botox. And, no, she's not alone. *New York Times*, pp. E1, E3.

Loury, G. (1996, January/February). Joy and doubt on the mall. *Utne Reader*, pp. 70–71.

Lovell, J. (2014, June 5). Leftover women: The resurgence of gender inequality in China—Review. *Guardian*. Retrieved from http://www.theguardian.com/books/2014/jun/05/leftover-women-gender-inequality-china

Luarn, P., Kuo, H.-C., Chiu, Y.-P., & Chang, S.-C. (2015). Social support on Facebook: The influence of tie strength and gender differences. *International Journal of Electronic Commerce Studies, 6*(1), 37–50. Retrieved from https://doi.org/10.7903/ijecs.1391

Ludden, J. (2014, June 5). Stay-at-home dads on the rise, and many of them are poor. *National Public Radio*. Retrieved from http://www.npr.org/2014/06/05/319214546/stay-at-homedads-on-the-rise-and-many-of-them-are-poor

Lugones, M., & Spelman, E. (1983). Have we got a theory for you! Feminist theory, cultural imperialism, and the demand for "the woman's voice." *Women's Studies International Forum, 6*, 573–581.

Luhby, T. (2016, May 4). The men America has left behind. *CNN*. Retrieved September 25, 2016, from http://money.cnn.com/2016/05/04/news/economy/america-left-behind-white-men/

Lukianoff, G. (2013, May 17). Feds to students: You can't say that. *Wall Street Journal*, p. A15.

Lukianoff, G., & Haidt, J. (2014, September). The coddling of the American mind. *The Atlantic*. Retrieved September 16, 2016, from http://www.theatlantic.com/magazine/archive/2014/09/the-coddling-of-the-American-mind/399356/

Lumsden, L. (2009). "Women's lib has no soul?" Analysis of women's movement coverage in black periodicals, 1968–73. *Journalism History, 35*, 118–130.

Luscombe, B. (2016, April 11). Porn and the threat to virility. *Time*, pp. 40–47.

Luster, T., & Okagaki, L. (Eds.). (2005). *Parenting: An ecological perspective* (2nd ed.). Mahwah, NJ: Erlbaum.

Maccoby, E. E. (1998). *The two sexes: Growing up apart, coming together*. Cambridge, MA: Belknap Press of the Harvard University Press.

MacGeorge, E., Gillihan, S. J., Samter, W., & Clark, R. A. (2003). Skill deficit or differential motivation? Accounting for sex differences in the provision of emotional support. *Communication Research, 30*, 272–293.

Macur, J. (2014, August 30). New N. F. L. policy is step on long road to regaining fans' trust. *New York Times*, p. B11.

Mai, M. (2006). *In the name of honor*. New York: Simon & Schuster/Atria.

Maltz, D. N., & Borker, R. (1982). A cultural approach to male–female miscommunication. In J. J. Gumperz (Ed.), *Language and social identity* (pp. 196–216). Cambridge, UK: Cambridge University Press.

Mandziuk, R. (2008). Dressing down Hillary. *Communication and Critical/Cultural Studies, 5*, 312–316.

Mangan, K. (2004, November 12). Does affirmative action hurt black law students? *Chronicle of Higher Education*, pp. A35–A36.

Mansson, D., & Myers, S. (2011). An initial examination of college students expressions of affection through Facebook. *Southern Communication Journal, 76*, 155–168.

Mapstone, E. (1998). *War of words: Women and men argue*. London: Random House.

Marcus, S. (2010). *Girls to the front: The true story of the Riot Grrrl Revolution*. New York: Harper Perennial.

Martocci, L. (2015). *Bullying: The destruction of self.* Philadelphia, PA: Temple University Press.

Martz, D., Petroff, A., Curtin, L., & Bazzini, D. (2009). Gender differences in fat talk among American adults. *Sex Roles, 61,* 34–41.

Marusak, J. (2017, April 3). Mayors denounce N.C. compromise legislation over HB2. *The Charlotte Observer.*

Marx, K. (1867/1975). *Capital* (B. Fowles, Ed., Vol. 1). New York: Vintage.

Marx, K. (1977). *Early writings.* (Q. Hoare, Ed.). New York: Vintage.

Mau, D. (2016, February 16). Zac Posen makes an important statement by casting models of color almost exclusively. Retrieved August 30, 2016, from http://fashionista.com/2016/02/zac-posen-fall-2016

McClelland, C. (2004, May 14). Man raised as a girl commits suicide at 38. *Raleigh News & Observer,* p. 9B.

McClish, G., & Bacon, J. (2002). "Telling the story her own way": The role of feminist standpoint theory in rhetorical studies. *Rhetoric Society Quarterly, 32,* 27–55.

McCloskey, D. (2000). *Crossing: A memoir.* Urbana, IL: University of Chicago Press.

McDonald, K. (2012). *Feminism, the left, and postwar literary culture.* Jackson, MS: University Press of Mississippi.

McDonald, M., Phipps, S., & Lethbridge, L. (2005). Taking its toll: The influences of paid and unpaid work on women's well-being. *Feminist Economics, 11,* 63–94.

McDonald, T. (2015, June 19). The rite to be men. *Raleigh News & Observer,* pp. IB, 2B.

McIntosh, P. (2007). White privilege: Unpacking the invisible knapsack. In M. Andersen & P. H. Collins (Eds.), *Race, Class & Gender* (pp. 98–102). Belmont, CA: Thomson Wadsworth.

McKinley, J. (2012, March 25). Ruling extends sex-discrimination protection to transgender woman denied federal job. *New York Times,* p. A14.

McMurtrie, B. (2013, August 30). Political science is rife with gender bias, scholars find. *Chronicle of Higher Education.* Retrieved July 9, 2014, from http://chronicle.com/article/Political-Science-Is-Rife-With/141319/

McQuade, J. D., Achufusi, A. K., Shoulberg, E. K., & Murray-Close, D. (2014). Biased self-perceptions of social competence and engagement in physical and relational aggression: The moderating role of peer status and sex: Biased self-perceptions of social competence. *Aggressive Behavior, 40*(6), 512–525. Retrieved from https://doi.org/10.1002/ab.21552

McRobbie, A. (2009). *The aftermath of feminism: Gender, culture and social change.* Thousand Oaks, CA: Sage.

Mead, M. (1935/1968). *Sex and temperament in three primitive societies.* New York: Dell.

Meân, L. J., & Kassing, J. W. (2008). "I would just like to be known as an athlete": Maintaining hegemony, femininity, and heterosexuality in female sport. *Western Journal of Communication, 72*(2), 126–144.

Mears, B. (2014, April 23). Michigan's ban on affirmative action upheld by Supreme Court. *CNN Justice.* Retrieved June 29, 2014, from http://www.cnn.com/2014/04/22/justice/scotus-michigan-affirmative-action/

Medved, C. E. (2016). Stay-at-home fathering as a feminist opportunity: Perpetuating, resisting, and transforming gender relations of caring and earning. *Journal of Family Communication, 16*(1), 16–31. Retrieved from https://doi.org/10.1080/15267431.2015.1112800

Mehrabian, A. (1981). *Silent messages: Implicit communication of emotion and attitudes (2nd ed.).* Belmont, CA: Wadsworth.

Meier, A., Musick, K., Flood, S., & Dunifon, R. (2016). Mothering experiences: How single parenthood and employment structure the emotional valence of parenting. *Demography, 53*(3), 649–674. Retrieved from https://doi.org/10.1007/s13524-016-0474-x

Men's Rights. (2016). Retrieved from http://mensrights.com

Merisotis, J., & Slaughter, A. M. (2016, July 5). College kids, with kids. *New York Times,* p. A23.

Merskin, D. (2011). Perpetuation of the hot-Latina stereotype in desperate housewives. In G. Dines & J. M. Humez (Eds.), *Gender, race and class in media: A critical reader* (3rd ed., pp. 27–334). Los Angeles, CA: Sage.

Messner, M. A. (2001). When bodies are weapons: Masculinity and violence in sports. In D. Vannoy (Ed.), *Gender mosaics* (pp. 94–105). Los Angeles, CA: Roxbury.

Messner, M. A. (2002, December 6). Needed: A fair assessment by a "budgetary umpire." *Chronicle of Higher Education,* pp. B8–B9.

Messner, M. A. (2005). Still a man's world? Studying masculinities and sport. In M. A. Messner, J. Hearn, & R. W. Connell (Eds.), *Handbook of studies on men & masculinities* (pp. 313–325). Thousand Oaks, CA: Sage Publications.

Messner, M. A. (2007). Masculinities and athletic careers. In M. Andersen & P. H. Collins (Eds.), *Race, class, gender: An anthology* (6th ed., pp. 172–184). Belmont, CA: Thomson.

Messner, M. A., & Sabo, D. F. (2006). Sport in the social construction of masculinity. In S. M. Whitehead (Ed.), *Men and masculinities: Critical concepts in sociology* (pp. 303–316). New York: Routledge.

Meston, C., & Buss, D. (2009). *Why women have sex: Understanding sexual motivations—from adventure to revenge (and everything in between).* New York: Times/Holt.

Metts, S. (2006a). Gendered communication in dating relationships. In B. Dow & J. T. Wood (Eds.), *The SAGE handbook of gender & communication* (pp. 25–10). Thousand Oaks, CA: Sage.

Metts, S. (2006b). Hanging out and doing lunch: Enacting friendship closeness. In J. T. Wood & S. W. Duck (Eds.), *Composing relationships: Communication in everyday life* (pp. 76–85). Belmont, CA: Thomson/Wadsworth.

Meyers, M. (2004). African American women and violence: Gender, race, and class in the news. *Critical Studies in Media Communication, 21,* 95–118.

Migliaccio, T. (2009). Men's friendships: Performances of masculinity. *The Journal of Men's Studies, 17*(3), 226–241. Retrieved from https://doi.org/10.3149/jms.1703.226

Miller, A. N. (2011, February). Men's and women's communication is different—sometimes. *Communication Currents,* p. 1.

Miller, B. (2015). "Dude, where's your face?" Self-presentation, self-description, and partner preferences on a social networking application for men who have sex with men: A content analysis. *Sexuality & Culture, 19*(4), 637–658. Retrieved from https://doi.org/10.1007/s12119-015-9283-4

Miller, B., & Behm-Morawitz, E. (2016). "Masculine guys only": The effects of femmephobic mobile dating application profiles on partner selection for men who have sex with men. *Computers in Human Behavior, 62,* 176–185. Retrieved from https://doi.org/10.1016/j.chb.2016.03.088

Miller, C. (2015a, October 22). A disadvantaged start in life harms boys more than girls. *New York Times,* p. A3.

Miller, C. (2015b, July 30). Millennial men aren't the dads they thought they'd be. *The New York Times.* Retrieved from http://www.nytimes.com/2015/07/31/upshot/millennial-men-find-work-and-family-hard-to-balance.html

Miller, C. (2015c, May 31). The problem with work is overwork. *New York Times,* p. BU4.

Miller, C. (2016a, January 17). What we can do to close the pay gap. *New York Times,* p. BU6.

Miller, C. (2016b, March 20). Why women still get the short end of the dollar. *New York Times,* pp. BU1, BU5.

Miller, C. (2016c, October 22). The powerful woman: A prime target for jabs. *New York Times,* P. A12.

Miller, C. C. (2014a, June 8). An elusive jackpot. *New York Times,* pp. BU1, BU5.

Miller, C. C. (2014b, September 7). For working mothers, a price to pay. *New York Times,* p. BU6.

Miller, C. C. (2017, April 20). How child care enriches mothers, and especially the sons they raise. *The New York Times.* Retrieved from https://www.nytimes.com/2017/04/20/upshot/how-child-care-enriches-mothers-and-especially-the-sons-they-raise.html

Miller, J. (2012). Girls face ACL woes. *Raleigh News & Observer,* pp. 1D, 2D.

Miller-Day, M., & Fisher, C. (2006). Communication in mother-adult daughter relationships. In K. Floyd & M. Morman (Eds.), *Widening the family circle: New research on family communication* (pp. 15–38). Newbury Park, CA: Sage.

Million, J. (2003). *Woman's voice, woman's place: Lucy Stone and the birth of the women's rights movement.* Westport, CT: Praeger.

Million Family March picks up where men's march ended 5 years before. (2000, October 14). *Raleigh News & Observer,* p. 6B.

Minhas, S. F. (2009). The politics of rape and honor in Pakistan. In L. Cuklanz & S. Moorti (Eds.), *Local violence, global media* (pp. 65–78). New York: Peter Lang.

Mischel, W. (1966). A social learning view of sex differences in behavior. In E. E. Maccoby (Ed.), *The development of sex differences* (pp. 93–106). Stanford, CA: Stanford University Press.

Misner, J. (2014, September 9). Women's colleges drop barriers to transgender students. *Chronicle of Higher Education.* Retrieved September 23, 2014, from http://chronicle.com/article/Women-s-Colleges-Drop/148705/?cid=at&utm_source=at&utm_medium=en

Misra, J., Hickes, L. J., Holmes, E., & Agiomavritis, S. (2011). The ivory ceiling of service work. *Academe, 97,* 22–26.

Mitchell, C. (2013, October 4). The sorority body-image problem. *The Atlantic.* Retrieved from http://www.theatlantic.com/health/archive/2013/10/the-sorority-body-image-problem/280256/

Mongeau, P., Serewicz, M., Henningsen, M., & Davis, K. (2006). Sex differences in the transition to a heterosexual romantic relationship. In K. Dindia & D. Canary (Eds.), *Sex differences and similarities in communication* (2nd ed., pp. 337–358). Mahwah, NJ: Lawrence Erlbaum.

Monsour, M. (2006). Gendered communication in friendships. In B. Dow & J. T. Wood (Eds.), *The SAGE handbook of gender and communication* (pp. 57–70). Thousand Oaks, CA: Sage.

Moore, T. (2015, October 22). Don't create a new surname with your spouse unless you're ready to piss people off. Retrieved May 31, 2016, from http://jezebel.com/dont-create-a-new-surname-with-your-spouse-unless-youre-1737392285

Moran, R. (2013). *Paid for: My journey through prostitution*. New York: W.W. Norton.

Morgan, J. (1999). *When chickenheads come home to roost: My life as a hip-hop feminist*. New York: Simon & Schuster.

Morgan, M. (1973). *The total woman*. New York: Pocket.

Morman, M. T., & Floyd, K. (2006). The good son: Men's perceptions of the characteristics of sonhood. In K. Floyd & M. T. Morman (Eds.), *Widening the family circle: New research on family communication* (pp. 37–55). Thousand Oaks, CA: Sage.

Moses, M. (2016). *Living with moral disagreement*. Chicago, IL: University of Chicago Press.

Moss-Racusin, C., Dovidio, J., Brescoll, V., Graham, M., & Handelsman, J. (2012). Science faculty's subtle gender biases favor male students. *PNAS, 109*, pp. 16474–16479. doi: 10.1073/pnas.1211286109.

Mulac, A. (2006). The gender-linked language effect: Do language differences really make a difference? In K. Dindia & D. Canary (Eds.), *Sex differences and similarities in communication* (pp. 219–239). Mahwah, NJ: Erlbaum.

Murphy, C. (2005). Grass-roots men's ministries growing. *Raleigh News & Observer*, p. 5E.

Muwakkil, S. (2005, December 19). Jump-starting a movement. *In These Times*, p. 13.

My secret self. (2009). *60 Minutes*. Retrieved June 21, 2014, from http://www.tvtonight.com.au/2009/09/60-minutes-my-secret-self.html

Nadal, K. (2013). *That's so gay!: Microaggressions and the lesbian, gay, bisexual, and trans community*. Washington, D.C.: American Psychological Association.

Nagem, S. (2015, July 17). I thee wed, but with my own name. *Raleigh News & Observer*, p. 2A.

Nakamura, D. (2015, October 11). A fresh call for justice in D.C. *Raleigh News & Observer*, p. 12A.

Nanda, S. (2004). Multiple genders among North American Indians. In J. Spade & C. Valentine (Eds.), *The kaleidoscope of gender* (pp. 64–70). Belmont, CA: Thomson/Wadsworth.

Natalier, K. (2003). 'I'm not his wife': Doing gender and doing housework in the absence of women. *Journal of Sociology, 39*, 253–269.

National Association of Anorexia Nervosa and Associated Disorders. (2014). Retrieved June 15, 2014, from http://www.anad.org/get-information/

National Association of Anorexia Nervosa and Associated Disorders. (2016). Retrieved August 30, 2016, from http://www.anad.org/get-information/about-eating-disorders/stats/

National Center for Transgender Equality. Retrieved April 14, 2016, from www.transequality.org

National Center for Transgender Equality. (2015). Know your rights: Schools. Retrieved September 29, 2016, from http://www.transequality.org/know-your-rights/schools

National Coalition of Anti-Violence Programs. (2013). "Hate violence against transgender communities." New York, NY: National Coalition of Anti-Violence Programs. Retrieved April 13, 2016, from http://avp.org/wp-content/uploads/2017/04/ncavp_transhvfactsheet.pdf

National Institute of Mental Health. (2016). Retrieved December 27, 2016, from http://www.nimh.nih.gov/health/publications/eating-disorders/what-are-eating-disorders.shtml

National Organization for Men against Sexism. (2014). *Tenets*. Retrieved July 11, 2014, from http://nomas.org/tenets/

National Women's Law Center. (2015). *Closing the wage gap is crucial for women of color and their families*. Washington DC: National Women's Law Center. Retrieved from https://nwlc.org/wp-content/uploads/2015/08/closing_the_wage_gap_is_crucial_for_woc_and_their_families_2015.pdf

Neighbors, C., Walker, D., Mbilinyi, L., O'Rourke, A., Edleson, J., Zegree, J., & Roffman, R. A. (2010). Normative misperceptions of abuse among perpetrators of intimate partner violence. *Violence against Women, 16*, 370–389.

Neinas, C. M. (2002, December 6). Can we avoid unintended consequences for men? *Chronicle of Higher Education*, p. B8.

Newcombe, N. (2002, December 14). Is sociobiology ready for prime time? *Chronicle of Higher Education*, pp. B10–B11.

Newsome, J. (Writer, director, and producer). (2011). *Miss representation* [Motion Picture]. United States: Los Angeles.

Newton-Small, J. (2016). *Broad influence*. New York: Time Books.

Nilsson, L. (2015, April 27). How to attract female engineers. *New York Times*, p. A17.

Noah, T. (2012). *The great divergence*. New York: Bloomsbury Press.

Nolen-Hoeksema, S. (2003). *Women who think too much*. New York: Henry Holt.

Nomas. (2016). Retrieved from http://nomas.org

Norlund, R., & Rubin, A. (2010, May 31). Escaping marriage, but not lashes. *New York Times*, p. A4.

Norplant: A new contraceptive with the potential for abuse. (1994, January). Retrieved from http://www.aclu.org/reproductive-freedom/norplant-new-contraceptive-potential-abuse Norplant.

(2012, July 7). *Rx list* (online). Retrieved from http://www.rxlist.com/nor-plant-drug.htm

No skinny models. (2016, June 4). *The Week*, p. 10/

NPR. (2014, June 23). *The new American man doesn't look like his father*. Retrieved from http://www.npr.org/2014/06/23/323966448/the-new-american-man-doesnt-look-like-hisfather

Nutt, A. E. (2015). *Becoming Nicole: The transformation of an American family*. New York: Random House.

O'Brien, S. A. (2015, August 4). Hip-hop dancer, college dropout: #ILookLikeAnEngineer. *CNN*. Retrieved August 30, 2016, from http://money.cnn.com/2015/08/04/technology/isis-wegner-i-look-like-an-engineer/index.html

Office for Victims of Crimes. (n.d.). Responding to transgender victims of sexual assault. Retrieved from https://www.ovc.gov/pubs/forge/sexual_numbers.html

Ofori-Atta, A. (2011, March 21). Is hip-hop feminism alive in 2011? *Root*. Retrieved from http://www.theroot.com/is-hip-hop-feminism-alive-in-2011-1790863203

Okun, R. A. (2014). *Voice male: The untold story of the profeminist men's movement*. Northhampton, MA: Interlink Publishing Group.

O'Leary, A. (2012, August 2). In virtual play, sex harassment is all too real. *New York Times*, pp. A1, A3.

Olson, K. R., Durwood, L., DeMeules, M., & McLaughlin, K. A. (2016). Mental health of transgender children who are supported in their identities. *PEDIATRICS*, *137*(3), e20153223–e20153223. Retrieved from http://doi.org/10.1542/peds.2015-3223

Olson, L., & Rauscher, E. (2011). We'll never be that kind of couple: The variability of intimate violence. In D. O. Braithwaite & J. T. Wood (Eds.), *Casing interpersonal communication* (pp. 149–156). Dubuque, IA: Kendall-Hunt.

O'Neill, O., & O'Reilly, C. (2011, December). Reducing the backlash effect: Self-monitoring and women's promotions. *Journal of Occupational Psychology*, *84*(4), 825–832. doi:10.1111/j.2044-8325.2010.02008.x

O'Neill, R., & Colley, A. (2006). Gender and status effects in student e-mails to staff. *Journal of Computer Assisted Learning*, *22*, 360–367.

Onishi, N. (2007, April 28). Japan court rules against sex slaves and laborers. *New York Times*, p. A5.

Ono, K., & Pham, V. (2009). *Asian Americans and the media*. Malden, MA: Polity Press.

Orenstein, P. (2011a). *Cinderella ate my daughter*. New York: Harper.

Orenstein, P. (2011b). Should the world of toys be gender-free? *New York Times*, p. A21.Orenstein, P. (2016a). *Girls and sex*. New York: Harper.

Orenstein, P. (2016b, April 11). How porn is changing a generation of girls. *Time*, p. 47.

Ostrow, N. (2010, May 19). Men, too, suffer postpartum depression. *Raleigh News & Observer*, p. 5A.

Our story: We are Fathers 4 Justice. (n.d.) *Fathers 4 Justice*. Retrieved July 1, 2014, from http://www.fathers-4-justice.org/about-f4j/our-story/

Padawer, R. (2016, June 28). The humiliating practice of sex-testing female athletes. *The New York Times Magazine*. Retrieved from http://www.nytimes.com/2016/07/03/magazine/the-humiliating-practice-of-sex-testing-female-athletes.html

Palczewski, C. H. (2005). The male Madonna and the feminine Uncle Sam: Visual argument, icons, and ideographs in 1909 anti-woman suffrage postcards. *Quarterly Journal of Speech*, *91*(4), 365–394.

Palomares, N. (2008). Gender salience and language. *Human Communication Research*, *34*, 263–286.

Palomares, N. A. (2010). Gender-based language use: Understanding how and why men communicate similarly and differently. In M. B. Hinner (Ed.), *The interrelationship of business and communication* (pp. 74–96). Frankfurt, Germany: Peter Lang.

Paludi, M., Martin, J., Gruber, J., & Fineran, J. (Eds.). (2015). *Sexual harassment in education and work settings*. Santa Barbara, CA: Praeger.

Paoletti, J. (2012). *Pink and blue*. Bloomington, IN: Indiana University Press.

Parker, K., & Wang, W. (2013, March 14). Modern parenthood: Roles of moms and dads converge as they balance work and family. In *Pew research: Social and demographic trends*. Retrieved June 20, 2014, from http://www.pewsocialtrends.org/2013/03/14/modern-parenthood-roles-of-moms-and-dads-converge-as-they-balance-work-and-family/

Parker, P. (2006). *Race, gender, and leadership: Re-envisioning organizational leadership from the perspective of African American women*. Mahwah, NJ: Erlbaum.

Parker-Pope, T. (2008, June 10). Gay unions shed light on gender in marriage. *New York Times*, p. D1.

Parker-Pope, T. (2010a, February 16). As girls become women, sports pay dividends. *New York Times*, p. D5.

Parker-Pope, T. (2010b, April 6). Surprisingly, family time has grown. *New York Times*, p. D5.

Parks, S. (2010). *Fierce angels: The strong black woman in American life and culture*. New York: Random House.

Parlee, M. B. (1979, May). Conversational politics. *Psychology Today*, pp. 48–56.

Patel, T. (2006). *Sex-selective abortion in India*. Thousand Oaks, CA: Sage.

Patten, E. (2015, November 4). How American parents balance work and family life when both work. Retrieved from http://www.pewresearch.org/fact-tank/2015/11/04/how-american-parents-balance-work-and-family-life-when-both-work/

Patterson, C. J. (2000). Family relationships of lesbians and gay men. *Journal of Marriage and the Family, 62,* 1052–1069.

Patton, S. (2012, November 2). From cellblock to campus, one black man defies the data. *Chronicle of Higher Education,* pp. B9–B13.

Pedelty, M., & Kuecker, M. (2014). Seen to be heard: Gender, voice, and body in television advertisements. *Communication and Critical/Cultural Studies, 11,* 2050–2069.

Peretti, P. O., & Abplanalp, R. R., Jr. (2004). Chemistry in the college dating process: Structure and function. *Social Behavior and Personality, 32,* 147–154.

Pérez-Peña, R. (2013). College groups connect to fight sexual assault. *New York Times,* pp. A14, A17.

Perrin, A. (2015, October 8). Social media usage 2005–2015. *Pew Research Center.* Retrieved May 18, 2016, from http://www.pewinternet .org/2015/10/8/social-networking-usage-2005-2015

Peter, J., & Valkenburg, P. (2010). Adolescents' use of sexually explicit Internet material and sexual uncertainty: The role of involvement and gender. *Communication Monographs, 77,* 357–375.

Peters, M., & Wessel, D. (2014, February 6). More men in their prime are out of work and at home. *Wall Street Journal,* pp. A1, A14.

Petri, A. (2015, October 13). Famous quotes the way a woman would have to say them during a meeting. *Washington Post.* Retrieved June 3, 2016, from http://www.washingtonpost.com/blogs/compost/ wp/2015/10/13/jennifer-lawrence-has-a-point-famous-quotes-the-way-a-woman-would-have-to-say-them-during-a-meeting/

Pew Research Center. (2015). *Raising kids and running a household: How working parents share the load* (pp. 1–23). Washington, DC: Pew Research Center. Retrieved from http://www.pewsocialtrends .org/2015/11/04/raising-kids-and-running-a-household-how-working-parents-share-the-load/

Phillips, M. (2011, June 13). *These "Slut Walks" prove feminism is now irrelevant to most women's lives.* Retrieved from http://www.dailymail.co.uk/debate/ article-2002887/Slut-Walks-prove-feminism-irrelevant-womenslives.html#ixzz1isfBlzEJ

Piaget, J. (1932/1965). *The moral judgment of the child.* New York: Free Press.

Pinsky, M. (2007, February 2). Churches ramp up to bring in men. *Raleigh News & Observer,* p. 4E.

Pollock, E. (2015). *The only woman in the room: Why science is still a boys club.* Boston, MA: Beacon.

Pollitt, K. (2011, July 18–25). Talk the talk, walk the SlutWalk. *Nation.* Retrieved from http://www.thenation.com/article/161728/ talk-talkwalk-slutwalk

Popenoe, D. (1996). *Life without father.* New York: Free Press.

Potârcă, G., Mills, M., & Neberich, W. (2015). Relationship preferences among gay and lesbian online daters: Individual and contextual influences. *Journal of Marriage and Family, 77*(2), 523–541. Retrieved from https://doi.org/10.1111/jomf.12177

Potok, M. (2014, Fall). War on women. *SPLC Intelligence Report,* pp. 38–41.

Potter, C. (2016). Not safe for work: Why feminist pornography matters. *Dissent, 63*(2), 104–114. Retrieved from http://doi.org/10.1353/ dss.2016.0041

Pough, G. D., Richardson, E., Raimist, R., & Durham, A. S. (2007). *Home girls make some noise: Hip-hop feminism anthology.* Mira Loma, CA: Parker Publishing, LLC.

Pozios, V. K., Kambam, P. R., & Bender, H. E. (2013, August 25). Does media violence lead to the real thing? *New York Times,* p. SR12.

Prevalence of domestic violence. (2013, August). *The advocates for human rights.* Retrieved July 3, 2014, from http://www.stopvaw.org/ prevalence_of_domestic_violence

Promise Keepers: "Men have dropped the ball." (1997, October 1). *USA Today,* p. 14A.

Pruett, M. K., & Pruett, K. (2009). *Partnership parenting.* Cambridge, MA: DaCapo Lifelong Books.

Pryor, D., & Hughes, M. (2013). Fear of rape among college women: A social psychological analysis. *Violence and Victims, 28,* 443–465.

Purewal, S. J. (2015, April 30). "4 anonymous social networking apps that are not secret." *CNET.* Retrieved June 20, 2016 from http://www.cnet .com/how-to/anonymous-social-networking-apps-that-are-not-secret/

Quart, A. (2014, April 27). Status update: A report of teenagers' online lives portrays them as neither passive consumers nor pliant sex objects. *New York Times Book Review,* p. 25.

Quenqua, D. (2014, August 3). Tell me, even if it hurts me. *New York Times,* p. 1, 8–9.

Rabin, R. (2012). Benefits of circumcision are said to outweigh risks. *New York Times,* p. A3.

Rabin, R. (2013, January 29). The drug-dose gender gap. *New York Times,* p. D4.

Raeburn, P. (2014). *Do fathers matter?* New York: Scientific American/ Farrar, Straus & Giroux.

RAINN: Rape, abuse, and incest national network. (2016). Children and teens: Statistics. Retrieved from https://www.rainn.org/statistics/ children-and-teens

Rancaño, V. (2015, December 22). Is it time to set weight minimums for the fashion industry? *NPR.* Retrieved September 5, 2016, from http://www.npr.org/sections/health-shots/2015/12/22/460682633/is-it-time-to-set-weight-minimums-for-the-fashion-industry

Ransby, B. (2003). *Ella Baker and the Black Freedom Movement: A radical democratic vision.* Chapel Hill, NC: University of North Carolina Press.

Rasmussen, J. L., & Moley, B. E. (1986). Impression formation as a function of the sex role appropriateness of linguistic behavior. *Sex Roles, 14,* 149–161.

Reby, D., Levréro, F., Gustafsson, E., & Mathevon, N. (2016). Sex stereotypes influence adults' perception of babies' cries. *BMC Psychology, 4*(1). Retrieved from http://doi.org/10.1186/s40359-016-0123-6

Recent legislative debate. (2013). *Harvard Law Review.* Retrieved November 10, 2014, from http://www.harvardlawreview.org/wp-content/uploads/pdfs/vol127_wendy_davis_filibusters_abortion_bill.pdf

Reeser, T. (2010). *Masculinities in theory.* Chichester; Malden, MA: Wiley-Blackwell.

Reeves, R. V., & Sawhill, I. V. (2015, November 14). Men's lib! *The New York Times.* Retrieved from http://www.nytimes.com/2015/11/15/opinion/sunday/mens-lib.html

Rehel, E. M. (2014). When dad stays home too: Paternity leave, gender, and parenting. *Gender & Society, 28*(1), 110–132.

Reich, M. (1991). *Toxic politics: Responding to chemical disasters.* Ithaca, NY: Cornell University Press.

Reid, E. (2015, April 8). Why some men pretend to work 80-hour weeks. *Harvard Business Review.* Retrieved from https://hbr.org/2015/04/why-some-men-pretend-to-work-to-80-hour-weeks

Reiner, A. (2016, April 10). The masculine mystique. *Education Life,* special section in the *New York Times,* pp. 11, 23.

Reisman, J. M. (1990). Intimacy in same-sex friendships. *Sex Roles, 23,* 65–82.

Remmick, D. (2015, March 23). Today's woman. *The New Yorker,* pp. 35–36.

Reuther, R. R. (Ed.). (1974). *Religion and sexism: Images of woman in the Jewish and Christian traditions.* New York: Simon & Schuster.

Reuther, R. R. (1983). *Sexism and Godtalk: Toward a feminist theology.* Boston, MA: Beacon.

Reuther, R. R. (2001). Ecofeminism and healing ourselves, healing the earth. In D. Vannoy (Ed.), *Gender mosaics* (pp. 406–414). Los Angeles, CA: Roxbury.

Rhode, D. (2010). *The beauty bias: The injustice of appearance in life and law.* New York: Oxford University Press.

Rich, M. (2008). Music videos: Media of the youth, by the youth, for the youth. In P. E. Jamieson & D. Romer (Eds.), *The changing portrayal of adolescents in the media since 1950* (pp. 78–102). New York: Oxford University Press.

Richardson, S. (2013). *Sex itself: The search for male and female in the human genome.* Urbana, IL: University of Chicago Press.

Riegle-Crumb, C., & Humphries, M. (2012). Exploring bias in math teachers' perceptions of students' ability by gender and race/ethnicity. *Gender & Society, 26,* 290–322.

Rimmerman, C. A. (2001). ACT UP. In R. A. Smith (Ed.), *Encyclopedia of AIDS: A social, political, cultural, and scientific record of the HIV epidemic* (pp. 3–7). New York: Penguin Books.

Ring, J. (2013). *Stolen bases: Why American girls don't play baseball.* Urbana, IL: University of Illinois Press.

Risman, B. J. (1989). Can men mother? Life as a single father. In B. J. Risman & P. Schwartz (Eds.), *Gender in intimate relationships* (pp. 155–164). Belmont, CA: Wadsworth.

Ritchie, J., & Ronald, K. (Eds.). (2001). *Available means: An anthology of women's rhetoric(s).* Pittsburgh, PA: University of Pittsburgh Press.

Rites of Passage. (2016). Retrieved from http://ritesofpassagedurham.weebly.com

Rivers, C., & Barnett, R. (2011). *The truth about girls and boys.* New York: Columbia University Press.

Roberts, D. (1997). *Killing the black body: Race, reproduction, and the meaning of liberty.* New York: Pantheon Books.

Roberts, D. (2001, April–May). *Ms.* Retrieved from http://www.msmagazine.com/apr01/roberts.html

Roberts, D. (2009, Summer). Race, gender, and genetic technologies: A new reproductive dystopia? *Signs: Journal of Women in Culture and Society, 34,* 783–804.

Roiphe, K. (1993). *The morning after: Sex, fear, and feminism on campus.* Boston, MA: Little, Brown.

Romano, A., & Dokoupil, T. (2010). Men's lib. *Newsweek.* Retrieved from http://www.thedailybeast.com/newsweek/2010/09/20/why-we-need-to-re-imagine-masculinity.html

Roodkowsky, M. (2016, August 5). Why the visceral Hillary hatred? *Raleigh News & Observer,* p. 13A.

Roosevelt, M. (2010, January 14). When the gym isn't enough. *New York Times,* pp. E1, E8.

Roscoe, W. (1993). How to become a Berdache: Toward a unified analysis of gender diversity. In G. Herdt (Ed.), *Third sex and third gender: Beyond sexual dimorphism in culture and history* (pp. 329–372). New York: Zone Books.

Rose, A. J., Smith, R. L., Glick, G. C., & Schwartz-Mette, R. A. (2016). Girls' and boys' problem talk: Implications for emotional closeness in friendships. *Developmental Psychology, 52*(4), 629–639. Retrieved from https://doi.org/10.1037/dev0000096

Rosenberger, J. G., Herbenick, D., Novak, D. S., & Reece, M. (2014). What's love got to do with it? Examinations of emotional perceptions and sexual behaviors among gay and bisexual men in the United States. *Archives of Sexual Behavior, 43,* 119–128.

Rosenthal, A. M., Sylva, D., Safron, A., & Bailey, J. M. (2011). Sexual arousal patterns of bisexual men revisited. *Biological Psychology, 8,* 112–115.

Ross, L. J. (2009). The movement for reproductive justice: Six years old and growing. *Collective Voices, 4,* 8–9.

Rosser, S. (2012). *Breaking into the lab: Engineering progress for women in science.* New York: NYU Press.

Rothstein, J., & Yoon, A. (2008). *Affirmative action in law school admissions: What do racial preferences do?* (No. w14276). Cambridge, MA: National Bureau of Economic Research. Retrieved from http://www.nber.org/papers/w14276.pdf

Rowe-Finkbeiner, K. (2014, April 30). The motherhood penalty. *Politico Magazine.* Retrieved from http://www.politico.com/magazine/story/2014/04/the-motherhood-penalty-106173.html#.U6aurdJOXq4

Roy, J. (2014, July 2). What I learned as a woman at a men's-rights conference. *Time.* Retrieved from http://time.com/2949435/what-i-learnedas-a-woman-at-a-mens-rights-conference/

Rubin, A. (2015, March 19). French debate setting weight standards for models. *New York Times,* p. A6.

Rubin, J. Z., Provenzano, F. J., & Luria, Z. (1974). The eye of the beholder: Parents' views on sex of newborns. *American Journal of Orthopsychiatry, 44,* 512–519.

Rudacille, D. (2006). *The riddle of gender.* New York: Anchor.

Ruddick, S. (1989). *Maternal thinking: Toward a politics of peace.* Boston, MA: Beacon.

Rudman, L., & Glick, P. (2010). *The social psychology of gender.* New York: Guilford Press.

Rudman, L. A., & Phelan, J. E. (2007). The interpersonal power feminism: Is feminism good for relationships? *Sex Roles, 57,* 787–799.

Runyowa, S. (2016, September). Microaggressions matter. *The Atlantic.* Retrieved September 17, 2016, from http://www.theatlantic.com/politics/archive/2015/09/microaggressions-matter/406090/

Rusbult, C. (1987). Responses to dissatisfaction in close relationships: The exit-voice-loyalty-neglect model. In D. Perlman & S. W. Duck (Eds.), *Intimate relationships: Development, dynamics, and deterioration* (pp. 209–238). London: Sage.

Russell, E. M., DelPriore, D. J., Butterfield, M. E., & Hill, S. E. (2013). Friends with benefits, but without the sex: Straight women and gay men exchange trustworthy mating advice. *Evolutionary Psychology, 11*(1). Retrieved from https://doi.org/10.1177/147470491301100113

Rutter, V., & Schwartz, P. (1996). Same-sex couples: Courtship, commitment, and context. In A. Auhagen & M. von Salisch (Eds.), *The diversity of human relationships* (pp. 197–226). New York: Cambridge University Press.

Ryan, B. (2004). Identity politics in the women's movement. In J. Spade & C. Valentine (Eds.), *The kaleidoscope of gender: Prisms, patterns, and possibilities* (pp. 104–113). Belmont, CA: Thomson/Wadsworth.

Ryle, R. (2015). *Questioning gender.* Thousand Oaks, CA: Sage.

Sagrestano, L., Heavey, C., & Christensen, A. (1998). Theoretical approaches to understanding sex differences and similarities in conflict behavior. In D. J. Canary & K. Dindia (Eds.), *Sex differences and similarities in communication: Critical essays and empirical investigations of sex and gender in interaction* (pp. 287–302). Mahwah, NJ: Erlbaum.

Sales, N. J. (2016). *American girls: Social media and the secret lives of teenagers.* New York: Alfred A. Knopf.

Salome, R. (2007). A place for women's colleges. *Chronicle of Higher Education,* p. B20. Sandberg, S. (2013). *Lean in: Women, work, and the will to lead.* New York: Knopf.

Sandberg, S., & Chávez, A. (2014, March 8–9). Don't call us bossy. *Wall Street Journal,* pp. C1–C2.

Sandberg, S., & Grant, A. (2015a, March 8). How men can succeed. *New York Times,* p. SR5.

Sandberg, S., & Grant, A. (2015b, January 11). Speaking while female. *New York Times,* p. SR3.

Sander, K., & Taylor, T. (2012). *Mismatch.* New York: Basic.

Sander, L. (2012, November 2). Colleges confront a gender gap in student engagement. *Chronicle of Higher Education,* pp. B14–B17.

Sander, R. H. (2004). A systemic analysis of affirmative action in American law schools. *Stanford Law Review, 57,* 367–483.

Sapolsky, R. (2013, December 7–8). Caught between male and female. *Wall Street Journal,* p. C2.

Sarkeesian, A. (2014). Women as background decoration: Tropes v. women. *Feminist Frequency.* Retrieved from http://www.feminist-frequency.com

Sarkela, S. J., Ross, S. R., & Lowe, M. A. (2003). *From megaphones to microphones: Speeches of American women, 1920–1960.* Westport, CT: Praeger.

Savage, C. (2012, January 7). U.S. to expand its definition of rape in statistics. *New York Times,* pp. A10, A15.

Sax, L. (2016a). *Boys adrift.* New York: Basic.

Sax, L. (2016b). *The collapse of parenting: How we hurt our kids when we treat them like grown-ups.* New York: Basic.

Saxen, R. (2007). *Good eater: The true story of one man's struggle with binge eating disorder.* Oakland, CA: New Harbinger Publications.

Scelfo, J. (2002, December 9). Kneed to know. *Newsweek*, pp. 88, 90.

Scelfo, J. (2006, November 6). Extreme makeovers. *Newsweek*, pp. 56–57.

Scelfo, J. (2015, February 8). They. *New York Times Education Life*, pp. 18–19.

Schaap, J. (2010). *Corrective rape* (Video shown on ESPN). Retrieved May 10, 2010, from https://www .ovguide.com/corrective-rape-9202a8c04000641f8 000000021b9bdb4

Schalet, A. (2011, April 7). Caring, romantic American boys. *New York Times*, p. A15.

Schalet, A. (2012). *Not under my roof: Parents, teens and the culture of sex*. Chicago, IL: University of Chicago Press.

Scheiber, N. (2015, September 16). Attitudes shift on paid leave: Dads sue, too. *New York Times*, pp. A1, B8.

Schiebinger, L., & Gilmartin, S. K. (2010, January–February). Housework is an academic issue. *Academe*, 96(1), 39–44.

Schieman, S., Schafer, M., & McIvor, M. (2013). The rewards of authority in the workplace: Do gender and age matter? *Sociological Perspectives*, 56, 75–96.

Schiff, S. (2006, October 13). Desperately seeking Susan. *New York Times*, p. A27.

Schlossberg, T. (2014, July 19). UConn to pay $ 1.3 million to end suit on rape cases. *New York Times*, p. A16.

Schmitz, A., Zillmann, D., & Blossfeld, H. -P. (2013). Do women pick up lies before men: The association between gender, deception patterns, and detection modes in online dating. *Online Journal of Communication and Media Technologies*, 3(3), 52–73.

Schneider, J., & Hacker, S. (1973). Sex role imagery and use of the generic "man" in introductory texts: A case in the sociology of sociology. *American Sociologist*, 8, 12–18.

Schroeder, L. O. (1986). A rose by any other name: Post-marital right to use maiden name: 1934–1982. *Sociology and Social Research*, 70, 290–293.

Schulevitz, J. (2015, May 10). Why mothers remain the designated worriers. *New York Times*, pp. SR 1, 6, 7.

Schulte, B. (2014). *Overwhelmed: Work, love and play when no one has the time*. New York: Sarah Crichton Books.

Schultz, J. (2014). *Qualifying times: Points of change in U.S. women's sport*. Urbana, IL: University of Illinois Press.

Schwalbe, M. (1996). *Unlocking the cage: The men's movement, gender, politics, and American culture*. Cambridge, MA: Oxford University Press.

Schwartz, P., & Rutter, V. (1998). *The gender of sexuality*. Newbury Park, CA: Pine Forge Press.

Scott-Bell, P. (2016). *The firebrand and the first lady*. New York: Knopf.

Searcey, D. (2016, February 5). Central Africa peacekeepers are accused of sex crimes. *New York Times*, p. A6.

Sedgwick, E. (1990). *Epistemology of the closet*. Berkeley, CA: University of California Press.

Segrin, C., & Flora, F. J. (2005). *Family communication*. Mahwah, NJ: Erlbaum.

Sex matters: Drugs can affect sexes differently. (2014, May 25). CBS 60 minutes (online). Retrieved June 15, 2014, from http://www.cbsnews.com/news/ sex-matters-drugs-canaffect-sexes-differently-2/

Sexton, J. (2016, October 13). America's toxic masculinity. *New York Times*, p. A25.

Shah, S. (2011, April 22). Pakistan frees 5 accused in court-ordered gang rape. *Raleigh News & Observer*, p. 4A.

Shapiro, T. (2007). The hidden cost of being African American. In M. Andersen & P. H. Collins (Eds.), *Race, class, & gender* (6th ed., pp. 127–135). Thousand Oaks, CA: Sage.

Sharp, S. (2011). Disciplining the housewife in *Desperate Housewives* and domestic reality television. In G. Dines & J. Humez (Eds.), *Gender, race, and class in media: A critical reader* (3rd ed., pp. 481–486). Los Angeles, CA: Sage.

Sheehy, G. (2010). *Passages in caregiving*. New York: William Morrow.

Sheeler, K. H., & Anderson, K. V. (2013). *Woman president: Confronting postfeminist political culture*. College Station, TX: Texas A&M University Press.

Sheridan-Rabideau, M. P. (2009). *Girls, feminism, and grassroots literacies: Activism in the girl-zone*. New York: SUNY Press.

Sherr, I. (2013, July 3). Fans take videogame damsels out of distress, put them in charge. *New York Times*, pp. A1, A12.

Sherrod, D. (1989). The influence of gender on same-sex friendships. In C. Hendrick (Ed.), *Close relationships* (pp. 164–186). Newbury Park, CA: Sage.

Shimron, Y. (1997, January 22). Men unite to live their faith. *Raleigh News & Observer*, pp. 1A–6A.

Shimron, Y. (2002, July 21). Promise Keepers fill the house—and heart. *Raleigh News & Observer*, pp. 1A, 17A.

Shoener, S. (2014, June 21). Two-parent households can be lethal. *New York Times*. Retrieved June 21, 2014, from http://mobile.nytimes. com/2014/06/22/opinion/sunday/domestic-violence-and-two-parent-households. html?_r=2&referrer=

Shulevitz, J. (2015, May 10). Mom: The designated worrier. *New York Times*, pp.SR 1, 6–7.

Silverstein, L., Auerbach, C., Grieco, L., & Dunkel, F. (1999). Do Promise Keepers dream of feminist sheep? *Sex Roles, 40*, 665–688.

Simmons, R. (2002). *Odd girl out: The hidden culture of aggression in girls* (Rev. ed.). New York: Mariner Books.

Simmons, R. (2004). *Odd girl speaks out: Girls write about bullies, cliques, popularity, and jealousy.* Orlando, FL: Harvest Books.

Simmons, R. (2011). *Odd girl out, revised and updated: The hidden culture of aggression in girls (Rev. ed.).* New York: Mariner Books

Slater, D. (2013, March 16). Does affirmative action do what it should? *The New York Times*. Retrieved from http://www.nytimes.com/2013/03/17/opinion/sunday/does-affirmative-action-do-what-it-should.html

Slaughter, A. (2012, June/July). Why women still can't have it all. *Atlantic*. Retrieved from http://www.theatlantic.com/magazine/archive/2012/07/why-women-still-can-8217-t-have-itall/9020/

Slaughter, A. (2013). Yes, you can. *New York Times Book Review*, pp. 1, 12–13.

Slaughter, A. (2015). *Unfinished business*. New York: Random House.

Sloop, J. (2006). Critical studies in gender/sexuality and media. In B. Dow & J. T. Wood (Eds.), The SAGE *Handbook of gender & communication* (pp. 319–333). Thousand Oaks, CA: Sage.

Smith, D. (2004). Schooling for inequality. In J. Spade & C. Valentine (Eds.), *The kaleidoscope of gender: Prisms, patterns, and possibilities* (pp. 183–186). Belmont, CA: Thomson/Wadsworth.

Smith, S., Choueiti, M., & Pieper, K. (2013). *Race/ethnicity in 500 popular films: Is the key to diversifying cinematic content held in the hand of the black director?* Retrieved from http://annenberg.usc.edu/sitecore/shell/Applications/~/media/PDFs/RaceEthnicity.ashx

Smith, S., Choueiti, M., Scofield, E., & Pieper, K. (2013). Gender inequality in 500 popular films: Examining on-screen portrayals and behind-the scenes employment patterns in mother pictures released between 2007–2012. Retrieved from https://www.scribd.com/document/235824941/Gender-Inequality-in-Film-2007-2013-Final-for-Publication

Snyder, K. (2014, August 26). The abrasiveness trap: High-achieving men and women are described differently in reviews. *Fortune*. Retrieved September 30, 2014, from http://fortune.com/2014/08/26/performance-review-gender-bias/

Solebello, N., & Elliott, S. (2011). "We want them to be as heterosexual as possible": Fathers talk about their teen children's sexuality. *Gender & Society, 25*, 293–315.

Solinger, R. (2005). *Pregnancy and power: A short history of reproductive politics in America*. New York: New York University Press.

Sommers, C. (2013). *Freedom feminism: Its surprising history and why it matters today*. Landham, MA: AEI Press.

Span, E. (2014, June 7). Is softball sexist? *New York Times*, p. A19.

Spar, D. (2013). *Wonder women: Sex, power and the quest for perfection*. New York: Sarah Crichton Books.

Spender, D. (1984a). Defining reality: A powerful tool. In C. Kramarae, M. Schultz, & W. O'Barr (Eds.), *Language and power* (pp. 195–205). Beverly Hills, CA: Sage.

Spender, D. (1984b). *Man-made language*. London: Routledge and Kegan Paul.

Spielhagen, F. (Ed.). (2013). *Debating single-sex education: Separate but equal?* Landham, MD: Rowman & Littlefield Education.

Spitzack, C., & Carter, K. (1987). Women in communication studies: A typology for revision. *Quarterly Journal of Speech, 73*, 401–423.

Spottswood, E. L., Walther, J. B., Holmstrom, A. J., & Ellison, N. B. (2013). Person-centered emotional support and gender attributions in computer-mediated communication: Social projections in CMC. *Human Communication Research, 39*(3), 295–316. Retrieved from https://doi.org/10.1111/hcre.12006

Stacey, J. (1996). *In the name of the father: Rethinking family values in a postmodern age*. Boston, MA: Beacon.

Stafford, L., Dutton, M., & Haas, S. (2000). Measuring routine maintenance: Scale revision, sex versus gender roles, and the prediction of relational characteristics. *Communication Monographs, 67*, 306–323.

Stampler, L. (2011, April 20). SlutWalks sweep the nation. *Huffington Post*. Retrieved from http://www.huffingtonpost.com/2011/04/20/slutwalk-united-states-city_n_851725.html

Stansell, C. (2010). *The feminist promise*. New York: Random House.

Stanton, E. C., Anthony, S. B., & Gage, M. J. (Eds.). (1882). *History of woman suffrage* (Vol. 1, p. 116). New York: Fowler & Wells.

Starecheski, L. (2014, August 18). The power of the peer group in preventing campus rape. *Morning Edition, National Public Radio*.

Stephens, N., Hamedani, M., & Destin, M. (2014). Closing the social-class achievement gap: A difference-education intervention improves first-generation students' academic performance and all students' college transition. *Psychological Science, 25*, 943–953.

Stewart, A. (2016, July 26). Female officers save lives. *New York Times*, p. A27

Stiglitz, J. (2012). *The price of inequality*. New York: W. W. Norton.

Stone, S. ([1992] 2006). The empire strikes back: A posttranssexual manifesto. In S. Stryker & S. Whittle (Eds.), *The transgender studies reader* (pp. 221–235). New York: Routledge.

Stonington, J. (2011, December 11). Recession increases number of stay-at-home dads. *Raleigh News & Observer*, p. 5A.

Straus, S. (2004). Escape from animal house. In J. Spade & C. Valentine (Eds.), *The kaleidoscope of gender* (pp. 462–465). Belmont, CA: Thomson/Wadsworth.

Streib, L. (2011, September 26). Power and progress. *Newsweek*, pp. 30–33.

Stripling, J. (2012, March 12). Survey finds drop in minority presdients leading colleges. *Chronicle of Higher Education*. Retrieved April 22, 2017, from http://www.chronicle.com/article/Who-Are-College-Presidents-/131138/

Stryker, S., & Bettcher, T. (2016). Introduction: Transfeminism. *TSQ: Transgender Studies Quarterly*, 3, 5–14.

Stryker, S., & Bettcher, T. M. (2016). Introduction: Trans/Feminisms. *TSQ: Transgender Studies Quarterly*, 3(1–2), 5–14. Retrieved from https://doi.org/10.1215/23289252-3334127

Sue, D. W. (2010a). *Microaggressions and marginality: Manifestation, dynamics, and impact*. New York: Wiley.

Sue, D. W. (2010b). *Microaggressions in everyday life: Race, gender, and sexual orientation*. New York: Wiley.

Sue, D. W. (2016). *Race talk and the conspiracy of silence*. New York: Wiley.

Suggs, W. (2005, July 1). Gender quotas? Not in college sports. *Chronicle of Higher Education*, pp. A24–A26.

Sullivan, L. (2014, April 2). Enforcing prison rape elimination standards proves tricky. *National Public Radio*. Retrieved from http://www.npr.org/2014/04/02/298332579/enforcing-prison-rape-elimination-standards-proves-tricky

Superson, A., & Cudd, A. (Eds.). (2002). *Theorizing backlash: Philosophical reflections on the resistance to feminism*. Oxford, UK: Rowman & Littlefield.

Surrey, J. L. (1983). The relational self in women: Clinical implications. In J. V. Jordan, J. L. Surrey, & A. G. Kaplan (Eds.), *Women and empathy: Implications for psychological development and psychotherapy* (pp. 6–11). Wellesley, MA: Stone Center for Developmental Services and Studies.

Suter, E., & Oswald, R. (2003). Do lesbians change their last names in the context of a committed relationship? *Journal of Lesbian Studies*, 7, 71–83.

Suter, E. A. (2014). Communication in lesbian and gay families. In L. H. Turner & R. L. West (Eds.), *The SAGE Handbook of Family Communication*. Thousand Oaks, CA: Sage.

Suter, E. A., Kellas, J. K., Webb, S. K., & Allen, J. A. (2016). A tale of two mommies: (Re)Storying family of origin narratives. *Journal of Family Communication*, 1–15. Retrieved from http://doi.org/10.1080/15267431.2016.1184150

Swaby, R. (2015). *Headstrong: 52 women who changed science—and the world*. New York: Broadway Books.

Swain, S. (1989). Covert intimacy: Closeness in men's friendships. In B. J. Risman & P. Schwartz (Eds.), *Gender and intimate relationships* (pp. 71–86). Belmont, CA: Wadsworth.

Sweet, E. (2011). *The "gendering" of our kids' toys and what we can do about it*. The Center for a New American Dream. Retrieved June 17, 2014, from http://www.newdream.org/blog/2011-10-gendering-of-kids-toys

Sweet, E. (2012, December 21). Gender-based toy marketing returns. *New York Times*. Retrieved June 17, 2014, from http://www.nytimes.com/2012/12/23/opinion/sunday/gender-based-toy-marketing-returns.html?_r=1&

Sweet, E. (2013). Guest blog: Is separate really equal when it comes to gender assigned toys? *Free Zone*. Retrieved June 17, 2014, from http://princessfreezone.com/pfz-blog/2013/11/26/guest-blog-is-separate-really-equal-when-it-comes-to-gender.html

Swim, J., & Becker, J. (2011). Seeing the unseen. *Psychology of Women Quarterly*, 35, 227–242.

Switzer, J. Y. (1990). The impact of generic word choices: An empirical investigation of age- and sex-related differences. *Sex Roles*, 22, 69–82.

Tabuchi, H. (2015, October 27). Sweeping away gender-specific toys and labels. *The New York Times*. Retrieved from http://www.nytimes.com/2015/10/28/business/sweeping-away-gender-specific-toys-and-labels.html

Tannen, D. (2017). *You're the only one I can tell: Inside the language of women's friendships*. New York: Random.

Tarkan, L. (2009). Fathers gain respect from experts (and mothers). *New York Times*, pp. D5–D6.

Tavernise, S. (2012, February 10). Rich and poor further apart in education. *New York Times*, pp. A1, A3.

Taylor, S. (2002). *The tending instinct: How nurturing is essential for who we are and how we live*. New York: Times Books.

Teens & online video. (2012). *Pew Internet and American Life Project.* Retrieved from http://www.pewinternet.org/Reports/2012/Teens-and-online-video.aspx

Television watching statistics. (2016, February 18). Retrieved May 16, 2016, from http://www.statistic-brain.com/televison-watching-statistics/

Terlecki, M., Brown, J., Harner-Steciw, L., Irvin-Hannum, J., Marchetto-Ryan, N., Ruhl, L., & Wiggins, J. (2011). Sex differences and similarities in video game experience, preferences, and self-efficacy: Implications for the gaming industry. *Current Psychology, 30,* 22–33.

Thomas, G. (2016). *Because of sex: One law, ten cases, and fifty years that changed American women's lives at work.* New York: St. Martin's Press.

Thomas, K. (2011, April 26). College teams, relying on deception, undermine gender equity. *New York Times,* pp. A1, A18.

Thomas, K. R. (2008). Macrononsense in multiculturalism. *American Psychologist, 63,* 274–275.

Thompson, B. (Summer 2002). Multiracial feminism: Recasting the chronology of second wave feminism. *Feminist Studies, 28*(2), 337–355.

Timm, J. (2014, July 11). "Men's rights" group's sad reality: Behind the doors of a depressing confab. *Salon.com.* Retrieved from http://www.salon.com/2014/07/11/mens_rights_groups_sad_reality_behind_the_doors_of_a_depressing_confab/?utm_source=facebook&utm_medium=socialflow

Title IX Q & A. (2008). Retrieved October 26, 2008, from https://feminist.org/education/TitleIXQA.pdf

Toldson, I. A. (2014, October 27). Black males aren't failing our schools. Our schools are failing them. *Chronicle of Higher Education.* Retrieved October 31, 2014, from http://chronicle.com/article/Black-Males-Aren-t-Failing/149573/

The toll of toxic sexism. (2016, December 9). *The Week,* p. 22.

Tobia, J. (2014, June 10). Why I'm genderqueer, professional and unafraid. Retrieved April 26, 2017, from http://www.huffingtonpost.com/jacob-tobia/genderqueer-professional-_b_5476239.html

Toma, C. L., & Hancock, J. T. (2010). Looks and lies: The role of physical attractiveness in online dating self-presentation and deception. *Communication Research, 37,* 335–351.

Tong, R. (2013). *Feminist thought* (4th ed). Philadelphia, PA: Westview Press.

Torabi, F. (2014). *When she makes more: 10 rules for breadwinning women.* New York: Penguin: Hudson St. Press.

Traister, R. (2012). *Can modern women have it all?* Retrieved June 25, 2012, from http://www.salon.com/2012/06/21/can_modern_women_have_it_all/

Traister, R. (2016). *All the single ladies: Unmarried women and the rise of an independent nation.* New York: Simon & Schuster.

Trangsrud, K. (1994). Female genital mutilation: Recommendations for education and policy. *Carolina Papers in International Health and Development,* 1, n.p.

Trebay, G. (2010, January 21). Disaster coverage without having to roll up the sleeves. *New York Times.* Retrieved from http://www.nytimes.com/2010/01/24/fashion/24tshirt.html?r=1

The truth about the pay gap. (2014, April 10). *New York Times,* p. A20.

Tumulty, K., & Smith, M. (2013, June 26). Texas state senator Wendy Davis filibusters her way to Democratic stardom. *Washington Post.* Retrieved from http://www.washingtonpost.com/politics/texas-state-senator-wendy-davis-filibusters-her-way-to-democratic-stardom/2013/06/26/aace267c-de85-11e2-b2d4-ea6d8-f477a01_story.html

Turkewitz, J. (2014, June 11). A fight as U.S. girls face genital cutting abroad. *New York Times,* pp. A1, A13.

Turkewitz, J. (2015, February 6). Effects of ancient custom present new challenges to U.S. doctors. *New York Times,* pp. A11, A15.

Turner, R. (1998, December 14). Back in the Ms. Biz. *Newsweek,* p. 67.

Tyre, P. (2006, January 30). The trouble with boys. *Newsweek,* pp. 44–52.

Tyre, P. (2009). *The trouble with boys: A surprising report card on our sons, their problems at school, and what parents and educators must do.* New York: Crown.

Ugwu-Oju, D. (2000, December 4). My turn: Should my tribal past shape Delia's future? *Newsweek,* p. 14.

Umberson, D., Thomeer, M. B., & Lodge, A. C. (2015). Intimacy and emotion work in lesbian, gay, and heterosexual relationships. *Journal of Marriage and Family, 77*(2), 542–556. Retrieved from https://doi.org/10.1111/jomf.12178

U.S. Department of Education. (2013). *Human trafficking of children in the United States—a fact sheet for schools.* Retrieved from http://www2.ed.gov/about/offices/list/oese/oshs/factsheet.html

U.S. Department of Education, National Center for Education Statistics. (2016). *Status and trends in the education of racial and ethnic groups 2016 (NCES 2016-007).* Retrieved from https://nces.ed.gov/fastfacts/display.asp?id=72

U.S. Department of Health & Human Services. (2014). *What is cyberbullying?* Retrieved from http://www.stopbullying.gov/cyberbullying/what-is-it/

Valenti, J. (2011, June 5). SlutWalks and the future of feminism. *Washington Post.* Retrieved from http://

www.washingtonpost.com/opinions/slutwalks-and-the-future-of-feminism/2011/06/01/AGjB-9LIH_story_1.html

Valentine, D. (2007). *Imagining transgender: An ethnography of a category*. Durham, NC: Duke University Press.

van Ogtrop, K. (2015, September 28). Why ambition isn't working for women. *Time*, pp. 52–55.

Vedantam, S. (2006, July 13). Male scientist writes of life as female scientist. *New York Times*, p. D1.

Vedantam, S. (2014). Evidence of racial, gender bias found in faculty mentoring. *National Public Radio*. Retrieved from http://www.npr.org/2014/04/22/305814367/evidence-of-racialgender-biases-found-in-faculty-mentoring

Vidal, M. (1971). Women: New voice of La Raza. *International Socialist Review*. Retrieved from http://library.duke.edu/rubenstein/scriptorium/wlm/chicana/

Villano, D. (2011, September/October). Balancing act. *Miller-McCune*, pp. 22–25.

Vive la différence. (2013, December 7). *Economist*, pp. 81–82.

Vivian, J. (2011). *The media of mass communication* (10th ed.). Boston, MA: Allyn & Bacon.

A voice for men. (n.d.). International Conference on Men's Issues. Retrieved May 25, 2016, from http://www.avoiceformen.com/international-conference-on-mens-issues-detroit-june-26-28-2014/

Vokey, M., Tefft, B., & Tysiaczny, C. (2013). An analysis of hyper-masculinity in magazine advertisements. *Sex Roles*. doi:10.1007/s11199-013-0268-1

Von Drehle, D. (2014, July 31). Manopause?! Aging, insecurity and the $2 billion testosterone industry. *Time*. Retrieved from http://time.com/3062889/manopause-aging-insecurityand-the-2-billion-testosterone-industry/

Vromen, A., Xenos, M. A., & Loader, B. (2015). Young people, social media and connective action: From organisational maintenance to everyday political talk. *Journal of Youth Studies*, *18*(1), 80–100. Retrieved from http://doi.org/10.1080/13676261.2014.933198

Waber, B. (2014, January 13). What data analytics says about gender inequality in the workplace. *Bloomberg BusinessWeek*. Retrieved June 28, 2014, from http://www.businessweek.com/articles/2014-01-30/gender-inequality-in-the-workplace-what-data-analytics-says

Wade, L. (2009, March 19). Dora the Explorer's makeover. *Sociological Images*. Retrieved from http://thesocietypages.org/socimages/2009/03/19/dora-the-explorers-makeover-gwen-and-i-saw-it-comin/

Wagenheim, J. (1996, January–February). Among the Promise Keepers. *Utne Reader*, pp. 74–77.

Waismel-Manor, R., & Tolbert, P. (2010). *Earnings differences in dual earner couples*. International Sociological Association Conference, Gothenburg, Sweden.

Walk a mile in her shoes: The international movement to stop rape, sexual assault, and gender violence. (2016). Retrieved May 4, 2016, from http://www.walkamileinhershoes.org

Walker, A. (1983). *In search of our mothers' gardens*. New York: Harcourt Brace Jovanovich.

Walker, K. (2004). Men, women, and friendship: What they say, what they do. In J. Spade & C. Valentine (Eds.), *The kaleidoscope of gender: Prisms, patterns, and possibilities* (pp. 403–413). Belmont, CA: Thomson/Wadsworth.

Walker, R. (1992, January–February). Doing the third wave. *Ms.*, *12*, pp. 86–87.

Walker, S. (2007). *Style and status: Selling beauty to African American women*. Lexington, KY: University of Kentucky Press.

Wallace, A. (2014, January 20). Life as a female journalist: Hot or not? *New York Times*, p. A15.

Walters, M. L., Chen, J., & Breiding, M. J. (2013). *The national intimate partner and sexual violence survey: 2010 findings on victimization by sexual orientation*. Atlanta, GA: National Center for Injury Prevention and Control, Centers for Disease Control and Prevention.

Walton, D. (2013, October 7). *Essence's* images study: Bonus insights. *Essence*. Retrieved from http://www.essence.com/2013/10/07/essence-images-study-bonus-insights

Walton, S. C., & Rice, R. E. (2013). Mediated disclosure on Twitter: The roles of gender and identity in boundary impermeability, valence, disclosure, and stage. *Computers in Human Behavior*, *29*, 1465–1474.

Wang, S. (2013, May 7). How autism is different in girls vs. boys. *Wall Street Journal*, pp. D1–D2.

Ware, S. (2014). *Title IX: A brief history with documents*. Long Grove, IL: Waveland Press.

Warner, J. (2012, December 14). The lesson of the boy in the pink ballet flats. *Time*. Retrieved from http://ideas.time.com/2012/12/14/the-lesson-of-the-boy-in-the-pink-ballet-flats/

Warner, J. (2013, August 7). Ready to rejoin the rat race? The opt out generation wants back in. *New York Times Magazine*, pp. 24–29, 38, 43, 49.

Wartik, N. (2002, June 23). Hurting more, helped less? *New York Times*, pp. 15–1, 15–6, 15–7.

Watson, R. J., Adjei, J., Saewyc, E., Homma, Y., & Goodenow, C. (2016). Trends and disparities in disordered eating among heterosexual and sexual minority adolescents: LGB eating disorders. *International Journal of Eating Disorders*. Retrieved from http://doi.org/10.1002/eat.22576

Watzlawick, P., Beavin, J., & Jackson, D. D. (1967). *Pragmatics of human communication.* New York: W. W. Norton.

Way, N. (2013). *Deep secrets: The hidden landscape of boys' friendships.* Cambridge, MA: Harvard University Press.

Weber, L., & Adamy, J. (2016, January 29). Plan would force pay disclosures by gender. *Wall Street Journal,* p. B1.

We marched everywhere. (2017, Spring). *Ms. Magazine, 27*(1), 20–27.

The Week. (2012). Retrieved from http:// theweek.com/article/index/225214/ rush-limbaugh-vssandra-fluke-a-timeline

The Week. (2016, April 22). p. 19.

Wegner, H., Jr. (2005). Disconfirming communication and self-verification in marriage: Associations among the demand/withdraw interaction pattern, feeling understood, and marital satisfaction. *Journal of Social and Personal Relationships, 22,* 19–31.

Weigel, J. (2010). Are you a good man? *Chicago Tribune.* Retrieved from http://www.chicagotri-bune.com/lifestyles/ct-tribu-weigel-good-men-20101202-column.html

Weiner, J. (2015, May 31). The pressure to look good. *New York Times,* p. SR8.

Weiss, D. M., & Sachs, J. (1991). Persuasive strategies used by preschool children. *Sociology, 97,* 114–142.

Weitz, R., & Kwan, S. (2013). *The politics of women's bodies* (4th ed.). New York: Oxford University Press.

Welter, B. (1966). The cult of true womanhood: 1820–1960. *American Quarterly, 18,* 151–174.

West, C. (2007). Black sexuality: The taboo subject. In M. Andersen & P. H. Collins (Eds.), *Race, class, gender: An anthology* (6th ed., pp. 247–252). Belmont, CA: Thomson.

West, C., & Zimmerman, D. H. (1983). Small insults: A study of interruptions in cross-sex conversations between unacquainted persons. In B. Thorne, C. Kramarae, & N. Henley (Eds.), *Language, gender and society* (pp. 102–117). Rowley, MA: Newbury House.

West, I. (2013). *Transforming citizenships: Transgender articulations of the law.* New York: New York University Press.

West, I. (2014, June 27). Trans*politics, solidarity, and ENDA. *From the Square: NYU Press Blog.* Retrieved June 30, 2014, from http://www .fromthesquare.org/?p=6434

White, A. M. (2008). *Ain't I a feminist? African American men speak out on fatherhood, friendship, forgiveness, and freedom.* New York: State University of New York Press.

White Ribbon Campaign. (n.d.). Retrieved May 20, 2003, from http://www.whiteribbon.com

Whitehead, B. (1997, October 3). Soccer dads march on Washington. *Wall Street Journal,* p. A10.

Whitefield-Madrano, A. (2016). *Face value.* New York: Simon & Schuster.

Whitmire, R. (2011). *Why boys fail.* New York: AMACOM.

Why it's not "Rain Woman." (2014, March 1). *Economist,* pp. 79–80.

Why STEM fields still don't draw more women. (2012, November 2). *Chronicle of Higher Education,* pp. B24–B27.

Widman, L., Choukas-Bradley, S., Noar, S. M., Nesi, J., & Garrett, K. (2016). Parent-adolescent sexual communication and adolescent safer sex behavior: A meta-analysis. *JAMA Pediatrics, 170*(1), 52. Retrieved from http://doi.org/10.1001/ jamapediatrics.2015.2731

Wiesmann, S., Boeije, H., van Doorne-Huiskes, A., & den Dulk, L. (2008). 'Not worth mentioning': The implicit and explicit nature of decision-making about the division of paid and domestic work. *Community, Work & Family, 11,* 341–363.

Wilchens, R. (2014). *Queer theory, gender theory.* New York: Riverdale Press.

Wilier, E. (2011). The queen and her bee: Social aggression in female friendship. In D. O. Braithwaite & J. T. Wood (Eds.), *Casing interpersonal communication* (pp. 189–196). Dubuque, IA: Kendall-Hunt.

Williams, C. (2014, July 5). App raises new bullying concerns. *Raleigh News & Observer,* p. 2B.

Williams, J. (2013, June 6). Paygap deniers. *Huffington Post.* Retrieved June 22, 2014, from http://www .huffingtonpost.com/joan-williams /pay-gap-deniers_b_3391524.html

Williams, J., & Dempsey, R. (2014). *What works for women at work: Four patterns working women need to know.* New York: New York University Press.

Williams, J. C. (2010). *Reshaping the work-family debate: Why men and class matter.* Cambridge, MA: Harvard University Press.

Williams, J. J. (2012, January 6). Queer 20: Judith "Jack" Halberstam complicates gender. *Chronicle of Higher Education,* pp. B13–B15.

Williams, N. (2010, March 11). Is Lady Gaga a feminist or isn't she? *Ms. Blog.* Retrieved from http://msmagazine.com/blog/blog/2010/03/11/ is-lady-gaga-a-feminist-or-isnt-she/

Williamson, G., & Silverman, J. (2001). Violence against female partners: Direct and interactive effects of family history, communal orientation, and peer-related variables. *Journal of Social and Personal Relationships, 18,* 535–549.

Wills, J. B., & Brauer, J. R. (2012). Have children adapted to their mothers working, or was adaptation unnecessary? Cohort effects and the relationship between maternal employment and child well-being. *Social Science Research, 41,* 425–443.

Wills, T. A., Weiss, R. L., & Patterson, G. R. (1974). A behavioral analysis of the determinants of marital satisfaction. *Journal of Consulting and Clinical Psychology, 42,* 802–811.

Wilson, E. (1975). *Sociobiology: The new synthesis.* Cambridge, MA: Harvard University Press, Belknap.

Wilson, E. (2013, January 14). The triumph of the size 12's. *New York Times,* pp. E1, E6.

Wilson, E. (2013, August 8). Fashion's blind spot. *New York Times,* pp. E1, E6.

Wilson, E., & Koo, H. (2010). Mothers, fathers, sons, and daughters: Gender differences in factors associated with parent-child communication about sexual topics. *Reproductive Health, 7,* pp. 18–31.

Wilson, G. (2014). *Your brain on porn: Internet pornography and the emerging science of addiction.* Richmond, VA: Commonwealth Publishing.

Wingfield, A. (2009). Racializing the glass escalator: Reconsidering men's experiences with women's work. *Gender & Society, 23,* 5–26.

Wingfield, A. H. (2013). *No more invisible man: Race and gender in men's work.* Philadelphia, PA: Temple University Press.

Wiseman, R. (2015, July 20). Why video games need more female heroes. *Time,* p. 27.

Wolf, N. (1993). *Fire with fire: The new female power and how it will change the 21st century.* New York: Random House.

Wolf, N. (2006, March 12). Wild things. *New York Times Book Review,* pp. 22–23.

Women still earn a lot less than men. (2015, April 14). *New York Times,* p. A22.

Women's Media Center. (2015). The status of women in the U.S. media 2015. Retrieved May 14, 2016, from http://wmc.3cdn.net/83bf6082a319460eb1_hsrm680x2.pdf

Wood, J. T. (1998). *But I thought you meant. Misunderstandings in human communication.* Mountain View, CA: Mayfield.

Wood, J. T. (2001). The normalization of violence in heterosexual romantic relationships: Women's narratives of love and violence. *Journal of Social and Personal Relationships, 18,* 239–262.

Wood, J. T. (2005). Feminist standpoint theory and muted group theory: Commonalities and divergences. *Women & Language, 28,* 61–64.

Wood, J. T. (2008). Critical, feminist theories of interpersonal communication. In L. A. Baxter & D. O. Braithwaite (Eds.), *Engaging theories in interpersonal communication* (pp. 323–334). Thousand Oaks, CA: Sage.

Wood, J. T. (2009). Gender as an area of study. In W. Eadie (Ed.), *21st century communication:*
A reference handbook (pp. 371–379). Thousand Oaks, CA: Sage.

Wood, J. T. (2010). The can-do discourse and young women's anticipations of future. *Women & Language, 33,* 103–107.

Wood, J. T. (2011). Which ruler? What are we measuring? Thoughts on theorizing the division of domestic labor. *Journal of Family Communication, 11,* 29–49.

Wood, J. T. (2013). Becoming gendered: Theories of gender development in families. In M. Fine & F. Fincham (Eds.), *Family theories: A content-based approach* (pp. 301–315). New York: Routledge.

Wood, J. T. (2015). He says/she says: Misunderstandings in communication between women and men. In D. O. Braithwaite & J. T. Wood (Eds.), *Casing interpersonal communication* 2nd ed., (pp. 59–65). Dubuque, IA: Kendall-Hunt.

Wood, J. T., & Conrad, C. R. (1983). Paradox in the experience of professional women. *Western Journal of Speech Communication, 47,* 305–322.

Wood, J. T., & Dow, B. J. (2010). The invisible politics of "choice" in the workplace: Naming the informal parenting support system. In S. Hayden & L. Obrien Hallstein (Eds.), *Contemplating maternity in an era of choice: Contemplating discourses of reproduction* (pp. 203–225). Lanham, MD: Lexington Books.

Wood, J. T., & Inman, C. (1993). In a different mode: Recognizing male modes of closeness. *Journal of Applied Communication Research, 21,* 279–295.

Wooten, S. C., & Mitchell, R. W. (Eds.). (2016). *Preventing sexual violence on campus.* New York: Routledge.

Workplace Bullying Institute. (2009). Retrieved from http://www.workplacebullying.org/2009/05/20/wow-bullying/

Wright, P. H. (1982). Men's friendships, women's friendships, and the alleged inferiority of the latter. *Sex Roles, 8,* 1–20.

Wright, P. H. (1988). Interpreting research on gender differences in friendship: A case for moderation and a plea for caution. *Journal of Social and Personal Relationships, 5,* 367–373.

Wright, P. H. (2006). Toward an expanded orientation to the comparative study of women's and men's same-sex friendships. In K. Dindia & D. Canary (Eds.), *Sex differences and similarities in communication* (pp. 37–57). Mahwah, NJ: Erlbaum.

Yalom, M. (with Theresa Donovan Brown). (2015). *The social sex: A history of female friendship.* New York: Harper Perennial.

Yan, H. (2016). Female hurricanes are deadlier than male hurricanes, study says. Retrieved December 21, 2016, from http://www.cnn.com/2016/09/01/health/female-hurricanes-deadlier-than-male-hurricanes-trnd/index.html

Yao, A. (2013, March 19). 'Never let them see you sweat': The myth of effortless perfection. *Huffington Post*. Retrieved June 24, 2014, from http://www.huffingtonpost.com/amy-yao/college-women-pressure_b_2898446.html

Yao, M., Mahood, C., & Linz, D. (2010). Sexual priming, gender stereotyping, and likelihood to sexually harass: Examining the cognitive effects of playing a sexually-explicit video game. *Sex Roles, 62*, 77–88.

Ye, Z., & Palomares, N. A. (2013). Effects of conversation partners' gender-language consistency on references to emotion, tentative language, and gender salience. *Journal of Language and Social Psychology, 32*, 433–451.

20 Years in, FMLA too weak. (2013, February 16). *Raleigh News & Observer*, p. 15A.

Zack, N. (2005). *Inclusive feminism: A third wave theory of women's commonality*. Lanham, MD: Rowman & Littlefield.

Zarocostas, J. (2014, May 14). U.S. alone in not paying maternity leave. *Raleigh News & Observer*, p. 3A.

Zarya, V. (2016, June 6). The percentage of female CEOs in the Fortune 500 drops to 4%. *Fortune*. Retrieved from http://fortune.com/2016/06/06/women-ceos-fortune-500-2016/

Zernike, K. (2012, March 17). Jury finds spying in Rutgers dorm was a hate crime. *New York Times*, pp. A1, A16.

Zhang, M. (2012, December 26). *Portraits of Albanian women who have lived their lives as men*. Petapixel. Retrieved from http://petapixel.com/2012/12/26/portraits-of-albanianwomen-who-have-lived-their-lives-as-men/

Zeisler, A. (2016). *We were feminists once: From Riot Grrrl to CoverGirl, the buying and selling of a political movement*. Philadelphia, PA: PublicAffairs Press.

Zimbalist, A. (2016, March 26). The N.C.A.A.'s women problem. *New York Times*, p. A19.

Zimmerman, A., & Geist-Martin, P. (2006). The hybrid identities of gender queer: Claiming neither/nor, both/and. In L. A. Samovar, R. E. Porter, & E. R. McDaniel (Eds.), *Intercultural communication: A reader* (11th ed., pp. 76–82). Belmont, CA: Thomson.

Ziobro, P. (2016, January 29). Mattel reshapes Barbie to reflect diversity. *Wall Street Journal*, p. B1.

Zuk, M., & O'Rourke, S. (2012, November 2). Is biology just another pink-collar profession? *Chronicle of Higher Education*, pp. B20–B21.

Index